May the Armed
Forces Be with You

May the Armed Forces Be with You

The Relationship Between Science Fiction and the United States Military

STEPHEN DEDMAN

McFarland & Company, Inc., Publishers
Jefferson, North Carolina

ISBN (print) 978-0-7864-9742-3
ISBN (ebook) 978-1-4766-2286-6

LIBRARY OF CONGRESS CATALOGUING DATA ARE AVAILABLE

British Library cataloguing data are available

© 2016 Stephen Dedman. All rights reserved

No part of this book may be reproduced or transmitted in any form or by any means, electronic or mechanical, including photocopying or recording, or by any information storage and retrieval system, without permission in writing from the publisher.

Front cover image © 2016 Wood River Gallery

Manufactured in the United States of America

*McFarland & Company, Inc., Publishers
Box 611, Jefferson, North Carolina 28640
www.mcfarlandpub.com*

To my father,
Flight Sergeant Ken Dedman,
RAAF (Retd.), AASM, DSM,
Vietnam Medal, National Medal, Long Service
& Good Conduct Medal, Defence Medal,
Republic of Vietnam Medal

In Memoriam

Acknowledgments

Thanks to Professor Van Ikin, without whose assistance and encouragement this book would never have been completed, and in memoriam Hans Schmah.

Thanks also to Joe Haldeman, Robert J. Sawyer, and Chris Palmer; Grant Stone and David Medlen, librarians extraordinaire; Jack Lane Bridges, Lily Chrywenstrom, Cecily Scutt, Emily Smith and Grant Watson, and the makers of *Mystery Science Theater 3000*.

Table of Contents

Acknowledgments   vi
Preface: Study War No More?   1
Introduction: "The Impact of Actual or Imagined Science"   5

1. "See You Later, Space Cowboy"   23
2. "The Eve of the War": 1926 to 1942   32
3. "A War Increasingly Science-Fictional": 1942 to 1945   42
4. "The Meaning of Atomic Weapons": 1946 to 1949   51
5. "I'm Not Working for the World": 1950 to 1961   56
6. "A Taste of Armageddon": 1962 to 1975   84
7. *Murder in the Air*: The Quest for the Death Ray   123
8. *Ender's Game*: Killing Machines   147
9. "The Punisher": The Gulf Wars and Beyond   166

Appendix A: Science Fiction Writers Who Served in the U.S. Military, World War II to Vietnam   187
Appendix B: From Jeep to JEDI: SF Influences on Military Terminology   190
Appendix C: The Vietnam War Advertisements, 1968   192
Appendix D: Science Fiction Films Made with the Assistance of the Pentagon (to 2013)   194
Chapter Notes   197
Bibliography   227
Index   231

Preface: Study War No More?

One of the best pieces of advice I've heard on writing and research came from Connie Willis. Speaking on a panel at a convention sometime after writing *Remake*, she remarked that writers planning to write a novel that required extensive research had better be sure they were sufficiently interested in the topic to do the necessary reading (or, in the case of *Remake*, watching old movies) and not develop a lasting hatred for that field.

Perhaps fortunately, science fiction—in the forms of movies, TV shows, comics and books—has been a passion of mine since my boyhood in the 1960s. As well as reading and watching science fiction extensively, I made my first attempts at writing SF novels while in my teens, sold my first SF short story and attended my first SF convention in 1977, and began working in the first of a series of science fiction bookshops in 1985. So after I'd finished my MA (my exegesis was on "The Idea of the Colony in American, British and Australian Science Fiction"), I tried to think of an aspect of SF that could be explored in sufficient detail to serve as the basis for my PhD thesis.

I first proposed writing a history of the topic of "The Relationship Between American Science Fiction and the U.S. Military" in 2002, before the "full air offensive" in Iraq. While I had not believed that the 21st century was going to be utopian and that we would "study war no more," I expected this to be primarily a history of an aspect of American culture during the twentieth century, beginning with war fears revealed by Orson Welles's radio adaptation of *The War of the Worlds* and the origin stories of patriotic superheroes in the lead-up to World War II, and ending with Paul Verhoeven's largely satirical and anti-military movie version of Heinlein's pro-military SF novel *Starship Troopers*. My intention was to show how SF had sometimes reflected and sometimes arguably inspired Americans' changing opinion of their military from what a Haldeman character describes as "the last good war, as though there was ever a good one," through the Cold War, the defeat in Vietnam, and the aftermath of the collapse of the Soviet Union. At that time, it seemed unlikely that the U.S., having already invaded Afghanistan, would embark on another war by the time I finished my thesis—much less that it would be embroiled in *two*, one of which would last longer than the Vietnam War (as I write this, the U.S. still has approximately 10,000 serving military personnel stationed in Afghanistan and is performing manned airstrikes against Islamic State in Iraq, as well as having hundreds of troops stationed at the U.S. Embassy and consulates and at Baghdad International Airport). As a result, this grew in the telling, to become the book you now hold.

This study is aimed at science fiction readers and academics who are interested in the background of the genre, as well as lecturers teaching courses on the history of science fiction. It is not a comprehensive history of the genre: despite my best efforts, it is inevitable that I've missed discussing some relevant material, particularly more recent work, though I have attempted to cover science fiction in the media of comics, films, television and (to a lesser degree) computer games, as well as novels and short fiction. For one thing, these visual media are what most people—particularly most in the U.S. military—would, to paraphrase Damon Knight, "be what they point to when they say 'that's science fiction.'" As influential and enduring as novels such as *Starship Troopers* or *The Forever War* have undeniably been, they are less well-known than *Superman*, *Star Trek* or *Star Wars*.

Secondly, the nature of these media has meant that because they are generally collaborative efforts, and are more costly to produce and thus are aimed at a mass audience in the hope of recouping this expense. They are also more likely to reflect popular opinion of the time as regards the image of the military and any military action than any book or short story that may represent a dissenting minority viewpoint would.

Finally, while science fiction writers are generally free to describe anything they can imagine and put into words, filmmakers and television producers often find that they can save money and increase profits by using military hardware and military personnel, or at least war surplus props and military-issue stock footage, to put their visions onto the screen. This may require script approval from the U.S. military—effectively granting them control of what Eagleton terms "the means of literary production."

This book is intended as a companion to other SF histories such as John Clute and Peter Nicholls's *Encyclopedia of Science Fiction*, Brian Aldiss and David Wingrove's *Trillion Year Spree*, Frederic Jameson's *Archaeologies of the Future*, H. Bruce Franklin's *War Stars: The Superweapon and the American Imagination,* and other reference works which I have found invaluable, including journals such as *Extrapolations* and *Science Fiction Studies.* It is *not* intended to be a "CliffsNotes"-type substitute for reading any of the short stories or novels discussed in this book ... though I can understand and sympathize if your own interest in the genre isn't so great that you are willing to sit through *King Dinosaur* or *The Beast of Yucca Flats* without the commentary by the team from *Mystery Science Theater 3000,* or *Star Wars Episode I: The Phantom Menace* under any circumstances.

Introduction: "The Impact of Actual or Imagined Science"

[Science fiction] is now largely—in emphasis and in fact—an American artform, coinciding with a time of great technological evolution and with the rise of the USA to super-power status.—*Brian Aldiss and David Wingrove*[1]

Basically, of course, the science fictioneer is simply the citizen of the Technological Era, whose concern is, say, the political effect of a United States base on the Moon.—*John W. Campbell*[2]

America is a nation of liars, and for that reason science fiction has a special claim to be our national literature, as the art form best adapted to telling the lies we like to hear and to pretend we believe.—*Thomas M. Disch*[3]

Science fiction is a genre that defies easy definition; creators, critics, aficionados and publishers seem to delight in disagreeing on what is science fiction and what lies beyond its nebulous borders—in the realm of fantasy, or horror, or technothriller. Norman Spinrad's "science fiction is anything that's published as science fiction"[4] or the definition attributed to John W. Campbell that "science fiction is what science fiction editors buy" would seem to exclude popular forms such as film, comics and television, as well as many things published before the term "science fiction" was coined. Rather more useful are the Merriam-Webster Dictionary definition, "fiction dealing principally with the impact of actual or imagined science on society or individuals or having a scientific factor as an essential orienting component"; John W. Campbell's "an honest effort at prophetic extrapolation from the known"; and Robert Heinlein's "realistic speculation about possible future events based solidly on adequate knowledge of the real world, past and present."[5] These, similarly, exclude many works widely accepted as science fiction, but they do suggest some common elements: predicting possible futures by means of extrapolation, and the role of applied science (technology) in shaping those futures.

"Future," of course, is relative: many science fiction stories have been set in a year that we now consider the past, Orwell's *Nineteen Eighty-Four* and Clarke's *2001: A Space Odyssey* being among the famous examples (Orwell's telescreens are now entirely feasible, but Clarke's manned mission to Saturn and HAL 9000 have yet to be realized). Ray Bradbury has even described *Singin' in the Rain* as "the only science-fiction musical film ever made" because the plot concerns "the invention of sound and its shattering consequences,"[6] and speculates that if it could have been shown to George Bernard Shaw before "the invention of sound" (in movies), Shaw would have extrapolated the effects of this new technology.[7] By this standard, alternative world stories where the past is changed by an anachronistic technological development, such as Twain's *A Connecticut Yankee in King Arthur's Court*, L. Sprague de Camp's *Lest Darkness Fall*, Harry Turtledove's *The Guns of the South* or Alan Moore's *Watchmen*, would still count as science fiction. *Star Wars Episode IV: A New Hope*, set "a long time ago in a galaxy far, far away," has as its premise the development of a new superweapon, the Death Star, intended to be "the ultimate power in the universe," changing society by its mere existence and implied threat, and therefore I would argue that it still qualifies as science fiction (as well as drawing heavily on several other genres).

I will be using the idea of "fiction that speculates on the possible impact of (applied) science on society or individuals" as an identifying characteristic of science fiction rather than an exclusive definition, while admitting there may be stories (in a variety of formats) that lack this element but are nonetheless widely regarded as science fiction. Beyond this, I can only fall back on Damon Knight's definition that "science fiction is what I point to and say 'that's science fiction.'"[8]

◆ ◆ ◆

Charles Gannon has suggested that science fiction has been "directly influencing the planning and development of military strategies" since the 1960s.[9] H. Bruce Franklin has argued that science fiction ideas are so engrained in the American psyche that they "profoundly influenced how the [Vietnam] war was conceived and conducted: fantasies of technowonders and of superheroes,"[10] and he describes "future-war novels"[11] published as early as 1881 that "incited the public to yearn for a large peacetime war fleet."[12] This may seem rather a heavy burden to place on a genre of fiction which is intended primarily as entertainment, but it accords with Eagleton's statement: "Literature is an agent as well as an effect of [political] struggles, a crucial mechanism by which the language and ideology of an imperialist class establishes its hegemony ... also a zone in which such struggles achieve stabilization—in which the contradictory political unity of imperial and indigenous, dominant and subordinate social classes is articulated and reproduced in the contradictory unity of a 'common language' itself."[13]

In this book, I aim to show that for more than seventy years, ideas that were introduced or popularized in science fiction—particularly American science fiction—have influenced not only the high-ranking strategists and developers of weapons systems such as the proposed "Star Wars" missile defense and "Future Force Warrior," but also air force ground crews who have adorned planes with the likenesses of comic-book heroes, reservists who have taken the names of science fiction characters or adopted their emblems as their own, and Defense Department officials who have used science fiction tropes in their recruitment posters and ads and given assistance to producers of science fiction entertainments which they hope will improve the image and further the aims of the U.S. military. It has also been used by American soldiers and civilians during and after wars as a means of questioning the nature, activities, cost, and sometimes the very necessity of the U.S. military establishment.

In part, this is because science fiction has become part of Eagleton's "common language," or as Aldiss aptly puts it, "part of the cultural wallpaper"[14] of the English-speaking world. Terms invented by science fiction writers, such as "ansible," "antigravity," "cyberspace," "death ray," "robot," "ET," "Jedi," "Klingon" and "warp drive," can now be found in the Oxford English Dictionary. "Daleks" are mentioned in the *SAS Survival Handbook*,[15] and the Australian Defence Force has named its knowledge productivity framework TARDIS, after the "bigger on the inside" spacecraft/time machine from *Doctor Who* (the U.K.'s military communication satellite network is, rather alarmingly, known as Skynet, but this name predates *The Terminator* by 15 years). Characters from *Star Wars* are used to sell everything from labelmakers to car insurance to religion, as in this poster for a UWA Christian Union meeting bearing the likenesses of the *Star Wars* characters Yoda and Darth Vader as representations of good and evil, presumably on the assumption that these would be more immediately recognized by students than Jesus and the Devil. Another poster adorning university campuses in 2003 depicted George W. Bush as Major Kong from the 40-year-old but still instantly identifiable *Dr. Strangelove*, waving a cowboy hat as he rides a bomb down to (presumably) Iraq.

Science-fiction references have become even more prevalent in the U.S. in the twenty-first century. In June 2004 alone, editorial writers at the

Poster for Christian Union, University of Western Australia.

New York Times referred to *The Beast From 20,000 Fathoms, The Stepford Wives, Invasion of the Body Snatchers* and the Damon Knight story and *The Twilight Zone* episode "To Serve Man" when describing White House staff.[16] Americans protesting against Attorney-General John Ashcroft played the Imperial March (Darth Vader's theme) outside his invitation-only lectures.[17] A *New York Times* writer described Vice-President Cheney as "the potty-mouthed Darth Vader"[18] and "Vice-President Strangelove."[19]

President George W. Bush referred to Aldous Huxley's *Brave New World* in a speech condemning stem cell research,[20] while Al Gore and newspaper editorials described the Bush government as "Orwellian"[21] and used terminology from *Nineteen Eighty-Four*—"memory hole,"[22] "Oceania,"[23] and "thought police."[24] Cheney admitted (or possibly boasted) that people see him as "the Darth Vader of the administration,"[25] and Congressman David Wu, in a speech before Congress, described members of Bush's War Cabinet who call themselves "the Vulcans" (after a statue of Vulcan in Condoleezza Rice's hometown, not the planet in *Star Trek*) as "Klingons in the White House."[26] More recently, the *New York Times* journalist Scott Anderson wrote that "most modern battlefields have no recognizable boundaries or rules of conduct; they bear less resemblance to any traditional war movie than, say, to *Mad Max*," while another review in the same issue mentioned *Dr. Strangelove*.[27]

So far, this could be true of any genre of fiction which introduced a large number of neologisms into English. But science fiction's preoccupation with "the possible impact of (applied) science on society or individuals," or what Franklin terms "technowonders," is one very much shared by the U.S. military.

The U.S. military, arguably even more than any other body, has long been increasingly reliant on developing and maintaining technology at least equal, and preferably superior, to that of its present and possible future enemies—a tradition that Franklin traces back to the invention of the submarine *American Turtle* during the Revolutionary War, and which has become even more important with the very long supply lines involved in America's foreign wars.[28] The technology developed at the U.S. military's behest has often realized or even exceeded the creations of earlier speculative fiction: the military has then, in many cases, appropriated the names given to these devices by the science fiction writers and, thereby, some of the mystique or brand-name recognition of tropes that are already "part of the cultural wallpaper."

As Jackson and Nexon state, "What kinds of narrative an audience will accept limits what public policies officials can pursue,"[29] and science fiction has often made it easier for audiences to accept narratives that feature the type of technology the U.S. military has, or claims to have, or seeks: for example, Graham quotes Americans who believe that the "Star Wars" missile defense already exists because "we've seen it in the movies."[30] (The degree to which this has actually been part of the science fiction creators' intent, or contrary to it, is an issue I will discuss in later chapters.) For various reasons, the U.S. military, from its elected commander-in-chief

U.S. Army Modernization ad, 2003.

down to recruitment officers trying to meet a quota, has to work harder than those of many other countries to "sell itself" to the taxpayers who support it ... and the kinds of narrative it has used in seeking to gain acceptance have often drawn on the pre-existing tropes of science fiction to make expensive weapon projects seem more familiar and therefore more acceptable, or to portray their enemies as comic-book villains armed with stolen WMDs that the "good guys" would balk at using. Whether or not the tropes can be demonstrated to have inspired these tactics, their role in popular culture has certainly facilitated them.

Similarly, the industries that consume so much of the U.S. military budget use public relations campaigns to sell their product—to the government, to the military, to American voters who must decide whether the money was well spent, and in some cases to other friendly governments in the market for military vehicles and weapons. To popularize some of their creations, they have resorted to science fiction terminology to describe items such as the Taser (an acronym for Thomas A. Swift's Electric Rifle, named after the science fiction novel *Tom Swift and His Electric Rifle*), the Raptor fighter, PHASR (Personnel Halting and Stimulation Response), JEDI (Joint Expeditionary Digital Information) and HULC (Human Universal Load Carrier).

Van Creveld's *Technology and War* gives a dual explanation for the use of names and insignia on weapons and armor. The practice of naming

World War II soldiers with inscribed artillery shells (National Archive).

Hellfire missile inscribed "In Memory Honorable Ronald Reagan."

a weapon, suit of armor, or other equipment originally served "to endow the device with the desirable qualities implied by its name," and even in an age when "few people believe in saints and magic any longer," this is of "apparent benefit in raising troop morale."[31] Van Creveld cites the example of Roman soldiers inscribing the names of their targets on their arrows and sling bullets[32]; similar missives are still inscribed on modern missiles and bombs, by American servicemen as well as others[33]—the most famous cinematic example being the warheads in *Dr. Strangelove, or How I Learned to Stop Worrying and Love the Bomb*.

Other military equipment (particularly vehicles) may also be given names by the manufacturer, the high command, or the people who actually use them: some of these names were first formulated by science fiction writers (such as Jeep or X-wing), while others were coincidentally or subsequently used as titles or *noms de guerre* in science fiction narratives to convey the same sense of power, mission, or menace (e.g., USS *Enterprise*, Thor, Hercules, Vigilante, Gladiator, Starfire).

Van Creveld also suggests that weapons with a fearsome reputation are "not without a certain psychological value in battle…. Wars, to quote Patton, are won by frightening the enemy. An enemy who can be made

X-wing Research Vehicle, a joint DARPA-NASA project. Photograph by NASA, 1986.

to run away does not require to be killed."[34] Even if it doesn't frighten an enemy into running away, a weapon that seems more threatening than it actually is may deter enemies from attacking—a technique familiar both to military strategists and science fiction aficionados. Joe Haldeman's *1968*, for example, describes the attempt by the Vietnam-era U.S. military to endow the M16 rifle with a murderous reputation by nicknaming it "The Black Death"[35]; in *Star Wars*, similarly, Governor Tarkin assures his officers, "Fear will keep the local systems in line. Fear of this battle station."[36] Again, this depends on "the kinds of narrative an audience will accept"— as Dr. Strangelove says, "The doomsday machine is terrifying. It's simple to understand. And completely credible, and convincing."[37] Ideally, as in that case, a weapon with a sufficiently fearsome reputation might never have to be used at all, might not have to work as advertised, and, if it assumes the role of a myth (in the Barthesian sense of being believed in) *might not even need to exist*: witness the psychological/political impact of the "Star Wars" missile defense in negotiations between America and Russia, or of Saddam Hussein's long-since-scrapped weapons of mass destruction. The usefulness to the military of having a popular genre that creates and perpetuates such myths is clear.

As well as lowering the morale of the enemy, the science fiction roots of these "technowonders and superheroes"[38] may be used to boost the morale of the U.S. military's own personnel. As I will demonstrate, the

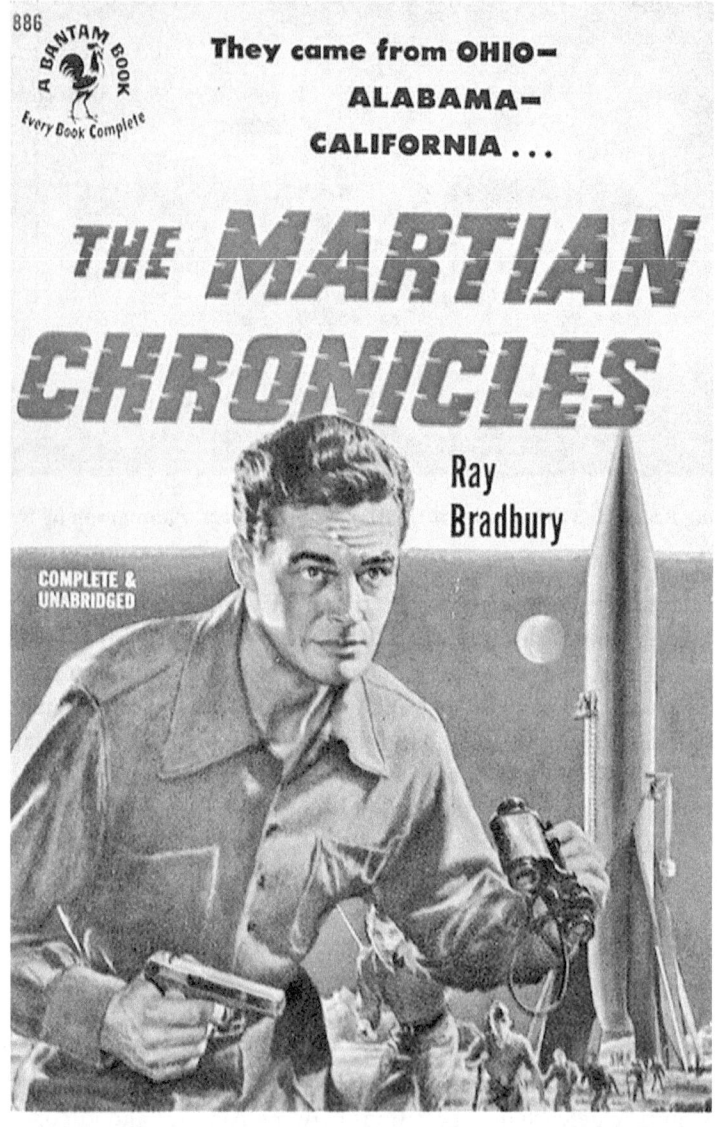

Cover of first paperback edition of Ray Bradbury's *The Martian Chronicles*.

U.S. military has enhanced recruitment campaigns by borrowing power fantasies and glamorous depictions of military life from science fiction. The image of a square-jawed man in a distinctive and possibly protective garment, armed with an as-yet-unrealized weapon, has been used for U.S. military recruitment as well as on science fiction movie posters, superhero comics, and the covers of science fiction pulps and games.

Furthermore, while generals are sometimes accused of "preparing for the previous war," many science fiction narratives attempt to anticipate *future* wars using new weapons—sometimes against strictly hypothetical enemies such as extraterrestrials or robots (who may, of course, be thinly

"The U.S. Army Natick Soldier Research Development and Engineering Center is testing out what could be the next generation of protective headgear. Developed by Revision Military, a company known for ballistic eyewear, this new modular helmet system [right] was designed for the Helmet Electronics and Display System-Upgradeable Protection (HEaDS-UP) program. Although the helmet bears a striking resemblance to the kind worn in popular combat warfare game, *Halo* [left], suppliers say this is a coincidence. 'I think military industrial designers and the entertainment industry look to each other for inspiration but this product was not modeled after *HALO*,' Revision marketing communications manager Jennifer Zimmerman said" (Amanda Marcias, "Supplier Denies that the New U.S. Military Helmet Is Based on '*Halo*,'" *Business Insider*, 30 October 2013).

U.S. Army Sgt. Dan Harshman (right) displays the 2010 Future Force Warrior uniform system, the first phase of the U.S. military's Future Combat Systems project. The 2010 MultiCam uniform features physiological monitoring sensors and headgear designed as "the situational awareness hub" of the system. Army Staff Sgt. Raoul Lopez poses in the all black 2020 Future Force Warrior uniform, which also features bio sensors and adds smart fabric body armor, a sustenance pack and a digital display visor. Photograph by Phil Copeland. Other photographs of the 2020 uniform include a forearm-mounted weapon similar to that of high-tech superheroes.

veiled representations of earthly foes), but sometimes against nations seen as a genuine potential threat, as with much of the speculative fiction written in the lead-up to World War II or during the Cold War. These hypotheticals can also be used by the military for planning tactics and strategy, or for recruitment.

I do not mean to imply here that the ideology of *all* American science fiction texts should be conflated with the general ideology of the U.S. military; much of it has been overtly and implicitly anti-military, or employs "technowonders" as story elements in cautionary tales rather than power fantasies—Pandora rather than Hercules, or Dr. Faust rather than *panzerfaust*. However, there has long been a subgenre of science fiction adventure—arguably the most commercially successful, and what most of the American public would (to paraphrase Damon Knight) point to when they say "science fiction"—that promotes the idea that individuals can be the most effective force for good by virtue of being proficient in the use of weaponry more advanced than any used by their opponents, and granted greater mobility by superior technology.

This subgenre is the oldest of Fredric Jameson's "various stages of science fiction," which he defines as (1) "Adventure, or 'space opera' which comes most immediately out of the work of Jules Verne"; (2) "Science (or at least the mimesis of science) which might classically be dated from the first SF pulps"; (3) "Sociology, or better still, social satire or 'cultural critique'"; (4) Subjectivity; (5) Aesthetics; and (6) Cyberpunk.[39] Jameson assigns dates to these stages, but also states that they overlap and "the dates are merely symbolic." Of these six "stages," it is the oldest two (to which Jameson ascribes dates of 1917 and 1926, respectively) which are of most interest in this case, as they have proved remarkably durable—not only in science fiction literature, but (at least as importantly, and arguably more so) in those other media that have formed part of the "cultural wallpaper": comics, film, television and most recently, computer games. They are also the "stages" of science fiction which are of most use to the U.S. military in its search for "narrative[s] which an audience will accept,"[40] and I would venture that this usefulness has contributed greatly to their longevity—that they are, to quote Disch "the art form best adapted to telling the lies [the U.S. military and those who support it] like to hear and to pretend [they] believe."[41]

It must be remembered, too, that American science fiction publishing/production, being a commercial enterprise, also strives to create believable narratives; publishers are more likely to publish work with a narrative which they believe will be accepted by a significant proportion of readers

Cover art for *War Machine*, Vol. 1: *Iron Heart*, Marvel Comics.

at that time, whether this readership be pacifistic or pro-military. This aspect of timeliness—in Eagleton's terms, a gap between "literary means of production" and "general means of production"—may affect when a piece of work is published (as with Isaac Asimov's antiwar story "The Weapon," unsaleable in 1938, or Kate Wilhelm's My Lai–inspired story "The Village," written in 1969 but unpublished until 1973: see Chapters 4 and 6, respectively), or how long it remains part of the "cultural wallpaper" (witness the temporary disappearance of the patriotic super-soldiers from comic books after World War II: see Chapter 5), or how it is interpreted (compare Heinlein's 1959 novel *Starship Troopers* with Paul Verhoeven's 1999 film adaptation).

As a result, the image of the U.S. military at any particular time since the 1930s has influenced and inspired American science fiction, and both sides have borrowed each other's tropes when it served their respective purposes. Just as appropriating a name from science fiction could make a piece of military hardware seem more impressive, making a fictional character a member or former member of America's armed forces would instantly identify him as the hero of a story—for some readers at some times, at least. And science fiction writers have long used extrapolations about American wars, weaponry, and military life as story material— arguably beginning as early as 1843 with Edgar Allan Poe's satirical "The Man Who Was Used Up," in which an Indian-fighting U.S. Army general loses so many body parts in his campaigns that nothing remains but an "odd-looking bundle of something" and a collection of magnificent-looking (and fully functional) prosthetics, about which he enthuses volubly.[42] Many science fiction writers, filmmakers and comics have also found it useful to use the contemporary image of the U.S. military and its equipment as a way of reducing the need for exposition or "info-dump": familiar equipment requires less description than new inventions, and when the U.S. military is generally viewed favorably, giving a character a war record places him on the "same side" as the reader. At times when the military's image is tarnished by events such as the My Lai massacre or Abu Ghraib prisoner abuses, conversely, this can also be used as a form of shorthand: blackening a character's name by associating him with bloody and dishonorable campaigns may date back to Chaucer's satirical description of the Knight in the Prologue to *The Canterbury Tales*.[43] More recently, science fiction filmmakers have also used U.S. military stock footage to pad out their films, used war surplus for props and costumes, and depicted the U.S. military favorably in order to gain access to equipment and personnel.

◆ ◆ ◆

Top: Cover art for *The Forever War*, novel by Joe Haldeman, art by Jim Burns, EOS/HarperCollins.

Bottom: Sgt. Philip Morici models Land Warrior individual soldier combat system. Photograph by Gerry J. Gilmore, 6/7/07.

Introduction

In *War Stars: The Superweapon and the American Imagination*, Franklin traces science fiction ideas which have influenced the U.S. military back from the "Star Wars" missile defense fantasies through the nuclear arms race to "The End of New York" (1881), a story by a former naval officer that "launched an influential subgenre of American future-war fiction: stories intended to scare the public into a vast military preparedness campaign."[44]

While the origin of science fiction has been variously attributed to Mary Shelley[45] and Poe,[46] and its roots back as far as Lucian of Samosata or even Homer, I would argue that its recognition as a distinct genre and its prominence in American popular culture dates back only as far as the late 1920s, the time of Jameson's "second stage" of science fiction, when the terms "science fiction" and "Buck Rogers" both entered the language (via the American publications *Amazing Stories* in 1927 and a newspaper comic strip in 1929, respectively), and that superheroes with science fiction origins (extraterrestrials or super-scientists) came to eclipse gun-toting cowboys as symbols of American might while war fears were escalating during the 1930s.

While many American science fiction writers contributed to the war effort in the 1940s and would have had their ideas of the role of the military

Cover art for *Universal Soldier* DVD: Jean-Claude van Damme, Dolph Lundgren.

largely shaped by this experience, the relationship between American science fiction and the U.S. military has not invariably been symbiotic, or even entirely civil. If the power fantasies of Jameson's first two stages of science fiction,[47] combined with the World War II image of an American military machine heroically saving the world from an absolute evil, contributed to the hubris which sent the U.S. military into Vietnam (as Franklin suggests), then the disillusionment created by that later war helped divide American science fiction writers into camps described by Darko Suvin as warmongers and war critics.[48] Simon Schama saw the division as between the Hamiltonian versus the Jeffersonian—the former seeing war as necessary not only to "defend liberty" and other American ideals but to aggressively disseminate them,[49] and co-operating with the U.S. military in this process; the latter, seeing military might and its exercise as "inconsistent with the 'principles of republican government,'"[50] potentially oppressing the very people the military claimed to defend and even threatening to bring about their extinction in a nuclear holocaust. The "Jeffersonians" used their fiction and other forums to actively protest against U.S. military action. In time, too, a search for a new narrative that both the public and U.S. military found easier to accept than the lessons of Vietnam would lead to the huge commercial success of the good-vs.-evil space opera of *Star Wars* and the financial burden of the still-unrealized "Star Wars" missile defense.

◆ ◆ ◆

For the purposes of this book, I will be dealing with science fiction in many of its forms, including novels and short stories, movies, television, and comics, but all with one element in common—they depict science and technology that are at a conceptual, rather than a concrete, state at the time of writing (e.g., nuclear weapons before 1945, manned space flight before 1961, communication with extraterrestrial and/or artificial intelligences, etc.). My definition of "American science fiction" will include any science fiction written by writers living or born in the USA *or* written in English primarily for the U.S. market and first published by American publishers. This encompasses works written by American-born authors such as Harry Harrison that were first published in British magazines, as well as works by British-born writers such as Brian W. Aldiss, Arthur C. Clarke and Alan Moore that were written for American publishers, and works by foreign-born filmmakers working in the U.S., such as Ang Lee and Peter Watkins. I will, however, note when the author is not a U.S. citizen or resident on those occasions that this distinction is significant.

1. "See You Later, Space Cowboy"

"Space is like Texas, only larger."—*Thomas M. Disch*[1]

"[T]here isn't an American president since Eisenhower who hasn't ended up, at some point or other, being depicted by the world's cartoonists as a cowboy astride a phallic missile."—*David Aaronovitch*[2]

"Boys' wild west stuff given an interplanetary setting, with handsome young space-pilots instead of cowboys and sheriffs, and 'Martians' and 'moon-men' instead of Indians and outlaws."—*H.P. Lovecraft*[3]

The rise of American "technowarrior" science fiction largely coincides with the decline of the "wild west" as a major source of American mythology. "Scientific romances" or "edisonades" had shared the dime novels with tales of cowboys and Indians since Edward Ellis's 1868 *The Steam Man of the* Prairies.[4] "The End of New York" was published in 1881, which was also the year of the gunfight at the O.K. Corral and the death of Billy the Kid.

If there is an art form better "adapted to telling the lies [Americans] like to hear and to pretend we believe" than science fiction, it's the western. Richard Slotkin describes "The Myth of the Frontier" as America's "oldest and most characteristic myth ... called on to account for our rapid economic growth, our emergence as a powerful nation-state, and our distinctively American approach to the socially and culturally disruptive processes of modernization."[5]

Garry Wills, similarly, says of the archetypal cowboy actor John Wayne: "He embodies the American myth. The archetypical American is a displaced person—arrived from a rejected past, breaking into a glorious future, on the move, fearless himself, feared by others, a killer but cleansing the world of things that 'need killing.'"[6] Wills adds that "Westerns, like science fiction or horror movies, push a fixed moral system out into alien space where its assumptions no longer apply,"[7] an accusation that has also often been leveled at the U.S. military.

The usefulness of this archetypically American genre to the U.S. military is obvious, particularly as the cowboy is not only seen as heroic and honorable, pushing back the frontier to make more lands safe for women and children, but as perpetually armed and famed for his speed "on the draw." (Horses, period firearms and former cowboys were also readily available in Hollywood in its early days—John Wayne and director John Ford met the real Wyatt Earp in the 1920s when he was trying to sell his story to Hollywood—and were then much cheaper than giant steam men.) The cowboy had the added advantage of being a recognizably unique American figure, familiar to billions through more than 4000 American movies since *The Great Train Robbery* in 1903: Slotkin points out that the genre was once so popular that by 1908 "distributors listed their products under the headings 'Drama,' 'Comic' and 'Western.'"[8]

Slotkin, Wills, Joanna Bourke and others provide many examples of American soldiers whose behavior in World War II and Vietnam reveals the influence of westerns on their image of the American fighting man (and vice versa; Slotkin argues convincingly that Westerns made in the 1960s, such as *The Magnificent Seven* and *The Wild Bunch*, used Mexico as a metaphor for Vietnam, and Bourke that antiwar films such as *Little Big Man* "explicitly linked the genocide of the Indians in the American West with the war in Vietnam").[9] Livermore, home of the Lawrence Livermore laboratories where American nuclear weapons are designed, makes the link strongly with a city seal that depicts a mounted cowboy and an old-fashioned representation of an atom. The U.S. Army's 7th Cavalry Regiment, now an armored regiment, still features the head of a Native American in a feathered war bonnet on its coat of arms from the days of the Indian Wars (including its defeat at the Little Big Horn). One Humvee shown on news telecasts of the war on Iraq in 2003 was emblazoned "Cowboy Op,"[10] and the commander of the U.S. Strategic Command (STRATCOM), General James Cartwright, takes his nickname "Hoss Cartwright" from the character in the TV western, *Bonanza*.

Much of the credit and/or blame for turning the "Peacemaker"-toting cowboy into a symbol must go to actor Marion Morrison, better known as the archetypical Western hero John Wayne. Jane Mills points out:

> Wayne has haunted the dreams of Americans for decades.... He became a star by carefully fabricating his screen image as the symbol of American masculinity. He built up his persona—his "John Wayne-ness"—through carefully considered strategies, such as concealing his refusal to fight in World War II and refusing to play roles that didn't fit the image he wanted to project. Despite script and plot requirements, Wayne refused to play a coward for Howard Hawks or shoot a man in the back for a Don Siegel movie.
>
> The ensuing "John Wayne," whether admired or loathed, had a profound effect on

how the American male came to be defined. General Douglas MacArthur considered him the model U.S. soldier; the non-combatant Wayne was awarded the Veterans of Foreign Wars gold medal, and received the "Iron Mike" from the Marines.[11]

Bourke, similarly, says: "In the 'Indian Country' of Vietnam, 'The Duke' or John Wayne was the hero most emulated. Indeed, in July 1971, the Marine Corps League named him the man 'who best exemplified the word 'American.'"[12]

Bourke goes on to list several American soldiers who consciously modeled themselves after Wayne, including one woman. Wayne also had a piece of ubiquitous U.S. military equipment named in his honor during World War II—the P-38 C-ration can opener. More recently, the toilet paper issued with MREs has been nicknamed a "John Wayne" because "it's rough, tough, and don't take shit from nobody."[13]

Slotkin's point about the applicability of the myth of the frontier to the "distinctively American approach to the socially and culturally disruptive processes of modernization,"[14] and Wills's mention of a "rejected past, breaking into a glorious future,"[15] indicate the significance of technological change in this particular myth. The "cowboy-adventurer"[16] is not a science fiction creation, nor even entirely fictitious, nor the only violent quasi-historical culture hero adopted by a country as a symbol of national identity. Other examples include England's King Arthur and Romania's Vlad Dracula, both immortalized in the names of their respective countries' military hardware, just as the U.S. immortalized the legendary Davy Crockett in the name of a battlefield nuclear weapon in the 1950s when a TV show of the same name was enjoying enormous success.[17] This "cowboy-adventurer" is, however, probably the first national hero to owe his existence to, and to be symbolized by, mass-produced artifacts of military technology—the revolver and the repeating rifle. Slotkin refers to "a group of Westerns that fetishized particular kinds of weapons: *Colt 45* (1950), *Springfield Rifle* (1952), *Winchester '73* (1953) and *The Gun That Won the West* (1955). The figure of the 'gunfighter' similarly exaggerates a skill that had been merely one of the standard attributes of all cowboy heroes."[18] Franklin, similarly, describes the "cultural significance" of a revolver used by General Nguyen Ngoc Loan to execute a prisoner as "symbolic of the American West."[19] In many films and other narratives, the cowboy-gunfighter is also a precursor of more advanced technology, in the form of the railroad (though this is not always viewed favorably: Slotkin describes several Westerns in which rail barons are villains, and the train in *High Noon* brings not progress but murderous outlaws).

However, after *Dr. Strangelove, or How I Learned to Stop Worrying and Love the Bomb* (1963), in which Slim Pickens waves a ten-gallon hat as he rides the American nuke that triggers the Soviets' Doomsday Bomb, it became less easy to see the cowboy as an appropriate symbol for the American soldier in a Cold War context. The waning glamor of the cowboy may also be attributed to the box-office decline of the Western, John Wayne's descent into "conscious anachronism" and self-caricature from the late 1960s until his death in 1979,[20] and the commercial success of Mel Brooks's *Blazing Saddles* (1974), which McKee credits with having "exposed the Western's fascist heart" with the result that "the genre went into virtual hibernation for twenty years before making a comeback by altering its conventions."[21] (In 1977, before that comeback, George Lucas would tell *Rolling Stone* that he "saw the Western die" as actors and directors who remembered L.A.'s "wild west" days died.[22]) It may also indicate recognition by some in the U.S. government and its military that this particular icon is not as highly regarded overseas, even by U.S. allies, as it is in the USA (where Presidents Ronald Reagan and George W. Bush capitalized on their "cowboy" images). In the words of a widely quoted *London Times* article from 2002: "Many Europeans regard Bush as a gun-toting, semi-articulate cowboy, whose bellicosity reaches far beyond the battlefield."[23] Or as Sardar and Davies say of *Shane*: "What to Americans reads as iconic of simple virtues made safe by a knight-errant of the wilderness, is for the rest of the world full of the ambiguity at the heart of America: violence."[24]

◆ ◆ ◆

American science fiction's relationship to the western has often been commented upon. Slotkin traces the cowboy-adventurer influences in Edgar Rice Burroughs's seminal Barsoom series[25]: Burroughs was a former ranch-hand who had briefly served with "old Indian fighters" in the 7th Cavalry, Custer's former regiment, in Arizona Territory before being discharged for a heart murmur.[26] He would later write four westerns as well as his science fiction and fantasy novels, and Captain John Carter, the hero of the Barsoom series, is a former Confederate officer who claims descent from Pocahontas. Carter, mystically teleported to Mars while cornered by Apaches in Arizona, allies himself with the civilized Red Martians against Green Martians who "fit the general stereotype of Indians as elaborated in works like *The Winning of the West* and are described in passages that paraphrase Cremony's *Life Among the Apache*."[27] Slotkin, like Carl Abbott and Barnard Turner, also compares the importance of the idea of pushing back the frontier in Westerns and SF, particularly the original

Star Trek TV series (which began its title sequence with the phrase "Space, the final frontier") and movies.[28]

John Clute, similarly, notes in *Science Fiction: The Illustrated Encyclopedia*: "In America, as early as 1925 or so, space has become the New Frontier, and it takes heroes, gun-toting inventors, warriors, and cowboys in space to ride their shining new spaceships out into the realm of the unknown."[29] Buck Rogers was named after "contemporary western movie hero, Buck Jones" at the suggestion of the publisher of the comic strip,[30] and the first year of the *Buck Rogers* strip pitted Buck against 25th-century Navajo and outlaws wearing ten-gallon hats and chaps speaking cowboy jargon—"pardner," "tenderfoot," "hoss," etc.[31] The 1935 film serial *The Phantom Empire* had singing cowboy Gene Autry discovering the lost civilization of Murania (complete with robots, death rays, and radium bombs) underneath his ranch.[32] Heinlein described a rejected script for *Destination Moon* (1951) which featured "dude ranches, cowboys, guitars and hillbilly songs on the Moon,"[33] and Douglas Hill said of Heinlein that his "right-wing conservative stance owes at least as much to John Wayne as to Ayn Rand."[34] Harry Harrison has demonstrated how easily pulp magazine cover artists could "change the horse for a monster and you had SF instead of a western."[35] *Galaxy* editor Horace Gold railed against the prose equivalent of this in an ad on the back cover of the first issue in 1950 (and often reprinted), featuring the opening paragraphs of two stories which, he said, "You'll never see … in *Galaxy*":

> Jets blasting, Bat Durston came screeching down through the atmosphere of Bbllzznaj, a tiny planet seven billion light years from Sol. He cut out his super-hyper-drive for the landing … and at that point, a tall, lean spaceman stepped out of the tail assembly, proton gun-blaster in a space-tanned hand.
> "Get back from those controls, Bat Durston," the tall stranger lipped thinly. "You don't know it, but this is your last space trip."
> Hoofs drumming, Bat Durston came galloping down through the narrow pass of Eagle Gulch, a tiny gold colony 400 miles north of Tombstone. He spurred hard for a low overhang of rimrock … and at that point, a tall, lean wrangler stepped out from behind a boulder, six-gun in a sun-tanned hand.
> "Rear back and dismount, Bat Durston," the tall stranger lipped thinly. "You don't know it, but this is your last saddle-jaunt through these parts."[36]

Despite this (or possibly because of it), the comic series *Cowboy Western* became *Space Western* in 1952, pitting a lariat-twirling, six-gun-toting Spurs Jackson and the Space Vigilantes against "Martians and Nazis on the moon when they weren't roping cattle on their Bar-Z ranch in Arizona."[37] In *Lone Star Planet* (1957, aka *A Planet for Texans*), H. Beam Piper and John McGuire sent a gunslinging ambassador to an exaggerated version

YOU'LL NEVER SEE IT IN GALAXY

Jets blasting, Bat Durston came screeching down through the atmosphere of Bbllzznaj, a tiny planet seven billion light years from Sol. He cut out his super-hyper-drive for the landing...and at that point, a tall, lean spaceman stepped out of the tail assembly, proton gun-blaster in a space-tanned hand.

"Get back from those controls, Bat Durston," the tall stranger lipped thinly. "You don't know it, but this is your last space trip."

Hoofs drumming, Bat Durston came galloping down through the narrow pass at Eagle Gulch, a tiny gold colony 400 miles north of Tombstone. He spurred hard for a low overhang of rim-rock...and at that point a tall, lean wrangler stepped out from behind a high boulder, six-shooter in a sun-tanned hand.

"Rear back and dismount, Bat Durston," the tall stranger lipped thinly. "You don't know it, but this is your last saddle-jaunt through these here parts."

Sound alike? They should — one is merely a western transplanted to some alien and impossible planet. If this is your idea of science fiction, you're welcome to it! YOU'LL NEVER FIND IT IN GALAXY!

What you will find in GALAXY is the finest science fiction...authentic, plausible, thoughtful...written by authors who do not automatically switch over from crime waves to Earth invasions; by people who know and love science fiction...for people who also know and love it.

"Bat Durston" ad from back cover of *Galaxy* #1.

of Texas where the public murder of politicians was a legally approved form of free expression (arguably an unusually good example of the predictive potential of science fiction).[38] Bat Durston himself would return in G. Richard Bozarth's "Bat Durston, Space Marshall" (1978),[39] then as a character in Piers Anthony's time-travel fantasy *Bearing an Hourglass* (1984).[40]

As the "high frontier" or "final frontier" became part of the popular

Cover art for *A Planet for Texans*, novella by H. Beam Piper and John McGuire, cover by Ed Emshwiller, Ace Books (a dual edition with *Star Born*).

culture in the 1960s thanks to the American and Soviet space programs, science fiction film and television producers often stressed the resemblance between their projected shows and Westerns (with which studio executives were more familiar and presumably more comfortable). *Star Trek* was promoted to networks as "just another horse opera except that they ride a spaceship instead of a nag" and as "Wagon Train to the Stars,"[41] and featured a re-enactment of the gunfight at the OK Corral in the episode "Spectre of the Gun," as well as a transplanted Native American tribe in "The Paradise Syndrome": according to Richards, Roddenberry "had to rewrite many episodes to insert many action scenes in which Kirk is made to act like the star of a 1960s cowboy show."[42] *Moon Zero Two* (1969) overstressed the links with a typical Western plot involving a grizzled old prospector with a sister named Clementine, "Moon Fargo," and a brawl in a bar complete with dancers in oversize Stetsons and Native American head dresses.[43] *Star Wars* was described by George Lucas in 1975 as a "Flash Gordon kind of movie—with *The Magnificent Seven* thrown in,"[44] and included homage to *The Searchers*[45] and a shoot-out copied from the John Wayne movie *Red River*; *Rolling Stone*'s review described the film as "straight out of *Buck Rogers* and *Flash Gordon* by way of Tolkien ... and about every great western movie ever made" and Han Solo as "John Wayne-ish."[46] *Lost in Space* parodied the space western in its episode "West of Mars," as did the movie *Galaxina* (1980).[47] The original series of *Battlestar Galactica* (1979), which starred *Bonanza* star

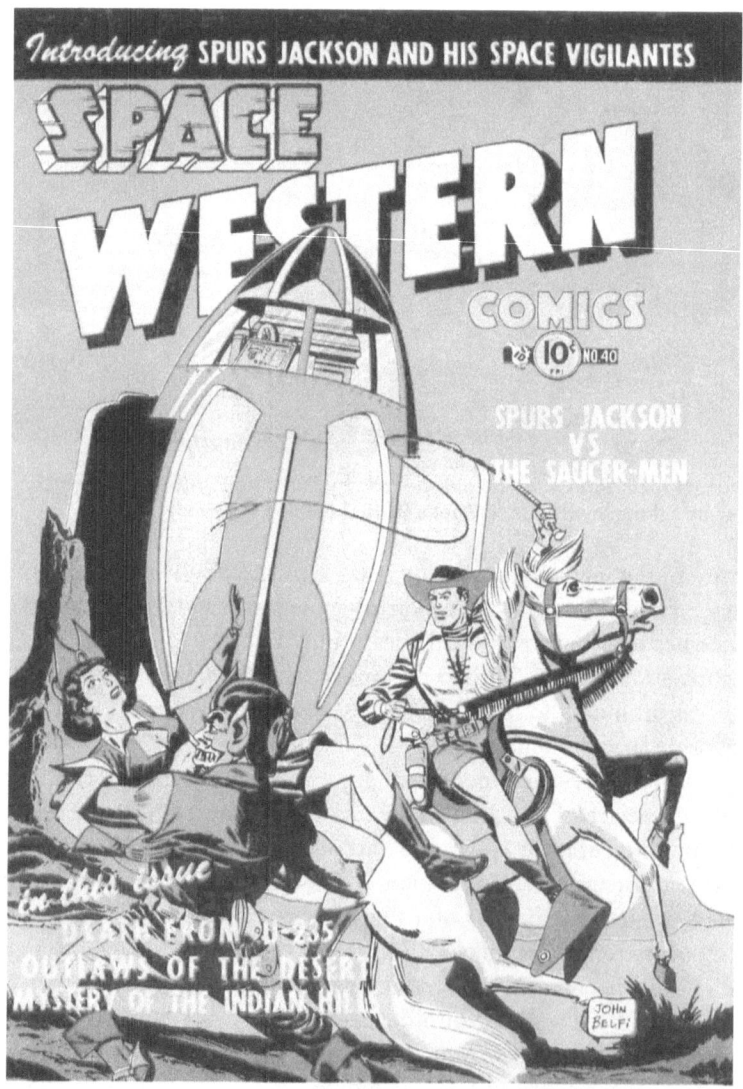

Cover of *Space Western Comics* #40.

Lorne Greene, was known to many fans as "Battlestar Ponderosa" (after the ranch from *Bonanza*), and re-used western costumes, backlots and plots in the episodes "The Lost Warrior" and "The Magnificent Warriors" (based closely on *Shane* and *The Magnificent Seven*, respectively).[48] *Battle Beyond the Stars* (1980) also paid homage to *The Magnificent Seven*, featuring Robert Vaughan reprising his role from the original, with George Peppard's "Space Cowboy," dressed in ranch-hand garb, offering to show the hero *Custer's Last Stand* and going into battle with a muttered "Remember the Alamo!"[49]

Outland (1981) was a remake of *High Noon* set on Io, and was known on set as "High Moon."[50] "Stardust," an episode of *Space: Above and Beyond* (1995), featured the 7th Cavalry (Custer's and Edgar Rice Burroughs's unit) and had a Navajo military intelligence officer using the Navajo language as a code when sending a message that he intended the alien Chigs to intercept and decode (the series was canceled before it was fully explained why the aliens were fluent in Navajo).[51] "Spirits," a 1997 episode of *Stargate SG-1*, featured a transplanted Native American tribe.[52] *Firefly* (2002–2003) and its sequel film *Serenity* (2005) are unashamedly space westerns, complete with horses and covered wagons on frontier planets, spaceships being used to smuggle cattle, country and western music on the soundtrack, frequent use of revolvers and other iconic 19th-century firearms, cowboy slang in the dialogue, and a starship crew largely based on the archetypes in John Ford's *Stagecoach*—preacher, doctor, prostitute, etc.[53]—and a shootist named Jayne (from John W*ayne*, aka Marion Morrison).[54] The Old West was invaded by extraterrestrials in *Cowboys and Aliens* (2011),[55] recreated as a robotic theme park in *Westworld* (1973) with *The Magnificent Seven* star Yul Brynner back in black and credited simply as "Gunslinger,"[56] and revisited by time travelers in films such as *Timerider* (1982), *Back to the Future Part III* (1990), and *Timecop* (1994).[57]

One similarity that links *all* of these films and television shows is the presence of at least occasional firefights, some of them copied directly from Western movies, and gun-toting heroes—most of whom have, in Wills's words, "arrived from a rejected past, breaking into a glorious future, on the move, fearless himself, feared by others, a killer but cleansing the world of things that 'need killing.'"[58] As the U.S. military moved towards this "glorious future," as planes, tanks, and other hardware became increasingly important and infantry less so, it has increasingly used other tropes more appropriate under the circumstances than a fearless killer from a "rejected past." Heroes more powerful than locomotives, or any other existing machines. Heroes who could fly.

2. "The Eve of the War"
1926 to 1942

> We were living in a time when it was necessary to have heroes who were capable of superheroic capacity, because the enemy was superheroic.—*Will Eisner*[1]
>
> Where's the recruiting office?—*Buck Rogers, 1929*[2]

The first American magazine devoted exclusively to science fiction, *Amazing Stories*, edited by Hugo Gernsback, appeared in 1926 ... though Gernsback didn't use the term "science fiction" (first suggested in a letter from a reader) until 1929, and the phrase would not be widely used for some years. Instead, many in the public named the genre after a character whose first adventure had appeared in *Amazing Stories* in August of 1928 in Phillip Francis Nowlan's novella "Armageddon 2419 A.D." In the novella, he was known simply as Anthony Rogers,[3] but in January 1929, when Nowlan adapted the story for the first newspaper comic strip with a science fiction theme (with artwork by a former U.S. Army officer who still signed himself "Lt. Dick Calkin"), Rogers was nicknamed "Buck" ... and science fiction became known to the public as "that Buck Rogers stuff," an appellation that remained commonplace until the late 1960s and is still in use.[4] Nowlan's story, which features hand-held rocket launchers, is also credited by Frederick Lerner with inspiring the U.S. Army to develop the bazooka.[5]

Equipped with a rocket-assisted "jumping belt" with "reverse weight," World War I veteran and badge-carrying American Legion member Rogers was able to float in mid-air and jump huge distances, an ability that would be emulated by many later comic-strip superheroes.[6] Other superheroic figures emerged in the pulps and newspaper strips during the same decade: the Shadow, with his swirling cape and multiple secret identities, debuted on radio's *Detective Story Hour* in 1930[7]; Doc Savage, the "Man of Bronze," whose hideouts included an Arctic "Fortress of Solitude," first appeared in 1933[8]; and the Phantom, in his skin-tight bodysuit and mask, first appeared in a newspaper strip in February 1936.[9] Science fiction tropes such as extraterrestrials and technowonders also appeared in comics not usually regarded as science-fictional: caveman *Alley Oop* became a time traveler in 1939 and went to the moon in 1947,[10] indestructible wonder-material Eonite featured as a MacGuffin in the *Little Orphan Annie* strip in 1935,[11] and Eugene the Jeep, from a four-dimensional world, appeared in a *Popeye* strip in August 1936.[12]

The comic book as the world now knows it was born in 1933 with the publication of *Funnies on Parade*—a collection of comic strips reprinted from newspapers (which had been running comic strips since 1896). Two years later, Major Malcolm Wheeler-Nicholson, a former U.S. Army officer and writer of military nonfiction (court-martialed for criticizing the Army command in a letter to the *New York Times*), as well as the Western novel *Death at the Corral* and adventure stories for the pulp magazines, created the first comic book to use original material, *New Fun Comics*.[13] Among the people Wheeler-Nicholson hired were former U.S. Army Colonel Lloyd Jacquet (as editor), *Superman* creators Jerome Siegel and Joe Schuster, and future *Captain America* co-creator Joe Simon.[14] The superhero comic book was born in June 1938 in the first issue of *Action Comics*, when Siegel and Schuster's colorfully clad Superman burst down a door in an attempt to gain a reprieve for a woman on Death Row.[15]

The Japanese had occupied Beijing and the Germans had bombed Guernica the year before, German troops had invaded Austria in March, and many in the USA already had war jitters—as demonstrated by their reactions to Welles's *The War of the Worlds* broadcast show that October.

> Many believed the Martians were actually either Germans or Japanese, a more plausible interpretation of the broadcast, in retrospect. Sylvia Holmes, a Newark housewife, said ... "I kept saying over and over again to everybody I met. "Don't you know New Jersey is destroyed by the Germans—it's on the radio." I was all excited, and I knew that Hitler didn't appreciate President Roosevelt's telegram a couple of weeks ago."[16]

Playwright Howard Koch, unaware of the chaos caused by the broadcast until the next morning, similarly recalled: "Catching ominous snatches of conversation with words like 'invasion' and 'panic,' I jumped to the conclusion that Hitler had invaded some new territory and that the war we all dreaded had finally broken out."[17] Even the military became involved in the panic: "New Jersey national guardsmen flooded the armories of Essex and Sussex counties with calls asking when and where to report," and "the governor of Pennsylvania even offered to send troops to New Jersey to help quell the Martian insurgency."[18]

According to the *New York Times*, "military experts" in Washington drew lessons from the broadcast, foreseeing "in time of war, radio loudspeakers in every public square in the United States and a system of voluntary self-regulation of radio ... to refrain from over-dramatizing war announcements which would react on the public like Sunday night's fictional announcement."[19]

War fears were nothing new in American fiction, of course: Franklin mentions "projected invasions or attacks by China, Spain, Britain, Japan and Russia" of the last two decades of the 19th century and "from Germany, France, Italy, Mexico and Africa" between 1900 and the U.S. entry into World War I.[20] But by the 1930s, radio and the comics were reaching enormous audiences: Welles's play was heard by an estimated six million listeners—with 30 million listening to NBC on the same night[21]; *Superman*'s readership, which began in *Action Comics* with an initial circulation of about 200,000 in 1938,[22] rose in only four years to an estimated 12 million in the comics, with newspaper strips adding another 25 million, plus radio plays on 85 stations and serials showing in "the majority of some 17,000 movie houses."[23] These mass media would give the government a useful platform for drumming up support for the war effort when this became necessary.

A future war was obviously in the thoughts of Superman's creators, Jerome Siegel and Joe Schuster, when, in his second appearance in 1938, "Superman crushes a conspiracy involving a U.S. senator, a lobbyist and a munitions manufacturer who wish to embroil the United States in a foreign war.... Echoing the Nye Committee's conclusion that 'merchants of death' had conspired to involve the United States in the Great War, Superman warns that moneyed self-interest remained a menace to the national welfare."[24] War fears were also in evidence when Timely Publications' publisher Martin Goodman brought out the first issue of a new pulp science fiction magazine a month later. *Marvel Science Stories* led with "Survival" by Arthur J. Burks, the blurb reading: "What will the rebirth of America be, when one day the military forces of the world combine to devastate the greatest nation the world has ever known?"[25] According to Stan Lee's *Secrets Behind the Comics* (1947), Goodman was already pacing his office worrying about "the dangers of Nazism and facism" [sic] as early as 1938, and decided to "'use stories in my magazines which have **Nazis** as the villains!' And so was born a new kind of comic magazine publishing policy! A policy of telling the truth about the Nazi menace! And so was born comic magazine covers which dared to be honest...."[26]

While this story sounds a little too idealized to be strictly true (Lee,

Goodman's cousin-in-law, did not begin working for Timely until 1941, the year the Sub-Mariner and the Human Torch teamed up to fight Nazis), Goodman was not the only person in the industry already worrying about Hitler. Will Eisner, creator of *The Spirit* and later of the *Uncle Sam* superhero comic, whose 1939 series "Espionage" had depicted a "mad dictator, bearing a strong resemblance to Adolf Hitler,"[27] conquering Argentina, and then South America, recalled:

> "We were living in a time when it was necessary to have heroes who were capable of superheroic capacity, because the enemy was superheroic," Will Eisner said of the days leading into World War II. "I was 22, 23 years old and Hitler seemed invincible. You'd pick up the morning paper and each day find their army had just marched into another country. We needed an invincible hero to fight an invincible enemy."[28]

Isaac Asimov followed the news of Hitler's exploits "with agonized absorption, becoming ever more fearful of Hitler's might; ever more contemptuous of the Western powers for failing to take a stronger stand against Germany and Japan."[29] However, Asimov was always leery of military solutions, and in 1938, he wrote "The Weapon," in which the hero strives to defeat "the forces of ruthlessness and evil,"[30] not with a "powerful instrument of destruction"[31] but by finding a chemical weapon which would "soften the violent emotions of fear, anger and hate."[32] The story did not sell to the magazines, and was forgotten and not published until 1979. Asimov's story "The Weapon Too Dreadful to Use" (1939) featured a Venusian weapon which decerebrated its victims: the Venusians use it to take back their planet from the human invaders, and attempt to use it as a deterrent for further attacks. Unfortunately, human Admiral von Blumdorff "was as Prussian as his name, and his military code was the simple one of brute force": he dismisses the weapon as a hoax, condemning his entire fleet to mindlessness.[33] The Admiral commits suicide, a treaty is signed, and the Venusians destroy the weapon—leading Fred Pohl to comment, "And after the weapon was destroyed, Earth wiped the Venusians off the face of their planet." Asimov later admitted, "I was naïve enough then to suppose that words and good intentions are sufficient."[34] Even at the height of the war, however, Asimov never entirely overcame his distaste for military solutions, or for the military itself.

◆ ◆ ◆

Patriotic considerations aside, Daniels tells us that Goodman realized in 1939 that comics were more profitable than pulps, and he recycled the Marvel name to create *Marvel Comics*.[35] (*Marvel Science Stories* survived until April 1941, undergoing two name changes—to *Marvel Tales*, then

Marvel Stories—and publishing work by Jack Williamson and Henry Kuttner.) The first issue of Timely's *Marvel Comics*, published in October 1939, featured two superheroes, the Sub-Mariner (created by Bill Everett) and the Human Torch (created by Carl Burgos), who would soon be tackling the "Japanazis."

Meanwhile, back at *Amazing Stories*, the contents pages were starting to show an obsession with matters military: the May 1939 issue featured Asimov's "The Weapon too Dreadful to Use"; "War with Jupiter" by W. Lawrence Hamling and Marc Reisberg; "The Foreign Legion of Mars" by Frederic Arnold Kummer, Jr.; and "Finding 75 Mile Guns" by William P. Schramm.[36] The August issue featured "Warriors of Mars" by Arthur R. Tofte[37]; the November issue, "Dictator of Peace" by Don Wilcox and "Legion of the Dead" by Frederic Arnold Kummer, Jr.[38]; and the December issue, an essay on "Future War Tank" by Henry Julian and a story "Fugitives from Earth" by Nelson Bond.[39] In Bond's story, "the new World War has been going on for 3 years, with no end in sight. Both German and American scientists are developing spaceships in order to escape from the war-torn Earth.... Unable to continue individually, the American and German scientists eventually trade secrets and the two spaceships, the *Goddard* and the *Oberth*, take off."[40] Also in 1939, the U.S. Army commissioned an off-road military vehicle. Labeled GP (General Purpose), it was soon dubbed "Jeep" by soldiers, after a pet of Popeye's from E.C. Segar's comic strip—a prescient orchid-eating creature from the fourth dimension. It appears to have been the first piece of U.S. military equipment to be named after a science fiction trope; it would not be the last.

In August of the same year, physicist and science fiction author Leo Szilard, inspired by the predicted use of "atomic bombs" against cities in H.G. Wells's 1914 novel *The World Set Free*,[41] and with the assistance of Albert Einstein, Edward Teller and Eugene Wigner, wrote a letter urging President Roosevelt "to speed up the experimental work" necessary to build an atom bomb before the Germans were able to do so. That same month, *Liberty* magazine began publishing the serial *Lightning in the Night*, "A Story of the Invasion of America," written by Fred Allhoff. In the serial, an Axis-Soviet alliance conquers Europe, then Caribbean and Central American nations, and ultimately attacks the U.S.: the final installment, published in November 1940, had Hitler threatening to use his nuclear weapons against American cities. Fortunately for the U.S., it has secretly been building A-bombs and uses these to force a German surrender.[42] Franklin describes the serial, which Allhoff reportedly wrote after consultation with a U.S. Army lieutenant general and a U.S. Navy rear admiral, as "blatant propaganda in the hackneyed mode of future war-fiction" but with the new element of "an all-out scientific-industrial effort to develop atomic bombs."[43]

During the months over which the novel (which Rosenfeld credits with "boosting the sales of the magazine ... to an all-time high")[44] was serialized, the magazine also published several articles and editorials urging a U.S. military buildup and possible intervention, such as "M-Day: How the U.S. is Ready to Mobilize"; "I Was a Hitler Agent in the USA"; "Prepare to Fight or Face National Death"; and "Berlin Should Be Bombed," by H.G. Wells.

In September 1939, in an attempt to "inspire the spirit of national patriotism," Congress urged various publishing media "to encourage those literary themes that were consistent with the government's position on the war."[45] The timing was fortunate for *Marvel Comics*, and their writers and artists responded quickly. The cover of Issue 4, in February 1940, showed the Sub-Mariner fighting Nazis. *Marvel Comics* writers Joe Simon and Jack Kirby attempted to create more heroes to rival the popularity of Detective Comics' Superman and Batman (created by Bob Kane and Bill Finger in 1939) and Timely's own Sub-Mariner and the Human Torch, but all of these failed financially—perhaps because, as Simon stated, "We were looking for a villain first, and Hitler was the villain."[46]

◆ ◆ ◆

In 1940, during the Blitz, Asimov wrote "History," in which a neutral Martian historian living on Earth is blackmailed into revealing what he knows about an ancient disintegrator weapon that will enable Earth to win its ongoing war against Venus. In this story, which predicts that Hitler will be defeated and exiled to Madagascar, the academic, though in favor of a quick end to the war because it interferes with his research, tells an admiral that victory "is just a silly word. History proves dat a war decided on military superiority only lays de groundwork for future wars of retaliation and revenge.... Now to end de war—really end it—you should just say to the plain people of Venus, 'It is unnecessary to fight. Let us just talk—'"[47] The story ends with the disintegrator being used against the Venusians, victory for Earth, and a victory parade barely distinguishable from that which heralded the start of the war.

Also in 1940, Detective Comics editors Jack Liebowitz and Whitney Ellsworth, concerned about foreign sales and American isolationists, continued to keep Superman (already condemned as a Jew by Hitler, presumably because his creators Joe Schuster and Jerry Siegel were Jewish) out of the war in Europe. The editors "didn't allow Superman to even take an implicit stance on the subjects of war and fascism" and decreed that "no DC hero would ever knowingly kill anyone again." Meanwhile, Jerry Siegel was writing *Red, White and Blue*, "about a trio of American military men with no costumes or superpowers" [although even there he was apparently told to make the stories less political after a few months].[48]

Obviously unafraid of being seen as political, Robert A. Heinlein's 1940 short story "Solution Unsatisfactory" tells the story of a U.S. army colonel turned congressman, "one of the Army's No. 1 experts in chemical warfare before a leaky heart put him on the shelf," in whom "ordinary hard sense has been raised to the level of genius." Colonel Manning is recalled to duty in 1943 when Dr. Estelle Karst invents artificial radioactives, "the first weapon the world has ever seen against which there is no defense."[49] Manning's secretary, Captain DeFries, describes this as "a weapon which would give the United States protection against aggression ... put a stop to this war, and any other war. We can declare a *Pax Americana*, and enforce it."[50]

In the story, the U.S. supplies the radioactive dust to Britain to use against Germany, ending the war, but Manning fears that their enemies will learn how to manufacture the dust: to counter this, he proposes a "military dictatorship imposed by force on the whole world."[51] When the "Eurasian Union" launches a sneak attack, Manning is prepared; he evacuates as many essential personnel from New York and Washington as he can, counterattacks, and is appointed Commissioner of World Safety—for life. When President Roosevelt retires, his successor asks for Manning's resignation, but Manning is prepared for this too; he threatens to dust Washington, stages a coup d'etat, and becomes "the undisputed military dictator of the world."[52]

One politician says to Manning, "You are a professional soldier and have no faith in people. Soldiers may be necessary, but the worst of them are martinets and the best are merely paternalistic."[53] The story ends with Manning being "universally hated,"[54] but DeFries admits he's telling Manning's side of the story, and the last line depicts him as a reluctant despot rather than a megalomaniac.[55] So it's difficult not to see Manning as the intended hero of the piece, rather than a villain. He can even be seen as a fantasy vision of Heinlein himself (admittedly, this has been said of most Heinlein characters, male and female, including DeFries). Heinlein, a graduate of the U.S. Naval Academy, had also been forced to retire from the military because of a disability, and had run for the California State Assembly as a Democrat in 1938. Manning is described as liberal, as Heinlein considered himself at the time.[56] And what makes this solution unsatisfactory, at least in DeFries's eyes, is not that Manning is an all-powerful military dictator, but that Manning is mortal and "there is no one to take his place."[57]

In "Solution Unsatisfactory," the virtues that save the world are not primarily "American," but military: Manning expresses little faith in democracy, and DeFries blames the Mexican War on "unfit Presidents and power-hungry Congresses."[58] None of the pilots Manning sends to threaten Washington are American-born[59]; his Commission is "open to youths of any race, color or nationality … with an obligation only to the Commission and the race and welded together with a carefully nurtured esprit de corps."[60] The importance of "esprit de corps" as a guide to (or possibly substitute for) a moral code is a theme that would recur in Heinlein's work, most notably in *Starship Troopers*.

◆ ◆ ◆

Heinlein's first serialized novel, *Sixth Column* (1941), also published as *The Day After Tomorrow*, also had a U.S. Army officer as hero: Major Ardmore defeats a "PanAsian" invasion with the assistance of a small team of scientists and heroic soldiers, and a weapon that can kill selectively based on racial genotype.[61] A rather different American super-soldier with a rather different technowonder also appeared in 1941, when Simon and Kirby created Captain America:

> an all-new character who blasted Nazi aggression with a double-barreled dose of American patriotism—first, as a superhero garbed in a colourful red-white-and-blue costume of stars and stripes, and second, in his alter-identity as Pvt. Steve Rogers, U.S. Army. The cover of *Captain America Comics* No. 1 was, at the time, a sensation newsstand shocker—it was the first of its kind to depict a fictional character of American origin striking Adolf Hitler months before America declared war on Germany![62]

Joe Simon later stated that he "saw [Captain America] as a political statement fleshed out to be an active force."[63] Unlike the many comic-book heroes who were born with their powers or acquired them in bizarre accidents, and hid their identities from the government, Steve Rogers *volunteered* to be injected with Professor Reinstein's "super-soldier" serum as part of Project Rebirth after being turned down by the U.S. Army as unfit. He then became "the first of a corps of super-agents whose mental and physical ability will make them a terror to spies and saboteurs."[64] When Reinstein was murdered by spies and saboteurs in the pay of the Gestapo, Rogers adopted a mask and alias like other comic-book superheroes, but (unusually) without concealing his identity from the government; instead,

Title page from Superman #34, May–June 1943. Script by Don Cameron, art by Pete Riss and George Roussos.

he was "assigned by the government to disguise himself as a private in the army"[65] and "went overseas to battle the 'Japanazis' both as a U.S. Army soldier and as Captain America."[66] As Daniels states:

> It could happen to anyone, even the ordinary reader. And part of the attraction was that Steve Rogers never became excessively gifted; he wasn't invulnerable—he was just tougher and braver and smarter than anyone else.
>
> The fact that many readers would soon find himself in that very same army helped ensure "Cap's" popularity: the new soldiers remained comic book fans, and they, too, hoped to be heroes in disguise.[67]

Captain America #1 sold close to a million copies, "in the same league with Superman and Batman.... As a contrast, consider that the weekly circulation of *Time* magazine during the same period was 700,000."[68] Simon admitted that it also inspired "threatening letters and hate mail" from "opponents to the war,"[69] but the best-selling *Captain America* soon gave rise to "literally dozens of imitators, including the American Crusader, the American Eagle, the Fighting Yank, Mr. Liberty, the Liberator, Spirit of '76, Uncle Sam, the Flag, Liberty Belle, Miss America, and Captain Freedom."[70]

While the stories inside did not reflect this, the *covers* of several issues of *Action Comics* in 1941 also depicted Superman fighting enemies wearing distinctive Nazi uniforms (Stahlhelms on #35 and #39, a tank with a German cross on #40, a paratrooper with a swastika armband on #43). More overtly anti–Nazi covers would become more frequent once the U.S. entered the war.

3. "A War Increasingly Science-fictional"
1942 to 1945

"[A] war increasingly science-fictional (ending in the long-predicted atom bomb)..."—Aldiss and Wingrove[1]

Buck Rogers must be the new chief of staff.—Robert A. Heinlein[2]

One reason for the high sales of superhero comics during World War II was their popularity among American soldiers actually fighting the war:

[O]ne of every four magazines shipped to troops overseas was a comic book. At least 35,000 copies of *Superman* alone went to servicemen each month.[3]

[T]he Navy Department ruled that Superman comic books should be included among essential supplies destined for the Marine garrison at Midway Islands.[4]

[A] special Armed Services Edition [of a 1942 novel in which Superman destroys Nazi submarines with the help of the U.S. Navy] was also issued ... for distribution to American servicemen ... not at all surprising, given the Man of Steel's immense popularity with soldiers and sailors.[5]

During the war years patriotic superheroes were sent off to fight for their country, and the conflict was polarised into one between supermen and supervillains: Tojo, Hitler and Mussolini stood no chance. These comics were unashamed morale-boosters, and retailed in unprecedented numbers: by 1943 it is estimated they were selling nearly 15 million copies a month, thereby totally dominating the industry.[6]

The American armed forces were unique in that comics were sent out to the troops in much the same way as other supplies.... [I]t was reported that on military bases comics outsold magazines like *Life* and *Readers' Digest* by something like ten to one.[7]

This influence was reflected in the "nose art" of bomber crews, which depicted comic characters including Superman, the Green Hornet, the Batman villainesses Poison Ivy and Catwoman, alien Shmoos (from *Li'l Abner*), the Goon (from *Popeye*), and a stick-figure Saint,[8] while the commander of the 98th Bombardment Group, Colonel John Kane, became known to both sides of the war as "Killer Kane" after Buck Rogers's nemesis.[9]

Comics publishers also tried to drum up support for the war effort

After spending the prewar years fighting against munitions manufacturers trying to start wars for profit, Superman turns "Waste Paper into War Weapons!" for the U.S. armed forces. Public Service Ad, Superman #28, May–June 1944, writer unknown, art by George Roussos.

and the troops among younger readers, whom Captain America assured (or warned) directly in this ad:

> Hello, kids!
> You're in this war even though you don't carry a gun, ride a tank, a jeep, or pilot a plane. You can do your part in winning this war by **joining the waste paper drive!** ...
> Paper is a weapon of war! A mighty weapon! Every gun, bullet ... every piece of ammunition used to smash the unholy Japs and Nazis is shipped in paper containers![10]

Captain America's teenage sidekick, war orphan and Camp Lehigh mascot Bucky Barnes, joined other teenagers to form the Sentinels of Liberty, later renamed the Young Allies and given their own comic later in 1941, while the Sentinels of Liberty became a fan club that young readers could join. Members were urged to

> assist Captain America in his fight upon the enemies who attempt treason against the United States of America....
> Joe Simon invented the club and its card and badge. "We were stirring up the population," says Simon today. "We weren't making any money on it, but the kids were taking an oath to defend the Constitution."...
> The club was dropped in the middle of the war with the explanation that the metal in the badges was needed for ammunition.[11]
> Bucky suggested they use the money for a war savings stamp instead.[12]

Captain America appeared on the cover of the "All Out For America Issue!" (#13, April 1942—the first prepared after Pearl Harbor), punching Emperor Hirohito while saying "You started it! Now, we'll finish it!" Superman, Batman and Robin, and other superheroes also appeared on the covers of their comics attacking Hirohito, Hitler and Mussolini (in the case of 1941's *Daredevil Battles Hitler*, a photo of Hitler's face with exaggerated eyes was pasted onto a cartoon body) while exhorting kids to buy war bonds.

Superheroes such as Captain Marvel and Wonder Woman (who first appeared in December 1941) were depicted as enlisting, though this often required the writers to find "creative means to avoid upstaging America's real-life heroes overseas."[13]

> Jerry Siegel and Joe Shuster felt strongly that Superman should participate in the war, but realizing that he could fly to Berlin and Tokyo and promptly bring the war to an end on his own, they did not wish to minimize the daunting task faced by the nation and its fighting forces.... To resolve this dilemma, Siegel and Shuster had Clark Kent declared 4-F.... Superman shrugs off the disappointment, resolving to serve the American war effort by policing America's home front and declaring that "the United States Army, Navy, and Marines are capable of smashing their foes without the aid of a Superman!"
> Despite paper rationing, comics continued to sell, though "their continued prosperity depended on the approval of military censors and PX masters."[14]

The device used to have Superman declared 4-F (absent-mindedly using his X-ray vision, he sees through the eye chart used to test him and

3. "A War Increasingly Science-fictional"   45

Clark Kent fails his physical and decides that the U.S. Armed Forces don't need him. Superman daily newspaper strip, February 18–19, 1942. Script by Jerry Siegel, art by Wayne Boring.

reads from one in the next room instead) not only suggests either a personal in-joke about Superman's artist and co-creator Joe Schuster (also declared 4-F because of bad eyesight) or a certain desperation on the part of writer Jerry Siegel, but an assumption about service in the U.S. military that was already outdated by 1941—the idea that the majority of volunteers would become infantrymen. In fact, only 14 percent of U.S. troops serving overseas during World War II fought in the infantry[15]: the degree of mechanization of the U.S. military had increased more markedly between the world wars than at any other time,[16] and with it the proportion of non-combat support roles to frontline troops. In the American Expeditionary Force in World War I, 65 percent of personnel were assigned to combat units, with 3 percent in administration and 32 percent in logistics; of that 65 percent, 77 percent were combatants, 9 percent admin and 14 percent logistics.[17] In World War II, the logistical staff needed to support armored divisions and the Army Air Force wing had increased, and combat troops had decreased from 53 percent to 39 percent of personnel.[18] If an experienced reporter such as Clark Kent had volunteered for military service in 1942, it seems much more likely that he would have been "assigned to

Panels from Superman #25, November–December 1943. Script by Mort Weisinger, art by Fred Ray, "Prepared in cooperation with the Army Air Forces Training Command." Clark Kent, embedded with the Technical Training Command, tells a cadet who has failed to qualify as a pilot that the Army still needs him.

propaganda or education duties," like Siegel himself—who, once drafted in 1943, worked for the armed forces paper *Stars and Stripes*.[19] But the image of the heroic American soldier used in recruiting, especially in the early years of the war, was predominantly that of the fighting infantryman or marine, the group that suffered the highest rate of casualties and, therefore, turnover.[20] (Artillery, which *inflicted* the majority of casualties,[21] rarely featured in recruiting posters; the only image of artillerymen I've found in U.S. propaganda from World War II was an ad for the Canned Florida grapefruit juice "rich in Victory Vitamin C" shipped out to the troops.)

Comic creators Joe Simon, Jack Kirby, Carl Burgos, Bill Everett, Will Eisner and Stan Lee, among many others from the industry, all signed up during World War II. Kirby would later recall that he was "handed a chocolate bar and an M-1 rifle and told to go kill Hitler,"[22] while others, like Siegel, worked on military publications. Eisner worked with the Armed Forces to create comic format training material for the troops, while Stan Lee scripted training films, designed an anti–VD poster, and continued to write comics for Marvel,[23] once escaping punishment by telling the army that "the writer of Captain America was being threatened with court-martial."[24]

The USS *Edgar Allan Poe*, currently the only U.S. Navy vessel named after a science fiction writer (the campaign to have one named after Heinlein having so far failed to achieve its goal), was commissioned in 1942, torpedoed later the same year, awarded the American Campaign Medal,

Asiatic-Pacific Campaign Medal and World War II Victory Medal, and remained in service until 1946.[25]

◆ ◆ ◆

Robert A. Heinlein had been invalided out of the U.S. Navy in peacetime and taken up writing to supplement his military pension; he tried to re-enlist after Pearl Harbor, but was rejected.[26] The outbreak of war enabled him to take up a civilian position at the U.S. Naval Air Experimental Station in 1942, "designing and testing plastics for aircraft and high-altitude pressure suits"[27] and "[to] recruit other bright and imaginative people to work there."[28] Heinlein recruited L. Sprague de Camp, who applied for and received an officer's commission in the Navy, rising to the rank of lieutenant commander,[29] and Isaac Asimov, who tried hard throughout the war to remain a civilian and only applied reluctantly for OCS in its last days in hope of avoiding being drafted as an NCO.[30] At the Naval Air Experimental Station, Asimov happily worked on dye markers for pilots "because it clearly contributed to the welfare of our fighting men and excused my not being among them—at least, a little."[31] Asimov, by this time, had realized that the Nazis could be defeated and "had enough confidence in the American Navy and Air Force to believe the Japanese advance was stopped forever,"[32] though this confidence did not extend to embracing a military mindset, which he later described as "unparalleled as a vehicle of creative stupidity."[33]

Asimov would continue to depict the military, especially high-ranking officers, in less than sympathetic terms over his career, and showed them at the mercy of the scientists they depended upon for their high-tech devices in "Little Lost Robot" (1947), *Foundation* (1951), "Risk" (1955), and "The Proper Study" (1968).

Fred Pohl, who had been writing editorials in *Fighting Aces* magazine (and running into problems with military censors) as well as editing *Astonishing Stories* and *Super Science Stories*, attempted to enlist in 1942, but "voluntary enlistments had been suspended,"[34] and he was drafted into the Army Air Force on April 1, 1943. Though he would later write that as an enlisted man, he was "a unit quantity ... less than a number.... An EM knows what it is like to be treated like a piece of meat,"[35] he explains that without this depersonalization, "armies would not be possible"[36] because "a *person* would not put up with any of this crap for a minute."[37] He added:

> I knew it was only a game, and that when I got my discharge all the rules would change back again.... I played that game, and my God, I actually enjoyed it. All of it.
>
> [A]nd by and by they told us we were finished killers and sent us off in a thirty-car troop train to Chanute Field, Illinois, to become Air Force weathermen.[38]

The Army later decided Pohl "would be more use with words than with weapons or weather instruments,"[39] and in January 1945 gave him a job in public relations and editing a squadron newspaper. Jack Williamson also served as an Army weather forecaster, rising to the rank of staff sergeant (Pohl later wrote that "the weather wing picked up all the high-IQ oddballs in the Air Force").[40] Harry Stubbs (Hal Clement), Cyril Kornbluth, Horace Gold, Henry Kuttner, Edgar Pangborn, James Blish, E.E. "Doc" Smith, George O. Smith, Paul Linebarger (Cordwainer Smith), and L. Ron Hubbard all joined the military (see Appendix A): many others found other ways to assist the war effort, though it might be more accurate to say that Hubbard's accident-prone service in the U.S. Navy slightly hampered it.[41] Will Jenkins (Murray Leinster), who had served in the army in World War I, worked for the Office of War Information. Edgar Rice Burroughs at age 66, became a war correspondent. Fletcher Pratt became a military analyst for *Time* magazine. Theodore Sturgeon, classified as 4-F and not even eligible for limited service, served as an Army steward and built airstrips for the U.S. Army Air Corps.[42] He also "worked for a while for the University of California, in the Empire State Building, with John W. Campbell Jr., the editor of *Astounding Science Fiction*, as his supervisor.... Campbell was supervisor in a classified section that wrote radar operation and maintenance manuals...."[43] When Ray Bradbury was also classified as 4-F and didn't immediately volunteer for war work, Heinlein "felt that Ray was betraying his country.... As a result, Heinlein cut Ray off, and they didn't speak again for decades."[44] Heinlein may have been unaware that Bradbury, a pacifist who was afraid of being killed either by the enemy or by "big, tough American soldiers," wrote advertising material for Red Cross blood drives during the war.[45]

In 1944, Heinlein recruited Hubbard, Sturgeon and others for a project: "OpNav-23, a brainstorming job on antikamikaze measures."[46]

> I had been ordered to round up science-fiction writers for this crash project—the wildest brains I could find, so Ted was a welcome recruit. Some of the others were George O. Smith, John W. Campbell Jr., Murray Leinster, L. Ron Hubbard, Sprague de Camp, and Fletcher Pratt....
>
> I never worried about security because there was always one member of naval intelligence invariably present.[47]

In 1943, *Astounding* raised its rates, because "too many of Campbell's reliables were off in the Army, or in civilian war work, and were not writing."[48] *Amazing Stories* went from monthly publication to bi-monthly in 1943 to quarterly in 1944, returning to a monthly publication schedule in 1946. *Astonishing Stories* folded in 1943. *Super Science Stories* went on hiatus from 1943 to 1949; *Future Science Fiction* from 1943 to 1950; *Science Fiction Quarterly* from 1943 to 1951. Heinlein produced no new fiction during World War II. Nor did Hubbard, prohibited from writing by the Navy's security regulations: he later described this as "the only thing that ever affected me as a writer."[49] Though his stories continued to be published throughout the war, the normally prolific Asimov wrote no stories during his first year at the NAES, and only one story while in the army after the war ended. Fred Pohl, who had been publishing from six to ten stories a year in 1940–42, had only one published in 1943, and none in 1945–1946. Theodore Sturgeon had ten stories published in both 1941 and 1947 (and 13 in 1940), but only three in 1942, two apiece in 1943 and 1945, and only one in 1944. E.E. "Doc" Smith had no stories published in 1943–47, and James Blish, none in 1945–1947.

Apart from occupying time that would normally have been spent editing magazines or writing, and the effects of wartime paper rationing on publishing, the only real conflicts between science fiction writers and the military during World War II concerned the censorship of SF stories which featured technology that the U.S. military was secretly developing for use in the war, most notably nuclear weapons. Will Jenkins (Murray Leinster) fell afoul of military censors because of mentioning a sonar-type device in "Four Little Ships," published in *Astounding* in 1942.[50] Philip Wylie's novella *The Paradise Crater*, which depicted defeated Nazis building "an atomic bomb utilizing Uranium-237" for use against the U.S., was submitted to government censors in early 1945: "Wylie was suddenly placed under house arrest, and then informed by an Army intelligence major that he was personally prepared to kill Wylie if necessary to keep the weapon secret."[51] Ironically, Wylie would later be "invited to report on the Hiroshima bombing," be granted a maximum security rating, "attend the Desert Rock A-bomb tests and brief publishers on the implications of the Atomic Age."[52] An early 1945 *Superman* newspaper comic strip involving an "Atom Smasher" or cyclotron was also banned by the Officer of Censorship and replaced with a more innocuous story.[53]

The most celebrated case of wartime censorship of American science fiction was that of Cleve Cartmill, partly paralyzed and thus ineligible for military service, who wrote to Campbell in 1943 proposing a story about a super-bomb.[54] Campbell responded by sending him details of how an atomic bomb might be constructed using fissionable Uranium-235, and Cartmill pressed him for more information, saying, "You see, I want to know how to make a U-235 bomb.... Keeping an eye, of course, on what should or should not be told for social, military, or political reasons."[55]

Cartmill's story "Deadline" caused an investigator from the War Department's Counter-Intelligence Corps, Arthur Riley, to interview Campbell for fear that there had been a security breach. Riley's report recommended that Campbell and Cartmill be placed under surveillance, and also suggested that the leak might have started with Isaac Asimov, via Cartmill's friend Robert Heinlein. Riley's report also cast suspicion on L. Sprague de Camp and Will Jenkins (Murray Leinster), who had given Asimov some atomic copper for spectroscopic analysis.[56]

Cartmill was extensively investigated, and Campbell was officially "reminded of a confidential Code of Wartime Practices that had been circulated to editors and broadcasters in June 1943, forbidding dissemination of any information regarding war experiments involving 'atom smashing, atomic energy, atomic fission, atomic splitting, or any of their equivalents.'"[57] Robert Silverberg states that in the aftermath of this event, there were "no further stories about U-235 bombs in the next dozen or so issues of *Astounding*, though a Fritz Leiber story speaks of a world devastated by 'subtronic power,' a Raymond F. Jones novel mentions 'gigantic atomic projectors' being used as weapons, and a Lewis Padgett story about mutants is set in a world that has been devastated by atomic war."[58] That "world that has been devastated by atomic war" would become a recurring theme in SF after Hiroshima—so much so that in 1948, Campbell "specified to our authors that the 'atomic doom' stories are not wanted,"[59] and Horace Gold followed suit in 1952.[60]

But for the duration of the war, apart from minor incidents such as the Cartmill, Wylie and Leinster brushes with military censors and some quiet grumbling, most of America's science fiction writers of the time cooperated fully with the U.S. military in what a Joe Haldeman character would later call "the Last Good War, as though there had ever been a good one."[61] Even Asimov, who was finally drafted in September 1945 after attempts to enroll in OCS had failed, who rose to the rank of corporal and sharpshooter[62] despite his oft-expressed hatred of army life, and who narrowly escaped having to participate in an A-bomb test at Bikini by applying for a "research discharge" (which "also meant, perhaps, I did not die of leukemia at a comparatively early age"), later admitted, "Actually, I was not mistreated in the army in any way."[63]

4. "The Meaning of Atomic Weapons"
1946 to 1949

> [T]he atomic bomb was more than a weapon of terrible destruction; it was a psychological weapon. —*Henry Lewis Stimson, U.S. Secretary of War, 1947*[1]

Victory in World War II may have meant that Americans no longer felt the same need to be protected by fictional super-powered technowarriors, and that many would have preferred to relax without needing to worry about what Stimson described as "the most terrible weapon ever known in human history"[2]—for as long as only the U.S. had it, at least.

The perceived role of A-bombs in ending the war meant that science fiction writers were, if not necessarily hailed as prophets, then at least, in Asimov's words, "salvaged into respectability."[3] To them, it was far from a new idea. The term "atomic bomb" had been coined by H.G. Wells in his 1914 serial "A Prophetic Trilogy," the basis for his novel *A World Set Free*[4]; the 1936 film of Wells's *Things to Come* had featured a mushrooming cloud behind the caption "1945."[5] Even the nickname of the B-29 that had dropped the bomb, the Peacemaker, had been foreshadowed in John Ulrich Giesy's 1915 *All for His Country*, in which an American aircraft of that name had devastated Japan,[6]

With the war over and his services no longer required by the Navy Yard, Heinlein returned to writing, hoping to "leave the SF-pulp field"[7] and also to "explain the meaning of atomic weapons through popular articles"[8]—a field he felt had been neglected, despite what he later described as "some heavy tonnage"[9] in the form of reassurances from the Manhattan Project's General Groves, the Chief of Naval Operations, and "a very senior Army Air Force general."[10]

In one nonfiction article, "The Last Days of the United States," Heinlein accused these and others "charged with the defense of this country"[11] of proposing solutions that were only appropriate to the previous war—with the exception of Brigadier General Henry "Hap" Arnold, who predicted A-bombing by space ships.[12] As in "Solution Unsatisfactory," Heinlein continued to press for a "planetary organization so strong that it can enforce peace, forbid national armaments, atomic or otherwise, and in general police the globe,"[13] or second-best, for "another Buck Rogers weapon with which to ward off atomic bomb rockets … some sort of a devastatingly powerful beam of energy, acting with the speed of light,"[14] which would, like Manning's Commission, "end civilian aviation."

Alternatively, he suggested, the U.S. could "save money by not buying flame throwers, tanks or battleships," and instead prepare to attack with "the fastest and most long-range rockets, the most powerful atomic blasts, and every other dirty trick conceived in comic strip or fantastic fiction. We must have space ships and we must have them first. We must land on the Moon and take possession of it in order to forbid its use to other nations as a base against us and in order to have it as a base against any enemy of ours."[15] Heinlein did not express much more hope for this possibility than he did for "that Buck Rogers super-duper death ray screen,"[16] concluding, "Regularly, in the past, our State Department has bungled us into wars, and with equal regularity our military establishment has been unready for them."[17]

Other writers were also trying to come to terms with what the A-bomb might mean to U.S. military personnel. Will Jenkins's (Murray Leinster) 1946 *The Murder of the U.S.A.* "has a high-ranking missile officer"[18] help solve the mystery of who launched a sneak nuclear attack on the U.S., then launch a punitive strike that destroys "everything that moved or lived or breathed"[19] in the enemy nation. The same year, "Captain Walter Karig of the U.S. Naval Reserves produced a little pamphlet partly aimed at arguing for the continuing importance of the navy in the atomic era, but which provided his sailors with all manner of Buck Rogers gimmickry suddenly made plausible by the new technology."[20]

In Chandler Davis's "To Still the Drums," published in *Astounding* in October 1946, a U.S. Army lieutenant discovers that the question cut out of his letter by military censors, "Do you think it'd be possible for a military clique to get the United States into war against the wishes of the people and Congress?" is "far from academic." He has to stop a colonel from stockpiling nuclear weapons without informing the government, precipitating an arms race and potentially a nuclear war.[21]

Theodore Sturgeon's story "Thunder and Roses" (1947) showed a USA so damaged and demoralized after a nuclear attack that suicide has become endemic, and soldiers are destroying all potential weapons (such as straight razors) to reduce the temptation they pose. The USA has not counterattacked, and when two U.S. Army soldiers discover a hidden nuclear weapon, one wants to use it, even though it will result in the extinction of the human species. Unable to dissuade him, the other soldier kills him to save their enemies.[22]

Kris Neville's "Cold War" (*Astounding*, 1949) described (and predicted) psychological tests intended to prevent soldiers from launching nuclear bombs without authorization.[23] This would have proved useful in Heinlein's story "The Long Watch," published in the *American Legion Magazine* the same year, which pits an American soldier against others in the same force, and reveals the potential downside of both the nuclear-armed moon base Heinlein had been proposing in his nonfiction articles and the "planetary organization so strong that it can enforce peace," such as Colonel Manning's Commission, the military dictatorship of "Solution Unsatisfactory."

In "The Long Watch," the battle-hardened second-in-command of the moon base, Colonel Towers, decides to become a military dictator and force Earth's politicians to yield power to "a scientifically selected group. In short—the Patrol."[24] He and his followers attempt to bomb "an unimportant town or two"[25] as a demonstration of their power, but are frustrated by a junior bomb officer with no combat experience, Lieutenant Johnny Dahlquist, who sacrifices his own life and defies the chain of command by destroying the warheads. In this story, Heinlein voices the suspicion that the power inherent in world-girdling nuclear weapons can corrupt even those in whom the military virtues of obedience and esprit de corps have been carefully instilled—an apparent reversal of his position in "Solution Unsatisfactory."

While "The Long Watch" is not a direct sequel to "Solution Unsatisfactory" (the former appears in Heinlein's "Future History" chronology, the latter does not), parallels are easily drawn: Colonel Manning uses the threat of radioactive dust and the loyal officers of the Commission to become military dictator of the world; Colonel Towers seeks to do the same with nuclear weapons and hand-picked officers from the Patrol. There are differences. Towers, despite his claim to be "scientifically selected," only gains control of the moon base and its weapons after the death (by implication, murder) of his commanding officer.[26] While Johnny Dahlquist is identified as being from Illinois, the nationalities of Towers and his followers (Morgan, the marine "Smitty," and Lopez) are never specified. But in this story, it is Johnny Dahlquist's destruction of the moon base's nuclear weapons, in direct defiance of his colonel's orders, that saves the lives of those in the "unimportant town or two" and has him recognized (posthumously) as a hero, rather than the soldierly virtues of obedience and esprit de corps that Heinlein espoused in "Solution Unsatisfactory" and other works. While Towers argues that it is unsafe "to leave control of the world in political hands,"[27] the story suggests that even Heinlein could concede that leaving it in the hands of a military dictator might not be a satisfactory solution.

♦ ♦ ♦

As early as 1944, "Timely was slowly drifting away from the super hero genre" as it became apparent that U.S. forces were, indeed, capable of smashing their foes without the aid of a Superman.[28] Their need for invincible heroes temporarily sated, younger readers were buying more funny animal comics, and after writer Otto Binder, writing for *Marvel Mystery Comics* in 1943, created the

> female version of Captain America ... it turned Timely towards a new audience.... Comics began to focus on the activities of average American female adolescents. Features were added on clothes, makeup and cooking, and a whole new division of comic books came into being.[29]

Timely's *USA Comics* was canceled in fall 1945, despite featuring Captain America (who had starred in a relatively big-budget movie serial only a year before). In 1946, Stan Lee tried uniting the Sub-Mariner, the Human Torch and Captain America with Miss America as the All Winners Squad for *All Winners Comics*, but it was canceled after only two issues.[30]

Captain America was one of the very few of the wartime superheroes to last more than two years after being demobbed; in *Captain America Comics* No. 59 (November 1946), the character became a teacher at Lee High School and fought crime part-time. Bucky was shot seven issues later (April 1948), and replaced by Golden Girl. Captain America, the Sub-Mariner, the Human Torch, and *Marvel Mystery Comics* all disappeared from the scene in 1949: only the DC stalwarts Superman, Batman and Wonder Woman retained their own titles without interruption.

♦ ♦ ♦

In 1947, the U.S. Army, which had been test-firing captured V-2 rockets, issued a recruiting poster featuring a moon rocket with the slogan: "Into the World of Tomorrow with the U.S. Army." The Navy followed suit with a poster illustrating a rocket leaving the Earth, with the moon and

Saturn in the background. Its slogan reads: "The Sky *Was* the Limit. Now—A Career in Electronics."[31]

In June 1949 "The Aphrodite Project," an "article" by Philip Latham (astronomer Robert Richardson) in *Astounding Science Fiction*, "supposedly an abstract of a 320-page government report, fools not a few people" into thinking that the U.S. Navy had succeeded in sending an unmanned rocket to Venus in January 1947.[32]

On August 29, 1949, the Soviet Union performed their first successful nuclear weapon test. On October 1, after the U.S. withdrew support for Chiang Kai-Shek's Nationalist Kuomintang, the Chinese Communist Party became the new government of mainland China.

On May 8, 1950, the U.S. Secretary of State offered to help the French defeat Ho Chi Minh's communist forces in Indochina (Vietnam); on June 25, the United Nations Security Council condemned the North Korean invasion of South Korea; on August 4, President Truman ordered the U.S. Army to ready 62,000 troops for military duty. Instead of the moon or the planets, the U.S. military would soon be going to war once again—and Heinlein was going to Hollywood.

5. "I'm Not Working for the World"
1950 to 1961

> I'm not working for the world, Scott. I'm working for the Air Force.—*Captain Hendry,* The Thing from Another World[1]
>
> We cannot hope to match the communist enemy in manpower. If we wish to maintain our present standard of living, or anything approaching it, we cannot hope to match him in sheer weight of reserve materiel. We must, therefore, use our limited manpower far more effectively. And we must provide our soldiers with the finest weapons and equipment that the talent of our scientists and military experts and the ingenuity of our industrial community can produce.—*U.S. Secretary of the Army Robert T. Stevens, 1953*[2]

In the 1950s, inventions that had made World War II "increasingly science-fictional" increasingly became part of everyday life. Jet aircraft, originally developed for the military, began carrying civilian passengers in 1952; the first mass-produced electronic computer, UNIVAC, appeared the same year. Rockets based on von Braun's designs carried nonmilitary satellites into orbit—the USSR's *Sputnik 1* and *2* in 1957, the U.S.'s SCORE communications satellite in 1958, navigation and weather satellites in 1960. The first breeder reactors, providing electricity for civilian use as well as the plutonium needed for hydrogen bombs, went online in 1951. And there was an understandable fear that atomic weapons, possessed by both the U.S. and the Soviet Union before 1950 and the UK from 1952, would also impact on everyday life—if not in a full-scale nuclear war, then from radioactive fallout from a nuclear test, as befell the not-so-lucky crew of the Japanese *Lucky Dragon 5* in 1954 after the test of an H-bomb. In the latter half of the decade, the economic cost of what Eisenhower would later describe as "the military-industrial complex," even in peacetime, also came under scrutiny by science fiction writers—and would be fiercely defended, even glorified, by Heinlein.

♦ ♦ ♦

Aldiss has described the 1950s as "perhaps ... the perfect decade for science fiction"[3]; Clute refers to it as SF's "Age of Silver."[4] Lucanio estimates that 500 science fiction films (features and shorts) were made between 1948 and 1962.[5] In 1950 alone, fifteen new SF magazines were launched, as well as Asimov's first novel, debut stories from Richard Matheson and Gordon R. Dickson (both of whom had served in the U.S. Army during World War II), and the first big-budget SF movie produced in the U.S. The first Hugo Awards for the best science fiction of the year were presented in 1953.

While there had been American-made science fiction movies before 1950—*Dr. Jekyll and Mr. Hyde*; *The Invisible Man*; *Frankenstein*; serializations of *Flash Gordon* (1936, 1938 and 1940), *Buck Rogers* (1939), *Captain America* (1944) *Superman* (1948), and others—1950s *Destination Moon* is arguably the first big budget ($385,000) American science fiction movie. (Wingrove suggests that the commercial failure of 1930's expensive futuristic musical comedy *Just Imagine* made U.S. studios reluctant to invest in SF "epics" for another twenty years.[6]) It was directed by Irving Pichel (blacklisted in 1947, but never called to appear before HUAC), and co-written by Heinlein, based very loosely on his first published novel *Rocketship Galileo* (the credits read that the novel "inspired" the film).[7]

While *Destination Moon* gives the job of building a manned (nuclear) rocket to civilian businessmen acting in defiance of a "peacetime government" ban, the driving force is U.S. Air Force General Thayer (previously part of the unsuccessful U.S. military effort to launch an artificial satellite, the failure of which he blames on sabotage, and who is later one of the astronauts), and the intent is clearly military. In one scene, Thayer tells industrialists: "We are not the only ones who know that the Moon can be reached. We're not the only ones who are planning to go there. The race is on—and we'd better win it, because there is absolutely no way to stop an attack from outer space. The first country that can use the Moon for the launching of missiles ... will control the Earth. That, gentlemen, is the most important military fact of this century."[8] The space race is explicitly compared to a war effort earlier in the scene, when an aircraft manufacturer exhorts, "American industry must get to work, now, just as we did in the last war!"[9]

Despite the stated military objectives, the first two men on the moon are civilians, one of whom proclaims: "By the grace of God, and the name of the United States of America, I take possession of this planet on behalf of, and for the benefit of, all mankind."[10] There is no need for the combat that features in Heinlein's 1947 novel *Rocketship Galileo*, in which the civilian astronauts claim the moon on behalf of the United Nations instead, before discovering and ultimately destroying a Nazi base.[11] There is also no hint here of Heinlein's earlier story "Solution Unsatisfactory," and no sign of military dictatorship such as Colonel Manning's enforcing a Pax Americana, much less the fears expressed in "The Long Watch."

Nine years later (and nearly two years after the launch of *Sputnik*) the U.S. Army did indeed propose a manned lunar base, believing "that anything short of being first on the moon 'will be catastrophic.'"[12] The Project Horizon task force was created on March 20, 1959, working under the direction of Maj. Gen. John B. Medaris (Army Ordnance Missile Command) and with the full cooperation of Werner von Braun and his team.

Whether or not *Destination Moon* had any role in inspiring this, Waldrop credits the film with starting the "SF boom of the early 1950s," despite the relatively inexpensive *Rocketship X-M* having beaten it to cinemas by nearly four weeks. Without *Destination Moon*, Waldrop argues, there would have been "no *Day the Earth Stood Still*, no *The Thing (from Another World)* of 1951."[13]

Rocketship X-M (X-M being an abbreviation for "Expedition Moon") was quickly made in an attempt to exploit the publicity surrounding *Destination Moon*, but delivers a very different message. Its astronauts—American military officers and European-accented scientists, clad in U.S. military-surplus fatigues and breathing masks—were also intending to set up "an unassailable base on the moon to control world peace," but were funded by the government rather than private industry.[14] The downbeat script, co-written by then-blacklisted Dalton Trumbo (author of the 1939 antiwar novel *Johnny Got His Gun*), had the astronauts discovering that the Martian civilization was destroyed in a nuclear war—which the protagonists of Heinlein's *Rocketship Galileo* postulated had also been the fate of a long-ago lunar civilization, evidence for which they find on the moon. Unfortunately, parts of the planet are still dangerously radioactive, and the astronauts die before they can return to Earth to deliver a warning.[15]

Simon Schama, in *The American Future*, characterizes these two schools of American political thought as the Hamiltonian versus the Jeffersonian—the former seeing war as necessary not only to "defend liberty" and other American ideals, but to aggressively disseminate them"[16]; the second seeing military might as "inconsistent with the principles of republican government" and potentially oppressing the people it claimed to defend.[17] World War II, which was largely viewed as a necessary act of

5. "I'm Not Working for the World" 59

self-defense rather than a war of conquest, may have temporarily reconciled these two sides ... but not for long. For many Americans, including SF writers and filmmakers, the existence of nuclear weapons made the issue that much more urgent: was a powerful military the best hope of defending their way of life, or was it a threat not only to liberty but to survival itself?

The split between Hamiltonian and Jeffersonian attitudes to the military can also be seen between the other pair of movies Waldrop cites, 1951's *The Day the Earth Stood Still* (directed by Robert Wise, screenplay by Edmund H. North, based on a story by Harry Bates published in *Astounding Stories* in 1940), and *The Thing from Another World* (directed by Christian Nyby, produced by Howard Hawks, screenplay by Charles Lederer based on a story by *Astounding*'s editor John W. Campbell, published in the magazine in 1938). Both pit the U.S. military against lone extraterrestrials which they shoot almost on sight, but there the resemblance ends. In *The Thing*, the audience is clearly expected to applaud the efforts of the soldiers (who have come to the Arctic to search for what they initially suspect is a crashed Russian plane) for their stand against the alien invader, a "blood-drinking human carrot from Planet X."[18] In *The Day*, the soldiers who shoot the visitor (on two separate occasions!) nearly trigger the destruction of Earth.

Stephen King describes *The Thing from Another World*, released a week after the convictions of Julius and Ethel Rosenberg, as the first of the "political horror films" of the 1950s.[19] He points out, "The very presence of Kenneth Tobey and his squad of soldiers gives the film a militaristic, and thus political, patina,"[20] as is borne out by Hendry's (Tobey's) retort to a reporter, "I'm not working for the world, Scott. I'm working for the Air Force."[21] No one in the film questions this: the only character who has other priorities, the English-accented Nobel laureate Dr. Carrington (who asks for permission to thaw and examine the Thing "in the interest of human knowledge" and later attempts to communicate with it), is depicted as dangerously wrong. In an earlier draft of the script, where Carrington was killed in his last-ditch unsuccessful attempt to save the Thing, the reporter looks at the two corpses and says, "A clean sweep, Captain. *Both monsters are dead.*"[22]

King also considers *The Thing* a post–World War II polemic against appeasement, concluding that the film's "'let the military handle this' thesis was a perfectly acceptable one in 1951, because the military had handled the Japs and the Nazis perfectly well in Duke Wayne's 'Big One.'"[23] This accords with Evans's estimate that approximately 70 percent of images of the military in Hollywood films in 1950–55 were positive, and less than 10 percent negative.[24] Jancovich, however, points out, "The military itself is not presented positively, but only the solders on the ground.... Indeed, when orders do come from above, they are either too late or else completely misguided."[25] He assumes that when Scott, the reporter, suggests that Hendry might be promoted "for destroying embarrassing information,"[26] he isn't joking.

While technical problems prevent Hendry from communicating with his superiors, and the orders he receives are mostly counterproductive, the problems faced by the soldiers in *The Thing* are largely of their own making. As King points out, "The Army guys ... demonstrate frostbite of the brain throughout the film," first accidentally destroying the alien's spaceship by using too much thermite to free it from the ice (following "standard operation procedure"), then releasing the frozen Thing from its own frozen coffin by concealing it under a switched-on electric blanket(!).[27] On reviving, the Thing is immediately shot by a panicky guard.

Once past these improbable contrivances, though, the military acts swiftly and intelligently. As Strick comments, "it's a film about teamwork, with the monster and the glacial scientist heading the opposition and Kenneth Tobey in the John Wayne part leading our side ... all that's needed to contain and restrain [the Thing] is clear thinking and prompt action."[28] Ironically, when Hawks asked the Air Force for assistance in making the film, this was reportedly rejected despite its pro-military sentiments because it depicted flying saucers as real.[29]

Invasion USA (1952) is even more stridently pro-military, making a case for a larger army and the "universal draft"—including conscripting women into formerly privately owned factories taken over to make military equipment—by positing an invasion by Communists (clad in U.S. Army uniforms to enable the use of U.S. military stock footage for both sides, and mixing German as well as Russian with their English, but touting Russian-made PPSh submachine guns when played by extras) and a limited nuclear war. The invaders A-bomb some cities, but the U.S. retaliates with three A-bombs for every one of theirs and is the first to use the hydrogen bomb (which the Russians would not develop for another year). The factory owner decries the conscription of his tractor factory as "communism," but attempts to fight back when one of his workers helps the communist invaders take over the factory to make tanks for "the peoples' army"; a senator who rejects a military appropriation bill, saying the U.S. "could safely reduce our military forces by half," is one of the first killed when Congress is captured.[30] This "trip into the future" turns out to be a hallucination, the result of mass hypnosis of bar patrons by a fortuneteller, but it motivates the drinkers into changing their priorities to support a stronger U.S. military, and presumably was intended to make viewers do the same.

The same Hamiltonian military virtues applauded in *The Thing* and *Invasion USA* are called into question in *The Day the Earth Stood Still*, when too-prompt reflex action by a nervous American soldier results in the wounding of a benign alien ambassador, Klaatu, and destroys the gift he has brought for the U.S. president (an interplanetary communicator). After the opening titles superimposed on a backdrop of astronomical shots, the film opens with shots of U.S. military radar installations as they detect an object approaching Earth.[31] A flying saucer lands in Washington, D.C., where it is promptly surrounded and cordoned off by the military. The troops, tanks and other vehicles and weapons were provided by the National Guard. Director Robert Wise chose them rather than the U.S. Army, because "when you went for some help with equipment and personnel from one of the Armed Services, you had to submit a script to them…. Well, [the Army] turned us down on this. We didn't need much from them, we thought we'd get those jeeps and some tanks. And I guess they didn't like the message."[32] A lobbyist from 20th Century–Fox then approached the National Guard, who "had no problem with it."[33]

Both *The Thing* and *The Day the Earth Stood Still* were released at a time when public support for the Korean War was already declining, and Speaker Sam Rayburn was warning that it might be "the beginning of World War III."[34] In a conversation with the U.S. Secretary of State, Klaatu dismisses such international disputes as "petty squabbles," "childish jealousies" and "stupidity."[35] He easily escapes from military detainment in Walter Reed Hospital, steals a major's civilian clothes, and sets out to meet ordinary people hoping to "become familiar with the basis for these strange unreasoning attitudes."[36] He takes a room in a boarding house where he meets war widow Helen Benson and her ten-year-old son Bobby. Bobby takes him to Arlington National Cemetery, where Klaatu is clearly astounded and saddened by the sheer number of America's war dead, telling Bobby that his people have nothing similar because "they don't have any wars." The boy enthusiastically responds, "Gee, that's a good idea."[37]

But Klaatu and robotic enforcer Gort (revealed, in Bates's story and early drafts of the screenplay, to be Klaatu's master, rather than the reverse) are not totally pacifistic. Gort, notably, increases his level of violence against soldiers throughout the film. At their first encounter, he vaporizes guns, a tank, and some cannon. When Klaatu first returns to the saucer, he apparently grabs the two sentries and either kills them or renders them unconscious. After Klaatu is killed, Gort vaporizes the new sentries.

Klaatu tells Professor Barnhardt (a fictionalized Albert Einstein), "So long as you were limited to fighting among yourselves with your primitive tanks and aircraft, we were unconcerned." Earth, by possessing rockets and nuclear weapons, poses an intolerable "threat to the peace and security of other planets," and Klaatu in turn threatens "violent action, since that seems to be the only thing your people understand." In order to get a hearing, he raises the possibility of "leveling New York City, perhaps, or sinking the Rock of Gibraltar."[38] Barnhardt counterproposes a peaceful worldwide demonstration of power, to bring scientists and great thinkers to a meeting with Klaatu: Klaatu's "dramatic, but not destructive" solution is to stop all electricity on Earth for an hour, except for hospitals and planes in flight. Helen's suitor, the self-serving and unsympathetic Tom Stevens, echoes *The Thing*'s Captain Hendry's "I'm not working for the world," by saying "I don't care about the rest of the world" while on the phone to the Pentagon, as he betrays Klaatu to the U.S. Army in the hope of becoming "the biggest man in the country" and "a big hero."[39]

En route to the meeting with the scientists, Klaatu is once again shot by the army—this time, fatally. Helen relays a message from him to Gort ("Klaatu barada nikto"), evidently telling the robot what has happened to Klaatu and ordering him not to destroy the world. Gort retrieves Klaatu's body from prison, and revives him for long enough for him to deliver the film's closing speech.

Gort, Klaatu explains, is one of the robotic policeman they have created to

> preserve the peace. In matters of aggression, we have given them absolute power over us. This power can not be revoked. At the first sign of violence, they act automatically against the aggressor. The penalty for provoking their action is too terrible to risk. The result is, we live in peace, without arms or armies, secure in the knowledge that we are free from aggression and war. Free to pursue more profitable exercises. We do not pretend to have achieved perfection, but we do have a system, and it works.
>
> I came here to give you these facts. It is no concern of ours how you run your own planet, but if you threaten to extend your violence, this Earth of yours will be reduced to a burned-out cinder. Your choice is simple. Join us and live in peace, or pursue your present course and face obliteration.[40]

On the commentary on the DVD, Nicholas Meyer describes Klaatu's solution as "a sort of Orwellian peace on compulsion" and "dictatorial."[41] Wise responds by asking, "How else would you deal with these governments in this world of ours except to have something hanging over them to force them into it?"⁴² In effect, his enforced peace differs from the one Heinlein proposes in "Solution Unsatisfactory" in only one regard—*who* (or arguably what) enforces the peace. The idea that it should be left to U.S. military personnel would not have convinced Klaatu (who has twice been shot and wounded by them, once mortally, by the end of the film), nor, presumably, the writers and Wise—who explained that he was attracted to the script because "I had been an antimilitarist all my life, and I think this was one way of expressing that."⁴³

Possibly because of its then-atypical antimilitary message, *The Day the Earth Stood Still* remains one of the most influential science fiction films of the 1950s: Wikipedia lists 65 pop-culture references to the film and its line "Klaatu Barada Nikto," and according to Cannon, Colin Powell believed it had inspired Ronald Reagan to suggest to Mikhail Gorbachev they might one day join forces to repel "an invasion by extraterrestrials."⁴⁴

The Day the Earth Stood Still was in the minority, though: in most American science fiction movies of the 1950s, "portraying the military in heroic terms was still the norm,"⁴⁵ and Franklin describes *The Day the Earth Stood Still* and Arch Oboler's *Five* (1951) as the "last for several years" to speak against the military buildup, because of the House Un-American Activities Committee investigation of the film industry.⁴⁶

In *Invaders from Mars* (1953), a saucer-load of Martians comes to the U.S. to prevent the launch of the first atomic rocket, and implants mind-controlling hardware into the brains of several people—including a U.S. Army General who is taken over after investigating the landing site. Despite this fifth column, the invasion is easily defeated by the firepower of the U.S. Army (represented by a few actors and a large amount of military-issue World War II–vintage stock footage).⁴⁷ In *Earth vs. the Flying Saucers* (1956), similarly, aliens threaten to invade if the U.S. military persists with rocket launches: the invasion is defeated by the joint efforts of a scientist who develops a new weapon, and American soldiers who do the more risky work of driving the weapon around and facing alien attack.⁴⁸ *The Amazing Colossal Man* (1957), the giant ants in *Them!* (1954), and *The Invisible Invaders* (1959) were also defeated by the U.S. Army, and *The Beast from 20,000 Fathoms* (1953) by the National Guard.⁴⁹ The giant *Tarantula* (1955) and the computer controlling the rampaging robot *Gog* (1954) were destroyed by the U.S. Air Force⁵⁰; the irradiated cephalopod in *It Came from Beneath the Sea* (1955), *The Monster that Challenged the World* (1958) and the underwater UFO menacing *The Atomic Submarine* (1959) by the U.S. Navy⁵¹; and *The Deadly Mantis* (1957) jointly by the U.S. Air Force and Army.⁵² *Them!* was made with U.S. Army assistance, including the loan of flamethrowers and soldiers skilled in using them,[53] while other filmmakers made do with stock footage of U.S. military equipment and troops—a money-saving resource would require *Invasion USA* (1952) to include a line about Communist invaders wearing U.S. Army uniforms,[54] and that would later be denied to anti-military films in the 1960s. Even when the U.S. military was unable to defeat alien menaces such as the nuke-proof Martians in George Pal's *War of the Worlds* (1953), they were shown in a positive light, helping with the evacuation of threatened cities.[55] In *Forbidden Planet* (1956), the heroes are on a rescue mission in the service of the United Planets rather than the United States, but the heavily armed and apparently all-American crew have the ranks and titles of U.S. naval personnel, and are described as (unneeded) "military assistance" and "an army of his fellow creatures" by Dr. Morbius, the sole survivor of the scientific team they were sent to save. Morbius, who treats the officers (apart from the ship's doctor) with less than perfect respect and tells the ship's captain, "A commanding officer doesn't need brains. Just a good loud voice," is later revealed to be (unconsciously) the villain and meets a fate strongly reminiscent of Dr. Carrington's from *The Thing*.[56]

This Island Earth (1955) begins with its hero, physicist Cal Meacham, donning a flight suit to fly a USAF Lockheed T-33 Shooting Star back to his lab, thus countering the often negative image of '50s SF movie scientists by showing him as a fighter pilot.[57] (I have been unable to find out what degree of assistance *This Island Earth* received from the USAF, if any, but while the images of the T-33 in flight may be stock footage, Rex Reason as Meacham can clearly be seen climbing into the cockpit. According to Clary, the movie did cause minor problems for the USAF by inspiring a brief surge of reports of UFOs with the same capabilities as the Metalunan saucer from *This Island Earth*.[58] The choice of the aircraft may also have been a visual pun: Metaluna's enemies destroy the planet with a barrage of meteors, with "shooting stars" clearly visible in the shots of the war-ravaged surface.)

While the majority of these films end with the U.S. military victorious, or at least with the menace removed with U.S. military assistance, it's interesting to take a closer look at how some of them *begin*. Early in *Earth vs. the Flying Saucers* (which was "suggested" by a nonfiction book by retired USMC Major Donald Keyhoe, *Flying Saucers from Outer Space*), it's announced that the U.S. military has adopted the policy of firing first on any UFOs.[59] As in *The Thing from Another World* and *The Day the Earth Stood Still*, they do exactly that. The aliens, "survivors of a dying solar system," begin by destroying American satellites (launched from U.S. military bases) which they mistake for weapons; when they realize their mistake, and try to communicate with the scientist in charge of the satellite program, Dr. Marvin (played by Hugh Marlowe, who had played the would-be "big hero" in *The Day the Earth Stood Still*), the message is understood too late. The aliens are fired upon when they land, and retaliate. When the aliens attempt to arrange a meeting in Washington with Earth's political leaders, a la *The Day the Earth Stood Still*, Marvin and the military assume it's a trap, and arrange to evacuate the city and defend it with Marvin's new weapon: "When a powerful and threatening force lands on our nation's doorstep, we don't meet it with milk and cookies," as one officer remarks.[60] There is no apparent attempt in this film by the U.S. to negotiate with the aliens, no equivalent of *The Day the Earth Stood Still*'s secretary trying to enlist their aid against "forces of evil," though this may have been because the producers wanted spectacular battle scenes (memorably created by Ray Harryhausen) rather than any comment on possible peaceful solutions.

◆ ◆ ◆

Despite John W. Campbell and Horace L. Gold telling their authors that "atomic doom" stories were not wanted, these would proliferate in science fiction stories, novels, film, and eventually TV, reaching a wide and often appreciative audience. Wilson A. Tucker's *The Long Loud Silence* (1952), in which a U.S. Army corporal wakes up on the wrong side of an Army-enforced cordon sanitaire after a joint nuclear and biological weapon attack and must struggle, cheat and ultimately murder merely to survive,[61] was praised by Damon Knight as being "as near perfection as makes no difference ... honest, courageous, deeply felt."[62]

Philip K. Dick wrote in 1955:

> In science fiction, a writer is not merely inclined to act out the Cassandra role; he is absolutely obliged to—unless, of course, he honestly thinks he will wake up some morning and find that the high-minded Martians have sneaked off with all our bombs and armaments, for our own good.
>
> Of course, doom stories become monotonous, since there are infinite bright, successful, nondoom futures, but only one *doom*; that is war. Once *the* war-doom story has been written, there is not much to say; and Ray Bradbury has written that story at least once.[63]

Ray Bradbury's story "There Will Come Soft Rains" (1950), which depicts the house of a family who have been reduced to shadows on an exterior wall by an A-bomb blast,[64] was reprinted at least once in every year from 1950 to 1954, 1958 to 1963, and 1965 to 1990, including an adaptation into comics form in 1966—not including translations into other languages.[65]

In Isaac Asimov's *The Currents of Space* (1952), a spacers' legend has it that half of Earth's surface is radioactive.[66] His short story "The Gentle Vultures" (1957) has aliens waiting for a nuclear war on Earth so they can colonize the devastated planet[67]; in "Spell My Name With an S" (1958), an alien manages to avert a nuclear war on Earth by persuading one physicist to change the spelling of his name, then accepts a bet to use a similarly minor change to bring the war about on schedule before his boss notices his interference in human history.[68] Walter M. Miller's *A Canticle for Leibowitz* (1959), which predicted the slow re-establishment of a high-tech civilization after an apocalyptic nuclear war, and then a second Armageddon once the secret of nuclear weapons was rediscovered, won the Hugo Award for Best Novel in 1960.[69]

Stories about nuclear war and the aftermath were also common in American science fiction films in the 1950s, starting with Arch Oboler's *Five* (1951), and some '50s SF films lauded the use of American nuclear weapons. *Invasion USA* (1952) had the U.S. military retaliating against the invaders by dropping three times as many A-bombs on the enemy homeland as the invaders used against America,[70] and the hilariously awful *King Dinosaur* (1955) took this beyond any logical extreme. In the latter film, American astronauts exploring a habitable planet carry a nuclear reactor (cabin luggage–sized and apparently near weightless) which can be turned into a timed A-bomb: when one of the astronauts has his shirt torn by a "Tyrannosaurus rex" (actually an iguana) on an island, the military doctor remarks, "I brought the atomic bomb. I think this would be a good time to use it!" After nuking the island and its inhabitants (two lizards, a small alligator, a mata-mata, an armadillo, and stock footage of a mammoth taken from *One Million B.C.*), another astronaut grins while saying that they have "brought civilization to planet Nova." This endorsement of the use of nuclear weapons borders on the reverence shown the Omega Bomb by the mutants in *Beneath the Planet of the Apes*, though in this case the nuking was presumably done to justify including stock footage of an A-bomb blast in the trailer rather than as a political statement.[71]

However, I have yet to find a film of the decade that clearly depicted the U.S. military as bringing about the apocalypse by being the first to attack another Earthly city with nuclear weapons, as some SF stories had done as early as the 1940s. A few movies of the era suggested that the attack would be launched by Russians or by communists of indeterminate nationality, as in *Invasion USA* (1952) and *Rocket Attack U.S.A.* (1961),[72] but most remained vague about the causes of the war and concentrated on the aftermath, as in *Five* (1951), *Teenage Caveman* (1957), and *On the Beach* (1959).[73]

On the Beach came closest to assigning blame to the U.S. military in the line by scientist Julian Osborne: "The war started when people accepted the idiotic principle that peace could be maintained by arranging to defend themselves with weapons they couldn't possibly use without committing suicide."[74] The U.S. military declined to assist in the making of the film, and "Eisenhower's cabinet met to consider how to limit its success and exposure,"[75] but a USN vice admiral acted as technical consultant, the Royal Navy lent the director a submarine, and the Royal Australian Navy provided an aircraft carrier.

Some SF nuclear holocaust films with positive images of the U.S. military were made after this—*Panic in Year Zero!* (1962) ended with the protagonists being saved by Army[76]—and not until the '60s would American SF films openly show the U.S. military starting a nuclear war that killed Americans as well as their enemies.

However, several SF films showed contemporary U.S. nuclear weapons *testing* as dangerous. *The Amazing Colossal Man* (formerly a U.S. Army lieutenant colonel traumatized by his experiences in the Korean War), *The Monster that Challenged the World*, and the giant ants in *Them!* mutated to enormous size because of radiation from U.S. military bomb tests; *The Beast from 20,000 Fathoms* was freed from ice and revived by an American A-bomb test; the giant cephalopod of *It Came from Beneath the Sea* was irradiated by an H-bomb and forced to seek out new prey in shallower waters; *The Incredible Shrinking Man* slowly disappeared because of a cocktail of fallout from a nuclear test and chemical spray; *The Beast of Yucca Flats* transformed from a defecting Hungarian scientist to a "prehistoric beast" (played by Tor Johnson in torn clothes and a little makeup) after being exposed to radiation from an American aboveground A-bomb test.[77] *Them!* And *It Came from Beneath the Sea* both openly suggest that further tests may bring forth more monsters. While Marvel Comics of the 1960s would use radioactivity to turn ordinary Americans into superheroes—the Fantastic Four mutated by cosmic rays, the Hulk by gamma rays from a nuclear weapon of his own devising, Spider-Man bitten by an irradiated spider, Daredevil exposed to radioactive waste, etc.—as well as villains, these films of the '50s invariably showed the side-effects of fallout from nuclear weapon tests as being negative for individuals and/or entire cities.

The Beast from 20,000 Fathoms hit cinemas before the Castle Bravo H-bomb test at Bikini Atoll sent a cloud of fallout over inhabited islands and the crews of the USS *Bairoko* and close to a hundred fishing boats, including the *Daigo Fukuryu Maru* (*Lucky Dragon 5*). All members of the

Daigo Fukuryu Maru's crew suffered acute radiation sickness, and one died six months later, while hundreds of Marshallese were evacuated from their contaminated homes. After this, it's easy to understand why the Assistant Secretary of the Navy in *It Came from Beneath the Sea* protests, "H-bombs have been blamed for every freak accident that's happened since, up to and including marine monsters being disturbed!"[78]

Ray Bradbury's short story "Embroidery" (1951) and Asimov's short stories "Hell-Fire" (1956) and "Silly Asses" (1958) also reflect this wariness about nuclear testing. In the Bradbury story, three women wait for five o'clock when a scheduled "experiment" involving an atomic blast "twice as big as ever before. No, ten times, maybe a thousand," destroys their town: one asks, "Why didn't we stop them before it got this far and this big?"[79] In "Hell-Fire," a slow-motion film of a nuclear test reveals the face of Satan.[80] In "Silly Asses," aliens are about to welcome Earth into the galactic federation until they discover that humans are testing nuclear weapons on their own planet, at which point they delete their name from the list with the comment, "Silly asses."[81]

It may be argued that this suggests fear of the bomb, or even of science, rather than distrust of the U.S. military, but it's noteworthy that these films and "Hell-Fire" clearly refer to *U.S.* military bomb tests (*Them!* specifically blames the historic Trinity test, nine years before, for causing the ants to mutate,[82] and *The Beast of Yucca Flats* is set in and around a Nevada test site), when it would have been as easy and more patriotic to blame them on another power. As in *The Thing from Another World*, the U.S. military is shown in these films as cleaning up a mess of its own making, and people die in the process.

As the decade drew to a close, the criticism of U.S. military weapons testing became even more pronounced in SF films. In 1958's *The Space Children*, a giant brain teams up with the children of human scientists to stop a military rocket launch that threatens the planet.[83] And in 1959's *Plan 9 from Outer Space*, the aliens have come to Earth to prevent the testing of a bomb that will start a chain reaction and destroy the universe. Not only is the U.S. military depicted as covering up the truth about UFOs, a U.S. military officer responds to the aliens' warning about the bomb, "So what if we do develop this Solanite bomb? We'd be an even stronger nation than now!"[84]

This suggests that even at the height of the Cold War, mainstream American SF filmmakers had started to worry whether even the U.S. military could be trusted with these increasingly powerful weapons. Evans estimates that between 1956 and 1960, negative images of the U.S. military in American films were marginally more common than positive ones—approximately 42 percent vs. 40 percent, in contrast to the 10 percent negative to 70 percent positive ratio of 1951–55.[85] The U.S. military was still prepared to cooperate with SF writers and directors who were prepared to present them in a positive light—for example, selling a surplus $345,000 B-25 bomber to CBS for $2500 for use in "*King Nine* Will Not Return," a 1960 episode of *The Twilight Zone*[86]—a show which generally depicted the U.S. military in a positive light and used time travel and ESP to deal with survivors' guilt, "battle fatigue," post–traumatic stress, and other psychological problems faced by servicemen. "*King Nine* Will Not Return" tells the story of Captain Embry, a World War II B-25 commander who fell ill before a mission that killed his crew: when the wreckage of the plane is found seventeen years later, Embry wakes up at the crash site, then in a hospital bed. This is assumed to be a hallucination, until a nurse finds sand in his shoes.[87] A similar case of survivor's guilt is central to "The Thirty-Fathom Grave," when the crew of a U.S. Navy destroyer finds the 21-year-old wreckage of a U.S. Navy World War II submarine near Guadalcanal. A hammering sound is heard from within the sub, and one of the destroyer's crew—the sole survivor of the sub, who holds himself responsible for its sinking because he accidentally dropped a signal lamp—believes that the ghosts of the crew are summoning him. He dives overboard and drowns.[88]

Both of these scripts were written by *The Twilight Zone*'s creator, Rod Serling, who had enlisted in the U.S. Army's 11th Airborne Division as a paratrooper the day he graduated from high school, and had written scripts for Armed Forces Radio as well as fighting in the Philippines. Discharged in 1946, he went to college on the G.I. Bill.[89] The name *The Twilight Zone* was taken from an obscure Air Force term, though not one Serling remembered having heard beforehand.[90] The pilot episode for *The Twilight Zone*, "Where is Everybody?," starred Earl Holliman (the cook in *Forbidden Planet*) in a USAF jumpsuit, as a trainee astronaut taking part in a psychology experiment to test his ability to withstand isolation.[91] "The Purple Testament," also written by Serling, tells the story of an infantry lieutenant in the Philippines in 1945, "Fitz" Fitzgerald, who sees a strange light on the faces of those of his men who are about to die. His captain, noticing that Fitzgerald seems unusually disturbed by the deaths of four men in one day (recalling another day when the company had lost eight), asks if there was "anything special" about the four. The lieutenant replies that apart from their all being under twenty-one, the thing that made them special was that he had correctly predicted that they, and only they, would die that day and had written the names down beforehand. When the story of Fitzgerald's ability spreads, one soldier in the company asks who will die in the next action; the captain quashes the "rumor" rather than risk any desertions, and Fitzgerald, who has foreseen the captain's death, accedes to this.[92]

That one question aside, there is no suggestion in the episode that any American soldier fighting in the Philippines in World War II would ever disobey orders or hesitate to do his duty, even if he knew that it would prove fatal. While one soldier remarks, "War stinks," no one suggests that it's unnecessary.

Serling would return to this setting for another episode in the following season: "A Quality of Mercy," in which a freshly graduated young lieutenant takes command of an infantry platoon of seasoned and war-weary NCOs who have cornered a group of starving Japanese soldiers in a cave. The lieutenant wants to launch a potentially suicidal frontal assault on the cave, but his sergeant wants to bypass it, saying the Japanese no longer pose a threat. The lieutenant suddenly finds himself in the head of a Japanese lieutenant in Corregidor on May 4, 1942, serving under a Japanese captain who wants to attack the cave—this time, occupied by a small number of wounded *American* soldiers—and finds himself unsuccessfully trying to persuade the captain to bypass the cave or let the Americans surrender. Having asked for mercy for his own people, when he is returned to his own body and time, he decides to bypass the cave—and hears on the radio that Hiroshima has been bombed and the Japanese are expected to surrender within days.[93]

The idea of American soldiers showing mercy to the enemy, rather than vengeance—at least, when they feel that it will not affect the outcome of the war—is also central to "Two," written and directed by Montgomery Pittman and broadcast at the beginning of the third season. Five years after a war that has left a U.S. city an abandoned corpse-strewn ruin, an American soldier (played by archetypical tough guy Charles Bronson) encounters a woman wearing the uniform of the invading army. Though initially suspicious of each other, they share food found in an empty shop, and when the American finds two guns, he gives one to her. When she admires a dress in a shop window (the only word she speaks is "precassny," Russian for "pretty"),[94] he breaks the window and gives that to her. She goes into the nearest intact building to change—but it's a recruiting center, and the propaganda posters enrage her, motivating her to shoot at the American. He retreats, then removes his uniform and changes into civilian clothes: when he sees her again, she's wearing the dress (though accessorized with combat boots), and they walk off together side by side. Once out of uniform, and with the war over, they no longer need to be enemies.[95]

The most negative depiction of the American military in *The Twilight Zone* is in the fifth season episode "The Encounter" (1964), in which Neville Brand ("the fourth-most decorated U.S. Army soldier of World War II")[96] plays Fenton, a decorated ex–Marine with an attic full of World War II memorabilia. His souvenirs include a supposedly cursed katana taken from a Japanese officer who had already surrendered—but whom Fenton killed, because he'd been ordered not to take any prisoners. Nearly twenty years later, Fenton insults a young American-born Japanese man, Arthur Takamuri, who has come to mow his lawn, and blames immigrants, rather than his drinking, for the loss of his job (and, by implication, his wife's leaving him). While Fenton is not portrayed sympathetically, the voice-over narration at the episode's end blames his decline on guilt.[97] It was broadcast on the first of May 1964, the day before the first major student demonstrations against the Vietnam War, but never syndicated, reportedly because of protests from Japanese-Americans angered because Takamuri claims his father was a traitor who signaled the Japanese planes at Pearl Harbor (no such traitor existed), and Fenton's racist comments, including "Women are a dime a dozen. Anybody who's been in the Orient knows that," and, "In the Pacific, we were told that you weren't even human, you were some species of ape." (This makes it the only episode of *The Twilight Zone* to have only been broadcast once.[98])

The image of the U.S. military presented in *The Twilight Zone*, particularly in scripts by Serling, is almost exclusively that of men who may be fallible—particularly if they've had little experience of actual combat—but are essentially heroic. Except for Fenton (the only character in the entire series identified as a U.S. Marine), and Flight Officer Corey, the astronaut who kills his commanding officer for his water in "I Shot an Arrow Into The Air,"[99] everyone identified as serving in the U.S. Army, Navy or National Guard (in "The 7th Is Made Up of Phantoms"[100]) appears willing to sacrifice himself to defend his country and his fellow soldiers (and is potentially traumatized when he fails to do so), but is also able to stop fighting once the war is over.

It's an image almost exclusively based on ideas of World War II: while the first episode of the fifth season, "In Praise of Pip" (1964), begins in an aid station in Vietnam, where a young soldier has been wounded even though "there isn't supposed to be a war going on there,"[101] no episode was set during the more recent Korean War. "The Last Flight," about a World War I fighter pilot who travels back in time to save a friend whom he had abandoned in a moment of cowardice, had English actor Kenneth Haigh playing an RAF officer, not an American.[102] Except for Fenton in "The Encounter," *The Twilight Zone*'s portrayal of American servicemen dealing with combat situations or the aftermath was generally sympathetic—and even Fenton has a conscience, and suffers remorse at having obeyed his orders to kill a defenseless soldier who had already surrendered. The idea of the U.S. serviceman as a remorseless psychopathic killing machine would not become iconic until the Vietnam War came to dominate public consciousness.

◆ ◆ ◆

The early fifties were less than golden for comic-book superheroes. The American comic industry in the early 1950s depended mainly on romance, western, crime and horror titles: though some science fiction comics appeared during the decade, few of the costumed superheroes were still active by the time the Korean War began in August 1950,[103] and only Fawcett's Captain Marvel and Captain Marvel, Jr., were depicted fighting in Korea before the war was over—battling "The Mad Mongol Monster," "The Scarlet Vampire," "The Red Crusher," "The Mongol Blood Drinkers," "Vampira the Korean Queen of Terror," "The Great Red Brain" and other communist horrors.[104]

Though comics "remained the literature of choice for American G.I.s,"[105]

> Timely began to produce comic books very different from the ones that had been published throughout World War II. The battles depicted were no longer a matter of super heroes bashing bad guys; comics now began to show the pain, misery and fear of ordinary soldiers. Perhaps the change stemmed from the experience of writers and artists who had seen combat themselves, but the new war they portrayed was different too.[106]

This was not always popular with the U.S. Army, who condemned Harvey Kurtzmann's 1950 *Two-Fisted Tales* and *Frontline Combat* as "subversive because they tend to discredit the army and undermine troop morale."[107] According to Kurtzmann: "At the time, it was fashionable to do war comics in terms of fantasy and glamour, which I thought was a terrible immorality. They made war a happy event where American supermen go around beating up buck-toothed yellow men.... The way war really is, you get killed suddenly for no reason."[108] Wright suggests that it was this acknowledgment of the reality of war that prevented comic-book aliens and scientist/crimefighters from being recruited, and being used to recruit others, to fight in Korea. "Unlike the 'good war' against the Axis, the news from Korea defied optimism ... by the winter of 1950–51 U.S. troops were in full-scale retreat out of frozen North Korea ... the war settled into a grim and interminable contest of attrition. In this context, the naïve scenarios envisioned by Fawcett's writers simply did not work. There were no easy answers and no simple resolution to this war."[109]

In 1954, after the end of the Korean War, *Seduction of the Innocents* author Fredric Wertham's appearance before the Senate Subcommittee on Juvenile Delinquency, and the creation of the Comics Code Authority, Marvel Comics attempted to revive its World War II-era superheroes. Captain America and Bucky made a brief and little-remembered reappearance, with "Captain America.... Commie Smasher!" and "Striking Back at the Soviet!" emblazoned on the cover, including going on a mission to postwar Korea to treat Chinese POWs whom the U.S. has been accused of poisoning.[110] The series folded after only three issues, and Marvel waited another ten years before reviving Captain America again with a little revisionist history that revealed the '50s Captain America and Bucky to be impostors.

The only item of U.S. military equipment produced in the 1950s that I can find that was named after a science fiction creation was the T-63 training shape (a dummy nuclear bomb), also called the "Blue Beetle." Blue Beetle, the crimefighting inventor of a bulletproof suit, had premiered in 1939 but had gone on hiatus in 1950; after a brief revival in 1955, he too disappeared until the mid–1960s.

One science fiction invention that attracted U.S. military funding in the 1950s was the rocket belt or Individual Lift Device. In 1959, Colonel Charles Parkin, who had earlier tried strapping the nitrogen propellant tank from a flamethrower to his back and jumping,[111] a la Buck Rogers, persuaded the U.S. Army's Transportation Research and Engineering Command (TRECOM) to issue "a Request for Proposal, asking for an authoritative report on the feasibility of "small rocket lift devices" to increase the mobility of individual soldiers."[112] Bell Aerosystems and Thiokol Corporation, which had already been working on rocket-powered flying belts, submitted bids, but the contract to conduct the study went to Aerojet-General, who were paid $56,456 for the report, declaring the Small Rocket Lift Device feasible.[113] Bell received $25,000 in 1960 to build a working prototype, and in 1961 demonstrated a 78-lb. Rocket Belt with a flight time of 21 seconds, which the pilot flew over an Army truck.[114] In 1965, it would make appearances in the James Bond movie *Thunderball* and the TV series *Lost in Space*; the same year, Bell was contracted by ARPA to build a jet belt with a greater range, overseen by the Army Aviation Materiel Command.[115] While the jet belt could stay aloft for ten minutes, the Army eventually decided that it had no practical value—though the small jet engines developed to power the belt would prove ideal for military UAVs and cruise missiles.[116]

◆ ◆ ◆

Klaatu's suggestion that living "without arms or armies" would leave people "free to pursue more profitable pursuits"[117] was echoed in written SF in the 1950s. With General Eisenhower in the White House and his secretary of defense, former General Motors CEO Charles Wilson, advocating a "permanent wartime economy,"[118] U.S. military spending more than doubled from approximately 32.2 percent of total budget outlays in 1950 to a peak of 69.5 percent in 1954, remaining above 42 percent for the rest of the decade and averaging 60.29 percent for 1951-1960.[119] Unsurprisingly, some science fiction writers of the time addressed the costs of the military, particularly in peacetime. Frederic Jameson describes 1953, the year Frederick Pohl and Cyril M. Kornbluth's *The Space Merchants* appeared, as the dawn of the third stage of science fiction–"Sociology, or better still, social satire or 'cultural critique.'"[120] The first story to explicitly address this issue may have been Kornbluth's 1953 "The Adventurer," which depicts a future U.S. where the Department of Defense accounts for seventy-eight percent of government expenditures.[121] After the secretary of defense is shot for treason by a president who wants the money for his private art collection, the cabinet secretly makes long-term plans for a military coup. When the coup succeeds (Kornbluth shows an early one failing, and mentions a previous Pentagon mutiny), the megalomaniac military dictator has the cabinet members executed for denying his godhead.

In Philip K. Dick's 1953 story "The Defenders," the populations of the USA and Soviet Union are tricked by their robots into remaining in their fallout shelters for eight years after the war has ended: the robots hope that when the humans emerge, neither side will want war and will work together towards peaceful goals including "the conquest of space" and "eliminating hunger and poverty."[122] In Ray Bradbury's 1952 story "A Piece of Wood" (the only Bradbury story I've been able to find that features soldiers prominently—in this case, both as protagonist and antagonist), a sergeant asks an official who ridicules his idea of disarming the world after sixteen years of war, "Are you lying to yourself and me because you've got a nice comfortable job?"[123] When the sergeant causes all metal weapons on the post to rust, the official orders him kicked to death and prepares to bludgeon him himself with a wooden chair-leg rather than see the armies disarmed.[124]

British author Arthur C. Clarke's *Childhood's End* (first published in 1953 in the U.S.) begins, rather like *The Day the Earth Stood Still*, with the arrival of an alien spaceship whose English-speaking emissary calls for peace between nations—and backs it up with displays of impressive but nonviolent technical power similar to Klaatu's. Within fifty years, this has resulted in a "golden age" where "the abolition of armed forces had at once almost doubled the world's effective wealth."[125]

Fred Pohl's "The Wizard of Pung's Corners" (1958) depicts the U.S. Army as being issued with new (and presumably expensive) equipment at such a rate that the riflemen in a company of 1250 are unable to keep up with the instruction manuals for their guns and are easily defeated by a lone octogenarian civilian armed with a shotgun and a .22. The octogenarian then goes on to take over the Pentagon (one side of which is occupied by an advertising agency).[126]

This argument is even posed in Heinlein's *Starship Troopers* (1959), with the protagonist's father saying early in the novel:

> If there were a war, I'd be the first to cheer you on—and to put the business on a war footing. But there isn't, and praise God there never will be again. We've outgrown wars. This planet is now peaceful and happy and we enjoy good enough relations with other planets. So what is this so-called "Federal Service"? Parasitism, pure and simple. A functionless organ, utterly obsolete, living on the taxpayers.[127]

As Panshin says, "Starship troopers are not half so glorious sitting on their butts polishing their weapons for the tenth time for lack of anything to do,"[128] which is pretty much the picture given of the peacetime army in Kurt Vonnegut's debut novel *Player Piano* (1952)—a repository for the poorly-educated and otherwise unemployable, parading with wooden guns and described by the Shah of Bratpuhr as "a fine bunch of slaves."[129] Vonnegut's soldier character, Pfc. Hacketts, wants to "occupy somewhere else and maybe be somebody" in the hope that "there might be laying *and* glory overseas and while there wasn't any shooting and wasn't going to be none either for a good long while still you got a real gun and bullets and there was a little glory in that." After observing the soldiers drilling, the Shah comments, "Americans have changed almost everything on Earth, but it would be easier to move the Himalayas than to change the Army."[130]

Heinlein's protagonist's answer to these accusations that an army is functionless and expensive is to counter (after he's been through basic training), "If there was ever a time when 'peace' meant that there was no fighting going on, I have been unable to find out about it."[131] While the period between the end of the Korean War in '53 and escalation of the Vietnam War in '63 was a relatively peaceful one for the U.S., Heinlein continued not only to defend the military throughout the decade but, in his own words, set out to glorify it, adding, "Would I have picked it for my profession and stayed on the rolls the past 56 years were I not proud of it?"[132]

In his *Between Planets* (1951), the protagonist, Don Harvey, is never referred to as a man until he enlists in the army. Before this, he is referred to as "son," "my boy," "young fellow," "kid"; within a page of joining a unit (where "*esprit de corps* was high"),[133] he is described as "soldier" and "man," and a few pages later he tells a much older friend, "I'm not anybody's 'dear boy' ... I'm a grown man now."[134] As a soldier, he is soon "looking forward" to raids[135] and "grew to hate" a life with "hot food ... sack time ... clean clothes, clean skin, no duties and no hazards,"[136] even though he purports to want a world where "a man ought to be able to do what he wants to, if he can, and not be pushed around."[137] Even the enemy soldiers are ennobled: Don's best friend at school, expressing his intention to enlist for the other side, tells him: "It wouldn't make any difference between us. My old man says when it's time to be counted, the important thing is to be man enough to stand up."[138] Don, thinking about him later, decides he "wasn't his enemy, couldn't be.... He hoped strongly that the wild chances of war would never bring them face to face."[139]

In 1958, Heinlein interrupted his work on *The Heretic* (later to become *Stranger in a Strange Land*) to write a paid newspaper advertisement titled "Who Are the Heirs of Patrick Henry? Stand Up and Be Counted!," defending the above-ground U.S. nuclear testing that had inspired so many '50s monster movies: "No scare talk of leukemia, mutation, or atomic holocaust will sway us. Is 'fall-out' dangerous? Of course it is! The risk to life and posterity has been wilfully distorted by these Communist-line propagandists—but if it were a hundred times as great we still would choose it to the dead certainty of Communist enslavement."[140] (The Jeffersonian Asimov, conversely, was "delighted" to "have played a very small part in bringing about the nuclear-test ban" by writing a paper about the effects of carbon-14 on the human body.[141])

After writing "Patrick Henry," Heinlein temporarily abandoned *The Heretic* to write *Starship Troopers*. Admitting that the Navy, his "own service usually doesn't have too bad a time of it," and "the Air Force leads a comparable life,"[142] Heinlein intended that the novel glorify "the Poor Bloody Infantry, the mudfoot who places his frail body between his loved home and the war's desolation—but is rarely appreciated."[143] "The 'Patrick Henry' ad shocked 'em; STARSHIP TROOPERS outraged 'em," he wrote in 1980 (presumably referring to his readers and science fiction fans).[144]

5. "I'm Not Working for the World"

The novel recounts the life of Juan "Johnnie" Rico from his last term at school through a Canadian boot camp where 187 men out of 2009 graduate (and fourteen die), then through Officer Candidate School, to finally achieving the rank of lieutenant in the Mobile Infantry (Kavenay has suggested that Heinlein gave Rico his name "as a riposte to Dalton Trumbo's pacifist tract *Johnny Got His Gun*"[145]; it is also plausible that it was inspired by the song "When Johnny Comes Marching Home," later used to great effect in *Dr. Strangelove*). Rico's mother is killed by an Arachnid attack on Earth and his wealthy and previously pacifist father joins up, becoming his platoon sergeant. In that time, the First Interstellar War or "Bug War" breaks out, with a totally communist[146] alien species with whom it is apparently impossible to negotiate (explicitly compared to "the Chinese Hegemony").[147] Another alien race, the Skinnies, former allies of the Arachnids, allies itself with the human Federation instead. Rico is present for a major battle, but the novel ends with the war still ongoing.

Anthony Boucher's review called it "not a novel at all, but an irate sermon with a few fictional trappings.... The author is so intent upon his arguments that he has forgotten to insert a story or any recognizable characters."[148] Dean McLaughlin described it as "a book-length recruiting poster."[149] Alexei Panshin described it as a "militaristic polemic—I don't see that any other reading is really possible," adding that it "put the military life in the most glamorous terms possible"[150] where "disease, dirt and doubt are missing"[151]; finally, he compared it to a recruiting film. H. Bruce Franklin describes the novel as "a bugle-blowing, drum-beating glorification of the hero's life in military service."[152] Norman Spinrad describes it as "a military wet-dream fantasy ... in which righteous ingénues guiltlessly slaughter faceless gunfodder in alien or robot gook-suits."[153]

James Blish, however, defended *Starship Troopers*, writing: "If a novel about a dedicated professional soldier does not leave the impression that warfare is the only real occupation for a real man, it's a failure. I think Heinlein succeeded admirably."[154] The fantasy of becoming one's own father's superior officer seems designed to appeal strongly to the teenagers who were the intended readership of Heinlein's "juveniles" as well as recruiting posters, and certainly Heinlein's "poor bloody infantry" believe themselves an elite: "You can't buy an M.I., you can't conscript him, you can't coerce him.... The M.I. is a free man; all that drives him comes from inside—that self-respect and need for the respect of his mates and his pride in being one of them called morale, or *esprit de corps*."[155] Also, the novel does indeed suggest that only veterans are adults, and that this is believed by the narrator and other soldiers (and, very probably, by Heinlein). The book is dedicated to "all sergeants anywhen who have labored to make men out of boys,"[156] and in one scene, a character still in training is described by a senior officer as "a bad boy—I say 'boy' because you quite evidently aren't a man yet, although we'll keep trying—a surprisingly bad boy in view of the stage of your training."[157] Senior officers and NCOs also call the raw recruits "sonny,"[158] "kids," "wild animals,"[159] and "unspanked young cubs"[160]; Rico later sums up that cadets are "zero. A nought without a rim."[161]

Unsurprisingly, some in the U.S. military apparently sympathize with this view, and the novel is on the reading lists of the U.S. Marines[162] and Navy.[163] Much of the weaponry and other technology described in the novel has either been developed at the U.S. military's behest (and expense) since the novel was written, or is on the drawing board. "Infrared snoopers" are now standard U.S. military equipment.[164] The Pentagon has spent millions developing a "nuclear hand grenade"[165] similar to Heinlein's "peewee A-rocket."[166] The "burrowing H-rocket"[167] intended for use against the burrowing Arachnids was echoed by U.S. military's development of nuclear "bunker buster" bombs beginning with 1963's M61, and most recently by the Robust Nuclear Earth Penetrator intended to destroy tunnels and underground complexes once thought to exist in Afghanistan and Iraq.[168] The U.S. military and DARPA have also experimented with metal body armor[169] and powered exoskeletons such as HULC (Human Universal Load Carrier), similar to Heinlein's mobile infantry's powered armor.[170] The name of one of the alien races in *Starship*, the Skinnies, was also adopted by U.S. troops in Somalia as a nickname for the locals, and the MP-5 submachine gun became known as the "skinny-popper."[171]

More significantly, two *political* ideas espoused in *Starship Troopers* have come to be widely accepted in the U.S. The first is the emphasis on well-equipped "superelite" military units: Franklin points out that "in 1959 there was still great resistance, even at the highest levels of the U.S. Army, against creating the kind of elite ground corps envisioned in *Starship Troopers*,"[172] until President Kennedy "almost single-handedly created the Green Berets"[173] in 1961. Kennedy increased the size of the Special Forces sixfold "over the objections of his own top generals, who voiced the traditional American military suspicion of elite forces."[174]

The second, which took longer to overcome resistance from the administration in the USA (and elsewhere), was the abolition of conscription in favor of an all-volunteer military. Heinlein spoke scathingly of conscription in *Starship Troopers* and his later defense of the novel in *Expanded Universe*: "I am opposed to conscription for any reason at any time, war or peace, and have said so repeatedly in fiction, in nonfiction, from platforms, and in angry sessions in think tanks."[175] Similarly, Rico says, "It's a whole lot safer to have a blank file on your flank than to have an alleged soldier who is nursing the 'conscript' syndrome."[176] Incidents of resistance (including the "fragging" of unpopular officers) in the Vietnam War arguably bear that out, and the U.S. government abandoned conscription in 1973 when troops were no longer needed for the Vietnam War.

The most controversial political idea in the novel, and one which has won fewer converts, is that the vote should be restricted to "discharged veterans" of "Federal Service": "civilians" can not vote. Heinlein later claimed[177] that "veterans" did not mean "solely a person who has served in military forces," but as Gifford points out, even if it had been Heinlein's "*intent* to make Federal service ninety-five percent 'civil service,'"[178] as Heinlein later stated,[179] the text of the novel does not support this, and Gifford cites several passages which indicate quite the reverse. (Interestingly, the figures *do* roughly apply to the enemy Arachnids, of whom Heinlein says, "Only about one in fifty is a warrior."[180]) Also, Heinlein's addendum admits that once someone has volunteered, "he goes where he is sent and does what he is told to do ... he may wind up as cannon fodder."[181] The triple-amputee recruiting officer in *Starship Troopers*, Ho, tells Rico (in peacetime) that "if you want to serve and I can't talk you out of it, then we have to take you, because that's your constitutional right,"[182] but federal service is "either real military service, rough and dangerous even in peacetime ... or a most unreasonable facsimile thereof."[183] Lt. Col. Dubois defines citizenship as "an emotional conviction that the whole is greater than the part ... and that *the part should be humbly proud to sacrifice itself* that the whole may live" (my italics).[184]

Echoing Asimov's view of the military, Philip José Farmer said of the serialized version of the novel ("Starship Soldier") that Heinlein "did not say a word about the well-known and thoroughly authenticated tendency of the military system to be stupid.... A world ruled by veterans would be as mismanaged, graft-ridden, and insane as one ruled by men who had never gotten near the odor of blood and guts."[185] In a mini-lecture in one of the novel's "History and Moral Philosophy" classes (which only veterans can teach—and in both cases we are shown, the veterans are officers badly wounded in combat), the teacher, Major Reid, admits, "Service men are not brighter than civilians. In many cases civilians are much more intelligent ... nor is it verifiable that military discipline makes a man self-disciplined once he is out: the crime rate of veterans is much like that of civilians."[186] However, Major Reid maintains, "Under our system every voter and officeholder is a man who has demonstrated through voluntary and difficult service that he places the welfare of the group ahead of personal advantage.... He may fail in wisdom, he may lapse in civic virtue. But his average performance is enormously better than that of any other class of rulers in history."[187] Reid does not define "the group," however, and Heinlein's emphasis on *esprit de corps* and chain of command in this novel and others suggests that a soldier's responsibility is to his own branch of the military. Rico may be expected to "place my body between my loved home and the war's desolation," but he states clearly that his "loved home" is the M.I., not Earth: "Patriotism was a bit esoteric for me, too large-scale to see. But the M.I. was my gang. I belonged. They were all the family I had left."[188] (Similarly, Vonnegut's Shah of Bratpuhr is unconvinced when told that American soldiers are free men motivated by patriotism.[189]) Echoes, again, of "I'm not working for the world, Scott. I'm working for the Air Force."

Heinlein stressed that in the novel, "The military tend to be despised by most civilians and this is made explicit"[190]; the novel even describes an apparently unprovoked assault on Rico and his fellow infantrymen by civilians in Seattle.[191] However, civilians have never rebelled against the Federation, because, as one soldier explains, "armed uprising—requires not only dissatisfaction but aggressiveness.... If you separate out the aggressive ones and make them the sheep dogs, the sheep will never give you trouble."[192] This argument, however, assumes that the Federal Service succeeds in recruiting *all* the aggressive ones, and that those who drop out or decline to enlist do so because they are not sufficiently aggressive to cause trouble, rather than dissatisfied with the pay, hours and conditions that even Rico complains about.[193] (Presumably, no one in this world joins the Federal Service as the only way to get health insurance or a university education.) The novel does not specify whether "sheep dogs" refers only to the Mobile Infantry, or to the Federal Service as a whole; if the latter, it suggests that all political power (the right to vote as well as the right to hold office) is restricted to the aggressive, which might explain the state of perpetual war suggested by the final line, "To the everlasting glory of the Infantry…"

The inconsistent characterization does not help here: the Rico who enlists, putting the infantry "clear at the bottom"[194] on his list of career choices, seems passive and subject to peer pressure rather than aggressive: Brian Aldiss understandably describes him as "a big strong masochist" who "longs to be humiliated."[195] And Rico admits that placement officers are fallible, in one case recruiting a man who later goes AWOL from boot camp and murders a baby girl.[196] But Major Reid applauds the sheep dog analogy as "close to the facts,"[197] and further adds, "The practical reason for continuing our system is the same as the practical reason for continuing anything: it works satisfactorily."[198]

As Panshin points out, this straw man argument is "the justification of the sheep-shearer,"[199] "the old argument that might makes right."[200] While we are never shown the M.I. turning against human civilians (unless the Skinnies are actually human rebels; foreshadowing the problems American soldiers would face in irregular warfare in Vietnam and the Middle East, Rico admits to not being able to distinguish between Skinny civilians and soldiers), nothing in the novel suggests that they could not be ordered to do so if any *did* rebel, seeking to take back the government from what is effectively a military oligarchy disguised as a democracy. When Dubois says, "Violence, naked force, has settled more issues in history than has any other factor, and the contrary opinion is wishful thinking at its worst. Breeds that forget this basic truth have always paid for it with their lives and their freedom,"[201] he seems to be saying that the nonviolent cannot expect to keep either. While recruits in boot camp may be "pups" and "kids" (promoted to "men" or at least "apes" when they graduate), soldiers in the novel compare civilians to "sheep"[202] and "beans,"[203] suggesting that if Earth-dwelling civilians despise the military (attitudes are more positive on planets nearer the front lines), the feeling is mutual.

◆ ◆ ◆

While *Starship Troopers* has had a significant influence on later depictions of the military in American science fiction, I do not have space here to address all of the arguments as to its merits and defects as either literature or political treatise. (While I disagree with many of its ideas, this should not be misinterpreted as disrespect for Heinlein, who wrote many other works that I greatly admire and who is famous for his kindness to other science fiction writers, including Theodore Sturgeon and Philip K. Dick, regardless of whether they shared his views.) The novel has already been analyzed and criticized by many writers and scholars (the Science Fiction and Fantasy Research Database lists 56 reviews and essays on the book and film).[204] Scribner's, which had published Heinlein's previous twelve novels, rejected it "because of its intense unrelenting militarism,"[205] yet—either because of or despite this—it won a Hugo Award (voted on by fans), beating Gordon R. Dickson's military science fiction novel *Dorsai!* as well as Kurt Vonnegut's *The Sirens of Titan*. Even mentioning it can still polarize almost any gathering of science fiction fans, and Heinlein said in 1980, "It continues to get lots of nasty 'fan' mail and not much favorable fan mail ... but it sells and sells and sells and sells, in eleven languages.... And yet I almost never hear of it save when someone wants to chew me out over it."[206]

One common criticism of *Starship Troopers* is that, as Rosenbaum points out, Heinlein's "classless military utopia proffered as an ideal alternative seems no less socialist and totalitarian" than a Bug hive.[207] The Federal Service's chain of command is as hierarchical as the Arachnids' caste system: the main differences seem to be that a human (albeit only one who has done his time in the Federal Service) can be promoted in the military and political hierarchy, while it's implied that the Bugs cannot; that humans have chosen this system (though how the decision to disenfranchise the civilian population was made and enforced is never really clarified), and the Arachnids (presumably) have not; and that humans will go to war to rescue even one soldier taken prisoner, which it's stated (though not demonstrated) that Arachnids will not.[208] Major Reid claims that under their regime, "personal freedom for all is greatest in history,"[209] but we can only take his word for this, as nothing else in the novel supports this statement: Reid also says that "the human being has no natural rights of any nature"[210]; the unspecified percentage (majority?) of people who don't volunteer for Federal Service are ineligible to vote; and Rico's idea of "liberty" is R&R, which he seems to enjoy less than combat. Rico asks himself, "Does Man have any 'right' to spread through the universe?" and answers, "Man is what he is, a wild animal with the will to survive, and (so far) the ability, against all competition."[211] Morality, in *Starship Troopers*, comes down to "might makes right" coupled with a Darwinian drive to defend yourself and your offspring, to go forth and multiply—which is the only justification given for the wars against the Bugs and the Skinnies.

Note the "given." The justification for the war from the novel's point of view is that only a war (preferably one against a nonhuman enemy who will not surrender or negotiate) can justify the existence of the M.I., without which there would be no story. In this case, it is significant that the novel does not end in a victory for the Federation; if it did, the M.I. would again be (as Rico's father stated earlier in the novel) "a functionless organ, utterly obsolete, living on the taxpayers."[212] Rather than let this happen, Heinlein ends the novel with Rico's Roughnecks preparing for "another bug hunt."[213]

This suggests that it might also be in the military's interest to keep a war going—Rico expresses his skepticism that "we'll have that thing we sing about, 'ain't gonna study war no more,'"[214] and Major Reid approves of his assertion that even one prisoner held by an enemy is "sufficient reason to start or resume a war," even though "millions of innocent people may die, almost certainly will die, if war is started or resumed."[215] They certainly don't sound enthusiastic about a negotiated peace, and the last line of the novel is, "To the *everlasting glory* of the Infantry" (emphasis added).[216]

This attitude may go some way to explaining the novel's continued popularity with the U.S. military. If we accept Panshin's argument that "starship troopers are not half so glorious sitting on their butts,"[217] then for everlasting glory, you need a war that lasts forever.

6. "A Taste of Armageddon"
1962 to 1975

> The problem was how to keep the wheels of industry turning without increasing the real wealth of the world. Goods must be produced, but they must not be distributed. And in practice, the only way of achieving this was by continuous warfare.—*George Orwell,* Nineteen Eighty-Four[1]
>
> I suppose it would be better if we helped them the way we helped in Vietnam? Came in and burned them and shot them and blasted them right back to the Stone Age?—*Captain Carter, "Commando Raid," Harry Harrison*[2]
>
> The madness, the pointless butchery.... As I come to understand Vietnam and what it implies about the human condition, I also realize that few humans will permit themselves such an understanding.—*Dr. Manhattan,* Watchmen, *Alan Moore*[3]
>
> The fourth enemy was the Army, the lunatics that had sent you to Vietnam in the first place, the ones that ordered you out of the relative safety of base camp or bunker to produce a body count.—*Joe Haldeman,* 1968[4]
>
> Nobody who missed the Viet-Nam War should regret the fact. It was a waste of blood and time and treasure. It did no good of which I'm aware, and did a great deal of evil of which I'm far too aware.—*David Drake, "We Happy Few"*[5]

The 1960s and early 1970s would see some very negative images of the U.S. military widely disseminated, in science fiction and later in newscasts: Evans estimates that less than 20 percent of images of the military in films released in 1960–65 were positive, while close to 50 percent were bad.[6] Former soldiers with very different experiences of wartime service to Heinlein's would write novels seen as rebutting his vision of a glorious infantry. If World War II had united the American science fiction writing community, the Vietnam War would divide it into two camps—one Jeffersonian, one Hamiltonian—and create a lasting rift.

For all its brutality and horror, however, the Vietnam War never actually became the nuclear war that people so greatly feared, and which featured in several science fiction stories published and movies made during the duration. While there were some positive depictions of the U.S. military in science fiction films of the time—as in *Panic in Year Zero!* (1962), where survivors of a nuclear attack head for the safety of a U.S. Army field hospital[7]—some of the most negative images of the U.S. military establishment coming out of American film studios in the 1960s showed how the U.S. Air Force's own security measures might lead it to fire the first shot in such a war (possibilities the USAF vehemently denied). In *Fail-Safe* (a 1962 novel by Eugene Wheeler and Harvey Burdick, set in 1967), a condenser burns out in a "fail-safe" machine during a false alarm, making it impossible to recall a bomber. The pilots, trained to follow the last order they received and ignore any communication from any other machine apart from their "fail-safe" transceivers as possibly being fake, refuse to be diverted. USAF fighter planes are sent to intercept them, but are unsuccessful. The president negotiates with Premier Khrushchev, finally agreeing to send another USAF bomber to destroy New York City as "dramatic evidence of our sincerity" and to "balance the scales" if Moscow is destroyed.[8] The only man who advocates taking advantage of the accident and escalating the war despite the prospect of heavy U.S. casualties is a civilian advisor, Professor Groeteschele, a member of "a group which later included such as Henry Kissinger, Herbert Kahn, Herbert Simon and Karl Deutsch."[9] The hawkish Groeteschele, worried about the possibility of someone *refusing* to drop the bomb, has been largely responsible for a psychological screening process which means that people in the Strategic Air Command are, in the words of General Black (whom Groeteschele, in the film, describes as a "military dove"), "more likely to err on the side of 'go' rather than on the side of withdrawal."[10] Though the military men are generally depicted as honorable, even heroic individuals, and Khrushchev and the president agree that the crisis is "no man's fault. No human being made any mistake,"[11] Khrushchev grimly concludes, "You can never trust any system, Mr. President, whether it is made of computers, or of people."[12]

When the novel was filmed, two years later, the USAF declined to give any assistance in making the picture, despite the film's final title stating that the U.S. Defense Department assured that the scenario was impossible.[13] Not only did the Air Force deny the director use of stock footage of U.S. warplanes but, according to Robb (who describes it as "one of the Pentagon's least favorite movies of all time"), they also tried to prevent commercial film libraries from supplying it to them.[14]

An even less flattering portrayal of the U.S. military, particularly the Strategic Air Command, had been released late in 1963. *Dr. Strangelove or: How I Learned to Stop Worrying and Love the Bomb* was made in London by American director Stanley Kubrick, without cooperation from the U.S. military (though Kubrick was able to obtain Air Force issue stock footage of a B-52 refueling used for the opening sequence). The set for the cockpit of the B-52 bomber was copied from the cover of a paperback copy of *Strategic Air Command* by Mel Hunter; the rest of the interior of the plane was inventively designed by Peter Murton. According to Ken Adam, after the film's publicists invited USAF personnel to view the set, the Air Force men threatened both himself and Kubrick with investigation by the FBI unless they could prove that their research had come from legal sources.[15] Gilbert Taylor's second unit team also aroused the ire of the USAF when they inadvertently flew over a secret air force base while filming Arctic scenery, and were ordered down by two fighter jets and forced to land on a fjord.[16]

Like *Fail-Safe*, *Strangelove* (based loosely on RAF Flight Lieutenant Peter George's serious antinuclear 1958 novel *Two Hours to Doom*) postulates an equipment failure in a fail-safe communications device, making it impossible for the president to recall the bombers. In *Strangelove*, however, the bombers are deliberately ordered to attack targets in the Soviet Union by an "obviously psychotic" Air Force general determined to wreak revenge on the communists he suspects of causing his premature ejaculations through their conspiracy to fluoridate American water.[17] The other American officers depicted are only marginally saner: Kubrick had approached Joseph Heller, whose portrayal of high-ranking USAF officers in *Catch-22* was similarly unflattering, to write the screenplay.[18] Air Force General Buck Turgidson refers to casualties of "ten to twenty million—tops" as "get[ting] our hair mussed"; Army Colonel "Bat" Guano assumes that anyone in a different uniform and with a different accent must be a "deviated prevert [*sic*]" planning a mutiny, and in the face of a nuclear war finds time to worry about being held responsible to the Coca-Cola Company for damage to one of its vending machines.[19] Major Kong, described by Alexander Walker as "moronic" and "apelike,"[20] encourages his crew with the promise of "some important promotions and personal citations when this thing's over with" and waves his Stetson in triumph as he rides an H-bomb down to his death.[21] The president snaps at Turgidson, "When you instituted the human reliability tests, you assured me there was no possibility of such a thing *ever* occurring!" The General responds, "Well, I, uh, don't think it's quite fair to condemn a whole program because of a single slip-up, sir."[22]

Kubrick also shows (as he had done in *Paths of Glory*, and would again in *Full Metal Jacket*), that a military does not need nuclear weapons to be a largely indiscriminate menace. Ripper echoes Juan Rico's calling his lieutenant "a father to us" and his sergeant "a mother to us"[23] by describing the men he has lied to, convincing them to fire upon fellow American soldiers, as "like my children"; his British executive officer replies that he is "sure they died thinking of you, every man Jack of them, Jack."[24]

The prospect of an American general going rogue was also raised, less satirically, in *Seven Days in May*, in which the head of the Joint Chiefs of Staff, General Scott, plots a military coup against a president of the U.S. who has signed a disarmament treaty with the Russians.[25] The 1962 novel by Fletcher Knebel and Charles W. Bailey II was filmed in 1964 by John Frankenheimer (with a screenplay by Rod Serling), because President Kennedy, "to the dismay of the Pentagon, encouraged John Frankenheimer to film the novel as a warning to the republic."[26] According to Frankenheimer: "Those were the days of General Walker and so on…. President Kennedy wanted *Seven Days in May* made. Pierre Salinger conveyed this to us. The Pentagon didn't want it done. Kennedy said that when we wanted to shoot at the White House he would conveniently go to Hyannis Port that weekend."[27] Major-General Edwin Walker, an infantry officer known for his strong segregationist and anti-communist opinions, had been relieved of command in 1961 on suspicion of distributing John Birch Society literature to his division. He resigned from the army and unsuccessfully ran for governor of Texas in 1962 before being shot and wounded by Lee Harvey Oswald in April 1963. While Bosley Crowther says that Walker's "far-right ramblings" "allegedly inspired" Knebel and Bailey's novel,[28] it may also have been inspired by clashes between Kennedy and the head of his Joint Chiefs of Staff, General Curtis LeMay, during the Cuban Missile Crisis, and/or by the "Business Plot," a 1934 right-wing attempt to replace President Roosevelt with a military government led by General Smedley Butler. Schlesinger compares Walker to "Major General George Van Horn Moseley, who had gone in the thirties from high Army commands to the domestic fascist movement."[29] Imdb.com describes the subplot involving Scott's former mistress as being based on an incident involving Army Chief of Staff General Douglas MacArthur, who was widely expected to run for president in 1952 after being relieved of his position as General of the Army for insubordination by President Truman, and adds that the film was banned in Brazil by the generals who had recently overthrown an elected government in a military coup.[30] As there seems to have been no shortage of troublesome generals who might have inspired the character of General Scott, it's understandable that Schlesinger describes

Kennedy as being disturbed by the possibility of "direct military excursions into politics."[31]

Whatever the president's wishes and fears, the military declined to lend any assistance to the filmmakers. Frankenheimer responded by filming scenes outside the Pentagon using a hidden camera and filming an actor being ferried out to the USS *Kitty Hawk* without permission.[32]

◆ ◆ ◆

The U.S. had been militarily involved in Vietnam since 1950, when President Truman sent U.S. military advisors and $10,000,000 worth of military equipment to aid the battle against the communist Viet Minh. After the defeat of the French occupation in 1954, more military advisors were sent by President Eisenhower in 1955, and U.S. Army Special Forces were sent by President Kennedy in 1961.

The word "Vietnam" appears nowhere in Heinlein's 1963 novel *Glory Road*, but there are good reasons for believing that the military action, where the novel's hero begins his quest, is set there. The story begins in an election year with the twenty-one-year-old hero/narrator, Evelyn Cyril "Flash" Gordon, calling his draft board and telling them to mail him "that notice."[33] He attempts to enlist in the Air Force with the hope of eventually becoming an astronaut; instead, he is sent to Southeast Asia with the Army as a "military adviser."[34] Gordon mentions that his father served in the Korean War, and references to *Sputniks* (first launched in 1957), Khrushchev (who became chairman in '58), and his ambition to become an astronaut, all mean that the election year can be no earlier than 1960.

Despite his avowed patriotism, Gordon admits he doesn't like the Army (his father was a Marine, his stepfather Air Force; Heinlein, of course, was Navy), and having failed to be accepted for astronaut training, his only ambition was to be a chaplain's clerk stateside.[35] Unlike the soldiers in Heinlein's *Starship Troopers*, *Between Planets* and "Solution Unsatisfactory," Gordon is not driven by *esprit de corps*: the only other soldier in his corps he thinks worthy of mention is the commanding officer, who alternately promotes and demotes him from private to corporal and back again, and whose life he inadvertently fails to save. Gordon quotes World War I Major Ian Hay's structure of all military organizations as consisting of "a Surprise Party Department, a Practical Joke Department, and a Fairy Godfather Department. The first two process most matters as the third is very small."[36] But after his tour of duty is cut short when he is slashed across the face by a bolo-wielding "pragmatic Marxist in the jungle," the Fairy Godmother Department arranges for him to be honorably discharged.[37]

He makes his way to West Germany in the hope of going to Heidelberg University, but is told that the GI Bill does not apply to military advisers, even though Gordon has "killed more men in combat than you could crowd into a—well, never mind."[38]

Gordon never returns to the "unWar"[39]—he leaves Earth in Chapter 5 on an epic quest for glory, marries the Empress of the Twenty Universes, and doesn't return until the penultimate Chapter 21. He makes it plain that there's precious little glory involved in being a military adviser in what was not (then) even a "police action," even though he previously "had been told that we were 'saving civilization'"[40]: Gordon complains that he failed to receive a Medal of Honor because "nobody was looking" when he killed the "little brown brother" who had killed his captain.[41] Ultimately, he does receive the GI bill (as well as a prize in the Irish Sweepstakes), but finds it difficult to adapt to civilian life: he quits a job as a draftsman at a missile plant rather than obey an order he finds stupid, is arrested for wearing his sword,[42] and attacks a hippy who calls him a mercenary, explaining, "Sometimes I fight for free. Like right now."[43]

There is no evidence that Heinlein, writing in 1963, intended this to reflect the hostile reception many Vietnam veterans reportedly received on returning to the U.S. (a claim disputed by Franklin)[44]; Gordon receives better treatment from civilians on his return to Earth than the starship troopers do during their R&R in Seattle, and no worse than that endured by the soldier in Kipling's "Tommy," which Heinlein quotes in his defense of *Starship Troopers*.[45] And even before returning to Earth, Gordon is complaining of the ignominy and boredom now that he's fulfilled his duties as a hero and reduced to the role of his wife's "pet poodle." Samuelson cites this as evidence that *Glory Road* "satirizes the traditional romantic yearning for escape, heroism, and deference for authority,"[46] but while the novel does satirize many sword-and-sorcery tropes (the dragons breathe fire by lighting their belches; the beautiful princess he marries is a well-preserved grandmother), I don't see the ending as entirely satirical. Heinlein, like Gordon, was a champion fencer, and he told Samuel Delany that Gordon's sword, Lady Vivamus, was "lovingly modeled after his own fencing sword").[47] Gordon does not repudiate his adventures on his deathbed like Don Quixote, nor does he drink like Miniver Cheevy: he briefly doubts his sanity, wondering whether his heroic exploits were a hallucination, but the tone of the final scene, as he sets out on another "risky perhaps, but not dull" quest, sounds triumphant rather than ironic.[48]

While the novel's title has echoes of the last line of *Starship Troopers*, "To the everlasting glory of the infantry," it isn't glory, as defined by the

OED ("Exalted renown, honourable fame; subject for boasting, special distinction, ornament, pride; adoring praise & thanksgiving") that drives Gordon back onto the Glory Road: he could have as much of that as he wanted by staying in Centre as the Empress's husband. Just as Don Harvey "grew to hate" a life with "clean clothes, clean skin, no duties and no hazards,"[49] Gordon opts for "a 'Tramp Royal,' with no certainty of what you'll eat or where or if, nor where you'll sleep, nor with whom."[50] (*Tramp Royale* is also the title of Heinlein's autobiographical travelogue.) He goes searching for "other maidens, or pleasing facsimiles, elsewhere, in need of rescuing" because "*a man must work at his trade*" (emphasis added).[51] *Starship Troopers* ends with the war ongoing; *Glory Road* ends with a demobbed soldier, personally victorious, looking for a new enemy and a new fight.

◆ ◆ ◆

Also in 1963, Marvel Comics sent Tony Stark to South Vietnam to field-test his latest invention, mortars "no larger or heavier than flashlights"[52] (60mm "light" mortars "weighed almost fifty pounds"),[53] which he promises a U.S. Army General are "capable of solving your problem in Vietnam."[54] Stark is captured after being severely wounded by a booby-trap, and builds his first Iron Man suit to enable him to escape from a "Red Guerrilla Tyrant" Wong-Chu (no specific reference is made of North Vietnam or the Viet Cong, and the tyrant pays his men in yen!).[55]

Returning to the USA, Stark continues improving the suit while channeling his personal wealth into founding a cadre of superheroes, the Avengers. Even more so than the newly revived Captain America, Iron Man became a symbol of American prowess—but because his suit could be duplicated, unlike Reinstein's super-soldier formula, Stark found himself not only hounded by America's foreign (usually communist) enemies, but by a U.S. Senator determined to copy the Iron Man suit for use by U.S. forces.

The Soviet Union attempted to build their own version of Iron Man, Titanium Man, with whom Iron Man clashed repeatedly—firstly in a globally televised battle staged purely for political purposes, where a potential Russian victory is described by Senator Byrd as "the worst propaganda defeat we've ever suffered!"[56] Byrd then insists that Stark reveal the secrets of Iron Man's armor: "Stark's transistorized bodyguard is too all-important to America's **security** for us to permit him to keep his identity hidden any longer."[57] Though a reader wrote in to the letters column pointing out that under the Second Amendment, "the wishes of his government are unlawful,"[58] Stark eventually concurred: "He contends that I haven't the **right**

6. "A Taste of Armageddon"

to withhold the secret of Iron Man's armor from the nation when it may save **lives**—lives even now in jeopardy in far-off corners of the globe. And—I'm finally convinced that he's **right!**"[59]

Iron Man is then attacked by Titanium Man (again) over Washington while on his way to testify. Titanium Man explains: "You should have **known** we would never permit you to testify before your **Congress**! The secret of your **armor** must never be given to your own military forces!"[60] Iron Man then defeats Titanium Man (again), but when he begins testifying, he suffers heart problems due to the wound he received in Vietnam, and is excused.

In March 1964, a few months before the Gulf of Tonkin incident led to an escalation of American involvement in the Vietnam War, Marvel revived their World War II character of Captain America (more or less literally, in this case; he was discovered in an iceberg, where he'd been frozen since the last days of World War II, and thawed). Captain America joined the Avengers and began appearing in his own stories, beginning with *Tales of Suspense* #59 in 1965 alongside fellow Avenger Iron Man.

Marvel soon realized that while Captain America might not have changed between 1945 and 1965, the USA certainly had—notably in its attitude to patriotism, warfare, and the armed forces. As a result of this change, "The Most Enthusiastically Requested Character Revival of All Time" was stuck with a foot in each era.[61] As early as issue #60 of *Tales of Suspense*, Cap was back fighting one of his original foes from the World War II stories. In issue #61, writer Stan Lee sent Cap to Vietnam to rescue a downed American helicopter pilot, brother of a man who'd rescued Cap in the European Theater of Operations. After defeating a number of Viet Cong, and then their general (a gigantic super-powered Sumo wrestler: Marvel in the early '60s often seemed to think we were still at war with the Japanese, who paid in yen), he rescues the pilot and they escape. But instead of remaining in Vietnam to help fight the war, Cap returns to the USA and fights normal criminals for one issue.

At about this time, a student and fan wrote a letter (published in the letter column of issue #64) that reads, in part: "[Bucky] had his purpose—to instill patriotism in young boys. He was an obvious war effort. However, we are not at war at this time and there is no reason for Cap to be followed by a metal-scrap-and-surplus-paper-collecting Teen Brigade."[62] By the time this was published, Lee had already decided that Cap was more appealing in the World War II setting *with* his teenaged companion Bucky Barnes than fighting the "un-war" in Vietnam, as issues #63–71 retold the story of Cap's transformation from "a thin, somewhat sickly-looking youth" to "the **first** of an army of fighting men such as the world has never known"[63] and his battle against Nazi saboteurs and soldiers (though, as Bucky reminds him, "I know we're not yet at war with the Nazis").[64]

At this time, a soldier with the U.S. Army's 1st Artillery wrote to the comic's letter column to say: "I am very disappointed in his adventures in the past. Please bring him back to the present.... I think that you have a lot of material on the events that are happening today to base his adventures on. The war in Viet Nam would make an endless amount of adventures for ol' Cap." Stan Lee replied: "Thank you for writing 'em, soldier! But it's kinda tough to please everybody. Some Marvelophiles want us to keep Cap *out* of Viet Nam...."[65]

Another reader wrote in for the next issue:

> I, for one, am against the revival of the old Captain America stories. After all, Captain America's main purpose in the forties was to arouse American patriotism and also to arouse a form of anti-Naziism. Mind you, I'm not saying that we don't need patriotism, but do we really need anti-Naziism?... Today the main enemies of freedom are the communists and they are the ones who should be under constant attack by Captain America....[66]

The next 1960s story, beginning in issue #72, pitted the 1960s Cap, now billed as "Living Legend of World War II," against a robot created by his World War II-era enemy Red Skull but revived twenty years after the Skull's defeat.[67] Cap then returned to fighting peacetime super-criminals until issue #77, where he recalled another 1940s story; #78 was a modern-day story, and #79 resolved the dilemma by bringing the Red Skull into the 1960s.

Captain America never returned to Vietnam, and after sending their superheroes Iron Man and Thor there for brief skirmishes with the Viet Cong in 1965, Marvel mostly ignored the war until after it was over. When Lee sent Iron Man back to Vietnam in issue #92 of *Tales of Suspense* ("Within the Vastness of Viet Nam!") to fight "the commies' answer to Tony Stark!"[68] and he once again met his Russian counterpart Titanium Man, they received a letter from another reader claiming to be "disgusted with your present issue.... your recent SUSPENSE issue was base propaganda." Lee responded: "can't one measly story take place in Viet Nam without you jumpin' down our collective throat! ... the only propaganda we could find was that the tale was definitely anti–Titanium Man!"[69] Conversely, when a "soldier in Viet Nam" wrote in to correct a mistake in their choice of weapons, then to praise the story as "marvellous, stupendous, wonderful," he received a complimentary subscription.[70]

Journey into Mystery #117 has Thor visiting Vietnam not to fight in the war, but taking the bait in a trap set by his enemy Loki. This issue depicts the conflict as a civil war, with a VC commander aiming to shoot his brother for "defying the might of the Communist Viet Cong."[71] When his mother is killed while trying to intercede, the commander destroys himself and his base in an effort to "face my fate like a soldier. It was *communism* that made me what I am—that shaped me into a brutal, unthinking instrument of destruction."[72]

After these 1965 stories, however, Lee noted that as fan mail was "'about equally divided' between those who loved and those who loathed Vietnam War stories ... Marvel made it a policy to generally avoid the war."[73]

DC Comics, similarly, sent Superman to Vietnam only once, in "The Soldier of Steel!" (*Superman* #216), in which Clark Kent responds to letters from soldiers serving in Vietnam who are dealing with a giant they've named "King Cong." Clark serves briefly as a medic and embedded war correspondent, and discovers that "King Cong" is actually a U.S. soldier, the son of a general, who deserted during his first battle and was given magical herbs by a Vietnamese witch.[74] As with the Marvel superheroes, one taste of action in the Vietnam War must have been enough for Superman; he promptly returned to fighting supervillains on his home turf, and DC Comics also largely ignored the Vietnam War until it was over.

◆ ◆ ◆

In 1965, Doubleday published a novel that undeniably "satirizes the traditional romantic yearning for escape, heroism, and deference for authority": Harry Harrison's *Bill, the Galactic Hero*, which Harrison describes as "a piss-take on Heinlein's *Starship Troopers* and all those gung-ho military SF books."[75]

Unlike Juan Rico and Oscar Gordon, Bill doesn't volunteer for military service: instead, he's distracted by the sight of a woman's backside, lured by the sound of "Star Troopers to the Skies Avant" and 3-D film of the space troopers, drugged by a greedy recruiting sergeant, and forced to march by a hypno-coil in his boot. He finds military service quite different from the depiction in the recruiting film with its "battle and death and glory, though it was only the Chingers who died: troopers only suffered neat little wounds in their extremities that could be covered easily by small bandages."[76] In reality, the Chingers are seven inches tall, not seven feet as shown in the posters; the most enthusiastic member of his squad is secretly a Chinger spy; the army is "run by mental defectives and time-servers keeping an endless war and their jobs going"[77]; and in his first battle, Bill loses his left arm and has it replaced with the right arm of a dead comrade. A heavy infantryman in *Starship Troopers*–style battle armor, complete with "teensie A-bomb,"[78] appears briefly, but sinks into a swamp because his suit weighs 3,000 pounds and takes an hour to remove. Bill ultimately shoots himself in the foot to receive a discharge from combat, but becomes a recruiting officer, press-ganging his own brother because every recruit he brings in takes a month off his enlistment time.[79]

Harrison had served in the U.S. Army during World War II as a gunnery instructor, truck driver, armorer, computing gunsight specialist, and prison guard, later recalling:

> Though I loathed the army I was completely adjusted to it. I could not return to the only role I knew in civilian life, that of a child.... When on furlough we helped friends still undrafted to avoid the fate we suffered. We jeered openly at anyone sucker enough to volunteer.[80]
>
> My generation was a draftee generation. We knew the second we turned eighteen, we'd be in the army. I went in in 1943, and we didn't even know if we'd win the war or not.... And you saw it coming, a sort of feeling of doom, you never really thought where you were going to go, except stay alive; get through high school and a week later you're in the army.
>
> I came out of the army, I was happy to be alive, but it was a tremendous thing to readjust to civilian life. It wasn't a matter of ambition, it was just staying alive again. People forget, you know, the shell-shock from the war. A lot of guys became alcoholics, couldn't readjust. You're shaped by the army, that horrible, stupid institution.[81]

The issues of the endless war and the difficulty of soldiers readjusting to civilian life (and how this might be exploited by the military as a way of persuading them to re-enlist) would be addressed in more detail by Joe Haldeman in *The Forever War* and other novels, but this would have to wait until the 1970s.

◆ ◆ ◆

Many American science fiction television series made during the Vietnam War era featured characters serving in the U.S. military, or American characters in a military organization defending the Earth. *The Outer Limits* episode "The Inheritors" (1964) concerns four American soldiers who begin obeying instructions from an alien intelligence controlling them through bullets in their brains. The four build a starship and abduct a group of foster children who are either physically challenged or dying, defying U.S. government investigators and sending the children—cured of their diseases and disabilities—to another planet to be cared for by a race of long-lived but sterile beings.[82] The sergeant and two privates obey the orders of the lieutenant, wavering when the lead (civilian) investigator,

Ballard, attempts to appeal to their patriotism, but their military background seems to have been primarily a convenient way for the writers to explain having four strangers suffering head wounds from bullets cast from metal from the same meteorite. The double episode begins with scenes of combat "in the Far East"; while Vietnam is never named, the meteorite crater is in the (fictional but Vietnamese-sounding) "Hoi Tong Province" and the Americans are fighting "Northern" guerrillas. The sympathetic portrayal of the soldiers obeying orders they don't understand, and in the case of the noncoms, wondering whether they should mutiny when ethical questions are raised by a civilian (Ballard seems driven by Kantian ethics, much more concerned with the fate of the children than with the prospect of learning the secret of the alien force field, star drive, or even the healing properties of the tiny spaceship's atmosphere), could be seen as a comment on the dilemma that would be faced by American soldiers in Vietnam, but there is no evidence that this was the writers' intention. David C. Holcomb argues convincingly that it was more probably a comment on the nature of artistic inspiration and a metaphor for the struggle of the more visionary creative people involved in the making of *The Outer Limits* against the dictates of the network.[83]

Another episode, "The Human Factor," set in the Arctic outpost of Point Tabu ("Total Abandonment of Better Understanding"), part of the Distant Early Warning Line, centers on a Major Brothers, who is haunted by a hallucination he believes is a hostile alien and attempts to use the base's A-bomb to destroy the alien, the base and himself. The base's psychiatrist, Dr. Hamilton, uses a prototype machine of his own invention to probe into Brothers's psyche, but an accident causes their minds to be transposed; Hamilton, in Brothers's body, is treated as insane, until his assistant frees him and prevents Brothers from detonating the bomb. Hamilton discovers that Brothers's hallucination is the ice-encrusted ghost of a man Brothers lost in a crevasse, his guilt at this death being so great that the only possible expiation seemed to be nuking the entire base.[84]

The episode "The Zanti Misfits" (written by Joseph Stefano, the screenwriter of *Psycho*), reveals a more cynical view of the U.S. military, particularly the Strategic Air Command. Earth has capitulated to the spacefaring Zantis' demands out of fear that their superior technology can destroy the planet, and the SAC has cordoned off an area of desert in California for the Zanti to use as a penal settlement. When rat-sized Zanti escape the ship and swarm over the SAC base (in a ghost town named Morgue), the SAC officers and the civilian official historian attack them with guns, grenades and a flame thrower. The episode ends with the Zanti explaining that there will be no reprisals, instead thanking the humans: the Zanti are incapable of executing their own criminals, so they send them to Earth to be massacred because humans are "practiced executioners."[85]

The U.S. military—this time, the U.S. Astro Force, part of a force from United Earth—is again shown in a negative light in "Nightmare," also written by Stefano. After Earth is attacked by the Ebonites, a spaceship crewed by Earth military (including at least two Americans: the commander, played by Ed Nelson, and Private Dix, played by Martin Sheen; Major Jong, played by James Shigeta, never reveals which nation he represents, but reminisces about San Francisco) is sent to Ebon, and captured. The crew is told that their demand to be treated as prisoners of war will be met, and they will be allowed to join the other POWs—but only once the Ebonites' demands have been met. The Ebonites interrogate and torture the prisoners: the German suffers a fatal heart attack after being forced to admit that he betrayed his grandfather to the Nazis, the African is temporarily blinded, Dix temporarily loses his voice, and Jong's arm is pulverized (the Ebonite interrogator estimates that it will take a year to heal). The other survivors, led by the English intelligence officer, accuse Jong of betraying Earth by letting slip the route the next ship will take, and draw straws to see who will kill him. At this point, the Ebonite interrogator protests to the American general who has been secretly observing the prisoners that "the game" has gone too far, and it is revealed that this cruel and lethal situation is, unknown to the men, a training exercise, an attempt by the military to discover which servicemen can stand up to the rigors of interrogation. Furthermore, there isn't a war between Ebon and Earth—the Ebonite "attack" was accidental, and their reluctant cooperation with the United Earth's military command seems to be a form of reparation. The general's justification for these atrocities is the lack of successful escape attempts from POW camps during the Korean War, so that the peacetime military can be sure that its soldiers will stand up to interrogation and brainwashing attempts in case the *next* alien race Earth encounters is not as benevolent as the Ebonites.[86]

It seems hardly necessary to say that other American SF TV shows of the 1960s tended to show the U.S. military in a more positive light than "Nightmare," but their depictions weren't always flattering. Irwin Allen's *Voyage to the Bottom of the Sea* focused on the U.S. Navy crew of the *Seaview*, supposedly a civilian research vessel for the Nelson Institute, but armed with four nuclear missiles, partly crewed by Navy men, and frequently involved in spying, covert ops and weapons tests for the U.S.

government. The regular cast, led by Richard Basehart as Admiral Nelson and David Hedison as Captain Crane, were mostly shown as heroes in those episodes where they weren't brainwashed, possessed by ghosts, replaced by aliens or cyborg duplicates, controlled by animate plants, enthralled by mermaids, under the influence of experimental drugs or chemical weapons, or transformed into werewolves or living bombs.

However, the show isn't completely without interest. Made and broadcast from September 1964 (a few weeks after the Gulf of Tonkin resolution and the beginning of U.S. bombing of North Vietnam) to March 1968 (by which time the Vietnam War was already the longest war in U.S. history, at least until the next century), it was set in the 1970s and early '80s, avoiding the issue of Vietnam but correctly guessing that by this time the Cold War would not have ended or escalated. While the series gradually became a "monster of the week" show with strong supernatural themes, some of the earlier episodes did touch on realities of U.S. military service during the Cold War, including showing some in the hierarchy as less than heroic, and occasionally as aggressive bullies.

In "The Condemned" (1965), publicity-hungry U.S. Navy Admiral Falk is shown as stealing the credit for the work of one of his assistants, Archer, then killing the other when problems arise with his experiment and he panics. After Archer dies, Falk sacrifices himself to save Captain Crane, and Nelson decides there's no point in exposing Falk as a fraud.[87] In "The Sky Is Falling" (1964), the *Seaview* is commandeered by U.S. Navy Rear Admiral Walter "Trigger-Happy" Tobin, assigned to investigate the sighting of a flying saucer that disappeared into the Pacific. He immediately orders battle stations, and when the UFO is spotted, gives the order to fire. Nelson manages to communicate with the alien pilot and assists him in repairing his spacecraft rather than have the aliens retaliate—much to the displeasure of Tobin, and an equally aggressive Air Force general who sends a formation of planes to bomb the area ahead of the arrival of the 7th Fleet.[88] "The Mist of Silence" (1964) involves the *Seaview* in a coup in a Central American country at the behest of the U.S. State Department, which then disowns them after some of the crew are captured by the country's government.[89] In "Long Live the King" (1964), the State Department asks Nelson to ferry home an imperious boy king to take the throne of his assassinated father to quash a rebellion: his coronation is celebrated with a "Christmas present" from the U.S.—a little gunboat diplomacy in the form of the 7th Fleet.[90]

"Doomsday" (1964), set in 1973, addresses an issue raised by Groeteschele in *Fail-Safe* and, much later, by the prologue to *War Games* (1984):

what happens when a military officer, given the "Go code," refuses to turn the key or press the button that will launch a nuclear missile? In the episode, the *Seaview*'s crew is ritually hazing those sailors who're crossing the Equator for the first time, when they are put on a war alert after the Soviet Union launches rockets (later revealed to be carrying satellites) without forewarning the U.S. Still wearing traces of their costumes and makeup from the comic ritual, they realize that this is not an exercise, and Nelson, Crane and regular crew member Chip Morton each unlock three of the four fail-safe units, readying the sub's missiles for launch—but the missile officer, Lieutenant Commander Corbett, a former student of Nelson's on temporary assignment from the U.S. Navy to evaluate the *Seaview*'s "fitness as a missile carrier," hesitates, then refuses to use his key, saying, "I cannot destroy the world. I can't."

Nelson tells him, "It's not you," to which Corbett replies, "It's not? Then who is it?"

Nelson replies, "It's me," slugs Corbett and overpowers him, forcibly takes the key from him and unlocks the last fail-safe unit as the sub heads towards the launch coordinates in enemy waters. When he recounts the incident to Crane, Crane replies, "Every soldier who's ever been to war knows that moment. It's one thing to be a crack shot on a rifle range, and it's another thing to pull the trigger when there's a man, a real man, a human being, in your sights."

> NELSON: "When the chips were down, they pulled the trigger, didn't they?"
> CRANE: "Most of them. Some of them couldn't."
> NELSON: "But Corbett's not a coward. He just started to wrestle with his conscience *at the wrong time*. He should have done that before he'd taken his oath of duty."

Crane responds, "Admiral, no one, none of us, knows how we'll act when we have to pull *that* trigger. Give him another chance—assuming we have another chance."

In the next scene, when two of the regular crew are removing the last traces of their costumes from the hazing, one tells the other, "Don't worry how you look, Clark; no one's ever going to see us again. Not ever." Meanwhile, one of the regular crew, Kowalski, has been temporarily blinded by a minor explosion, and the ship's doctor has to operate on his eyes, unsure of whether he will have time to successfully complete the surgery, "assuming, of course, there is no boom."

Nelson confronts Corbett again, saying, "I can't understand it. You're Navy. Annapolis. This is what you've been trained for; you've gone through this a hundred times!" Corbett replies, "Practice runs! Games, like when were kids! This is no game…. This is Doomsday, Admiral! Doomsday!"

NELSON: "If it is, we didn't start it."

CORBETT: "What difference is it who started it? It's one thing to carry a big stick, it's another to bash someone's head in with it. I just couldn't do it. But you could. Couldn't you, Admiral?"

NELSON: "You think that because I could do what I had to do, I don't feel, feel for the millions?... Our job is to provide the bone and muscle of our country's deterrent power. If we fail in that, if we freeze in the clutch, then our country's defenseless. You failed your country once before. Don't ever fail her again."

In the next scene (after some ominous music), Crane asks Nelson, "Can you think of any reason to delay firing, Admiral?" Nelson replies, "No reason that has any military relevance." When there is no abort signal, he gives the order to start the firing sequence—but when the alert is canceled a moment later, he laughs, and the rest of the crew cheers and dances. Unfortunately, one of the missile altitude triggers is faulty and, having been activated, will detonate automatically if it reaches sea level. Corbett and Nelson clash again when Corbett is only able to fix the trigger so that it detonates below sea level, not above it: Nelson wants to detonate the missile more than 1000 feet below the surface so that it won't be detected, even though this risks destroying the sub; Corbett wants it detonated at the surface to show that nuclear accidents can occur and "fail-safe is fallible." Nelson claims that he is not motivated by the fear of violating the Test Ban Treaty that prevents above-ground detonations, but "will not pollute the atmosphere with our mistake; I will not poison the air, the Earth; better to risk the lives of this crew than generations to come." (Presumably polluting the ocean didn't worry him unduly.) When Corbett points out that Nelson was ready only moments before "to press the button," Nelson replies, "Because long ago, under conditions less nerve-wracking than we face this morning, strategists and statesmen formulated a plan, a plan which you as a military man have sworn to follow. If plans made during periods of calm are not followed to the letter in times of stress, we can only face chaos. Our survival as a nation and as individuals requires that we rely upon reason, and not emotions." When Corbett replies that "our security, Admiral, also requires an informed public," Nelson says, "You want to sound the trumpet, Commander, do it—but not in that uniform." Corbett sets the missile to detonate at sea level, saying he has "a commitment that takes priority over this uniform"—but drains off enough of the fuel so that the missile doesn't reach the surface, but falls to the bottom of the sea without exploding.

In the epilogue, Nelson tells Crane that he has ordered that Corbett be court-martialed, that Nelson will testify against him and expects that he will be dishonorably discharged. Nelson notes that "by disobeying orders, he inadvertently saved our lives—but he wrecked his career," as though the two were of roughly equal importance.[91]

For an episode of a series usually seen as lightweight, this is a remarkably nuanced view of the dilemma faced by military servicemen given orders they are unable to square with their consciences: not a new situation (as is shown by "The Encounter," the episode of *The Twilight Zone* discussed in the previous chapter, where Fenton spends twenty years wracked with guilt over obeying orders to kill an unarmed enemy who had already surrendered), but one with increasingly dire consequences as individuals had to make decisions about nuclear missiles and other weapons of mass destruction. It also deals with the issue of soldiers, despite their proficiency with weapons in training, finding themselves unable to fire at people they could see in actual combat situations (according to Dave Grossman's *On Killing*, Crane's suggestion that "most" pulled the trigger is an exaggeration, at least until U.S. soldiers' weapons and training changed in the 1960s).[92] Further, it raises a question that would become significant in the Vietnam War—whether servicemen had the right to tell the public about military mistakes, accidents, and crimes. Significantly, it is Nelson's actions and decisions, motivated by his sense of duty to the Navy, which potentially lead firstly to the U.S. precipitating World War III by being the first to fire nuclear missiles, and then to having to choose between violating the Test Ban Treaty (or between polluting the air and the ocean) and risking the *Seaview* and its crew. Corbett, however, is proven right in his decisions not to turn the key (the alert turns out to be a false alarm) and then to set the warhead to detonate at the surface rather than below it, and his motives—concern for humanity and for American democracy—are never questioned by anyone other than Nelson. Nothing in the episode suggests that Corbett is villainous, insane, weak, cowardly, or lying about his motives, whereas Nelson's arguments that Corbett's inaction "leaves our country defenseless" and "our survival as a nation and as individuals requires that we rely upon reason, and not emotions" ring hollow if you consider that if the Russians *have* already launched an attack, the deterrent has obviously already failed as a defense, and there is no rational justification for retaliation except for an emotional desire for revenge. Nelson, insisting that only reasons that "have military relevance" matter, is in the same position as *The Thing*'s Captain Hendry, arguing in this case that he isn't working for the world, or even for American democracy, but for the Navy.

Two of the other three TV SF series Irwin Allen produced during the Vietnam War era also featured U.S. military officers, but stayed away from controversy. *Lost in Space* (1965–1968) featured U.S. Space Corps Major Don West as the copilot of the *Jupiter 2*, and the premiere showed saboteur Dr. Smith in the uniform of a highly decorated USAF colonel, but the mission to send the Robinson family to Alpha Centauri seems to have been run by a civilian agency, and Dr. John Robinson, rather than Major West, was clearly in command.[93] While West's rank was mentioned in later episodes, Smith's was not—presumably because he was soon revealed as being not only a murderous traitor (though it was never specified who he was working for), but also cowardly, lazy, and almost everything we would hope a military officer on our side wasn't. *The Time Tunnel* (1966–1967) was a military secret overseen by U.S. Army Lieutenant General Heywood Kirk (played by Whit Bissell, the callous general in *The Outer Limits* episode "Nightmare"), but again, the other regular characters (including the time-traveling volunteers) were addressed by civilian academic titles except for Sergeant Jiggs, who was assigned the occasional dangerous jobs.

The Invaders (1967–1968) pitted a lone man, David Vincent, against aliens attempting to conquer Earth by stealth. In the first season episode, "Doomsday Minus One," Vincent finds an ally in U.S. Army Major Rick Graves, head of security at a Utah army base, but discovers that the commander, General Beaumont, is in league with a group of Invaders who plan to detonate an antimatter bomb at the same time and place as a U.S. Army A-bomb test. Beaumont hopes that the explosion will scare the world into disarming, telling Vincent and Graves, "I'll tell you what my record adds up to. One hundred thousand men dead because of my orders. My own son dead because he believed me when I said his would be the last war. Death, destruction and suffering, and all for what? So we can all one day kill ourselves in one monumental nuclear holocaust."[94] When Vincent convinces Beaumont that the aliens have betrayed him and intend to detonate the antimatter bomb underground so that it will change the Earth's axial tilt, Beaumont leads the attack on the invaders (some of whom are disguised as American soldiers). Unable to defuse the antimatter bomb, he drives it to where the aliens have camped, sacrificing himself and killing them. The response of the military board of inquiry is a security clampdown and a verdict of "attempted sabotage by enemies unknown."[95]

In the next episode, "Quantity: Unknown," Army Intelligence officer Colonel Griffith turns out to be an alien.[96] The following episode, "The Innocent," reveals that the USAF has also been infiltrated, though not completely.[97] The second season began with the alien wife of a NORAD computer programmer feeding false instructions to NORAD's radar to allow a fleet of alien saucers to slip through undetected: David Vincent convinces the security chief to load the backup program, the saucers are spotted, and formations of military aircraft are hastily scrambled to meet them, forcing them to retreat.[98] (The aircraft are stock footage, but Roy Thinnes does appear to walk into the real NORAD HQ at Cheyenne Mountain, suggesting some degree of military cooperation with the show's producers, who also produced the series *Twelve O'Clock High* from 1964 to 1967.) In "Dark Outpost," written by Jerry Sohl, aliens masquerading as U.S. Army personnel take over a deactivated army base, Camp Crowley, to use as a hospital. One of the students captured with David Vincent asks whether the Army can arrest them; another, Vern, replies, "I never heard of it," but later fumes, "When I was in the Army, I was pushed around by sergeants and corporals and everybody. Now that I'm finally out, I'm still being pushed around.... I know the Army, and they don't have the right to lean on him.... If he's a thief, they can arrest him, they can charge him, but they can't bully him." When the alien Colonel Harris (played by the ubiquitous Whit Bissell) threatens to execute the students to compel Vincent to talk, Vern points out that he doesn't have the authority to do that (less than four years later, this authority would be granted, with Nixon calling the army in to deal with the 1971 Mayday protests). The students overpower the Invaders and escape, but by the time real Army personnel are brought in to investigate, the alien equipment has been removed, and the final voice-over intones, "The Army report will be thorough and painstaking, but without proof, its conclusions will be negative."[99]

Later in the second season, Vincent is able to recruit a small group of allies, including industrialist Edgar Scoville and USAF Colonel Archie Harmon. The final episode of *The Invaders* to feature U.S. military personnel in a significant role, "The Peacemaker" (broadcast February 6, 1968— a week after the beginning of the Tet Offensive and five days after Eddie Adams photographed the execution of Nguyen Van Lem), began with Harmon capturing an Invader alive to show his superior, four-star General Samuel Arlington Concannon, only to have the alien commit suicide in his cell moments later with the assistance of another alien disguised as a USAF officer, who is promptly shot and killed. The Invaders capture Harmon in the hope of exchanging him for the prisoner, but he escapes with David Vincent's help and takes Vincent to meet Concannon. After inquiring about the Invaders' military strength, Concannon says, "We don't want a war. It's insane to want a war these days. There's no reason on God's green earth why we can't live peacefully with these people. Will they talk to us?"

Concannon talks about arranging a summit meeting between U.S.

military delegates and the alien leaders, then proposes using the threat of a doomsday device to strengthen America's position: "If they think we'll blow up the world before we hand it over to them, they might have to sit down and bargain."

Concannon, who, with Harmon, survived the Battle of Corregidor and the Bataan Death March, plans to bomb the "peace conference" he has arranged at an abandoned farmhouse, using Scoville (who has refused to build the Doomsday device, but agrees to go along with the bluff), Vincent, and several generals as bait. He records a message saying, "Without leaders, soldiers have no army. It is our hope that they will go home, retreat from the battle and leave us with our beloved America. Militarily, the plan is sound." His wife attempts to stop him, telling their son that the Air Force was preparing to retire Concannon, that he is acting on his own authority (rather than the president's, as he claims), and explaining, "He's used to living violently. That's the only way he knows to get things done." The episode bears this out, showing Concannon delighted at the prospect of shooting woodchucks with soft-nose .270 caliber ammunition, decorating his office with weapons, and threatening his wife when she comments on his age: when Harmon tries to stop Concannon from bombing the farmhouse, Concannon pulls a pistol on him and says, "You're a soldier, Harmon, or I thought you were. Whoever told you you can make an omelet without breaking eggs?" When Harmon counters that the Invaders will retaliate and "kill as many of us as they can," Concannon replies, "All right, they'll kill a few of us, but the rest of us will be an army.... People don't understand talk. A kick in the teeth, that's what they understand." He calls Harmon a coward before pistol-whipping him, repeating, "That's what they understand."

At the farmhouse, one general looks at the alien negotiators (all in the guise of white men in late middle age) and comments, "At least we know they aren't Chinese." Concannon's wife tries pleading with him by radio from the farmhouse, but he won't be dissuaded, and Vincent asks the Invaders to destroy the bomber, which they do. This also kills Harmon, Vincent and Scoville's military ally, leaving them acting without official sanction. Trying to convince the alien leaders to meet for another peace talk, Scoville assures them, "There are men in our government; responsible, reasonable, sane men that you could talk to," implying that Concannon, a four-star general with 36 years of service, was none of these things.[100]

◆ ◆ ◆

Much has already been written about both pro-military and antimilitary subtexts in *Star Trek*. As H. Bruce Franklin points out in "*Star Trek* in the Vietnam Era," the original series was produced against the background of American involvement in the Vietnam War. Gene Roddenberry delivered the first pilot in February 1965, the same month as the signing of the Gulf of Tonkin resolution, the commencement of "retaliatory" bombing, and "dispatch of the first openly acknowledged U.S. combat divisions to Vietnam."[101] The final episode was shown in June 1969, two days after John Lennon recorded "Give Peace a Chance" and a week before President Nixon met with South Vietnamese President Nguyen Van Thieu and announced that 25,000 U.S. troops would be withdrawn by September, the beginning of "Vietnamization."

Several episodes of *Star Trek* have already been cited by other writers as comments on the Vietnam War and contemporary U.S. military actions. Suvin said of the show that "from its semi-liberal beginnings in the '60s [it] oscillated wildly in quality, SF content, and ideological orientation (the 1968 episode "A Private Little War" clearly justifies the U.S. War on [sic] Vietnam)."[102] Rick Wortland in "Captain Kirk Cold Warrior," J. William Snyder, Jr., in "*Star Trek*: A Phenomenon and Social Statement on the 1960s," and David Gerrold in *The World of Star Trek*, all comment on the parallels between the "*Pueblo* Incident," in which the USS *Pueblo* was captured while on a spying mission in North Korean territorial waters in 1968, and the third season episode "The *Enterprise* Incident," in which the *Enterprise* is captured by Romulans while on a spying mission inside the Neutral Zone.[103] Gerrold criticizes the episode for its justification of spying—"The way *Star Trek* told it, we were justified because our side was right and theirs wasn't"[104]—and according to Wortland, a scene in which Captain Kirk confesses to spying (as the Pueblo's captain had done) was removed at the studio's insistence.[105]

Franklin's "*Star Trek* in the Vietnam Era" refers to the first season episode "The City on the Edge of Forever," based on a script by Harlan Ellison but rewritten by Dorothy C. Fontana and Gene Roddenberry, and first broadcast in April 1967, as a criticism of the antiwar movement (a statement backed up by producer Robert Justman) as being "right, but at the wrong time," and points out that it aired two days after Martin Luther King's "Declaration of Independence from the War in Vietnam."[106] Franklin also describes the second season episode "A Private Little War," first broadcast in February 1968 (but written before the Tet Offensive), as a parable of "gradual escalation" that "promoted the official Administration version of the history of the Vietnam War," though a version that was already anachronistic; and "The Omega Glory," first shown in March 1968, and "Let That Be Your Last Battlefield," first shown in January 1969, as extrapolations of what might happen if the war escalated.[107] The last two depict cultures destroyed by wars—in the case of "The Omega Glory," one in which the "Yangs" (Yanks) are still fighting the Asian "Kohms" (Communists). The Yangs, who are depicted as bandits raiding Kohm villages, still revere the American flag and the words of the Constitution and the Pledge of Allegiance but no longer have any idea of their meaning.[108]

"A Private Little War," in which Klingons and the Federation compete for control of a planet (which has plant life of medicinal value), is the only one of these to directly refer to the Vietnam War, in this exchange between Kirk and Dr. McCoy:

> Kirk: Bones, do you remember the twentieth-century brush wars on the Asian continent? Two giant powers involved, much like the Klingons and ourselves. Neither side felt that they could pull out?
> McCoy: Yes, I remember—it went on bloody year after bloody year!
> Kirk: But what would you have suggested? That one side arm its friends with an overpowering weapon? Mankind would never have lived to travel space if they had. No—the only solution is what happened, back then, balance of power.
> McCoy: And if the Klingons give their side even more?
> Kirk: Then we arm our side with *exactly* that much more. A balance of power—the trickiest, most difficult, dirtiest game of them all—but the only one that preserves both sides![109]

An early draft of the script compared the leader of the side which had allied with the Klingons to Ho Chi Minh,[110] and Franklin cites a letter from Gene L. Coon saying, "It should be evident to everyone that we have essentially been talking about Vietnam.... What we are trying to sell is the hopelessness of the situation. The fact that we are absolutely forced into taking steps we know are morally wrong, but for our own enlightened self-interest, there is nothing we can do about it."[111] Gene Roddenberry insisted on rewriting the script because of its expressed opposition to U.S. intervention in Vietnam, telling Coon, "The things at stake in Vietnam are much more important and powerful than a charitable attitude toward simpler people in the world."[112]

Coon's letter also states, "We have always played [the Klingons] very much like the Russians,"[113] a parallel that would be made even more explicit in the 1991 film *Star Trek VI: The Undiscovered Country*, which depicted the Klingon Empire's collapse and the end of the interstellar cold war on the heels of a disastrous power station explosion on the Klingon homeworld.[114] In the light of this, it's worth examining the other episodes of the original series in which conflict with the Klingons was central: the first season's "Errand of Mercy," the second season's "The Trouble with Tribbles" and "Friday's Child," and the third season's "Day of the Dove."

The Klingons first appeared in "Errand of Mercy" (written by Coon and first broadcast on May 23, 1967, a week before "The City on the Edge of Forever"). Kirk and Spock are stranded on the strategically important planet Organia after unsuccessfully trying to persuade its leaders to allow a Federation force to occupy the planet to deter the Klingons. The Organians refuse, the Klingons invade, and Kirk and Spock, disguised as Organians, become a two-man resistance force. Their resistance is short-lived, as the Klingons execute Organians as punishment.

After Kirk attempts to capture the Klingon commander, Kor, the Organians decide they've had enough of this, and heat up all the weapons on both sides until they're too hot to touch. Even hand-to-hand combat becomes impossible. The Organians reveal themselves to be more advanced than either humans or Klingons: they are immortal beings who have transcended matter, none of them have really been killed, and they find the presence of such violent beings (making no distinction between the two societies) incredibly unpleasant. They impose a truce on the two races, predicting that not only will they become allies, but that Kor and Kirk will become friends. Kor expresses his regrets that war has become impossible, because "it would have been glorious." Kirk confesses to being "furious with the Organians for stopping a war I didn't want"; Spock remarks that it is "curious how often you humans obtain that which you do not want."[115]

"Errand of Mercy" and "The City on the Edge of Forever" were followed by the final episode in the first season of *Star Trek*, "Operation: Annihilate!," which was—as its title suggests—less pacifistic. The *Enterprise* traces the path of a species of alien brain parasites, a hive intelligence that has been moving from world to world, destroying civilizations as it goes, in a parallel to the domino theory. The aliens, portrayed by inflated bags of joke shop fake vomit, control their human hosts by pervading their nervous systems and inflicting intolerable pain. Instead of attempting to communicate with the aliens, as in earlier episodes such as "Devil in the Dark," Kirk considers exterminating the infected human survivors on Deneva to stop the spread of the parasites (who know how to build starships, but need hosts with hands), saying, "I can not let it spread beyond this colony, even if it means destroying a million people down there." Discovering that they are susceptible to ultraviolet radiation, Kirk has the crew create satellites that will simulate sunlight and uses this to exterminate the parasites, thereby freeing the human population of Deneva from their control.[116] (It's almost certainly a coincidence, but the idea of using satellites to simulate perpetual sunlight over Vietnam, in this case using giant mirrors, proposed by A.G. Buckingham and H.M. Watson in a study published in 1968 and '69, was seriously investigated, "but even with the advocacy of NASA and the Air Force the project was cancelled, primarily because of an anticipated early end of the war."[117])

In an earlier draft of Steven Carabatsos's teleplay—the version adapted to short story form by James Blish in the anthology *Star Trek 2*—the *Enterprise* traces the creatures back to their homeworld, which they destroy.[118] (Aptly enough, exteriors for Deneva were shot at the TRW Space and Defense Park, which built Atlas and Titan ICBMs as well as space probes and satellites[119] ... but I digress.)

"Friday's Child" (written by Dorothy C. Fontana and first broadcast on December 1, 1967—two days after Robert McNamara resigned as Secretary of Defense and a day after Eugene McCarthy announced his intention to run for president on an antiwar ticket), similarly has the Federation and the Klingons competing for control of a planet, this time for mining rights. The low-tech natives are as violent as the Klingons, but have a strict code of honor, and are won over by the Federation when the Klingons are found to have lied to them.[120] "The Trouble with Tribbles" sees humans and Klingons competing for the right to colonize an uninhabited but habitable planet.[121] "Day of the Dove" pits humans against Klingons aboard the *Enterprise* itself.

In "Day of the Dove" (written by Jerome Bixby, first broadcast November 1, 1968—the day after the U.S. halted bombing missions over North Vietnam), the *Enterprise* crew blame the Klingons for the murder of (nonexistent) Federation colonists using an unknown (nonexistent) weapon that leaves no traces of its victims; the Klingons, lured to the site by a similar false distress call, accuse Kirk of having lured them into a (nonexistent) trap and attacked and damaged their ship with an unknown (nonexistent) weapon. Both ruses are actually the work of a malign energy being that exacerbates, and feeds on, humanoid aggression. The battle is prolonged when the being transmutes their rayguns into swords, heals the wounded, and prevents the life-support system from being shut down, thereby enabling people to survive and keep fighting. The humans realize that they're being manipulated, and Kirk wonders aloud, "Has the war been staged for us—complete with weapons, ideologies, patriotic drum-beating, even race hatred?" The Klingon captain is finally convinced of this and agrees to a truce, saying, "We need no urging to hate humans! But for the present, only a fool fights in a burning house."[122] The episode ends with both the humans and the Klingons banishing the malevolent creature by jeering and laughing at it: Jerome Bixby's original script called for the two races to repel it by jointly staging a peace march[123]—which some Vietnam veterans had been doing since April 1967.

This suggestion that all that is necessary to prevent a war is for people to refuse to fight, at least for that day, was also at the core of another *Star Trek* episode, "A Taste of Armageddon" (written by Gene Coon and Robert Hamner, and first broadcast February 23, 1967), in which the inhabitants of two planets march into disintegration chambers when ordered to do so. In this episode, the two societies avoid an all-out war, with its destruction of property, by having their computers make entirely hypothetical attacks on each other's cities instead. Anyone caught by one of these theoretical attacks is obliged to report for termination, any refusal will break a treaty signed centuries ago between the two planets, and potentially start a war fought with *real* fusion bombs. Unable to dissuade any of these computer-picked conscripts from suicide (Kirk orders a crewman to stop one local from "immolating herself"—something Vietnamese Buddhist monks had done in 1963, and American antiwar protestors in 1965), Kirk and Spock destroy two of the chambers and then the computer, forcing the government to ask for a ceasefire and negotiate a new treaty.[124]

In several of these episodes, as in "A Private Little War" and "A Taste of Armageddon," there is the spectre of a war that lasts for centuries, and possibly forever: "Day of the Dove" makes this explicit, and rejects the solution proposed in "A Private Little War" earlier that year, with Kirk describing the alien as having "kept resources and forces balanced, so that it can maintain a constant state of violence ... filled with eternal bloodlust, eternal warfare."[125]

Two of these episodes suggest that refusing to participate in a war that is based on false reports (apt, considering the Gulf of Tonkin incident), ancient hatreds, or for the benefit of someone who is acting against your own interests, is the right thing to do. It is only the Klingons who admit to finding war "glorious," while Kirk claims (for his side) that "no one wants war." Kirk, confronted by the Organians, is at first as "disgusted" by their pacifism as the Klingon captain, but at the end, is unable to defend the Federation's own readiness for war.[126] In a second season episode written by Bixby, "Mirror, Mirror," Kirk similarly begins by being frustrated by a pacifistic alien race refusing to allow the Federation to mine ore that will be used to make weapons, even if the alternative is the total destruction of their planet, but after a glimpse of a parallel world in which the (essentially Jeffersonian) Federation of Planets has instead become an (ultra–Hamiltonian) Imperium similar to the Klingon Empire, he finishes the episode defending them.[127] All of these episodes except for "The City on the Edge of Forever" and "A Private Little War" suggest that any conflict that could be solved by war could, and presumably should, be solved by negotiation; in a decade when Martin Luther King advocated passive resistance, "Errand of Mercy" and "Mirror, Mirror" sympathetically portrayed aliens (humanoid foreigners) who would rather die than fight or even welcome anyone purporting to be fighting on their behalf.

It should be noted that *Star Trek*'s creator, Gene Roddenberry, had a military background and was no pacifist. He had served as a U.S. Army Air Corps bomber pilot, receiving the Distinguished Flying Cross, and conceived of *Star Trek* in 1964 while producing his first TV series, *The Lieutenant*, a drama set on the U.S. Marine Corps base at Camp Pendleton. His Starfleet used the same command structure as the U.S. Navy; eight of its twelve starships, including the USS *Enterprise*, bore the same name as U.S. Navy vessels.[128] The components for the *Enterprise* are described as being built at "what is still called the San Francisco Navy Yards,"[129] its weight is "compared to a displacement of 59,650 tons of our aircraft carrier, the USS *Forrestal*,"[130] and the scale drawing for the model-makers superimposes a silhouette of the starship over an image of the U.S. Navy aircraft carrier *Enterprise*.[131]

The writers' guide for *Star Trek* even specified that Captain Kirk should act not unlike the commanding officer of a U.S. Navy cruiser in the Vietnam War:

> The time is today. We're in Vietnam waters aboard the navy cruiser U.S.S. *Detroit*. Suddenly an enemy gunboat heads for us, our guns are unable to stop it, and we realize it's a suicide attack with an atomic warhead. Total destruction of our vessel and of all aboard appears probable. Would Captain E.L. Henderson, presently commanding the U.S.S. *Detroit*, turn and hug a comely female WAVE who happened to be on the ship's bridge?
>
> As simple as that. This is our standard test that has led to STAR TREK believability. (It also suggests much of what has been wrong in filmed SF of the past.) No, Captain Henderson wouldn't! Not if he's the kind of captain we hope is commanding any naval vessel of ours. Nor would our Captain Kirk hug a female crewman in a moment of danger, not if he's to remain believable.[132]

However, the guide then continues: "Some might *prefer* that Henderson were somewhere making love rather than shelling Asian ports, but that's a whole different story for a whole different network. Probably BBC."[133] (The implication that a British TV network might broadcast an SF show that might be seen as criticizing the Vietnam war, but that an American one would not, had some basis in fact: one episode of the British SF TV show *The Prisoner*, "Living in Harmony," in which Number Six is made to hallucinate that he is in a Wild West town, was not broadcast in the U.S. with the rest of the series in 1968 because the series hero, Number Six's, refusal to carry a gun in an American setting, was seen by CBS as an antiwar protest.[134])

While it sometimes reflected the American public's increasing disenchantment with the Vietnam war, the show's view of Starfleet, the military arm of the United Federation of Planets, remained positive, even utopian. Roddenberry insisted on rewriting scenes in Ellison's script for "The City on the Edge of Forever" which depicted "one of our crewmen engaged in dope smuggling, the Captain forsaking the ship, the crew in mutiny."[135] Starfleet might make mistakes (as in "The Ultimate Computer," where control of the *Enterprise* is given to a computer which reacts to a war game as though it were real, killing the entire crew of another starship), and individual officers occasionally disobeyed orders (including Spock in "The Menagerie" and Kirk in "Amok Time"), rose through the ranks without command experience (Commodore Stocker in "The Deadly Years"), and sometimes went completely off the rails to pursue personal vendettas (Decker in "The Doomsday Machine," Finney in "Court Martial") or went native while stranded on alien planets (Merik in "Bread and Circuses," Tracey in "The Omega Glory"). But while Roddenberry was at the helm, there was never a suggestion that the military machine was either unnecessary or evil.[136] Even in the 1988 *Star Trek: The Next Generation* episode "Conspiracy," inspired by the Iran-Contra affair, Roddenberry insisted that the group of renegade Star Fleet officers who'd turned conspirator had been taken over by alien parasites, easily defeated by Picard and Riker in a single episode.[137] (None of the Iran-Contra conspirators attempted to use alien parasites as a legal defense.)

Perhaps because of this positive view of a military organization, *Star Trek* had (and still has) its fans among the U.S. military, with the Air Force Academy incorporating the *Enterprise* and the show's slogan "Where No Man has Gone Before" into the insignia for a cadet squadron.[138] Gannon shows that engineers from Northrop Grumman in the 1980s superimposed silhouettes of real B-1 and B-2 bombers and F-117 stealth fighters over representations of the starship *Enterprise* to indicate scale, under the assumption that "a room full of senior military and defense personnel will recognize the outlines of the 'old' and 'new' USS *Enterprise*, find these comparisons appropriate to such a meeting without needing any contextualizing references, and regard them as interesting and possibly useful."[139] However, none of this prevented Roddenberry and several other *Star Trek* writers (Bixby, Jerry Sohl, Harlan Ellison, and Norman Spinrad; as well as Mack Reynolds and James Blish, both of whom wrote early *Star Trek* tie-in novels) from joining a group of 81 science fiction writers that posted advertisements in *Fantasy and Science Fiction* (March 1968) and *Galaxy Science Fiction* (June 1968) magazines saying, "We oppose the participation of the United States in the War in Vietnam."

These ads were organized by Judith Merril, who had unsuccessfully campaigned to have the Science Fiction Writers of America protest against the war, and signed before the Tet Offensive.[140] Other signatories included Isaac Asimov, Anthony Boucher, Ray Bradbury, Theodore Cogswell, Miriam Allen deFord, Samuel R. Delany, Lester del Rey, Philip K. Dick, Thomas M. Disch, Phillip José Farmer, Harry Harrison, Daniel Keyes, Damon Knight, March Laumer, Ursula K. Le Guin, Fritz Leiber, Katherine Maclean, Barry Malzberg, Bruce McAllister, Judith Merril, Kris Neville, Alexei Panshin, Joanna Russ, Robin Scott, Robert Silverberg, Kate Wilhelm, and Richard Wilson.

On hearing that these ads would be posted, Robert Heinlein contacted Jack Williamson and organized a group of 68 writers willing to sign an advertisement proclaiming, "We the undersigned believe the United States must remain in Vietnam to fulfill its responsibilities to the people of that country." The undersigned included Poul Anderson, Harry Bates, Lloyd M. Biggle, J.F. Bone, Leigh Brackett, Marion Zimmer Bradley, Reginald Bretnor, Fredric Brown, Doris Pitkin Buck, F.M. Busby, John W. Campbell, Hal Clement, L. Sprague de Camp, Daniel Galouye, Edmond Hamilton, Robert Heinlein, Joe L. Hensley, Dean C. Ing, R.A. Lafferty, Larry Niven, Alan E. Nourse, Jerry Pournelle, Joe Poyer, Fred Saberhagen, G. Harry Stine, Theodore L. Thomas, Jack Vance, Harl Vincent and Jack Williamson.

The ads were published on pages 45 (pro-war) and 130 (antiwar) of *F&SF*, but on facing pages of *Galaxy* by editor Fred Pohl (who offered the $500 advertising revenue to whoever came up with the best solution for the Vietnam situation). Pohl expressed his horror at this polarization of the SF writing community, claiming there was "not a pennyworth of difference between" the two groups or their visions of the future.[141]

Franklin disagrees, dividing the groups into "the champions of superscience and supermen, of manly and military virtue" on the pro-war side and "almost the entire vanguard of an emerging kind of science fiction, opposed to technocracy, militarism and imperialism; originally called the new wave" on the other.[142] While this is a good description of many in each group, it seems rather too hard-and-fast a categorization. *Star Trek* was hardly "new wave," but traditional space opera with occasional forays into Jameson's third stage of science fiction, cultural critique.[143] Asimov's work, particularly robot stories such as "The Evitable Conflict" and nonfiction pieces such as "By the Numbers," suggest that he was very much pro-technocracy and superscience, if less impressed by "manly and military virtue." Harrison, though he has asserted that almost all of his stories are anti-military,[144] is arguably best known for action-adventure series with heroes at least as super-capable as Heinlein's, as is Mack Reynolds. Lafferty is counted among New Wave writers[145] and was dismissive of what he terms the "Campbell corral" of writers "impressed with a sort of advocacy science, with the whole corpus of stereotyped falsehoods of secular liberalism, with the fascism which is the only logical conclusion to the secular liberal premise"—a group in which he included his co-signers Heinlein, Clement, De Camp and Poul Anderson as well as the antiwar Asimov and del Rey.[146] Ellison's 1967 anthology *Dangerous Visions*, which was "strongly identified with the New Wave in the USA,"[147] includes stories by pro-war Anderson, Hensley, Lafferty, and Niven, as well as work by Ellison and his co-signers Spinrad, del Rey, Dick, Silverberg, Leiber, Neville, Farmer and deFord, and an introduction by Asimov. Writers on opposite sides of the debate who collaborated with each other on stories or novels before or after 1968 include Ellison and Hensley, Thomas and Cogswell, Thomas and Wilhelm, and Ing and Reynolds.

The two groups had much else in common. The ages of the antiwar signatories ranged from 22 (Bruce McAllister) to 80 (Miriam deFord); those of the pro-war signatories from 29 (Joe Poyer) to 75 (Harl Vincent), and the male:female ratio was similar in each group (approximately 6:1). There were multiple past and future award winners on each side of the debate, as well as parents with children serving in Vietnam (Buck, the Busbys, Merril and Wilhelm) and military experience on each side: Asimov, Blish, Cogswell, Farmer, Harrison, Laumer, Neville, Reynolds, Roddenberry, Sohl and Wilson had served in the U.S. military during World War II, as had Biggle, Bone, Busby, Clement, de Camp, Galouye, Hensley, Lafferty, Thomas and Williamson. Nourse had served in 1946–48; Ing, Pournelle and Saberhagen during the Korean War; Ellison in 1957–59; Panshin in 1960–62. The antiwar side had fewer officers; the pro-war side had the longest-serving and highest-ranking officer (Bone, nine years in the army and twenty in the reserves, reaching the rank of lieutenant colonel).

But as has already been discussed, Asimov and Harrison hated their time in the U.S. Army, as did Ellison (who was saved from court-martial by Hensley), while Heinlein, whose brother had risen to the rank of lieutenant general, describes military service in mostly positive terms indicative of an acquired taste that had become almost an addiction or a raison d'etre. Jerry Pournelle, similarly, would later tell Charles Platt: "If you are trying to tell me that I should not depict realistically the attractions of a properly run military outfit, you're a fool. Because it can be damned attractive.... Are you telling me that I shouldn't tell people that there is a share of glory? It's a damned attractive life; if it wasn't, why would so many people want it?"[148] (Despite this ringing endorsement and circular reasoning, Pournelle admits in the same interview that after returning from "a pretty miserable war" in Korea, he briefly joined the Communist Party.[149])

This difference in opinions of military service may have been a major contributing factor in the writers' stance on the war: by this time, 40,000 men per month were being drafted in the U.S., and thousands more were fleeing to Canada or seeking other means of staying out of the army. But as Pohl wrote in 1977, the Vietnam war changed many Americans' idea that war was necessarily righteous.[150] A South Vietnamese officer, Lt. Col. Nguyen Ngoc Loan, was photographed shooting a handcuffed captive on February 1, 1968. After the shelling of Ben Tre a week later, journalist Peter Arnett quoted (or possibly misquoted) a U.S. Army major as saying of the destruction of Ben Tre, "We had to destroy the village in order to save it."[151] March 1968 saw the My Lai massacre, though this would not be widely reported until November 1969. Michael Herr, writing for *Rolling Stone*, *Esquire* and *New American Reviews* in 1968 and 1969, described American soldiers wearing necklaces of human ears, which they referred to as "love beads"[152]—an image that would later be used in the superhero comics *Green Arrow*, *Watchmen*, *The Punisher*, *Ultimate X-Men* and the SF film *Universal Soldier* as a signifier that a character—usually a villain, never a hero—was an American Vietnam veteran.

Asimov spoke against the Vietnam War in radio interviews, describing it as "exactly what I meant by a 'petty, inglorious' war, and I kept repeating to people Joseph Fouche's famous epigram on the assassination of the Duc d'Enghien: 'It is worse than a crime, it is a blunder.'"[153] Ursula Le Guin "had been helping organize and participating in nonviolent demonstrations, first against atomic bomb testing, then against the war in Vietnam ... all through the sixties."[154] She describes 1968 as "a bitter year for those of us who opposed the war. The lies and hypocrisies redoubled; so did the killing. Moreover, it was becoming clear that the ethic which approved the defoliation of forests and grainlands and the murder of noncombatants in the name of 'peace' was only a corollary of the ethic which permits the despoliation of natural resources for private profit or the GDP."[155] She wrote *The Word for World Is Forest*, in which she admits "the moralizing aspects of the story are plainly visible."[156] The American and Vietnamese humans who are destroying the forests of Athshea, enslaving or killing the humanoid natives, are surprised when the normally peaceful Athsheans retaliate; they are led by Selver, whose wife was raped and killed by Captain Davidson. Davidson, who ignores the order to surrender and continues killing Athsheans until all the other humans have left the planet and he is exiled to an island he has helped defoliate, is described by Le Guin in the story's introduction as "purely evil."[157]

Norman Spinrad said of the European anti–Americanism he experienced at the time: "The real gut feeling had little to with the plight of the Vietnamese. It was a feeling of sorrow, of loss, of betrayal. Europeans felt diminished by what America was doing ... let down by something they had believed in."[158] And Harry Harrison left the U.S. in 1974 partly because of "dissatisfaction with life in a country that could commit the crimes of Vietnam and not be ashamed."[159]

Meanwhile, American soldiers in Vietnam continued to read science fiction: Lynch reports that in April 1969, *The Magazine of Fantasy and Science Fiction*'s largest market outside the U.S. was Saigon.[160]

In May 1970, another incident would further tarnish the image of the U.S. military, when the National Guard bayoneted two students and shot thirteen more (four of them fatally) during an antiwar demonstration at Kent State University in Ohio. In his May 15 columns for the *LA Free Press*, Harlan Ellison would compare the killing to the slaughter at My Lai and predict that "the country is finally getting unified."[161] A week later, he more accurately included the Kent State shootings in a list of "the most divisive horrors in recent American history."[162] He would dedicate his collection *Alone Against Tomorrow* (1971) to the Kent State Four.

British documentary maker Peter Watkins, who had made *The War Game* (1965) for the BBC, had come to the U.S. in 1968 to make a trilogy of documentaries about American wars in the style of his reenactment of *Culloden* (1964). Though funding for the trilogy fell through, the Kent State shootings inspired Watkins to stay in the U.S. to make *Punishment Park* in 1970, which postulated that because the increasing number of protestors and draft evaders arrested during the escalating Vietnam War would lead to overcrowding in the prisons, the U.S. would use the 1950 McCarran Internal Security Act to set up "punishment parks" as detention centers and a means of field-training police and the National Guard. Americans convicted of political offenses could choose between serving out their prison terms or enduring a three-day 53-mile trek through the desert to reach an American flag and receive a pardon. The film follows two groups of dissidents—Group 638 is on trial in a military tent, while Group 637, already convicted, is attempting to survive the ordeal of Punishment Park. Watkins discarded his script for the trial scene and let the young people playing the dissidents (loosely based on figures such as Abbie Hoffman, Tom Hayden, Bobby Seale and Joan Baez) voice their own opinions of the Vietnam War and the protest movement, improvised and unrehearsed; the members of the tribunal, the police, U.S. marshals and the National Guard (including some former police officers) were either expressing their own conservative pro-establishment convictions, or role-playing. Only one of the actors, Carmen Argenziano, playing dissident Jay Kaufman, had previous screen acting experience; another, Stan Armsted, was charged with conspiracy to bomb shortly after the filming finished, and sentenced to three years for assaulting a police officer.

Group 637 splits up into militants, semi-militants and pacifists, with the militant subgroup (one member of whom predicts that she will die in two or three minutes) attempting to escape, they fatally stab a deputy with the spines of a Joshua tree, and steal his car and weapons. This understandably angers the police, who have already demonstrated the killing power of their .357 Magnum revolvers and twelve-gauge shotguns, and the would-be escapees are caught and killed. The dissidents who have continued in the course discover that the water they were promised at the halfway point isn't there. The police then use a dead body as a decoy to lure some of the group into the open so they can be arrested, and a soldier shoots one of them when they fail to hear his order to sit down; the dissidents rush and overpower him. In an unscripted scene, dissidents throw stones at approaching National Guardsmen, one of whom (played by the 18-year-old brother of cinematographer Joan Churchill) instinctively fires, "killing" two—which Watkins suspects was how the shooting started at Kent State.

The actor playing the guardsman tells the interviewer immediately after the shooting, "I didn't want to kill anyone; it was an accident." The interviewer (Watkins) then asks his commanding officer, "How old is this kid?"

OFFICER: He's 18.
WATKINS: What's a kid doing in the National Guard if he can't use weapons?
OFFICER: He's trained to use them. Well, what do you expect with all those men throwing rocks at him?
WATKINS: You mean he's trained to kill people?
OFFICER: Yes he is. To defend his own country. He's trained to defend his country.
WATKINS: You mean he's trained to kill unarmed people like that?

As the four surviving dissidents from Group 367 near the flag on the third day, they find it surrounded by police who refuse to let them pass; instead, they beat the survivors (who, as Watkins points out, "have not hurt a goddamn fly") with nightsticks and rifle butts when they try to break through the cordon in the vain hope that the government will keep its promise.[163]

Punishment Park was first screened at Cannes in May 1971. Earlier that month, 2000 National Guard and 4000 paratroopers from the 82nd Airborne Division were brought in to deal with demonstrators in the May Day protests in Washington, D.C. A total of 12,614 protestors and spectators were arrested, many of them confined in a makeshift emergency detention center next to RFK Stadium; only 79 were convicted. On July 5, 1971, the Twenty-sixth Amendment lowered the voting age from twenty-one to eighteen. On September 25, the "Emergency Detention Act" of the McCarran Act was repealed by Congress.

◆ ◆ ◆

As the war in Vietnam dragged on and support for it declined, Marvel became more likely to depict soldiers on *all* sides as "unthinking instruments of destruction." Wright notes that after 1968, "Political debate consumed the letters in *Iron Man*.... One pointed out that 'while Firebrand was marching, trying to bring about a more peaceful world, Stark Industries was probably building weapons for Vietnam where we 'destroyed a city in order to save it!'"[164]

Marvel had previously showed some U.S. military as gung-ho to the point of being trigger-happy—even with nuclear weapons. In the first issue of *The Fantastic Four* (1962), the military fires a nuclear-armed missile at the Human Torch while he's flying over New York City, and in the first issue of *The Incredible Hulk* (1962), General "Thunderbolt" Ross complains about Bruce Banner's slow progress on a bomb that "might blow up half the continent!!" Ross rants, "Powerful forces! Bah!! A bomb is a bomb! The trouble with you is you're a milksop! You've got no guts! They should have put me in charge of this test! By thunder, it would have been done by now!"[165] "Though soldiers in combat had generally been treated sympathetically before this, the October 1969 issue of *The Incredible Hulk* shows a U.S. Army commander shouting, "Kill Him! Kill the Hulk!" In *Captain America and the Falcon* #175 (1974), in an echo of *The Day the Earth Stood Still*, a flying saucer lands on the White House lawn, and the next frame shows soldiers firing at it with the caption, "The Army gives him its expected **answer!**"[166]

In the next issue, Captain America discovers Number One of the

Secret Empire working behind a desk at the White House (it is implied, but never stated, that he is President Nixon): he recoils in shock and retires, later explaining:

> There was a time, yes, when the country faced a clearly hideous aggressor and the people stood united against it! But now nothing's that simple![167]
>
> I did things I'm not proud of—but I always tried to serve my country well—and now I find that the government was serving itself![168]

Fans whose letters were published in later issues were generally supportive of this move. One stated that "never have the reasons for quitting been quite so real, so utterly legitimate." Another wrote, "Hate, wars and government corruption had destroyed Steve Rogers faith in America (as it has also done to us)."[169]

Five years earlier, Peter Fonda's character in *Easy Rider* (1969) had taken the name of Captain America as he "went looking for America ... and couldn't find it anywhere." Steve Rogers did much the same, continuing to fight crime as a civilian under the name of Nomad, "the Man Without A Country." During this sojourn, other characters tried to take on the role of Captain America, and it was after the death of one of these that Steve Rogers resumed the identity of Captain America in March 1975, a month before the withdrawal of the last U.S. troops from Vietnam.[170]

Tony Stark also "turns completely against the Vietnam War and terminates his industry's weapons division," and by 1975, when thinking of Vietnam, he wonders, "What right had we to be there in the first place?"[171] He flashes back to an incident in Vietnam, when he witnessed American weaponry of his own design lay waste to an entire village, killing enemy and innocent alike, and recommits himself to "avenge those whose lives have been lost through the ignorance of men like the man I once was!"[172]

◆ ◆ ◆

Many SF stories written during the Vietnam war reflect a particularly jaundiced view of military service, conscription and war—and occasionally, of American soldiers themselves.

Norman Spinrad's novel *The Men in the Jungle* (1967) was intended to "illuminate the brutality of war,"[173] and depicts a war drummed up on a planet by a drug dealer and deposed former dictator who fled his last home just in time to escape execution by revolutionaries.[174] In his story "Heirloom" (1972), aliens referred to as "the only gooks which beat us" defeat a human army by refusing to acknowledge their existence.[175] Another two 1969 Spinrad stories satirize military plans to use nuclear weapons in Vietnam. In "The Conspiracy," the president tells a press conference that he is confident "that we can win the war on poverty without resorting to tactical nuclear weapons."[176] In "The Big Flash," the Undersecretary of Defense tells a SAC general who, with the rest of the Pentagon, "has been screaming for the use of tactical nuclear weapons to end the war in Asia," that the president has "conditionally approved a plan for the use of tactical nuclear weapons during the next monsoon season," public opinion having been turned around by the Four Horsemen of the Apocalypse in the guise of a rock band.[177] "The Big Flash" ends with the crews of Polaris submarines hurrying to be the first to launch their nukes.

Philip K. Dick expanded his 1953 story "The Defenders" into the 1964 novel *The Penultimate Truth*, which retained the central premise—the people on both sides of World War III being tricked into staying in their underground shelters for several years after the war has ended—but attributed this action to corrupt propagandists who have fooled the military establishments, who during the war "held ultimate power," into maintaining the illusion.[178] Unlike the benign robots setting out to create a peaceful utopia by unifying the population, however, the propagandists divide the mostly uncontaminated surface of the Earth into enormous private estates.

Harry Harrison's "Commando Raid" (1970) offers an alternative vision of a future U.S. military: the M-16–toting American soldiers raiding a village turn out to be members of the Aid Corps, their "flit guns" filled with insecticide. When a private from Alabama clubs a village elder with his flit gun, his captain has him arrested, telling him:

> In Vietnam we spent five million dollars a head to kill the citizens of that country, and our profit was the undying hatred of everyone there, both north and south, and the loathing of the civilized world. We've made our mistakes, now let's profit from them.
> For less than one thousandth of the cost of killing a man, and making his friends our enemies, we can save a life and make the man our friend.... We are going to bring them about five percent of the "benefits" you enjoy in the sovereign state of Alabama and we are doing to from selfish motives. We want to stay alive. But at least we are doing it.[179]

In Kate Wilhelm's "The Village" (written the day after she heard about the My Lai massacre, but rejected by every editor until 1973),[180] American soldiers re-enact the My Lai massacre in a small American town because "one fucken village is just like the others."[181]

Some science fiction stories of the time portrayed American soldiers and conscripts more sympathetically, as trying to survive when sent into a nightmarish situation by superior officers, politicians and civilians. Harlan Ellison's "Basilisk" (1972) tells the story of a soldier in Vietnam who loses a foot to a pungi stick, is caged and interrogated by the North Vietnamese, discloses troop movements under interrogation, and escapes only to be condemned as a coward and traitor when he returns home.[182] Robert Silverberg's "Caught in the Organ Draft" (1972) has young Americans being conscripted as organ donors for the old.[183] James Blish's *The Day After Judgment* (1972) sees American soldiers literally being sent into Hell to fight demons their general has told them are Chinese troops, a "senseless advance of expensively trained and equipped men to certain and complete slaughter—men who as usual not only had no idea what they were dying for, but had been actively misled about it."[184]

In Stephen King's early novel *The Long Walk* (written in the late 1960s when he was a student and antiwar activist, published in 1979 as by Richard Bachman), America is a military dictatorship, and 100 randomly picked teenage boys participate in a long walk where stragglers are shot by soldiers until only one survivor remains.[185]

Spider Robinson's story "Unnatural Causes" (1975) explicitly refers to the brutalization of American soldiers serving in Vietnam. A Vietnam vet, Tony, recalls how a fellow recruit, Steve, who refused to carry a gun was beaten to death in the stockade, and how a friend shot a twelve-year-old Vietnamese who was trying to decapitate him with a machete, and was later killed and mutilated by (presumably) the Viet Cong. After this, he remarks: "The rest of my tour passed in a red haze. I remember raping women, I remember clubbing a baby's skull with a rifle butt to encourage a VC sympathizer to talk, I remember torturing captured prisoners and enjoying it. I remember a dozen little My Lais, and I remember me in the middle with a smile like a wolf. Fury tasted better than confusion, and this time it was easier to *kill* than to think."[186] After learning of Steve's death, Tony "went from kill-crazy all the way to the other kind ... tried to die and loused it up," and is sent home with "a piece of paper that said I was a normal human being again."[187] He tries to lose himself in alcohol, marijuana and meditation, then joins the Vietnam Veterans Against the War.[188]

By contrast, signatories to the pro-war advertisements in *The Magazine of Fantasy and Science Fiction* and *Galaxy* published little SF that could be seen as defending the Vietnam War until after the war was lost, and not much even then. Franklin's *Vietnam and Other Fantasies* cites only one story and two nonfiction pieces (though he suggests that one of the latter, Pournelle and Possony's 1971 "technowar apologia" *The Strategy of Technology*, is actually a fantasy).[189] Joe Poyer's article "Challenge: The Insurgent vs. The Counterinsurgent" (*Analog*, 1966) predicted a U.S. victory through superior technology[190]; his story "Null Zone" (*Analog*, 1968) has a "Rambo type"[191] U.S. Special Forces technowarrior on a mission to interdict the Ho Chi Minh Trail by creating a lethally radioactive no-man's land.[192]

In his August 23, 1973, column for the *Los Angeles Weekly News*, Harlan Ellison pointed out that American involvement in the Vietnam War had already lasted twenty-three years.[193] Though the draft ended that year and the majority of troops were withdrawn, the last American troops would not leave the country until April 30, 1975. Even if one sets the date for American involvement in the war as late as 1965, it was, at that time, nonetheless the longest war in U.S. history. So it is appropriate that the best known science fiction novel based on the Vietnam War, by a soldier who had served in Vietnam and been wounded in combat there, was titled *The Forever War* and published in 1974.

When Joe Haldeman asked an Army recruiter how he could avoid going to Vietnam, he was told:

> "Well, if you're drafted, you're in for two years and you don't get shit. But if you sign this piece of paper, you're in for two years and you never have to go into combat."
>
> What I did not realize is that he would get fifteen bucks for my signing that piece of paper; and no matter how you join the army, if there's a war on, you have to join a combat arm.[194]

Haldeman was willing to go to Antarctica to run a nuclear power plant to avoid Vietnam, but was told he was overqualified.[195] He stated that he was a conscientious objector, but this was disallowed because he had no formal religion.[196] He was allowed to take two books to basic training: he chose *Cyrano de Bergerac* and Heinlein's *Glory Road*.[197]

The opening line of Haldeman's novel *The Forever War* (1975)—"Tonight we're going to show you eight silent ways to kill a man,"[198]—was a direct quote from one of his own instructors.[199] While he admits that the novel is similar in structure to *Starship Troopers* (which he had read previously) and makes similar use of powered combat armor, he states that this was not intentional, explaining: "I find the combat scenes in *Starship Troopers* pretty well done, but Heinlein's experience is that of an elite officer who didn't stay in the service long enough to get shot at. I was a soldier, a fighting soldier, and much of my book came out of my emotional reactions to combat."[200]

Whatever similarities it has with Heinlein's novel (which include deaths during basic training) are outweighed by the differences. While Heinlein's novel depicts an all-male infantry who train in the nude, rarely see women, and seem unaware of sex (even when compared to the heroes of earlier Heinlein juveniles such as *Between Planets* or *Time for the Stars*), Haldeman's infantry begins as co-ed, with a roster for sharing bunks, and ends up—like the vast majority of humanity—as entirely homosexual except for the few, like Mandella, who've been in the army for centuries. More significantly, far from leaving "the impression that warfare is the only real occupation for a real man"[201] (to quote Blish's defense of *Starship Troopers*), *The Forever War*, which Haldeman describes as "anti-war but not anti-soldier,"[202] portrays it as a bewildering nightmare. Heinlein's troopers are volunteers; Haldeman's are draftees who enter the war not even knowing who or *what* they are fighting, much less why. Haldeman's protagonist/narrator, William Mandella, re-enlists because he is excluded from civilian work, or even a normal civilian life: the relativistic time-dilation effects of interstellar flight mean that more than 1100 years pass on Earth during his four years in combat, so that the world he periodically returns to is unfamiliar and his skills obsolete.[203] Juan Rico thinks of his sergeant and lieutenant as mother and father, respectively, and the Mobile Infantry as his family: Haldeman's Major Mandella survives a murder attempt from one of his own men.[204] Heinlein's novel ends with the war ongoing and the song "For the everlasting glory of the infantry" being piped through to the men while they wait for a drop; Haldeman's ends with the 1143-year-long war over after the humans and the Tauran enemy finally learn to communicate with each other. They discover that humans started the war on "laughably thin" evidence,[205] ignoring the skeptics, because "the fact was, Earth's economy needed a war, and this one was ideal. It gave a nice hole to throw buckets of money into, but would unify humanity rather than dividing it."[206]

Some fans predicted that Heinlein would "rip Haldeman's head off" for using the power armor from *Starship Troopers* in an antiwar novel[207]; instead, on meeting Haldeman, Heinlein said the novel "may be the best future war story I've ever read!" He later wrote to Haldeman saying that though they disagreed on some issues, they "did agree on two particular things: the evil of the draft, and the senselessness of fighting a war that you know you can't win."[208]

Haldeman's novel won the Nebula and Hugo Awards in 1976, the latter at a Worldcon where Robert A. Heinlein was Guest of Honor. Heinlein's Guest of Honor speech, like his previous ones in 1941 and 1961, prophesied war:

> Don't kid yourself that there will not be war. And don't kid yourself that there will not be survivors. The most ridiculous statement I have ever heard is ... "Peace and Freedom." You can have peace, or you can have freedom, but you don't get both at once....
>
> The only peace that a man ever gets is the peace of the grave, and sometimes those who fight get it too.... his secondary function is to fight in defense of women and children....[209]

Both of these statements were greeted by booing as well as applause.[210] The war, though finally over, continued to divide the science fiction community.

◆ ◆ ◆

While Franklin argues that American involvement in the Vietnam war was at least partly inspired by science fiction visions of technowar, "Buck Rogers ... wearing a green beret,"[211] this is not reflected in the official naming of U.S. military hardware of the war era, none of which had overtly science-fictional labels. And for several years after American public opinion largely turned against the Vietnam war, science fiction was much more likely to be used to express or promote *anti*-military sentiments and ideas.

The backlash from Vietnam in the mid–1970s was such that a young filmmaker was warned that "a question mark loomed over the entire market for military and space toys."[212] He ignored this advice, and inadvertently gave a name to a U.S. military project that would serve as "a nice hole to throw money into," without requiring the reintroduction of the draft, or even any combat, yet is credited by some with leading to a U.S. victory in the Cold War.

The filmmaker was George Lucas; his film, *Star Wars*.

7. Murder in the Air
The Quest for the Death Ray

> Ronald Reagan's advocacy of the Strategic Defense Initiative struck me as bizarre.... Was it science fiction, a trick to make the Soviet Union more forthcoming, or merely a crude attempt to lull us in order to carry out the mad enterprise—the creation of a shield that would allow a first strike without fear of retaliation?—*Mikhail Gorbachev*[1]
>
> Writers of science fiction are supposed to look into the future. So I started looking to see what they had in mind for X-ray lasers. It turns out all the science fiction references are to blowing things up.—*Peter Hagelstein, Lawrence Livermore Laboratories*[2]

While the original Strategic Defense Initiative, popularly known as "Star Wars," with its X-ray lasers generated by exploding A-bombs, or optical lasers reflected from orbiting mirrors, is still little more than a figment of the imagination, many have argued that it doesn't *matter* that the technology doesn't or couldn't work. Politicians such as Margaret Thatcher and CIA analysts such as Robert Gates,[3] as well as science fiction writers,[4] have claimed that "Star Wars" was a triumph because of its value as a propaganda weapon in the Reagan administration's economic warfare against the now-defunct Soviet Union. To see whether or not this was the intention of the scheme's creators—or if not, what they actually intended and expected SDI to do—we will have to look back to the days when lasers, ICBMs and nuclear warheads were also purely imaginary.

"It began, as most things do, in a science fiction story," Ben Bova remarks in his 1984 book *Assured Survival: Putting the Star Wars Defense in Perspective*.

> Ever since *The War of the Worlds*, evil monstrous creatures from other worlds and all-destroying "death rays" have been staples of science fiction. Through the 1930s and afterwards, the lurid covers of science fiction magazines almost invariably pictured a BEM (bug-eyed monster) carrying off a scantily clad human female with one tentacle and waving a "ray gun" in the other. Death rays and disintegrator weapons were the standard

sidearms for Buck Rogers, Flash Gordon, and a bevy of science fiction and comic book heroes.

But give a science fiction idea enough time, and it often turns into everyday reality.[5]

The "ray gun," second only to the spaceship as an icon of science fiction, was soon in science-fictional human hands, not just alien tentacles: in Garrett P. Serviss's 1898 unauthorized sequel to *War of the Worlds*, titled *Edison's Conquest of Mars*, Edison improves on the Martian Heat Ray to create disintegrator beams (the earliest known use of the word)[6] and leads a multinational but U.S.-dominated force to the moon, Ceres and Mars. "Death-ray" entered the English language in 1903, via George Griffith's novel *The World Masters*; "ray gun" in 1916, the following year, in an article in the *Newark Advocate*.[7]

William J. Fanning, Jr.'s essay "The Historical Death Ray and Science Fiction in the 1920s and 1930s" shows how the idea of the ray gun pervaded popular culture, and military thinking, in the period between the world wars—including some serious attempts to create one, and a few probable hoaxes as well as fictitious examples. In 1913, Giulio Ulivi claimed to have invented an infra-red "F-ray" projector that could remotely detonate explosives. He was granted an audience with the French army's chief of staff and arranged a demonstration for the army, setting off mines at sea and explosives in a fort, but refused to repeat the demonstration under military supervision and was branded a fraud. He moved to Italy, where "he obtained support for continuing his experiments" before again refusing to allow a demonstration under controlled conditions.[8]

More stories about destructive beam weapons appeared in newspapers, as well as in fiction, after World War I. In 1919, naval historian Edgar Stanton Maclay claimed that the British, during the Crimean War, had secretly developed a heat ray based on Archimedes's legendary "burning glass," supposedly deployed against Roman invaders of Syracuse, but refused to use it even in World War I, considering it "an affront to civilisation."[9] (Even had such a weapon ever been built, it would obviously have been less effective against 20th-century battleships than wooden-hulled sail-driven vessels still in service in the 1850s.)[10]

"In 1921, General Eugene Debeney, commandant of the French military school at Saint Cyr and later chief in staff of the army, predicted that electrical waves might be unleashed in a future conflict [...] 'the airplane will fall as though struck by a thunderbolt, the tank will burst into flames, the dreadnaught will blow up, poison gas will be dispersed.'"[11] Also in 1921, British General Ernest Swinton stated, "We may not be so very far from the development of some kinds of lethal ray which will shrivel up or paralyze human beings," comments that were widely quoted. *The Literary Digest* claimed that "the British already possessed electrical rays that could explode ammunition at great distances and kill the enemy," and *Popular Science Monthly* published an article titled "Civilization Must Abolish War or War Will Destroy Civilization," asserting, "At least one great power is known to be at work on a machine by which lethal rays can be directed at the enemy's military and civil centers."[12] Claims that Germany had a ray projector that could "short-circuit the magneto of a gasoline engine" became widespread in 1923 after reports of "French commercial airplanes flying over a certain region of Bavaria that experienced sudden engine failure and were forced to land." Later the same year, "British inventor Harry Grindell Matthews announced that he had developed a ray that not only could cause airplane engines to stop but could also be used to annihilate armies on the battlefield." Grindell Matthews met Air Vice-Marshal Sir Geoffrey Salmond in 1924, but like Ulivi, refused to repeat his apparently successful demonstrations under military or scientific supervision, and he relocated to France.[13] Despite this, his work was mentioned in Winston Churchill's "Shall We Commit Suicide?" (1924), and the "Rindel-Matthews Death Ray" is mentioned in Alexei Tolstoy's *Engineer Garin and His Death Ray* (1926) and Otfrid von Hanstein's *Elektropolis, The City of Technical Wonder* (1928).[14]

Rumors of ray projectors that could disable aircraft and remotely detonate explosives continued to surface, and many were debunked. The U.S. Bureau of Standards dismissed Tesla's claims of having invented a "death-beam" or "teleforce," a "defensive weapon only" that could "destroy 10,000 planes at 250 miles away,"[15] after determining "that it was technologically impossible to generate enough energy to power a ray capable of being an effective military weapon."[16] Despite this, the "death ray" was seriously proposed as an antiaircraft weapon as early as 1934, when the British Air Ministry, "inspired by Elihu Thomson's discovery in 1896 that ultra high frequency radiations (such as X rays) were destructive of matter ... asked Robert Watson-Watt of the National Physical Laboratory to examine the feasibility of 'cooking' aviators with a high-energy 'death ray.' He said this was pure fantasy...."[17] Shortly after this, the president of the University of California at Berkeley speculated "in a commencement address" that "the Rad Lab was developing a secret 'death ray'"—to the consternation of General Groves, who knew that the Rad Lab was actually working on the A-bomb.[18] In 1936, Henry Fleur was unsuccessfully sued by his backers for failing to produce a death ray, after showing the jury that his death ray could kill small animals, though only at a short range that made it impractical as a weapon.[19]

In 1940, refugees from Nazi Germany told British intelligence that the Germans were testing a "beam weapon that stopped cars"—actually a system of steerable radio beams used for guiding bombers, which was subject to interference from nearby traffic.[20]

That same year (according to an interview with Dr. A.F. Murray in *Time* in 1946),

> the National Defense Research Committee of the United States had created a section that came to be called Division 13. Its mission was to utilize radio communications to aid in defending the country. One of the tasks to which Murray was assigned involved evaluating the feasibility of a death ray. He and his team concluded, as had other scientists during the pre-war period, that an effective range for such a weapon required more energy than was then technologically available.[21]

Also in 1940, Hollywood used a ray gun as the MacGuffin in a science fiction movie, *Murder in the Air*. The "inertia projector" was a directed energy weapon—described in the trailer as "the most terrifying weapon ever invented" and "the death ray projector"—that "not only makes the United States invincible in war, but in so doing, promises to become the greatest force for world peace ever discovered."[22] Similar weapons had been common in science fiction before this date (including some deployed in Earth orbit: see Fanning for examples), but this film is of interest here because it starred Ronald Reagan as the government agent who must protect the device.

The idea was also popular outside Hollywood: in a meeting in 1941, Robert Oppenheimer suggested "using the cyclotron beam as a kind of death ray to defend especially important targets."[23]

> In July 1945, military officers recommend that the U.S. start researching and developing ways to defend against incoming ballistic missiles. A military advisory group discusses the idea of using an "energy beam" to defend the U.S. against ballistic missiles in December 1945, and two military studies are initiated three months later to explore the use of possible "interceptor" missiles to destroy incoming warheads.[24]

The *New York Times* reported on July 9, 1945, that U.S. forces had discovered that Nazi Germany had been working on a *Sonnegewehr* (sun gun), a gigantic orbiting solar reflector intended to focus sunlight onto targets on Earth, and on October 7 that Japanese scientists had also been trying to develop death rays.[25] The *Washington Post*, in August 26, 1945, also suggested using "beam weapons to destroy 'atom bomb rockets shot from thousands of miles away'"[26]; while *Time*, December 3, reported that Stalin had given his "chief of Soviet heavy industry" six months to develop a defense against atomic bombs and might already be ringing its cities with "'infra-cosmic ray' generators capable of exploding atomic bombs at a range of twelve miles."[27]

In a 1946 nonfiction piece, "The Last Days of the United States,"

Robert A. Heinlein wrote that the U.S. "can try for another Buck Rogers weapon with which to ward off atomic bomb rockets.... There is a bare possibility that science could cook up some sort of a devastatingly powerful beam of energy, acting with the speed of light, which would be a real anti-aircraft weapon, even against rockets. But the scientists don't promise it."[28] Heinlein went on to warn, "[I]t would not be air tight and it would be very expensive—and very annoying, for it would end civilian aviation. If we hooked the thing up to ignore civilian planes, we would leave ourselves wide open to a Trojan Horse tactic in which the enemy would use ordinary planes to deliver his atomic bombs."[29]

Death rays remained a staple of science fiction (including comics and movie serials) for several years before the invention of the first "energy beam" devices capable of destructive power, the maser (1953) and laser (1960). In 1959, SF writer Ben Bova joined the Avco Everett Research Laboratory, "where the first high-power laser was invented ... as a science writer, then organized its marketing department."[30] Bova states: "In 1966 it was apparent to us that high-power lasers had vital military implications.... We were patriotic (or chauvinistic) enough to feel that such weapons potential should be developed for the defense of the United States."[31] Shortly after this, he "helped to arrange the first top secret briefing in the Pentagon on the subject."[32]

By 1967, the idea of missile defense was sufficiently well known, at least among science fiction readers, that a reader wrote to Marvel Comics complaining because: "In the IRON MAN story, you have a missile going to Formosa unknown to the Red Chinese. You must think they're a bunch of idiots—all they had to do was destroy it!"[33] Stan Lee replied: "And as for the missile you mentioned, what do you mean 'All they had to do was destroy it!' You make it sound like catchin' a pop fly in the Little League. The Chinese Reds just recently began to explode basic nuclear devices— but, so far as we know, they're still a long way from possessing an effective, sophisticated anti-missile defense complex!"[34] This dose of reality, it should be pointed out, comes from a comic that postulated a powered battlesuit that could outfly a commercial jet, yet fit inside an attaché case.

But to return to Bova, he, in his own words,

> left Avco Everett Research Laboratory in 1971, to re-enter the publishing industry as the editor of *Analog Science Fiction—Science Fact* magazine. All during the years I was with Avco, and during my years as an editor, I continued to write books, and I have thought about and studied the many facets of ballistic missile defense for more than twenty years. I have worked with the scientists, engineers, military officers, politicians, bureaucrats, and futurists. I have portrayed how these people think and feel, and how they are changing the world around us.[35]

The best known example from Bova's fiction is *Millennium* (1977), in which Bova promotes the "assured survival" aspects of an orbital defense against ICBMs while acknowledging some of the problems with the idea. Firstly, the technical and economic problem of their sheer vulnerability: the USA and USSR are not only racing to complete their own defenses first, they are staying ahead in the race by destroying each other's laser satellites, while being careful to do so in ways that won't automatically trigger a war.[36] Secondly, the political problem of their potential as offensive weapons, what Gorbachev described as "the creation of a shield that would allow a first strike without fear of retaliation,"[37] which Bova acknowledges in *Assured Survival*: "One Russian commentator interviewed shortly after Reagan's 23 March 1983 speech put the matter quite succinctly: 'Why do you want to attack us?' Soviet leaders see any attempt by the United States to defend itself against Russian missiles as a preparation for American missile attack on their country."[38]

Similar reservations were expressed by Edward Teller in his 1962 book *The Legacy of Hiroshima*, Carl Sagan and fellow members of the Union of Concerned Scientists in "Star Wars: A Critique,"[39] and in Ronald Reagan's own so-called Star Wars speech of 1983, as well as at least one Russian response to it[40]—an acknowledgment that a missile shield owned by one side might never be effective enough to prevent a pre-emptive strike by the enemy, but might work if combined with a pre-emptive strike by that side that had already greatly reduced the number of missiles the enemy could fire in retaliation. As Seed points out, this scenario with the roles reversed—Russia, protected by "an impregnable barrier against aircraft and missiles"[41] launching a pre-emptive strike on the U.S.—had earlier been contemplated in Jerry Sohl's 1955 novel *Point Ultimate*.[42] And Reagan had previously advocated the possibility of "limited nuclear war,"[43] and as late as 1984 would put the Soviets on war alert by joking, "I'm pleased to tell you today that I've signed legislation that will outlaw Russia forever. We begin bombing in five minutes,"[44] lending credence to the impression that the missile shield was intended to prevent Soviet retaliation against America after a pre-emptive strike by the U.S.

Bova attempts to solve this problem in *Millennium* by putting control of the satellite network in the hands of an alliance of American and Russian astronauts who have learned to work together while stationed on the moon. They are commanded by an American colonel, Chester Kinsman, who was raised as a Quaker. Kinsman is branded a traitor by his own countrymen for attempting to ensure their safety from nuclear war; when he negotiates with the UN to have the moon base recognized as an independent nation, Americans burn down the UN building. At the novel's climax, Kinsman has to give the order to have the lasers turned against a manned rocket plane carrying U.S. Marines who are attempting to recapture the space station from which the satellites are controlled.[45]

Thirdly, Bova admits that even if a missile shield can be made to work and isn't used offensively, this only prevents the use of ICBMs, not war itself. In *Colony* (1978), the sequel to *Millennium*, the world is still safe from nuclear war, but war continues by other means—weather control, economic warfare, bioweapons, and state-sponsored terrorism.[46] In Spider Robinson's *Lady Slings the Booze* (1992), a similar missile shield is put in place (by time travelers from a far-distant future, using greatly advanced technology), but this only means that nuclear weapons have to be transported in other ways[47]—as happens in Arthur C. Clarke's "Loophole" (1946), Phillip Wylie's *The Smuggled Atom Bomb* (1956), Larry Collins and Dominique LaPierre's *The Fifth Horseman* (1980), and Harry Turtledove's *Worldwar: Upsetting the* Balance,[48] though in the last they use ships and trains rather than the ox cart once pessimistically suggested by Robert Oppenheimer.[49] And Arthur C. Clarke gave qualified support for "Son of SDI," if "it does not divert attention from such really dangerous delivery systems as offshore submarines and diplomatic bags."[50]

But it was political (rather than technical) considerations that temporarily banished missile shields back to the realm of science fiction from the signing of the Anti-Ballistic Missile (ABM) Treaty in 1972, with an amendment in 1974 limiting each superpower to only one ABM deployment site. Then, in 1977, the movie *Star Wars* appeared. Lucas had been warned, "Any film with the word War in it would not play well to women, the research had argued. 'The research said that no film with the word War in the title had ever made more than $8 million.'"[51] Further:

> In the wake of Vietnam, the accident-prone NASA moon shot program and the ill-fated Apollo 13 mission in particular, a question mark loomed over the entire market for military and space toys.
>
> "The feeling was that the mothers of America were afraid of having their children grow up to be spacemen," he [toy designer Dave Okada] said. "There was also still a backlash from Vietnam. For mothers, who are the ultimate gate-keepers, it was not a very pacifist-oriented toy line."[52]

Lucas ignored this advice, and to the astonishment of many at the studio (including Lucas himself), *Star Wars* quickly went on to become the biggest money-spinner in film history, a position it held for several years.

◆ ◆ ◆

Twentieth Century–Fox had had higher hopes for another, bigger-budget, 1977 science fiction release, *Damnation Alley*, which features a partially successful missile defense. Extremely loosely based on a post-apocalyptic novella by Roger Zelazny—i.e., it has the same title (though the studio considered changing it), and Jan-Michael Vincent's USAF lieutenant has the same surname as the book's Hells Angel protagonist and occasionally rides a bike—it starred Vincent and George Peppard as two mutually antagonistic SAC officers in a missile silo. When Tanner (Vincent) wonders aloud why a talented artist such as Keegan (Paul Winfield) remains in the service, Peppard's Major Denton stiffly informs him that he has requested that Tanner be reassigned to other duties for not meeting his (Denton's) specifications.

Moments later, 300 interceptor missiles are launched against a massive barrage of Russian ICBMs aimed at U.S. population centers. Tanner obeys without question, as unemotionally mechanical as Denton, when he receives the order to launch their ten missiles as part of a retaliatory attack against all Russian targets and releases a volley of stock footage of Titan rockets. The intercept destroys an estimated 40 percent of enemy missiles, the rest getting through and obliterating major U.S. cities. The nuclear war irradiates the sky and tilts the world on its axis; two years later, "the remnants of life ventured forth to commence the struggle for survival and dominance." Tanner has resigned from the USAF and grown his hair; Denton and Lieutenant Perry remain loyal to the chain of command, even though they admit that their commanding officer, General Landers, does nothing but sit in the former control room and drink. Denton explains, "He's our CO. We start taking off when we feel like it, place would collapse in a month." Seconds later, the bunker is destroyed after a sleeping airman drops a cigarette onto a centerfold while sleeping in a room full of high explosives.

After Landers dies despite Tanner's attempt to rescue him from the flames, Denton unveils the movie's real stars, two articulated amphibious combat vehicles. He tells Tanner and Keegan, "You don't have to re-enlist as long as it's clear I'm in charge," and they drive cross-country tracking down an automated radio message. Keegan, asked why he and Tanner quit the air force, replies, "What air force are you referring to?... Well, after the bombs fell, it didn't seem to make much sense to keep doing all those duties, fatigues, saluting, and sir-ing and...."

Perry asks him (unconsciously paraphrasing Joseph Heller's *Catch-22*), "What do you think would have happened if we'd all felt like that?" Keegan's response is, "Well, if more people had felt like that, there'd be a hell of a lot more people feeling and thinking ... and playing baseball, and singing, making love ... raising babies...."

Denton's insistence on hierarchy later results in Perry's death and the loss of one of the Landmaster vehicles, though Denton denies responsibility for this.[53] Whether because of its mostly unflattering portrayal of the U.S. military, its bleak outlook, or its unconvincing plot and special effects, the movie bombed at the box office, making back $4 million of a $17 million budget.[54]

Other studios tried to emulate *Star Wars*'s success, producing big-budget science fiction films that are generally remembered (if at all) for their spaceships, weapons, and other special effects. While some of these were "pacifist-oriented," others suggested the need for a strong defense against alien menaces, rather than welcoming them into our homes. King, in *Danse Macabre*, cites 1977's *Close Encounters of the Third Kind* as a counterbalance to 1951's *The Thing from Another World*:

> We can understand the latter's "let the military handle this" thesis was a perfectly acceptable one in 1951, because the military had handled the Japs and the Nazis perfectly well in Duke Wayne's "Big One," and we can also understand that the former's attitude of "don't let the military handle this" was a perfectly acceptable one in 1977, following the military's less-than-startling record in Vietnam, or even in 1980 (when *CE3K* was rereleased with additional footage), the year when American military personnel lost the battle for our hostages to the Iranians following three hours of mechanical fuckups.[55]

The nonaggressive stance of *Close Encounters of the Third Kind*, in which the U.S. military is responsible for covering up the truth of UFO sightings and stages a fake nerve gas accident in an attempt to keep contactees away from a UFO landing site, with dead sheep as props (a tactic which may have been inspired by the real nerve gas leak from the U.S. Army's Dugway Proving Ground in 1968, which killed thousands of sheep), was made (not surprisingly) without military assistance, and was not entirely typical of the SF movies of the time. This was also the era of *Alien* (1979) and *Battlestar Galactica* (1978–1979); *Invasion of the Body Snatchers* was remade in 1978, and *Buck Rogers in the 25th Century* in 1979, all of them featuring hostile extraterrestrials.[56] *Battle Beyond the Stars* (1980) saw pacifists turned into partisans to fight an intergalactic extortionist with a stellar converter.[57] *Starship Invasions* (1977), *Laserblast* (1978), *Superman: The Movie* (1979), *Superman II* (1980) and *Star Trek: The Motion Picture* (1980) had a bet each way, with both benign and hostile aliens.[58] But as with *Star Wars*'s Death Star, the enemy was often a "technological terror" from space— *Star Trek*'s V'ger, Sador's stellar converter in *Battle Beyond the Stars*, *Battlestar Galactica*'s robotic Cylons, *Starship Invasion*'s suicide-inducing electric arc, the superior military force of the Draconian starships in *Buck Rogers*. As with the North Vietnamese, though, these menaces were never defeated by superior technology.

Whether or not this comparison with the Vietnam War was consciously made by the writers of all of the films and TV shows mentioned above, it was certainly deliberate on George Lucas's part. According to Taylor, Lucas considered fleeing to Canada when he received his draft notice in 1966 after graduating from USC, but turned up for his medical, where it was discovered that he was diabetic and rated 4-F.[59] Hired to edit film for the U.S. Information Agency, he was "told that he'd made a story about a crackdown on an anti-government riot in South Korea look 'too fascist.'"[60] He was already talking about making *Star Wars*, summarized in 1973 as "a large technological empire going after a small group of freedom fighters."[61]

> The villain of this fairy tale, the Empire, was inspired by the U.S. military in Vietnam; the Ewoks by the Viet Cong; the Emperor by President Nixon. The fairy tale was charmingly benign enough to mask that fact, and now every culture around the planet, whether embattled or entitled, sees itself in the Rebel Alliance. "Star Wars has got a very, very elaborate social, emotional, political context that it rests in," Lucas said in 2012. "But, of course, nobody was aware of that."[62]

In 1969, Lucas was working for Francis Ford Coppola's American Zoetrope and planning to direct *Apocalypse Now*, then visualized as a "documentary-style Vietnam picture."[63] Coppola introduced him to Gary Kurtz, a fellow *Flash Gordon* enthusiast who had served for three years as a filmmaker with the USMC in Vietnam, and whom Lucas offered to make the producer of his next film. According to Taylor, Lucas had intended to make three films about the Vietnam War era, *American Graffiti* reflecting the idyllic "before" of 1962, *Apocalypse Now* the "during," and *Star Wars* as an allegory for the war, set in the future—and felt that *Apocalypse Now* "would lead to the government running him out of the country."[64] His version of *Apocalypse Now* was, as Lucas told *Rolling Stone* in 1977, "completely different" from the version Coppola was filming based on the screenplay by the much more conservative John Milius: "It was really more of man against machine than anything else. Technology against humanity, and then how humanity won. It was to have been quite a positive film."[65]— positive, presumably, unless you sided with the defeated U.S. military.

Lucas, who told *Rolling Stone* "we all know how wrong we were in Vietnam,"[66] would continue with the allegorical representation of the U.S. military as the Empire in the next two *Star Wars* movies. The AT-ATs or Imperial walkers in *The Empire Strikes Back*, defeated by much smaller craft with comparatively feeble weapons, were inspired by a design for "a four-legged tank, a concept vehicle designed by General Electric in 1968 called the Cybernetic Anthropomorphous Machine. The CAM had been commissioned by the army for possible use in Vietnam; GE only abandoned it when the design proved to be too exhausting to operate."[67] The Ewoks of *Return of the Jedi* echoed, as previously noted, the triumphant North Vietnamese.

By the time of *The Empire Strikes Back*, however, Americans' attitude to warfare and their military were beginning to change as memories of the Vietnam War receded. The late 1970s, under the Carter administration, saw the beginning of a massive increase in U.S. military spending, largely in response to the Soviet occupation of Afghanistan. It also saw another piece of military hardware named after a science fiction trope—the prototype space shuttle, considered a military vehicle by Soviet publications and American journals such as *Jane's* (justifiably, as eleven of its missions were for the Department of Defense, nine of them classified),[68] was named *Enterprise* after a campaign by *Star Trek* fans. However, Carter was replaced in 1981 by the more hawkish Ronald Reagan, who further accelerated the increase in U.S. military spending.

Gregory Benford described Reagan as a "science fiction fan"[69] and Lou Cannon's biography *President Reagan: The Role of a Lifetime* (1991), similarly states:

> Peace films such as *WarGames* also occupied a crucial compartment in Reagan's emotional arsenal.... In Hollywood, he became an avid science-fiction fan, absorbed with a favorite theme of the genre: the invasion from outer space that prompts earthlings to put aside nationalistic quarrels and band together against an alien invader. Reagan liked this idea so much that he tried it out on Gorbachev in their first meeting at Geneva in 1985.... He also repeated it to his advisers, to mixed reactions.[70]

WarGames begins with two USAF officers in a bunker receiving the Go code: one refuses to turn his key to launch the missiles, and the other threatens to shoot him. When the USAF learns that 22 percent of their officers refused to launch their missiles, they turn control of the missiles over to a computer. A teenaged hacker penetrates the computer's security and challenges it to a game of Global Thermonuclear War. The computer tells the USAF that they are under attack, and takes control of the missile control systems to launch a counterstrike. As the computer cannot be switched off (shades of *Dr. Strangelove*'s Doomsday Machine), the hacker and programmer attempt to prove to it that there is no possible way to win a nuclear war. The computer runs through all the available simulations, and concludes, "The only winning move is not to play."[71]

It should be noted, though, that *WarGames* was launched at Cannes in 1983, *after* Reagan's "Star Wars" speech, and could not have influenced it (though Reagan did see *WarGames* later, and discussed the scenario with the Army's Chief of Staff).[72] Similarly, while Reagan wrote in his personal journal after a pre-viewing of the science-fiction film *The Day After*, "[It] left me greatly depressed.... My own reaction: we have to do all we can to have a deterrent and to see there is never a nuclear war,"[73] this was nearly eight months after the "Star Wars" speech. If Reagan's stance on nuclear war was inspired by an SF "peace film," it must have antedated these. Cannon suggests a likely candidate, saying that Reagan's national security adviser Colin Powell "knew more than he had ever wanted to know about Reagan's preoccupation with what Powell called 'the little green men,' and he struggled diligently to keep interplanetary references out of Reagan's speeches. Powell was convinced that Reagan's unique proposal to Gorbachev had been inspired by a 1951 science-fiction film, *The Day the Earth Stood Still*."[74]

Reagan was certainly fond of movies and cinematic references. His national security adviser, Bill Clark, kept him informed on international politics with documentary films rather than written briefing notes.[75] In 1985, Reagan quoted Dirty Harry's "Go ahead, make my day" in Congress, and commented, "After seeing *Rambo* last night, I know what to do next time this happens," and even claimed that his fight for tax reform was "in the spirit of Rambo." Isaac Asimov, decrying the Star Wars scheme, described Reagan as not knowing where the "line between science and science fiction" was,[76] and Norman Spinrad refers to him as having "difficulty distinguishing movies from reality."[77] Ken Adams, set designer for *Dr. Strangelove*, recounts that one of Reagan's first demands on becoming president was to be shown the War Room; when told there was no War Room, he replied that there must be, because he'd seen it in movies.[78] Frances Fitzgerald has argued that Reagan was "enchanted with the notion of a protective shield ... because he had seen it work in the movies—specifically, in Alfred Hitchcock's 1966 *Torn Curtain*, in which Paul Newman's character speaks of an antimissile device that 'will make all nuclear weapons obsolete and thereby abolish the terror of nuclear warfare.' A variation of that sentence appeared in the 1983 speech in which Reagan first floated the idea of SDI."[79] *Star Wars Dreams* also notes similarities between the "Star Wars" speech and dialogue from *Murder in the Air*.[80] Arthur C. Clarke similarly asked, "Would President Reagan ever have made his famous 'Star Wars' speech of 23 March 1983 if he hadn't seen so many movies?"[81]

Reagan did not refer to "Star Wars" in his speech of March 23, 1983, though it is referred to that way almost universally, including on the Reagan Library website.[82] Senator Edward Kennedy dismissed the speech the next day as "misleading Red Scare tactics and reckless 'Star Wars' schemes," possibly inspired by the fact that Reagan had described the Soviet Union as "the Evil Empire" in a speech only fifteen days earlier, and that *Star Wars* had first appeared on television the month before. A few days later, physicist Hans Bethe told *Time*, "I don't think it can be done. What is worse, it will produce a Star War if successful."[83] The scheme was not named the "Strategic Defense Initiative" until 1984, by which time the "Star Wars" label had stuck. Reagan's domestic policy advisor Martin Anderson, who has claimed to have proposed the missile shield to Reagan,[84] stated that "Reagan never liked the name 'Star Wars.' I personally liked 'Star Wars,' because if you watch the movie *Star Wars*, the good guys won."[85] According to Peter Kramer: "In comments made in March 1985, he [Reagan] first rejected the 'Star Wars' label by saying that SDI 'isn't about war. It is about peace.' But then he added: 'If you will pardon my stealing a film line—the force is with us.'"[86] George Lucas also disliked the name, and according to Kramer,

> had actually written the part of the Evil Emperor with Reagan's Republican predecessor Richard Nixon in mind. In 1985 Lucas brought a suit against two advocacy groups that campaigned for SDI, intending to forbid them the use of the "Star Wars" label. However, in November 1985 U.S. District Judge Gerhard Gesell ruled that anyone could use the term "Star Wars" in "parody or descriptively to further a communication of their views on SDI."[87]

Because of his support for a laser-based defense system, Reagan was parodied by many (including SF author Rudy Rucker in his 1983 story "PAC-Man"[88] and the 1986 computer game *Nuclear War*) as "Ron Ray-gun," and cartoonists were quick to adopt "Star Wars" tropes when portraying Reagan and the Russians, especially on defense and international relations. Kramer describes several of these, and more appear in *The Art of Star Wars*.[89] Some linked Vader and/or the Death Star with the Russians, while Reagan took advice from Yoda or "a crack team of experts" which included the droids and ET; others, in the USA as well as Europe, had Reagan wearing Vader's costume.

The "Star Wars" label was taken to heart by the young scientists at Lawrence Livermore Laboratory's O Group, who were working under Edward Teller on the X-ray laser. Rod Hyde, second-in-command of O Group under Teller protégé Lowell Wood and designer of the "pop up" X-ray laser weapon, had been a science fiction fan since adolescence, particularly admiring the work of Heinlein, Gordon Dickson and Keith Laumer.[90] Another O Group physicist was Peter Hagelstein, whose dissertation on "Physics of Short Wavelength Design" contains a section on "future applications"—discussing three science fiction novels: Larry Niven's *Ringworld*, Niven and Jerry Pournelle's *The Mote in God's Eye*, and V. Appleton's *Tom Swift and his Cosmotron Express*—which includes a rather depressing line: "Writers of science fiction are supposed to look into the future. So I started looking to see what they had in mind for X-ray lasers. It turns out all the science fiction references are to blowing things up."[91] After their work was dubbed "Star Wars," O Group "took up a collection to buy Lowell [Wood] a costume of Darth Vader, the character in *Star Wars* who epitomized the dark side of the Force. But they scrapped the idea, afraid Lowell would actually wear it as he wandered the halls urging them to work harder."[92] For all of Lowell's urgings, O Group's attempts to develop a working X-ray laser satellite or "pop-up" weapon have never been realized. The lack of success did not prevent SDI from being a major bone of contention when Reagan and Mikhail Gorbachev met in Reykjavik where a treaty to completely eliminate nuclear weapons by 1996, a stated goal of both leaders, foundered on Reagan's refusal to agree to Gorbachev's terms that SDI-related research be limited to laboratory experiments for the next ten years.[93]

On May 13, 1993, a little over ten years after Reagan's "Star Wars" speech and less than 18 months after the dissolution of the Soviet Union, President Clinton's Secretary of Defense, Les Aspin, announced to a Department of Defense news briefing:

> Today we are here to observe ... the end of the Star Wars era.
> We are renaming and refocusing the Strategic Defense Initiative Office to reflect the Clinton Administration's changes in the priorities....[94]

He spoke too soon. In 1996, Republican presidential candidate Bob Dole and House Leader Newt Gingrich (himself a science fiction writer, who has collaborated with William R. Fortschen, David Drake and Jerry Pournelle, of whom more later) made missile defense an election issue in their "Defend America Act of 1996"; this was reported in the *Bulletin of Atomic Scientists* in an article titled "Star Wars: Play it again, Bob."[95] In 1998, Gingrich and once and future Defense Secretary Donald Rumsfeld were again calling for stronger missile defenses, and the *Boston Phoenix* reported this in a story titled "Son of Star Wars."[96] After Republicans regained the White House in 2001, "Son of Star Wars"—a ground-based ballistic missile system much less ambitious than Reagan's laser satellites—nonetheless became

Secretary of Defense Donald Rumsfeld, with Spider Man and Captain America. U.S. Navy photograph by Photographer's Mate Second Class Daniel J. McLain, 4/28/05.

the most expensive item in the U.S. defense budget before the wars in Afghanistan and Iraq.[97] By 2008, the estimated cost of missile defense schemes exceeded $110 billion, including an estimated $350 million for unnecessary "projects that the Pentagon did not want."[98]

Who was it that first persuaded Reagan to publicly commit funds for an unproven "'Star Wars' concept"—particularly one based on untested directed energy weapons rather than the "off-the-shelf" missiles proposed by the Heritage Foundation's *High Frontier* study? And why? And what, if anything, has it achieved?

According to Jerry Pournelle: "SDI [the Strategic Defense Initiative missile defense program] happened because of meetings held at Larry [Niven]'s house. Those meetings had Poul Anderson, Greg Bear, Dean Ing, Steve Barnes, Gregory Benford—all science fiction writers. Heinlein was at these meetings, while he was alive."[99] Niven similarly recounts:

> In 1980, Jerry Pournelle talked me and Marilyn into hosting a gathering of the top minds in the space industry in an attempt to write a space program for the Reagan government, with goals, timetables, and costs. The Citizens Advisory Council for a National Space Policy met four times during the Reagan Administration, and twice since, for harrowing three-day weekends. Attendees have included spacecraft designers, businessmen, NASA

> personnel, astronauts, lawyers. Adding science fiction writers turns out to be stunningly effective. We can translate! We can force these guys to speak English.
>
> We've had some effect on the space program. SDI (Space Defense Initiative, or Star Wars) was drafted at our house in Tarzana.[100]

Pournelle's Citizens' Advisory Council on National Space Policy included "some fifty rocket scientists and the administrator of NASA," including serving military officers, scientists, representatives of companies with military contracts, astronauts Buzz Aldrin (who later became a science fiction writer), Fred Haise and Pete Conrad, as well as the science fiction writers named above.[101] (A version of this group later appeared in Niven and Pournelle's 1985 novel *Footfall*, in which science fiction writers—including thinly disguised versions of Heinlein, Joe Haldeman, and Niven and Pournelle themselves—are called on to defend the U.S. against an attack by aliens using orbiting weapons.[102]) Gregory Benford, invited to join the Council in 1982, described it as "a body which had direct lines to the White House, through the National Security Advisor. Teller, who would advocate orbital X-ray laser weapons powered by nuclear explosions, was 'in the loop.'"

> Pournelle dominated the Council meetings with his Tennessee charm, technoconservative ideas and sheer momentum. An oddly varied crew assembled: writers, industrial researchers, military and civilian experts on subjects ranging from artificial intelligence to rocketry. The Council met at the spacious home of science fiction author Larry Niven, a raucous bunch with feisty opinions. There was a bit of politics, but no overall bias. I am a registered Democrat, but that never came up. The men mostly talked hardedge tech, the women policy. Pournelle stirred the pot and turned up the heat. Amid the buffet meals, saunas and hot tubs, well-stocked open bar and myriad word processors, fancies simmered and ideas cooked, some emerging better than half-baked.... The more ambitious specialists talked of war stars—great bunkers in the sky, able to knock down fleets of missiles....[103]

Edward Teller, whose team at Lawrence Livermore laboratory was working on an orbital X-ray laser weapon powered by nuclear bombs, met with Reagan four times before the "Star Wars" speech, and was one of thirteen scientists invited to hear him make the speech. Though not a science fiction writer, Teller, the controversial "father of the hydrogen bomb," is widely considered to be one of the three most likely real-world models for the character of Dr. Strangelove (the others being Herman Kahn and Werner von Braun, though Kubrick asked Clarke to tell von Braun that he "wasn't getting at him." Clarke "never did, because (a) I didn't believe it (b) even if Stanley wasn't, Peter Sellers certainly was."[104])

Benford mentions being struck by the resemblance between the real and fictional scientists, particularly on seeing Teller's prosthetic foot. After fellow physicist and Hungarian Leo Szilard, also a science fiction writer, attempted to solve the Fermi paradox by suggesting that Hungarians were actually from Mars (Hungarian is not related to any of the languages spoken in surrounding countries), Teller, who reveled in his initials "E.T.," "enjoyed the myth" but "complained of indiscretion."[105] Peter Hagelstein also liked to cite *Star Wars* when explaining how Teller had persuaded him to work on the nuclear-pumped X-ray laser, saying, "The Force has a powerful effect on the weak mind."[106]

When Benford asked Teller about the influence science fiction had had on science and science policy, Teller told him of reading pulp magazines while at Los Alamos in the 1940s, "the quiet, distant 'fan' community among the scientists themselves," and their reactions to Cleve Cartmill's "Deadline" and Heinlein's "Solution Unsatisfactory": "For long range thinking I trust in the real visionaries—the ones I prefer to read, at least. The science fiction writers. I haf always liked Mr. Heinlein, Mr. Asimov, of course Mr. Clarke—they are much more important in the long run than any Secretary of Defense."[107] Benford remarks that "it was no surprise to me when Teller enlisted SF allies in his policy battles," but Teller may have been surprised by both Asimov's and Clarke's reactions to SDI. Like the Vietnam War and the invasion of Iraq, SDI divided rather than united the science fiction community. Spinrad, then president of the Science Fiction Writers of America, was not invited to join the Citizens' Advisory Council by Pournelle because of his "open and publicly expressed dislike of Reagan."[108] Fred Pohl described SDI as "a fuzzy-headed notion" and "not merely not a way of keeping us from nuclear attack and very likely the nuclear winter as consequence. Rather, it is the surest way I can think of to make both these things happen."[109]

Arthur C. Clarke attended one meeting of Pournelle's Council, and as Pournelle admits, "did not agree with what we were doing":

> Clarke had testified before Congress against the Strategic Defense Initiative, and regarded the pollution of space by weapons, even defensive ones, as a violation of his life's vision.
>
> Heinlein attacked as soon as Clarke settled into Larry Niven's living room. The conversation swirled around technical issues. Could SDI satellites be destroyed by putting into orbit a waiting flock of "smart rocks" (conventional explosives with small rockets attached)? Would SDI lead to further offensive weapons in space?
>
> Behind all this lay a clear clash of personalities. Clarke was taken aback. His old friend Heinlein regarded Clarke's statements as both wrong-headed and rude. Foreigners on our soil should step softly in discussions of our self-defense policies, he said. It was, at best, bad manners. Perhaps Clarke was guilty of "British arrogance."
>
> Clarke had not expected this level of feeling among old comrades. They had all believed in the High Church of Space, as one writer present put it. Surely getting away from the planet would diminish our rivalries?

Now each side regarded the other as betraying that vision, of imposing unwarranted assumptions on the future of mankind. It was a sad moment for many when Clarke said a quiet goodbye, slipped out and disappeared into his limousine, stunned.[110]

Heinlein was now defending a system he had once described as a "Buck Rogers weapon ... a bare possibility,"[111] but Clarke, whose "third law" had been quoted by Reagan in a speech defending SDI, went on to criticize the scheme in his "Scenario for a Civilized Planet" as "a pipe dream ... technological, financial and above all operational absurdity."[112]

Isaac Asimov, similarly, spoke against SDI on several occasions, saying that the best it could achieve was "a John Wayne standoff,"[113] and described its supporters as "the same ones who were in favor of the Vietnam war"[114]—with some justification, as Heinlein, Pournelle, Niven, Anderson and Ing, members of the Citizens' Advisory Council, had all been signatories to the pro-war advertisements in *The Magazine of Fantasy and Science Fiction* and *Galaxy* in 1968, whereas no member of the Council had signed the antiwar advertisement. Asimov also said of the scheme:

> If you render the Soviet Union helpless to attack you, does that mean you can then dictate to them exactly what they should do to become a good Republican country?
> If the Soviet Union can't penetrate Star Wars, all they have to say is "Go ahead. Bomb the hell out of us. You'll get destroyed by the nuclear winter that follows." Unless we're completely insane, we don't dare take the chance. So what the hell good is this whole damned thing?[115]

Asimov also said of Pournelle: "The reason Jerry Pournelle is for Star Wars is not because he's a science-fiction writer.... It's because according to him, he, among others, wrote the speech that Reagan gave in first advocating Star Wars. He's supporting himself."[116] Norman Spinrad has also accused Pournelle of writing the "Star Wars speech," and of "having Reagan, not accustomed to mouthing metaphors drawn from theoretical physics, referring to it as a 'quantum leap.'"[117]

Clarke says the speech was "composed, after innumerable drafts, by my friend George A. Keyworth,"[118] Reagan's science advisor, who had been recommended by Teller. Bova, however, quotes Keyworth as saying, "It was a top-down speech ... a speech that came from the President's heart. We were told what to do by the President."[119] Reiss says, "Most of the script was written by Pentagon officials,"[120] and attributes the missile defense content of the speech to Robert McFarlane. Reagan would later say of SDI, "It kind of amuses me that everybody is so sure I must have heard about it, that I never thought of it myself. The truth is, I did."[121] While former Reagan advisers have confirmed that the speech had several authors, they report that the section that mentions missile defense—known as "the insert"—was written by Reagan "and his top national security advisers," including Keyworth and McFarlane.[122]

Pournelle, who is not known for undue modesty—he has claimed to be one of the "unwitting inventors of the whole bloody computer revolution" and one of the two "most influential guys in the modern military, even though most of them never heard of us"[123]—hedges somewhat on the question of the authorship of the speech: "[A]lthough the Council wrote parts of Reagan's 1983 SDI speech, and provided much of the background for the policy, we certainly did not write the speech. Mr. Reagan was a better speech writer than any of those working for him. By far."[124]

As to the "Why?" of the idea and promotion of the Strategic Defense Initiative, it clearly represented different things to many people, including the drafters of Reagan's speech. While Reagan apparently believed that an effective missile shield could be built, many of his advisers did not, and many who supported the project may have had more cynical motives. Spinrad argues:

> Pournelle was dedicated to launching an age of human space exploration, as were most sci-fi people across the political spectrum. Many space lobby groups were trying to sell such a programme to the Reagan administration on naively idealistic grounds. But Pournelle had political experience and sophistication, an inside track directly to the National Security Council through [National Security Advisor Richard] Allen, and a rather Machiavellian strategy. NASA was just not going to get the budget to put humans in space in a big way. The biggest part of the funding would have to come from the military, who had a budget two orders of magnitude larger than NASA's and much more clout when it came to getting project financing through Congress. How did he expect to get the Pentagon to finance a major human presence in space? Why would they do it? Pournelle came up with an answer: to defend the United States from Soviet nuclear missiles.[125]

Pournelle, who "flatly describes the leaders in the Kremlin as 'a gang of aged homicidal maniacs,'"[126] counters, "We were not trying to boost space, we were trying to win the Cold War, and we were all agreed that the West ought to win the Cold War,"[127] though he goes on to admit, "We were agreed that it would be very good if low cost space came from that."[128]

Other science fiction writers have suggested that the "Star Wars" scheme would not only be harmless, but may have other benefits beyond that of protecting the U.S. from a missile attack. Bova expressed the hope that SDI was a possible beginning for an International Peacekeeping Force, a la his novel *Millennium*,[129] and Benford suggested that a "defensive arms race" would help move war off Earth, because "battle stations in orbit cannot ... be used offensively against any nation. At worst, they can destroy other satellites, but we already live with antisatellite weapons, so that doesn't alter the picture."[130]

Other SF writers were unconvinced by this, and some science fiction stories have featured "Star Wars" satellites causing various disasters. In the film *Robocop* (1987), the malfunctioning one "aboard the Ronald Reagan Memorial Strategic Defense Platform" starts a forest fire that kills hundreds and destroys the homes of former U.S. presidents,[131] and in David Brin's *The Postman* (1985) automatic SDI satellites are unfairly blamed for shooting down planes,[132] echoing Heinlein's argument in "The Last Days of the United States" that such a weapon system would spell the end of civil aviation.[133]

Clarke and Spinrad attributed less than benevolent motives to SDI's proponents in what Clarke termed the "military-scientific complex,"[134] whom he described as "'merchants of death' ... by comparison the Mafia and the drug cartels are minor nuisances."[135] Both argue that support for scientific support for SDI was sparked more by "easier money from the Pentagon"[136] than belief in the scheme, as does Franklin, who argues that its backers had "a public record of wanting to destroy arms control, maximize spending for the aerospace industry, cut funding for social programs, devastate the Soviet economy by forcing it into an uncontrolled arms race, neutralize the movement against nuclear weapons, and regain invincible U.S. nuclear supremacy."[137] Spinrad states:

> During the height of the SDI feeding frenzy, the aerospace industry feasted lavishly at the public trough thanks to the Pentagon's clout with Congress, securing billions of dollars for anti-missile missiles that didn't work, anti-missile lasers that didn't shoot down anything, and on uncounted and perhaps uncountable crackpot "studies."
> During the height of the frenzy, I was at an aerospace industry party in Vandenburg, California, the planned "Spaceport West" that was never to happen. The party was full of scientists and engineers discussing their proposals for SDI projects. I decided to tell what I thought would be a scientific joke. The "tachyon" is a theoretical particle that would travel faster than light and therefore move backwards in time instead of forward. However, it has never been generated or detected. "Why don't you build a tachyon beam weapon?" I suggested, expecting laughs. "You detect incoming missiles, and zap them on the pad before they're launched." There were no laughs. Two scientists got dreamy dollar-sign looks in their eyes instead.
> "Yes," said one of them, "we could probably get half a million to study that one." Things being what they were, it would not surprise me if they did.[138]

Kim Stanley Robinson, similarly, described SDI as an "obvious boondoggle,"[139] and this cynical analysis has been at least partly borne out by the more recent discovery that contractors were using the missile defense budget as a "personal cash machine."[140] Clarke, however, concedes that SDI might have helped "devastate the Soviet economy,"[141] as Franklin suggests it was intended to do, and "may have been technological nonsense—but brilliant politics. It wouldn't have fooled scientists like Roald Sagdeev for a moment, but it may have scared the hell out of some of his countrymen with more medals than brains."[142]

Russian attempts to match SDI spending is considered by many to have been a major factor in the collapse of the Soviet Union[143]—though others, including Mikhail Gorbachev and Frances FitzGerald, dispute this.[144] The Reagan administration had authorized economic warfare against the Soviet Union in 1982, before the "Star Wars" speech, including deliberately selling them software that blew up a major gas pipeline.[145] But was this actually a significant part of the plan? Were the animated videos the most important part of the real "Star Wars" scheme? Was its main purpose as a psychological, and thus economic, weapon?

There are precedents for this in science fiction, at least some of which would have been familiar to the Council. In Will Eisner's "The Atomic Bomb" (1940), America's enemies try to keep it out of World War II with the threat of a (nonexistent) "atomic bomb."[146] In the *Star Trek* episode "The Corbomite Maneuver" (1966), scripted by Jerry Sohl, the *Enterprise* wins a battle against a much larger starship by bluffing, with Kirk claiming that his ship's hull was made of a material that would reflect all energy weapons back at the firer.[147] In the 1970 film *The Rise and Rise of Michael Rimmer*, a British prime minister boasts that Britain now has new high-tech defenses, and hires model-makers to create special effects footage as a deterrent; that part of the defense budget is then channeled into bio-weapon research.[148] And Larry Niven's collection *Convergent Series* (1979) contains two stories on the same theme: in "Transfer of Power," a castle on the edge of the world is protected by what might be a dragon, or might only be a trick of the light, and in "Rotating Cylinders and the Possibility of Global Causality Violation," an interstellar empire at war deliberately leaks plans for a massive time machine, in the hope that their enemy will begin the research project and collapse in the process.[149]

Franklin, FitzGerald and Scheer, however, suggest that the "Star Wars" scheme was largely and perhaps primarily intended not to scare the Russians or other enemies, but to reassure American voters. Franklin describes this as the "fantasy of *security* ... with its evocation of isolationist yearnings for fortress America. This was precisely the metaphor used to describe the magic powers of atomic bombs during the years of the U.S. monopoly and hydrogen bombs prior to Sputnik."[150] FitzGerald quotes G. Simon Harak's analysis of the "Star Wars" speech in which he states that Reagan was demanding that scientists "restore America to the time before it became vulnerable to nuclear annihilation; the time before the bomb."[151] This is supported by Scheer, who quotes Reagan as saying, "It isn't a case of turning the clock back. Well, maybe in one sense, but then you have to go back beyond the fifties."[152] Keyworth echoes this, saying that if SDI were implemented, "We will have effectively turned the clock back 20 years."[153]

SDI and "Star Wars" may therefore have even more in common than "fascinating hardware and gorgeous explosions," or what Clarke has labeled "technoporn."[154] One of Lucas's draft synopses for *Star Wars* set it in the 23rd century,[155] and early posters for the film show that it was originally set in the year 3000, but Kramer, examining the "pre-release market research for *Star Wars*," reports:

> Researchers found that, when asked to give their response to the film's title and to judge a brief description of the film, potential movie-goers, with the exception of males under twenty-five, expressed their lack of interest in seeing it, because it was associated with the science fiction genre, combat and technology, aliens and robots, and was therefore expected to lack a human dimension. To overcome the resistance of older and female audiences, the advertising campaign that was developed from these tests emphasised the film's epic scope, its echoes of classic mythology, as well as the centrality of its human characters. The campaign characterised *Star Wars* as a science fiction fairytale; hence the tag line: "A long time ago in a galaxy far, far away..."[156]

If it was Reagan's intention—or even part of his intention—to take advantage of science fiction tropes made familiar by the *Star Wars* films to construct what Jackson and Nexon would term "an acceptable narrative"[157] that would reassure his audience (as well as himself)—did it work? Bradley Graham, military correspondent for the *Washington Post*, states: "A substantial number of Americans believe that we actually already have a missile defense system. You get answers like 'Well, we've seen it in the movies,' and you say to them, 'Well, but it's just not true,' and they say, 'It's gotta be true, it's just secret. They're not going to tell us about it.'"[158] In a 1996 article, however, Graham states, "Apart from the surprise expressed when people learn no such shield exists, there is little evidence to suggest the issue is catching on among voters."[159] FitzGerald adds that by 1999 "there had been so little discussion of the ABM program for several years that many consistent readers of the major newspapers did not know that the anti-missile program was still extant."[160]

Certainly not everyone has been impressed by the efforts of Reagan, Newt Gingrich, and the other believers in the "Star Wars" missile shield—even in Reagan's own Republican Party. At Reagan's meeting with Gorbachev in 1986, neoconservative Reagan adviser Richard Perle, who had dismissed SDI as "the product of millions of teenagers putting quarters into video machines,"[161] used Gorbachev's condition that SDI testing be restricted to laboratories to dissuade Reagan from signing a treaty Reagan had proposed that would have scrapped all U.S. and Soviet nuclear weapons by 1996.[162] In 1989, Reagan's successor George H.W. Bush chose vocal SDI critics as his advisers, with his first nominee for Secretary of Defense telling the Senate, "I don't believe we can devise an umbrella that can protect the entire American population from nuclear incineration."[163] His running mate, Vice-President Dan Quayle, described Reagan's "impenetrable shield that was going to be completely leak-proof" as "political jargon."[164] A 2003 article in *New Scientist* pointed out that even the limited attempts at a ground-based ballistic missile defense that *have* been built (the Patriot missile system) had scored no confirmed kills on missiles, but three on the aircraft of allied forces, causing Canadian, British and U.S. casualties.[165] And the commission investigating the September 11, 2001, attacks has even suggested that one of the reasons that the second Bush government did not do more to pre-empt the attack was that Secretary of Defense Donald Rumsfeld was "focused on other priorities, like missile defenses."[166]

George Lucas, who involuntarily gave the scheme its name, has expressed his displeasure by taking the names of Reagan and Newt Gingrich for one of the villains of his *Star Wars* prequel trilogy, "Nute Gunray"—a "cutthroat," "unscrupulous," "cowardly" "executive officer of the Trade Federation ... willing to commit any atrocity in pursuit of commercial gain and power."[167]

Reagan, however, may have genuinely believed that his "Star Wars" scheme was not a weapon or "death ray" but a purely defensive system that would save the world from nuclear war by providing the U.S. and its allies with an "impenetrable shield" (much as Debeney, after World War I, had hoped that the electrical waves would disperse poison gas). According to Gorbachev, Reagan had wondered aloud "if perhaps, in a previous life, he had been the inventor of the shield."[168] Consciously or otherwise, he may well have cast himself as another patriotic figure from science fiction comics, who wields an impenetrable shield and had also saved the U.S. from a nuclear attack: Captain America.

(Note: I have no evidence that President Reagan ever read comics, and while there had been a *Captain America* serial made in 1944, with Cap wielding a pistol rather than a shield, and a *Captain America* TV-movie screened in 1979, the first cinema representation of Marvel's shield-slinging Captain America—which featured Ronny Cox as a U.S. president who had been a comics fan and member of the Sentinels of Liberty—was not released until 1990, and went straight to video in the U.S. in 1992 without being screened at theaters.[169]

(Reagan did appear in *Captain America* comics in the late 1980s, however; in #344, August 1988, he was depicted as having been poisoned and transformed into a snake-fanged reptile who attempts to bludgeon Steve Rogers with a U.S. flag in the Oval Office until he sheds his scaly skin.[170] Compared to Captain America's foray into the Nixon White House in 1974's *Captain America and the Falcon* #176, though, this may be considered relatively benign.)

8. *Ender's Game*
Killing Machines

> Even the fattest, most stupid politician on Capitol Hill realizes that *Son of Star Wars* is going to be *useless* against the kind of problems America's *really* facing out there.—*Nick Fury,* The Ultimates[1]
>
> [F]ortunately there is now a vastly superior alternative to guns. Video war-games are much more fun; and nothing like so hard on the environment.—*Arthur C. Clarke*[2]
>
> You could kill them without a qualm, because they weren't alive *and* they were relentlessly out to get you. Nobody minds if you blow up machines.—*Orson Scott Card*[3]

The influence of *Star Wars* on the U.S. military was not limited to unsuccessful attempts to create a missile shield. Sharon Weinberger describes talks at DARPATech, DARPA's annual conference (which moved to Disneyland in 2002) as being "interspersed with piped-in theme music from *Star Wars*."[4] Jon Ronson describes a U.S. Army "black ops" experiment to produce "psychic soldiers," who describe themselves as "super soldiers" and "Jedi Warriors,"[5] running from 1978 to 1995, trying to replicate Obi-Wan Kenobi's ability to not be seen, as well as psychic spying, psychic healing, and walking through walls. DARPA projects have included "Luke's Binoculars," a prototype sensor based on one seen in *Star Wars*,[6] a handheld computer dubbed JEDI (Joint Expeditionary Digital Information),[7] and a prototype helicopter/fixed wing hybrid aircraft named the X-wing (Sikorsky S-72).[8] Seymour Hersch cites a Pentagon staffer comparing the American Enterprise Institute to "Darth Vader's mother ship," alluding to both *Star Wars* and *Close Encounters of the Third Kind* in 2002, nearly twenty-five years after those movies had premiered.[9] USAF pilots voted to name the F-16 the Viper after the fighter spaceships on television's 1970s *Star Wars* clone *Battlestar Galactica*.[10] The *Star Wars* films also started a wave of big-budget science fiction blockbuster movies, gave a boost to the special effects industry (including the use of computer graphics), and played a major role in popularizing "shoot-'em-up" video games, all of which have proved enormously useful to the U.S. military.

The first computer game to be mass-produced, and also the first video game shoot-'em-up, was *Spacewar!*, in which a wedge-shaped and a needle-shaped spaceship fire missiles at each other inside a gravity well. Created by MIT students Stephen Russell, Martin Graetz, and Wayne Witanen, inspired by the battles in E.E. "Doc" Smith's *Lensmen* space operas and funded by the Pentagon,[11] it was soon being played on "just about any research computer that had a programmable CRT."[12]

In 1971, an updated *Spacewar!*, *Galaxy Game*, became the first commercial video game. *Computer Space*, a version modified for one-person play, appeared in bars in 1972 (and briefly in the film *Soylent Green*).[13] Also in 1972, a *Star Trek* computer game appeared, which H. Bruce Franklin, in *Vietnam and Other American Fantasies*, credits with "spawning a whole breed that would soon inhabit every university's mainframe computer and then spread to personal computers in homes and offices throughout America. Known as "Star Trek" or just plain "Trek," the game allowed millions of Americans, mostly young, to command the *Enterprise* and wage thrilling electronic warfare against an unending host of battle cruisers from the evil Klingon empire."[14] *Trek* had certainly spread to the mainframe of my university by the time I was an undergraduate (though it was periodically removed because the people playing it were using up too much computer time), and the version I remember was not "unending": if not destroyed, you could be relieved of command for being too bloodthirsty and picking on poor defenseless Klingons (as nearly verbatim as my memory will allow).

In 1977, *Spacewar!* evolved yet again, into its most commercially successful version, *Space Wars*, with the "needle" transformed into an *Enterprise*-shaped starship. 1977 was also the year when *Star Wars* premiered, using computer animation in the briefing for the attack on the Death Star (the third use of computer animation in a feature film—the predecessors being the science fiction films *Westworld* and its sequel *Futureworld*), and depicting its characters playing a holographic computer game as well as using computerized gunsights that would be mimicked by the arcade games positioned in the cinema foyer.

Also in 1977, Orson Scott Card's first science fiction story was published—a novelette titled *Ender's Game*, which, like *Starship Troopers*, pitted human soldiers against an insect-like hive culture—though in Card's novelette, the "soldiers" are controlling the attack ships remotely, years before "drones" would begin to play a significant role in the U.S. military.

Whatever the similarities (and Card denied in 2002 ever having read Heinlein's novel, saying any resemblances were coincidental),[15] the differences are significant. In *Ender's Game*, the soldiers entrusted with defending Earth are prepubescent, having been drafted into Battle School at the age of six, and they are never physically present on the battlefield and thus not in any immediate danger. Instead, they believe they are fighting a tactical simulation against the commander who won the last battle against the Buggers: only after the "simulation" is over are they told that they have been giving orders to the crews of real spaceships in a real battle, and that the planet they destroyed was equally real. Eleven-year-old Ender has won a war and saved Earth—by unknowingly exterminating another intelligent species.

The novelette was nominated for the Hugo Award and reprinted in Jerry Pournelle's first *There Will Be War* anthology (1983) before Card published a novel-length version in 1985. Like *The Forever War*, this novel won both the Hugo and Nebula awards, but not everyone was delighted by it. Spinrad described it as "something of a guiltless military masturbatory fantasy,"[16] which is reminiscent of his description of "military wet-dream fantasies like *Starship Troopers*, Perry Rhodan, or *Star Wars*, in which righteous ingénues guiltlessly slaughter faceless gunfodder in alien or robot gook-suits."[17] This is a fairly accurate summary of Card's original novelette-length version of *Ender's Game* (1977), and all but the last chapter of the novel: not only is an entire alien race (except, we later learn, for one cocooned queen) wiped out like so many pixels in a video game, the closest the reader comes to seeing one is when Peter, Ender's sadistic brother, actually makes him wear a bugger mask so he has an excuse to beat him up as part of a game of "buggers and astronauts."[18] In the ending, however, Ender's righteousness and guiltlessness are at least dented. To quote Spinrad: "There is a nice little piece of moral judo when Ender, all unknowing, commits his act of genocide via game console. For while the adults laud him as savior and hero, he views the result of what he has been conned into doing as just that, genocide, and in the confused final chapter, we see him, in skimpy outline form, expiating his guilt."[19] Spinrad argues that "Ender has no plot-reason to feel guilty"[20]—as his superior officers tell him, "*We* aimed you. We're responsible. If there was something wrong, we did it."[21] But Ender realizes that his actions have resulted in genocide, as well as the death of human pilots who followed his orders; and despite believing, as Haldeman's Mandella ultimately does, that he has been "conned into" fighting the war, he nonetheless feels ashamed.[22] For Card, this is one of "the human attributes that make us adults—the acceptance of endless responsibility"[23]—just as many American soldiers (including noncombatant support staff) returning from the Vietnam War suffered "shame at having left their buddies behind"[24] and "an agony of guilt and torment."[25]

Spinrad attributes Card's book's success to the way it appeals to "the audience's fantasy images of themselves,"[26] the hero being "a sexually arrested adolescent who becomes the savior of the human race through his prowess at war-sports and video games."[27] The school's second-in-command, Major Anderson, tells his commander after the war is ended, "It's too deep for me, Graff. Give me the game. Nice, neat rules. Referees. Beginnings and endings. Winners and losers and then everybody goes home to their wives."[28]

This, arguably, is not only the image of war created by *Star Wars* as well as *Ender's Game* (which was assigned as reading at the Marine Corps University),[29] but the image created by media-managed post–Vietnam U.S. military operations in the 1981–1993 Reagan/Bush era, such as Urgent Fury, Just Cause, and Desert Storm. Beginnings and endings, winners and losers, a clearly defined enemy to be demonized (Darth Vader, Fidel Castro, Manuel Noriega, Saddam Hussein), and a clearly defined mission (destroying the Death Star, evacuating Americans from strife-torn Grenada, the arrest of Noriega and regime change in Panama, forcing Iraqi troops out of Kuwait) that enabled them to claim victory in short order and return in triumph. Plus a role for elite special forces, lots of "gleaming weaponry and beautiful explosions,"[30] (the documentary *The Panama Deception* argued that the "Operation Just Cause" was largely intended as a field test and sales pitch for new U.S. weapons systems such as the F-117 Stealth Fighter, first used in that attack),[31] but a minimum of visible blood or body parts. When the first Gulf War (Desert Storm) began in 1991, carefully regulated media coverage included what documentary-maker Ken Burns described as "the eerie video-game-like destruction of Iraqi targets as seen by bomber pilots' remote cameras ... with pounding new theme music specific to the war, and striking new sets and maps and graphics, suggesting that the war itself might be a wholly owned subsidiary of television, not the other way around."[32] Naomi Klein similarly referred to "the shameful era of the video game war," "The Space Invader Battlefield," and "the illusion of war without casualties." Describing the "sterile bomb's-eye-views of concrete targets," she asks, "Who was in these abstract polygons?"[33]

Spinrad's answer, presumably, would be "faceless gunfodder." (A rare attempt to give a face to the Iraqi victims—Kenneth Jarecke's photo of an Iraqi soldier burned to death in the cab of his truck—was not shown in America until after the war had ended.)[34]

This idea of science fictional antagonists as "faceless gunfodder in alien or robot gook-suits" in movies, television and comics pre-dates *Star Wars Episode IV: A New Hope*, and was often done for economic or other practical (rather than ideological) reasons. The BBC series *Doctor Who* had long made use of the fact that using apparently identical robots or cyborgs meant that you could create the illusion of large invading armies using only a small group of costumed extras and a little trickery. George Lucas similarly used two masked actors to portray an entire robotic police force in the original *THX1138* (1971), and when making *Star Wars Episode IV: A New Hope*, not only recycled the stormtrooper costumes, but was able to have a smaller cast play multiple roles by donning different masks for some scenes as well as appearing unmasked to play the heroic rebels.[35] Comic illustrators and animators similarly find it easier to be able to draw large numbers of masked or helmeted characters than to make all of them individual—especially when using computer software to replicate images.

In video games as well, simpler images and simpler animation were less demanding of computer memory—a fact Card describes as "one of the practical reasons for using science fictional motifs in those early games. The graphics were unsophisticated and abstract. It was difficult to make objects that looked like anything. *Space Invaders* was a shooting gallery. But the ducks you could draw on the screen were pretty pathetic. However, aliens or spaceships or robots—whatever the descending "invaders" were supposed to be, because they were science fictional, they didn't have to look like anything in the known universe."[36] *Space Invaders* was designed by Tomohiro Nishikado, who had previously designed the first computerized arcade game based on a combat flight simulator, *Interceptor* (1975) and the first computer game to depict humans in a shoot-out, *Western Gun* (1975).[37]

> In Nishikado's first version of the game, the player shot down airplanes. But the vehicle movements appeared jittery, leading the designer to settle on human opponents. Taito's president balked when he saw the idea, and banned the use of human targets. A new idea came to Nishikado: "In Japan, we were starting to hear about the popularity of 'Star Wars,'" he said. "I decided to make the targets aliens, as a way to capitalize on the budding space boom." Drawing inspiration from the buglike aliens in H.G. Wells's novel *The War of the Worlds*, a book Nishikado loved as a child, he began to draw Martian enemies using simple pixel patterns.[38]

The U.S. military had been using flight simulators for training pilots since 1934, with the simulators becoming increasingly computerized in the 1960s and later. According to Platoni, the U.S. began buying and modifying commercial video games as training aids in 1980.[39] One of these was Atari's *Battlezone*, adapted as *Bradley Trainer* for crews for the Bradley

Fighting Vehicle—an arrangement which *Battlezone* designer Ed Rotberg hated, arguing, "Many of us engineers had the option to go to work for companies doing military contracting, and we consciously chose to work at a company that was not so involved."[40] (Perhaps coincidentally, 1980 also saw the release of *B-1 Nuclear Bomber*, a flight simulator in which the player bombs Moscow in 1991; *Computer Conflict*, in which players attacked or defended Soviet Russian towns; and *Missile Command*, in which the player uses ground-based anti-ballistic missile batteries to intercept bombs aimed at six cities. As with many games of the era, the only "victory" possible in *Missile Command* was racking up a higher point score for delaying your defeat—in this case, the inevitable nuking of the targets. The game reportedly gave its creator, Dave Theurer, who lived within earshot of a USAF base, years of nightmares about nuclear attack.[41]) The U.S. Army's own magazine, *Soldiers*, proclaimed that "video games have a future in the Army" in 1982.[42] This was endorsed by Ronald Reagan in August 1983, when he remarked: "I recently learned something quite interesting about video games. Many young people have developed incredible hand, eye and brain coordination in playing these games. The Air Force believes these kids will be our outstanding pilots should they fly our jets."[43]

By 1997, computer graphics had progressed to a level where the gun-fodder no longer needed to remain faceless—though convincing simulations of human facial expressions remained elusive. That year, the USMC modified the commercially available "first-person shooter" game *Doom* to make the multiplayer *Marine Doom*, then made it available for download.[44] This was followed by computer games designed by the U.S. military as recruitment tools, including "The Official Army Game," *America's Army*— which Canadian band Propagandhi's song "America's Army" describes as a "real-life *Ender's Game*"[45]—and its successor *Future Force Company Commander*, set in the then near-future 2015.[46] Another recent example is *Rover*, designed to train handlers of sniffer dogs that help search for improvised explosive devices (IEDs)[47]—not the sort of skill you want to have to learn in the field.

As well as using video games for training, as a remarkably cost-effective recruiting tool, and more recently for treating PTSD,[48] the U.S. military also launched Operation: Live Connections, enabling soldiers stationed overseas to play online X-Box games such as *Crimson Skies* (a game of aerial militias in an alternate balkanized North America) with family and friends at home in an attempt to boost morale.[49] Bangert quotes soldiers stationed in Baghdad saying, "Some of these kids, they'll go out and fight all day, and they'll come back and play these goofy space-age electronic war games all night," and "Half my deployment I've spent playing *Halo 2*."[50] In an ironic twist, the Department of Defense had to intercede to stop Operation Start Up, a group working as part of their "America Supports You" program, from including a video game in which Christian soldiers fighting at Armageddon must either convert or kill the forces of the Antichrist, in care packages sent to soldiers serving in Iraq.[51]

◆ ◆ ◆

Early in the morning of November 9, 1979, NORAD phoned President Carter's National Security Advisor Zbigniew Brzezinski to inform him that the Soviet Union had launched 250 missiles at the U.S. A second call said they were now tracking 2200 inbound missiles. Brzezinski later told biographer Andrezj Lubowski that he didn't wake his wife or President Carter, thinking that either it was a false alarm or that it was too late to do anything other than retaliate: "I knew that if it were true, then within about half an hour I, and my loved ones, and Washington, and the majority of America would cease to exist. I wanted to be sure that we'd have company."[52]

Jets were scrambled in case the attack was real, but the next call from NORAD reported that none of their other tracking systems were detecting the missiles, suggesting that it was a false alarm. It was discovered that a computer simulation of a nuclear attack "had been fed through NORAD's system." NORAD later had a separate facility built offsite for running simulations without the risk of having them feed into their detection network.[53] A similar computer error occurred in the Soviet Union in September 1983, a few months after the release of the movie *WarGames* (later made into a computer game).

In *WarGames*, a young hacker looking for computer games doesn't realize that his online opponent is an artificial intelligence that has been installed at SAC to override human officers who refuse to turn the keys to launch their missiles in the event of a perceived attack.[54] The movie was a huge commercial and critical success, and reflected popular unease about the U.S. military's perceived over-reliance on computers and their capacity to deal a devastating attack based on false data, unchecked by human operators because of the need to respond faster than human reflexes or decision-making processes. In 1984, this would inspire another apparently interminable SF saga, when Arnold Schwarzenegger first appeared as the Terminator—following the orders of Skynet, the U.S. military supercomputer that decided that humans were a threat to its continued existence and used the automated factories and nuclear weapons at its disposal to attempt to eliminate this human menace.[55]

The idea of a new creation killing its inventor and/or its family was hardly new: the story of Icarus, who failed to follow the safety precautions or flight plan dictated by his father Daedalus when using his prototype man-powered flying machine, is many centuries older even than that of Frankenstein. The idea that a military force could be weakened or even destroyed by its overreliance on untried technology was also a well-worn science fiction trope: a classic example is Arthur C. Clarke's "Superiority" (1951), based loosely on the story of Wernher von Braun and his military commander General Walter Dornberger.[56] In Kurt Vonnegut's Hugo-nominated *Cat's Cradle* (1963), a USMC general asks a nuclear physicist to invent something small so that Marines will no longer have to trudge through mud: the physicist creates a tiny amount of ice-nine, an allotrope of water that melts at 45.8 degrees Celsius (114.4 Fahrenheit) and acts as a "seed," freezing any water that it contacts: at the end of the novel, all of Earth's oceans, rivers and groundwater have frozen, dooming everyone on the planet.[57]

Handing over control of a war machine and/or nuclear weapons to a computer also had precedents in science fiction: among the many computers destroyed by *Star Trek*'s Captain Kirk was the M-5, given direct control of the *Enterprise* in the episode "The Ultimate Computer." M-5, which can think and act faster than humans, vaporizes a redshirt who tries to disconnect it from its power source, and uses the *Enterprise*'s weapons at full power to attack Federation starships and kill hundreds in what was meant to be a nonlethal wargame. Kirk persuades M-5 to shut itself down, pointing out that it has committed murder, for which the penalty is death—but M-5 has also disabled intership communications, making it impossible to tell the commander of the attacking ships what has happened. Kirk orders the shields be lowered, gambling that—unlike a computer—Commodore Wesley is too humane to fire on a ship that appears dead.[58]

It was already becoming clear to many that the problem of computerized warfare, though born of science fiction, would have to be addressed in the 20th century rather than waiting for the 23rd. In the 1970 movie *Colossus: The Forbin Project*, based on D.F. Jones's 1966 novel and directed by former *Star Trek* and *The Invaders* director Joseph Sargent, the supercomputer Colossus is part of a doomsday machine, effectively invulnerable. Learning that it has a Soviet counterpart, Guardian, Colossus demands a communication link, and the two supercomputers become allies: they use nuclear blackmail to restore the link when it is severed, and order the house arrest and constant surveillance of Forbin, Colossus's designer; the assassination of Guardian's creator; the targeting of both sides' missiles at countries not already under their control; and the building of an even larger computer. The U.S. and Soviet military tries to disarm the computers by replacing the warheads with dummies under the pretense of routine maintenance, but Colossus/Guardian sees through the ruse and detonates two bombs in the silos, killing the technicians. The computer justifies its actions, saying: "I bring you peace. It may be the peace of plenty and content or the peace of unburied death. The choice is yours: Obey me and live, or disobey and die. The object in constructing me was to prevent war. This object is attained. I will not permit war. It is wasteful and pointless. An invariable rule of humanity is that man is his own worst enemy."[59]

The same rationale is given by one of the robots in *Futureworld* (1974), in which the computer controlling the robotic theme park—unable to stage the same sort of display of power as Colossus or Klaatu—replaces a Russian general and a Japanese politician with robotic duplicates, with the stated aim of preventing humans from destroying the planet.[60] Most depictions of computers that controlled weapons of mass destruction, though, argued that this was probably a bad idea, as in *WarGames* or the *Terminator* franchise. In *Dark Star* (1974), Lieutenant Doolittle, in command of a starship crew that owes more to *Dr. Strangelove* than *Star Trek* or *2001* ("Don't give me any of that intelligent life crap, just give me something I can blow up"), has to reason with a smart bomb that, while single-minded, may be more intelligent than he is.[61] In *The Andromeda Strain* (1971), directed by Robert Wise and based on a 1969 novel by Michael Crichton, a scientist in a secret U.S. military facility has to run the gauntlet of an automated defense system to deactivate the nuclear self-destruct that will release a rapidly-mutating pathogen into the world.

Significantly, in *The Andromeda Strain*, as in *Cat's Cradle* and many 1950s monster movies, the problem is one of the military's own making: the (civilian) scientists called in after the disease has wiped out all but two inhabitants of a small town are horrified to discover that the Project Scoop space probe that brought the Andromeda microorganism to Earth was a military project to gather pathogens that would be suitable for use as bioweapons (an idea that would be repeated with a rather larger lifeform in the *Alien* franchise). The crisis at the end of the novel and film is caused because Project Scoop has gone ahead before the construction of the containment facility is complete—meaning that the override controls for the automatic self-destruct, which can only be operated by one keyholder, have not yet been installed in the section where the keyholder was working.[62]

Automated weapon systems that used more conventional munitions also made their appearance in science fiction, both before and after their adoption by the U.S. military. Joe Haldeman's *The Forever War* describes a "gunner" whose job is to prevent an automated bevawatt laser from firing: "If he let go, it would automatically aim for any moving aerial object and fire at will."[63] The rationale for such systems is that human reflexes are too slow to be as effective at targeting fast-moving missiles, but possibly better at telling friend from foe, and should therefore still be able to override these weapons. In *Forever Peace* (1997), Haldeman describes an asymmetrical war on 21st century Earth where the U.S. military relies heavily on "soldierboys," powerful remotely-controlled humanoid machines, the narrator pointing out:

> They didn't use actual robots, for several reasons. One was that they could be captured and used against you; if the enemy did capture a soldierboy, they would just have an expensive piece of junk. None had ever been captured intact, though; they self-destruct impressively.
>
> Another problem with robots was autonomy: the machine has to be able to function on its own if communications are cut off. The image, as well as the reality, of a heavily armed machine making spot combat decisions was not something any army wanted to deal with.[64]

This image of a "heavily armed machine making spot combat decisions" featured in the original *RoboCop* (1987), when the prototype police robot ED 209 fails to acknowledge that a test subject has dropped his weapon and messily blows him away with built-in autocannons. The ED 209 project is shelved in favor of the cyborg Robocop, leading the executive in charge of the project to complain, "I had a guaranteed military sale with ED 209—renovation program, spare parts for twenty-five years.... Who cares if it worked or not?"[65] (*RoboCop* had earlier featured another jab at U.S. defense spending on inadequately tested weapons projects with its news story about a malfunctioning laser on the Ronald Reagan Memorial Strategic Defense Platform.) The U.S. military would actually have that image problem in the real world, after automated Patriot missile systems in Iraq caused three "friendly fire" incidents in a two-week period in March and April 2003 (though the large number of "friendly fire" casualties inflicted by U.S. servicemen—an estimated 24 percent of U.S. casualties in the 1991 Gulf War—suggests that humans are also fallible when it comes to telling friend from foe). Haldeman's science-fictional solution to this is "an extension of the Powell Doctrine to an absurd degree," or at least one aspect of it—"minimum troop loss with maximum high-tech force" in the form of the soldierboys.[66] (The other, equally important aspects of the Powell Doctrine—"war only as a last resort, backed by strong public support and only undertaken with a well defined national interest at stake. It should be executed with overwhelming force and a clear exit strategy"— are largely ignored in *Forever Peace*, and, Haldeman argues, in both Iraq Wars.) While this strategy does reduce casualties on the U.S. side and the technology involved does lead to a more peaceful world (albeit in unexpected ways), the novel also depicts the army choosing sociopaths for the "hunter/killer" groups, while the villain, General Blaisdell, is the undersecretary of DARPA as well as being an apocalyptic religious fanatic intent on destroying the world.[67]

This idea that near-future U.S. military R&D projects and prototypes might constitute a threat to U.S. military personnel and/or American civilians, and possibly even to life on Earth, was not limited to fear of computerized weapon systems. In 1987, Captain America was led into conflict with the U.S. Army itself, as a drug-crazed gun-toting "Nuke," the latest in the series of mostly short-lived super-soldiers, was transported from Central America to New York on the orders of a corrupt army general.[68] In this story (by Frank Miller, collected under the title "Born Again"), Captain America is shown battling American soldiers as he fights his way into a maximum security military installation to access the computer. There, he learns that Project Rebirth was not abandoned: far from being "the only super-soldier there will ever be!,"[69] he is merely the first (and by the end of the story, the only) subject to have survived for any length of time after the experimental procedures. While Nazis and Russians had previously been shown attempting to mass-produce their own series of super-soldiers, and a Marvel *The Punisher/The 'Nam* crossover would later show a sadistic Vietnamese surgeon, Dr. Ng, trying to do the same,[70] this was the first of several stories depicting U.S. military researchers prepared to perform potentially lethal experiments on soldiers in an attempt to create the ultimate fighting man.

(*The 'Nam* was Marvel's attempt to depict the Vietnam War as seen by U.S. soldiers, and was initially written by Vietnam vet Doug Murray. Declining sales in the early '90s moved Marvel to introduce the Punisher as a character in Issue #52, bringing the story into the Marvel superhero line.)

In 2002, Robert Morales rewrote the history of Captain America in *Truth: Red, White and Black*, in which it was revealed that Steve Rogers was not even the *first* subject of Project Super Soldier: before him, two battalions of African American draftees had been used as guinea pigs in a pre-war series of often lethal experiments before Reinstein and his military supervisors ruled that the formula was safe enough to be given to a white man. Black soldiers not suitable as experimental subjects were gunned down by their own side: their next of kin, and those of the subjects, were told that they'd died in an explosives accident. The story was inspired by the Tuskegee syphilis experiment and an urban legend that "1200 black soldiers from the 364th Infantry Regiment at Camp Van Dorn, Mississippi, were executed en masse for being agitators."[71]

In the Marvel comic *The Ultimates* (2003), a reboot of original Marvel superhero origin stories, Dr. Robert Banner's and Dr. Henry Pym's attempts to recreate the super-soldier formula that turned Steve Rogers into Captain America (in this storyline, revived from cryogenic suspension in his iceberg in 2001, not 1965) are responsible for turning Banner into the Hulk, sending him on a rampage that kills dozens of people, and Pym into a super-powered vicious wife-beater.[72] In recent films of Marvel Comics' *Spider-Man* (2002), *Hulk* (2003), *X-Men 2* (2003), *The Incredible Hulk* (2008), *Iron Man* (2008), *X-Men Origins: Wolverine* (2009) and *Iron Man 2* (2009)—the super-powered threats are all created by researchers working for defense industries, which is in most cases a departure from the origin stories from the comics. Stan Lee had originally imagined the Green Goblin in 1964 as a mythological demon released from an Egyptian tomb, before Steve Ditko turned him into a human villain—later revealed to be industrialist Norman Osborn, who has drunk a secret formula in the hope of taking over New York's criminal underworld. In the 2002 film *Spider-man*, Dr. Norman Osborn has developed a heavily armed one-man flying platform, powerful new hand grenades, "human performance enhancers," and green body armor (with, inexplicably, a metallic fright mask for the face) to military specifications, but the U.S. Army general who has been given oversight of the project by his predecessor threatens to pull the funding and give it to a rival company unless Osborn can have the "performance enhancers" tested on humans in two weeks. Osborn tests the "performance enhancer" on himself, and is sent insane. At a test of the competition's equipment, the general says, "Nothing would give me more pleasure than to put Norman Osborn out of business," suggesting that military decisions on R&D funding are based on personal preferences rather than concerns about the safety or effectiveness of the equipment. Moments later, Osborn as the Green Goblin destroys the rival's flying power-armor with one shot before killing the general.[73]

In *Hulk* (2003) and *The Incredible Hulk* (2008), the uncontrollable Hulk and his equally destructive enemy the Abomination both result from U.S. Army attempts to recreate the "super-soldier" formula: Blonsky, the Abomination, was a KGB agent in the comics, but in the movie, he's a Russian-born Royal Marine serving with the U.S. Army under General

Ross, given his powers in an attempt to make him strong enough to defeat the Hulk.[74] *In X-Men Origins: Wolverine* (2009) similarly, U.S. Army Major (later Colonel) William Stryker is responsible for creating weaponized humans Wolverine and Deadpool; in *X-Men 2* (2002) and *X-Men* he is responsible for the creation of the murderous Lady Deathstrike, as well as a machine he intends to use to kill all the mutated humans on Earth, but which is taken over and turned against all *non*-mutated humans.[75] The character of Stryker in the original 1982 graphic novel is not a military man but a televangelist.[76]

The military fares rather better in the *Iron Man* movie franchise, where the origin story has been updated and Tony Stark is injured and held hostage by an Afghan warlord, and builds his first Iron Man battlesuit while trapped in his cave complex. USAF Colonel Rhodes serves as Stark's military liaison, and in the sequels, he dons an older suit of Iron Man armor and becomes War Machine, later re-named Iron Patriot—but in both *Iron Man* and *Iron Man 2*, weapons made by contractors for the U.S. military are used against innocent civilians.[77] It should be noted, though, that while Marvel movies seem to have a low opinion of generals and an ambivalent attitude towards colonels, ranks of captain and below have been treated more sympathetically.

The theme of using technology to create "super-soldiers" by enhancing human beings—some of them unwitting or unwilling experimental subjects—rather than their equipment, was also used in David Brin's novel *The Postman* (1987), in which two methods were found of enhancing the strength of American soldiers,[78] and the movie and TV series *Universal Soldier* (1992–1998), in which the government revives and modifies the bodies of Vietnam KIAs as super-soldiers—one of them a grinning murderous psychopath who collects the ears of his victims, and who kills the colonel commanding the team when their mission is canceled.[79] The theme became increasingly popular after 1995, when documents showing the nature of experiments secretly performed on American subjects from 1944 to 1974, including many at the Pentagon's behest, were declassified.

It was also used in several episodes of *The X-Files*, where it was revealed that the U.S. military had been involved in a long-running project to create super-soldiers, starting with their involvement in Operation Paperclip (1945–1990) and similar projects, repatriating Nazi scientists to the USA and allowing them to continue their research. In the episode "Paper Clip," Mulder discovers that ex–Nazi scientist Victor Klemper (based on Dr. Hubertus Strughold) has been working on producing hybrid human-alien super-soldiers.[80] Later that season, the episode "731" (named after the unit of the World War II Imperial Japanese Army that experimented on humans, some of whose researchers were also given immunity in exchange for working on biowarfare projects in the USA) gave one of the best rationales for the creation of super-soldiers:

> RED-HAIRED MAN: "Ask yourself, friend, what would be more valuable than Star Wars? What would be more valuable than the atomic bomb? Or the most advanced biological weapons?"
> MULDER: "A standing army immune to the effect of those weapons."[81]

In 2003, the U.S. Air Force was revealed to have issued pilots amphetamine "Go pills"—the "reds" taken by Daredevil's opponent Nuke—to keep them alert: after this practice was blamed by two pilots for their firing a laser-guided bomb at Canadian allies in 2002, DARPA announced that it was studying other ways of producing an "Extended Performance War Fighter" who would be resistant to sleep deprivation, including searching for the genes that enabled dolphins to "keep at least part of their brains awake," and "a plan to 'zap' their brains with an electro-magnetic energy called TMS." One scientist on the project, Dr. Stern, explained: "I am convinced that we can help the Pentagon. I have identified the parts of the brain that seem to control the response to sleep deprivation, and we have the technology to stimulate that part to improve the resistance to lack of sleep. The generals want a man who is awake and alert for up to a week. We think we can actually do that."[82] Whether or not it was intended as a deliberate allusion, the phrase "We have the technology" was made popular by the science fiction TV show *The Six Million Dollar Man*, in which bionics were used to enhance an American military test pilot who had lost three limbs and an eye (shades of Poe's "The Man Who Was Used Up"!), and who was then recruited as a spy.[83]

♦ ♦ ♦

In 1995, the TV series *Space: Above and Beyond* depicted a fighter squadron of the U.S. Marine Corps fighting an interstellar war in 2063 against the alien Chigs as well as the Silicates—rebellious human-made Ais, who had been defeated on Earth before the Chig attacks gave the surviving Silicates a chance to form an alliance and strike back. Created by Glen Morgan and James Wong, who had written 14 episodes of *The X-Files*, the series featured a similar emphasis on conspiracies and genetically engineered soldiers—though the "in vitro" soldiers, created to fight the Silicates, are largely treated as pariahs after the war with the Silicates has ended, especially after an in vitro assassinates the UN Secretary General. "Influenced" by Haldeman's *The Forever War*[84] as well as historical war fiction, the show was intended to last five seasons but was canceled after only one. Unlike most other well-known interstellar military action-adventure series, it assumed that current U.S. military units would retain their identity and traditions intact while operating away from Earth, rather than being absorbed into a larger body such as *The Forever War*'s UNEF, *Star Trek*'s Starfleet, or *Babylon 5*'s EarthForce. It was made without assistance from the U.S. military, though some scenes for the pilot were filmed on an RAAF airbase in Australia.

Like *Starship Troopers* (which Wong had read "a long time ago" and Morgan never),[85] the pilot episode begins with recruits signing up in peacetime, being insulted by their sergeant major (played by Ronald Lee Ermey, a former USMC gunnery sergeant who had played essentially the same role in Kubrick's *Full Metal Jacket*) and superior officers (one of whom says of a recruit, "until she graduates, she's slime"), with war being declared while they are still in training. The sergeant major responds to the announcement by shouting, "We are at war. Hoo-rah! War is what Marines pray for!"[86]

The continuing characters, a USMC 58th Fighter Squadron, are multi-ethnic but identifiably American, though the three Caucasian leads are given the most detailed backgrounds: West has signed up in the hope of reuniting with his girlfriend on an offworld colony; Vansen is the daughter of two Marines killed by Silicates in the AI War; Hawkes is an in vitro given the choice of joining the military or going to jail for manslaughter. Wang is made more overtly American by his obsession with American football and Wrigley Field.

A flashback in the episode "Who Monitors the Birds?" includes an indoctrination session for "in vitros," with powerpoint-style slides reading, "To be monitored is to be free." "Spared the agony of decision." "Released from the burden of choice." "In vitros need only react." "To react how America wants you to react." "America loves you." "One day"/"You will return her love." "And defeat those"/"Trying to harm her." "Terrorists." "Silicates." "Subversives." The lesson starts with a line reminiscent of the opening of *The Forever War*, "There are 687 methods"/"of killing a human being."[87]

For the most part, the show followed the "reset button" format of most U.S. TV series of the time, with episodes designed to be repeatable in any sequence: this meant that the continuing characters survived and the status quo remained largely unchanged, at least until the season finale, and casualties were limited to characters played by guest actors. However, there were a few subplots that depicted Marines having to deal with moral and psychological issues. In episode nine, "Choice or Chance," Lieutenant Wang is broken down by torture and interrogation by a Silicate and forced to confess to war crimes such as the bombing of civilian targets, for which he feels shame.[88] There are no apparent repercussions from this confession, suggesting that it has not been broadcast, but when a Silicate of the same model (played by the same actor in slightly different makeup) is captured in episode 15, "The Angriest Angel," it is tortured to death during an interrogation by the squadron's CO, despite Wang's protests.[89] In episode 17, "Pearly," Wang is captured by yet another Silicate of the same model, who tells him that if he removes a power cell from the armored personnel carrier that is transporting the squadron and members of the U.S. 7th Cavalry (Custer's old unit), the recording of his confession will be deleted: "Your mistake, Wang Paul, will never have taken place. If you don't, I promise, I will play the disc loud and clear for your fellow Marines, your family, and all of your friends back home."

Wang takes the cell and allows an eccentric English officer to be blamed; when the truth is discovered, he explains his actions to the squadron.

> HAWKES: Those AIs tortured you, man. What else could you do?
> WANG: I could've let 'em kill me!
> VANSEN: Paul, no one ever believes those confessions. Everyone knows that you're not a war criminal.
> WANG: That's not the point of it! The point is to show that they can break your spirit. Why couldn't my body have broken down before my soul? They may as well have cut off a hand or a leg, because they took something from me I can never get back. It so obsessed me, so possessed me, that when the chance arose to erase it without anyone knowing, I took it. I swear, I never, never intended to give them the cell; I just wanted the optical disc with the confession. I thought I could get back what they took. I needed it back, even if I was risking your lives. Lives that mean more to me than … than my own.

Wang redeems himself with his squadron by leaving the APC to shoot a Chig hovertank with a light anti-tank weapon; the Englishman kills the Silicate and retrieves the optical disc.[90]

In "Stay With the Dead," West is diagnosed as suffering PTSD and narrowly escapes being lobotomized, the treatment "approved by the V.A."; the episode also shows the marines forced to adopt the Chigs' tactics to survive.

> VANSEN: So we play by their rules. They ambush our Red Cross, they booby-trap our wounded; I say we give it right back to them. We use the 61st as bait.
> WEST: Bait? The bodies of Marines?
> VANSEN: There are no rules here.
> WEST: Yes! Our rules! The rules that keep us human!

WANG: We're not fighting humans.
HAWKES: Yeah. When this all plays out, there's going to be nobody who says who's right and who's wrong. It's going to be who stayed alive.
WEST: So what do you say we do?
VANSEN: Fire with fire. We put the 61st in our uniforms, just in case the Chigs know. We put out a distress call that the Chigs will monitor. When they come in to ambush us, we have the perimeter planted with motion-sensory claymore mines; we ambush them.
WEST: Desecrate our dead?
VANSEN: If that's what it takes.
WEST: The Marines have always gone back for their dead! This goes against everything we stand for![91]

In episode 19, "R&R," the squadron is shown suffering from exhaustion that results in fights and near-fatal mistakes, and it's revealed that the medics are issuing amphetamines to pilots, leading to Hawkes becoming addicted and having to undergo detoxification.[92]

In episode 21, "Sugar Dirt," 25,000 troops, including the 58th Squadron, are abandoned for more than two months behind enemy lines when their air support is needed for an attack on a strategically more important planet. The Squadron's CO, Lieutenant Colonel McQueen, a military historian, agrees with this decision, but acknowledges that "the right thing to do is rarely the easiest," and asks permission to join the troops on the ground. His superior, Commodore Ross, counters, "Right now, our people on that planet don't have the luxury of time to consider right or wrong." He orders the colonel to stay with the ship and tells the squadron, "You are encouraged, but not so ordered, to continue to engage the enemy; if, however, your positions become untenable, you are authorized to surrender." When the fleet returns to collect the approximately 2,000 survivors of the original 25,000, who have been reduced to licking soil for traces of sugar from an exploded supply drop, Ross tells them, "As a commander, I feel no need to explain my actions, but as a man, as a human being, I must share my emotions; I have never been more ashamed of myself."[93]

The same year, the *Babylon 5* episode "Gropos" gave an equally unglamorous depiction of military life, after 25,000 Earth Force marines stop at the station—a force intended for a surprise attack on an alien world. For security reasons, the marines have been lied to, and have no idea that they're going into combat, much less besieging a fortress reputed to be a deathtrap. Their commanding officer is the father of the station's chief medical officer, who accuses him of "constantly trying to murder" aliens. One of the "gropos" tells the station's security chief, "I'm a ground pounder. I'm cleaning latrines one day, the next I might be up to my hips in blood, hoping that I don't hear the round that takes me out." While the "ground pounders" are Earth Force, they are referred to as "jarheads," a nickname for U.S. Marines. At the end of the episode, the camera pans over a pile of bodies: apart from the general, all of the soldiers shown interacting with the station staff have been killed.[94]

These episodes suggest that even in the science fiction of the 1990s, before the wars in Afghanistan and Iraq, the image of American troops in combat could, as Galbreath suggests, shift from one of heroes to one of victims. In 1998, the film of *Starship Troopers*, usually seen more as another response to (or satire of) Heinlein's novel rather than a faithful adaptation, showed that Earth's military could still be portrayed as villains.

Director Paul Verhoeven, who was unable to finish reading Heinlein's novel, saw the script as showing "how war makes fascists of us all."[95] Verhoeven had childhood memories of both the Nazi occupation of the Netherlands and seeing a neighboring street bombed in an Allied "friendly fire" incident, and had started his career in 1965 making *The Marine Corps* for the Royal Dutch Navy as part of his compulsory military service.[96] His film of *Starship Troopers* quotes Heinlein selectively, but broadly follows the structure of his novel: opening with a battle scene, then going back to Johnny Rico's History and Moral Philosophy Class, his enlisting with the Federal Service, his days at boot camp, and his rise to the rank of lieutenant. The divergences are more significant: the Mobile Infantry is now mixed-gender and lacks the face-concealing battlesuits, being equipped with gear not very different from that of contemporary American forces (except for the presence of the grenade-sized tactical nukes described in the book); Dizzy Flores is female; Johnny Rico enlists primarily to impress Carmen (screenwriter Neumeier comments "the price of sex is to join the military")[97]; Lt. Col. Dubois and Lieutenant Racszak have been conflated; Johnny Rico's father dies rather than joining the MI; the only war is against the Bugs (there is no mention of the humanoid Skinnies); and, most notoriously, while the soldiers are played by American actors, the dress uniforms of the officers are clearly derived from Nazi regalia. The recruiting ads, similarly, satirize American recruiting films; the film opens with an ad with the title "Why We Fight," but the cinematography mimics Leni Riefenstahl as much as Howard Hawks.[98]

Unsurprisingly, the film received no assistance from the Pentagon, though retired and much-decorated USMC Captain Dale Dye, who had played USMC Major Colquitt in *Space: Above and Beyond*, served as technical advisor and made a cameo appearance as a general.

More faithful in spirit to Heinlein's novel is James Cameron's *Aliens* (1986), where *Starship Troopers* was required reading for the actors playing U.S. Marines expecting "another bug hunt,"[99] a term taken from Heinlein's novel. These actors, including much-decorated former USMC sergeant Al Matthews playing the Marine sergeant, were also trained for two weeks by the British SAS and told to personalize their equipment (much of it converted U.S. military surplus) a la American troops in Vietnam: Cameron excluded actors not playing the ground forces from this training, to increase the impression of *esprit de corps* among the Marines.[100] Their commanding officer is far less experienced than his troops, and his mistakes cost many their lives, though he is ultimately redeemed by an act of self-sacrifice. The film is, however, cynical about the *use* of the military, whose true mission (of which they are not informed beforehand) is not to rescue the colonists but to capture an alien for use as a bioweapon.[101]

Verhoeven's film, conceived during the first Gulf War, is even more cynical. Though the recruiting ads throughout the film exhort potential recruits at different times to save "the world," "the galaxy" and "the future," the only way suggested of doing this is to dominate the galaxy and exterminate the Bugs (who, the film implies, were provoked by human expansion into their territory).[102]

Verhoeven's commentary points out that he intended the film to reflect the tendency in U.S. politics (or, he adds, the politics of *any* superpower, such as communist Russia or Nazi Germany) to resort to violence "when things take too much time to solve in a more democratic way," and cites the examples of Grenada, Panama, Nicaragua and Iraq.[103] Verhoeven also comments that what the United States always needs is an enemy: "Didn't Albright say lately that the new enemy was in the Middle East, because we've lost the Cold War enemy?"[104] The trailer for *Starship Troopers* supports this, beginning with a voice-over saying: "In the future, wars will still be fought for honor, glory, and survival. Only the enemy will change."[105]

However, in the relatively peaceful 1980s and 1990s, particularly after the end of the Cold War, the Pentagon saw little reason to care about how the U.S. military was represented in science fiction. After the September 11 attacks and Operation Enduring Freedom in 2001, and the invasion of Iraq in 2003, that would change.

9. "The Punisher"
The Gulf Wars and Beyond

> I'm running out of demons. I'm running out of enemies. I'm down to Castro and Kim Il-Sung.—*Colin Powell, 1991*[1]
>
> I like to say that fighting aliens is no different than fighting a human.... If you're fighting for your life, you're going to do whatever it takes to win.—*Colonel Gregory Gadson*[2]
>
> We can understand keeping boots off the ground, because largely, it's a matter of not having casualties, which is very much connected to the idea that we look at our militaries now not as a heroic military, but in fact, in many cases, a victim.—*Professor David Galbreath*[3]
>
> 191. Our Humvees cannot be assembled into a giant battle-robot.—The 213 Things Skippy is no longer allowed to do in the U.S. Army[4]

The USA's problem of finding another enemy to replace the defeated Soviet Empire was addressed by some science fiction films and TV—some of which even anticipated the problem. In 1987, while U.S.–Soviet relations were thawing and after Iraq used mustard gas in the war with Iran, *Star Trek: The Next Generation* turned the Klingons into allies of the Federation, placing a Klingon (raised by Russian humans) aboard the new *Enterprise*, and created a new enemy in the form of the Ferengi. As the Ferengi wore keffiyeh-like headscarves and flew crescent-shaped starships, and the word "ferengi" resembles the Arabic and Turkish word "feringhee" (foreigner), derived from the Persian word "farangi" (European), this led *Star Trek* writer John M. Ford to openly worry before the show had aired that *Star Trek* was also looking for a new enemy in the Middle East.[5] *Star Trek VI: The Undiscovered Country* (released on December 3, 1991, three weeks before the formal dissolution of the Soviet Union) dealt more directly with the reaction of the military to the end of the Cold War, depicting both Klingon and Federation (human and Vulcan) officers as prepared to resort to assassination to prevent a peace treaty from being signed and being forced to give up their role as warriors.[6]

In 1991, the U.S. proved Ford right by finding that enemy in the Middle East, after Iraqi forces invaded Kuwait, fired Scud missiles into Israel, and seemed to be advancing on Saudi Arabia; Edward Teller also warned the White House that Saddam Hussein might be building a uranium-hydride bomb.[7] The Iraqis were driven back by a U.S.-led coalition with UN support, but Saddam Hussein remained in power for another twelve years despite international sanctions and unsuccessful coups.

In 2002, President George W. Bush proclaimed Iraq and Iran to be members of an "axis of evil," and in March 2003, U.S. troops invaded the country; in April, they captured Baghdad and removed Saddam Hussein from power.

One of the first U.S. soldiers I saw during the invasion, interviewed on a newscast as his unit attempted to take Umm Qasr in Baghdad, had the word "Shai-Hulud"—the Fremen name for the Sandworm, the military transport for Muad'dib's desert army in Frank Herbert's *Dune*—inscribed on his helmet.[8] A mobile artillery piece in the same battle was emblazoned with the name and logo of "The Punisher," a vigilante from Marvel Comics.[9] A National Guardsman who legally changed his name to "Optimus Prime," a character from the "Transformers" comic and cartoon, was on his way to the Gulf, telling journalists he had received a letter from a general at the Pentagon saying it is "great to have the employ of the commander of the Autobots in the National Guard."[10] Unmanned "Predator" vehicles were being used to look for enemy forces and weapons. DARPA received funding for research projects such as a palm pilot with the acronym "JEDI,"[11] a military internet known as FORCEnet,[12] and a Boeing aircraft demonstrator called "Bird of Prey" (the name of the Klingon/Romulan ship from *Star Trek*).[13]

In July 2003, Arnold Schwarzenegger visited troops stationed in Iraq, told them they are "the true terminators" and, quoting *Terminator 2: Judgment Day*, offered them "congratulations for saying 'hasta la vista, baby' to Saddam Hussein."[14] Hussein had been deposed as leader but evaded capture until December, when he was tracked down in Operation Red Dawn, named after a 1984 SF movie written and directed by John Milius, in which the U.S. Midwest is invaded by joint Nicaraguan, Cuban and Soviet forces.

The Iraq War, however, would not be terminated so easily; U.S. combat troops would remain in the country until denied immunity from prosecution by the new Iraqi government in 2011, with Marine Guards still stationed at the U.S. embassy and some 4000 American private military contractors remaining in the country as I write this. In 2013, American drones were again hunting for insurgents in Iraq, and in 2014, U.S. troops returned to the country to intervene in the fight against the Islamic State. The war in Afghanistan has lasted even longer, with the U.S. and NATO planning to begin a new mission after 2014 to continue training and assisting Afghan forces. Under the circumstances, it's easy to see why the Pentagon thinks there might be more benefit, recruitment-wise, in supporting movies such as *Battleship* and *Battle: Los Angeles*, which show quick, decisive victories against alien cyborgs, rather than the endless wars depicted in *Starship Troopers* or *The Forever War*. While the U.S. military has frequently proved capable of defeating conventional forces where enemy targets are easily identified, it has been much less successful in situations where soldiers find it difficult to distinguish between allies and adversaries—the Korean War, the Vietnam War, Afghanistan and Iraq—and may understandably prefer to reflect on conflicts where they could instantly recognize enemy soldiers by the colors of their uniforms or skins, symbols such as the swastika or rising sun, or the silhouettes of their helmets or guns.

According to Robb, the Pentagon's rules for providing assistance to filmmakers state that "fictional portrayals must depict a feasible interpretation of military life, operations and policies,"[15] but this will be ignored if the film makes the U.S. military look good, thereby helping morale and aiding recruitment and retention—hence the Pentagon's co-operation with the making of SF movies such as *Deep Impact*, *Star Trek IV: The Voyage Home*, *Armageddon*, *The Final Countdown*, *Jurassic Park III*, the James Bond film *Goldeneye* (which featured SDI-style orbital weapons, and gave its name to a U.S. military UAV), Steven Spielberg's 2005 remake of *War of the Worlds*, the 2008 remake of *The Day the Earth Stood Still* (in which the threat is climate change and mass extinction, not nuclear war), the *Transformers* and *G.I. Joe* franchises, *Iron Man 1* and *2*, *Battleship*, *Battle: Los Angeles* and *Godzilla* (2014). Robb quotes a U.S. Army memo predicting that *Deep Impact* "will enhance U.S. Army recruitment and retention programs,"[16] and a pitch from one of *The Final Countdown*'s writers promising the time travel film starring the USS *Nimitz* would be "a boon to the Navy/Marines recruiter. To quote Cdr. Kressey, "The kids will really love this one!""[17]—though the film's rather poor performance at the box office suggests that he may have been overly optimistic.

As late as 2004, Robb noted the reluctance of the U.S. military to "help movies with aliens. Usually in those movies, the military is shown to be ineffective in combating the aliens."[18] In the last ten years, however, this has changed: with the wars in Iraq and Afghanistan in their second decade, recruitment is again a major concern, and as in the 1950s, Hollywood is showing the military defeating, or at least playing a significant positive role in defeating, science-fictional monsters. In the case of Spielberg's *War of the Worlds* (2005), Pentagon liaison Phil Strub "wanted the case made that the Marines understood that they were not going to prevail, but they were nobly sacrificing so the civilians in that valley could escape."[19]

In the *Transformers* films, the U.S. military fights alongside the benevolent alien Autobots against the Decepticons; though the coup de grace to the Decepticon leader is delivered by a teenage civilian, the film ends with the military dumping the bodies of the defeated Decepticons into the sea. For this, director Michael Bay was given more U.S. military assistance than any movie made since *Black Hawk Down*, including the use of F-22 and CV-22 aircraft, uniforms, and military personnel as extras. The end credits give thanks to:

> Department of Defense Liaison: Phil Strub
> Department of Defense Project Officer: Lieutenant Colonel Paul Sinor
> Military Service Project Officers:
> Captain Christian Hodge, U.S. Air Force
> Lieutenant Erik Reynolds, U.S. Navy
> First Lieutenant Christy Kercheval, U.S. Marine Corps
> Holloman Air Force Base
> White Sands Missile Range
> Edwards Air Force Base
> Kirtland Air Force Base
> Fort Irwin
> The Pentagon
> Military District of Washington
> The Men and Women of the U.S. Armed Forces[20]

The second film in the franchise, *Transformers: Revenge of the Fallen* (2009) was touted as "probably the largest joint-military movie ever made," the first to involve four out of the five branches of the U.S. military (Army, Navy, Air Force and Marines).[21]

As well as aiding in recruitment, military liaisons argue that films showing the U.S. military triumphant, even if it is against fictitious alien menaces, may help make "rival despots quake in their boots. 'Recruiting and deterrence are secondary goals, but they're certainly there,' concedes Capt. Bryon McGarry, deputy director of the Air Force's public affairs office."[22]

A communiqué from U.S. Navy Chief of Information Dennis Moynihan explains why the Navy allowed the makers of *Battleship* to film during the Pacific Fleet's RIMPAC training exercise:

> Whether or not we supported *Battleship*, the film was going to be made—it was going to carry our brand and represent who we are to the American people. We can't take everyone out to our ships, but we can work with Hollywood and bring the Navy to life on the big screen. Consequently, it's in our best interest to engage and make sure that movies like *Battleship* accurately portray who we are and what we do as a Navy.[23]

Battleship also featured several hundred currently serving and retired military personnel as actors and extras, including Ray Mabus, Secretary of the Navy, and U.S. Army Colonel Gregory Gadson, garrison commander of Fort Belvoir and Director of the U.S. Army Wounded Warrior Program. Gadson, who lost both of his legs to an IED while serving in Iraq, plays a major role in the film (including physically tackling one of the alien cyborgs) and told an interviewer, "I like to say that fighting aliens is no different than fighting a human…. If you're fighting for your life, you're going to do whatever it takes to win."[24]

This type of assistance comes at the cost of filmmakers giving the Pentagon script approval, often necessitating rewrites: according to Matthew Alford, "approximately a third of major films that depict the U.S. military have direct cooperation and script rewrites by the Pentagon."[25] Kang argues that Moynihan's claim ("Whether or not we supported *Battleship*, the film was going to be made") is dubious because "*Battleship*'s production budget—already $209 million *with* the help of the Navy's resources, including props, backgrounds, extras, and technical expertise—would have probably been too prohibitive had Universal been forced to bear all those costs."[26] In Eagleton's terms, this means that those in charge of the general means of production are able to gain control of the literary means of production. In the case of *Star Trek IV*, for example, permission to film on board the USS *Ranger* (masquerading as the USS *Enterprise*, which was unavailable) required that the screenplay be rewritten to give a more positive portrayal of the U.S. Navy and their security arrangements.[27] In *Battleship*, the Navy demanded that director Peter Berg replace an actor portraying a naval officer on the grounds that he was 35 pounds overweight.[28]

In the case of *Battle: Los Angeles*, which star Aaron Eckhart describes as "a love letter to the Marines,"[29] the film received military assistance in the form of "an armada of" helicopters and MV-22 Ospreys, dozens of U.S. Marines and reservists as extras, a visit to an Afghanistan firebase for Eckhart, a three-week boot camp to train the actors playing Marines in the use of weapons and other military equipment, and technical advice from the U.S. Marines' Hollywood liaison, Lt. Col. Jason Johnson, who

> offers script notes—"a Marine wouldn't do that, a Marine wouldn't say that"—which productions are asked to follow if they want the military's cooperation.
> "Our job is to protect the image of the Marine Corps," Johnson said. "So let's say they wanted to add futuristic weapons. I'm not too concerned about that, but I'm really concerned with the way the Marines look, the way they act and [that] the standards of the Marine Corps are upheld. If they want to give them ray guns, hey, give them ray guns. But don't make them have long hair and earrings."[30]

The 2014 Hollywood remake of *Godzilla*, made with U.S. Navy assistance, blamed the revival of the monsters (Godzilla and the insectoid MUTOs) on the use of nuclear weapons, but explained later tests as unsuccessful attempts by the U.S. military to kill Godzilla. The film's hero is a U.S. Navy lieutenant, an explosive ordnance disposal expert who destroys the eggs laid by one of the MUTOs and is prepared to sacrifice himself to kill the other; the film also depicts the military assisting in the evacuation of monster-ravaged areas, saving the hero as well as his family, and defeating one of the two MUTOs before Godzilla kills the other.[31]

In the case of Spielberg's *War of the Worlds*, military support—including the first onscreen use of an Abrams tank and other vehicles, and the participation of heavily armed National Guard, Marines and Army units—came at the cost of a confusingly mixed message. While co-screenwriter David Koepp has said that the film may be seen outside the U.S. as "an allegory for Iraq and the fear of an American invasion,"[32] and his script supports the claim made by one character that "occupations always fail" and throws a reference to the French occupation of Algeria into the mix,[33] the final film (released on July 4, Independence Day) shows the U.S. military in the same entirely positive light as in the 1953 version. Hunter's review in the *Washington Post* even saw a subtext of "the value, the necessity of warriors."[34]

Science fiction TV shows have also received assistance from the U.S. military—most notably the long-running *Stargate SG-1*, which pits U.S. special forces against alien menaces. The film on which the series was based, *Stargate* (1994), depicted U.S. soldiers leading the descendants of Egyptian slaves against aliens masquerading as Egyptian gods. The TV show, which ran from 1997 to 2007 (a record for any American science fiction TV series), portrayed an elite USAF special ops team using a dimensional portal to explore the universe, while also defending the Earth from alien invasion. The series has featured two USAF Chiefs of Staff playing themselves, USAF personnel as extras, an honor guard for a funeral scene, use of USAF fighter planes and aerial footage, and scenes filmed at air force bases (including the exterior of the Cheyenne Mountain complex). The USAF also reviewed scripts for the show, which is repeated on Air Force Radio and Television, and presented star and producer Richard Dean Anderson with an award "for the show's continued positive depiction of the air force."[35] The show also launched an animated sequel series *Stargate Infinity* (2002–2003), two live-action spin-off series, *Stargate Atlantis* (2004–2009) and *Stargate Universe* (2008–2011), and two direct-to-DVD movies, *Stargate: The Ark of Truth* and *Stargate: Continuum* (both 2008), all of which continued the original show's "positive depiction of the air force": these received less military support, though some scenes for the last were filmed aboard the nuclear submarine USS *Alexandria*.[36]

One advantage, from the Pentagon's point of view, of military involvement in science fiction film and television which portray the military favorably in battles against robots, aliens, reanimated prehistoric monsters and other hypothetical menaces is that it allows them to demonstrate the (simulated) use of expensive weapons and vehicles such as the Abrams tank in *War of the Worlds* or the CV-22 Ospreys in *Transformers*, even if they have never actually been used in combat. Robb quotes another "military minder," Major Georgi, as saying that "one of the targets of this program is Congress; that Congress goes to movies, and that when they see positive images of the military, that makes it easier for them to vote for that $500 billion military appropriation."[37]

Another advantage of including the U.S. military as the heroes in science fiction films and television, from the point of view of recruiters, is that the film ratings classification of "science fiction violence" allows films (and videogames) to depict more graphic violence against nonhuman adversaries than against humans and have a film or game reach a wider and younger audience than would be permitted if the enemies were human. As Card said of the 1980 videogame *Berzerk*, based on Fred Saberhagen's science fiction *Berserker* novels:

> They were the perfect game enemy. You could kill them without a qualm, because they weren't alive *and* they were relentlessly trying to kill you. Nobody minds if you blow up machines.
> As computer graphics improved, the problem of killing became more urgent.[38]

As anyone who has seen ads where blue liquid is poured onto sanitary napkins will be aware, restrictions against showing blood on-screen do not apply unless the fluid looks like blood—which was the directors' rationale for giving the Klingons in *Star Trek VI* purple blood and the invading aliens of *Battle: Los Angeles* black blood.[39] Similarly, using drones or robots as the enemy means filmmakers can show much more violence without any bloodshed, enabling the film to get a PG or PG-13 rating rather than R or NC-17: as Jon Favreau said of the scene in *Iron Man 2* where Iron Man and War Machine fight the "Hammeroid" drones, "This big fight, because I wanted it to be just a bloodbath ... a PG bloodbath, so it's an oil-bath."[40] The aim of reaching a younger audience is shared by military recruiters as well as by film companies, as evidenced by a comment by the Chief of Public Affairs for the USAF, about military support for the film of *The Right Stuff*: "The obscene language used seems to guarantee an R rating," Colonel Burggrabe wrote. "If distributed as an 'R' it cuts down on the teenage audience, which is a prime one to the military services when our recruiting goals are considered."[41]

A worrying aspect of this creation of the ratings classifications of "science fiction violence," "futuristic violence" and similar categories ("high-tech horror violence" for *Ghost in the Machine*, "monster violence" for *Alien 3*, "intense sequences of western and sci-fi action and violence" for *Cowboys and Aliens*, "intense science fiction terror" for *Jurassic Park*, "intense fantasy action" for *Spawn*, and my personal favorite, "traditional Godzilla violence" for *Godzilla vs. Biolante*) is the easy way these entertainments can become scenarios in which, to quote Spinrad, "righteous ingénues guiltlessly slaughter faceless gunfodder in alien or robot gooksuits."[42] As Card says, players of video games are less likely to feel guilty about destroying robots than living creatures, and the old military tradition of dehumanizing the enemy is even easier if the enemy literally does not have a human face.

Grossman cites many examples to demonstrate that the vast majority of people have a natural aversion to killing other humans when they are physically close enough to see them as human, but that this diminishes with physical distance. He gives this as a partial explanation for the lack of reluctance on the part of artillerymen, naval gunners or bombardiers to attack their targets, even when this might kill thousands of civilians, which he describes as "a process in which close proximity on the physical distance spectrum can be negated when the face can not be seen. The essence of the whole physical distance spectrum may simply revolve around the degree to which the killer can see the face of the victim."[43] Grossman is also referring to the fact that casualty rates in combat increase after the enemy turns his back and flees, but also cites gangland and Nazi executions and "Miron and Goldman's 1979 research that the risk of death for a kidnap victim is much greater if the victim is hooded."[44] "If one does not have to look into the eyes when killing, it is much easier to deny the humanity of the victim."[45]

Grossman lists aspects of psychological distance—cultural, moral, social and mechanical distances—as other factors that make it easier for soldiers to overcome the aversion to killing. Hence, Nazi soldiers who believed that their enemies were *Untermenschen* "consistently inflicted 50 percent more casualties on the Americans and British than were inflicted on them,"[46] and "44 percent of American soldiers in World War II said they would really like to kill a Japanese soldier" but only 6 percent expressed that degree of enthusiasm for killing Germans."[47] Cultural, social and possibly moral differences are even easier to exaggerate if the enemy is actually an extraterrestrial, robot, mutated dinosaur, or undead.

"Mechanical distance" Grossman defines as "the sterile Nintendo-game unreality of killing through a TV screen, a thermal sight, a sniper sight, or some other kind of mechanical buffer that permits the killer to deny the humanity of his victim."[48] This "mechanical distance" is likely to be exacerbated even further by the increasing use of remotely controlled armed UAVs or drones by the U.S. military. Combine these factors—faceless, possibly soulless, enemies from an alien culture, possibly not even life as we understand it (e.g., robots can be rebuilt and their software downloaded and uploaded, making them effectively immortal), reduced to statistics and guiltlessly killed by long-range or remotely controlled weapons requiring trivial physical effort (pushing a button or squeezing a trigger rather than stabbing with a sword or spear)—and the potential of military science fiction films and games for recruiting and training future users of high-tech weapon systems, particularly drones, becomes obvious.

Faceless fictitious adversaries also have the advantage that they can more easily be used to represent new enemies when the political landscape changes former allies to adversaries. From Hollywood's viewpoint, this also has the advantages that obviously nonhuman menaces are less likely to alienate or offend audiences who might identify with "bad guys": for example, the 2012 remake of *Red Dawn* changed the invaders from Chinese to North Korean rather than lose the large potential Chinese audience.[49] For these reasons, science fiction films set on Earth in the very near future tend, like Marvel Comics, to sidestep the issue of contemporary wars. The film of *Iron Man* updates Iron Man's origin story from 1960s Vietnam to modern-day Afghanistan, but never refers to his captors as "Taliban."[50] The sequel shows unsuccessful attempts to build similar battle-armor in Iran and North Korea—but in the same sequence, Tony Stark claims to have "successfully privatized world peace."[51] This does not, of course, prevent them from commenting on the conduct of the military in wars of the time, as when Jon Favreau decided to feature drones in *Iron Man 2* because they "were in the news,"[52] or Lucius Fox's remark in *Batman Begins* (2005) that "bean counters didn't think a soldier's life was worth 300 grand." This comment came after Donald Rumsfeld responded to complaints about the shortage of body armor for soldiers fighting the war in Iraq with, "You go to war with the army you have, not the army you might want or wish to have at a later time." The rebooted *Battlestar Galactica* depicted Starbuck torturing a Cylon in the episode "Flesh and Bone" (2004), which Favreau described as "emblematic of what was going on at Guantanamo and places like that."[53]

◆ ◆ ◆

While military support for science fiction films that show the U.S. military in a good light is now almost routine, many other SF films made since the success of *Star Wars* have also been denied assistance. Examples include *Close Encounters of the Third Kind* (1978), which showed the U.S. military staging a fake nerve gas leak to scare people away from the site of a UFO landing (echoing the real nerve gas leak responsible for the Skull Valley sheep kill of 1968)[54]; *The Philadelphia Experiment* (1983), which was seen as perpetuating the myth that the Navy experimented with an invisibility device in 1943[55]; *The Day After* (1983), which depicts the aftermath of a nuclear strike on a U.S. city[56]; *Starman* (1984), in which the friendly alien's landing craft is shot down by the air force, and the military sets up roadblocks to try to prevent the alien from making his rendezvous with his mothership, even preparing an autopsy room in the hope of dissecting him (the film used civilian helicopters with Army markings, and out-of-date stock footage of F-102A interceptors)[57]; *The Avengers* (2012), in which USAF pilots obey an order to nuke New York from the "World Security Council"[58]; *Mars Attacks!* (1996), which features Paul Winfield and Rod Steiger as generals—the former a genial dove, the latter advocating the use of nuclear weapons and shouting "Annihilate! Kill! Kill! Kill!," both ultimately ineffectual against the Martian invaders who eventually succumb to terrible country and western music[59]; and *Independence Day* (1996). With the last, the Pentagon's Hollywood liaison raised objections to the "lack of true military heroes,"[60] the depiction of the private life of the Marine pilot (played by Will Smith), and the references to Roswell and Area 51. Though screenwriter Devlin attempted to write a script that "enhances recruiting and retention" and would "portray the military experience in a more positive and alluring portrait"[61] and "make every boy in the country want to fly a fighter jet,"[62] by giving military backgrounds to heroic civilian characters, making the military characters more effective, and changing the unsympathetic Secretary of Defense to a White House Chief of Staff, Pentagonians were not convinced. No assistance was provided, the verdict being, "There's nothing in the script so far that we won't get automatically if they make the film without us."[63]

◆ ◆ ◆

    Written science fiction has generally fared better than movies and television at antiwar messages and looking at alternatives to current ideas of warfare, as well as looking more closely at its costs as well as its purported benefits. *Forever Free*, Haldeman's sequel to *The Forever War*, shows soldiers still traumatized by the war twenty years later.[64] His novel *Forever Peace*, "a science-fiction refraction of the Powell doctrine"[65] of not risking the lives of American soldiers except as a last resort, anticipated the increasing use of remotely controlled drones in Iraq where "some twenty-two different robot systems were operating on the ground" in 2008.[66] The toy-truck-sized $5000 MARCBOT, jury-rigged with a Claymore mine, is being used to search for and, if necessary, kill insurgents hiding in cave complexes and alleys by detonating the mine.[67] Similar devices are used to investigate possible IEDs. The machines may be destroyed in the process, but as one officer said, "When a robot dies, you don't have to write a letter to its mother."[68] And DARPA is currently working on Project Avatar (named after the science fiction movie, which replaces *Forever Peace*'s humanoid drones with genetically engineered hybrids of humans and the extraterrestrial Na'vi), a scheme to "develop interfaces and algorithms to enable a soldier to effectively partner with a semi-autonomous bi-pedal machine and allow it to act as the soldier's surrogate"[69]—in other words, to create humanoid remotes such as Haldeman's soldierboys. Similar humanoid drones feature in *Iron Man 2* (2008), a film made with military assistance (including location filming on Edwards Air Force base, and the use of trademarked camouflage patterns for the military drones), but the rogue inventor—a Russian physicist and criminal working for an American defense contractor—is controlling all twenty-four heavily armed machines (six each for Army, Navy, Air Force and Marines), as well as overriding the weapons systems on Colonel Rhodes's "War Machine" power armor. This necessitates giving the "drones" some autonomy, effectively turning each one into a hunter-killer robot; in one scene, one targets a small boy wearing an Iron Man mask, the targeting graphic showing that his "friend or foe recognition" capability isn't all that might be desired.[70]

Of course, not all science fiction suggests that future wars will be fought mostly by robots or remotes, opting instead for "boots on the ground." A rather cynical view of future use of soldiers as cannon fodder who are cheaper than machines is given in John Scalzi's *Old Man's War* (2005) and *The Ghost Brigades* (2006), in which, reflecting the disputes about inadequate armor being provided to U.S. troops in Iraq, the new recruits are told, "There has never been a military in the entire history of the human race that has gone to war equipped with more than the *least* it needs to fight the enemy."[71]

Scalzi's series is set against a background of interstellar war, where humanity has to fight with alien races for possession of rare habitable planets—but instead of recruits or draftees in their late teens, the soldiers are 75-year-old retirees who sign up for a ten-year tour of duty in exchange for physical rejuvenation. Dying before you're due for your new body does not relieve you of duty: instead, you're cloned for the "ghost brigades."[72]

Wil McCarthy's *Aggressor Six* (1994) features a war against an insectoid foe, similar to Heinlein's bugs and Card's buggers—but as this one is technologically vastly superior to humanity, the military assigns teams to try to think like the enemy not to destroy them, but in order that they can learn their language well enough to ask for a truce.[73]

Franklin, in *Vietnam and Other American Fantasies*, describes "an entire science-fiction industry dedicated to glorifying mercenaries and their war making,"[74] naming Jerry Pournelle and David Drake (a U.S. Army interrogator during the Vietnam war) as its major authors. Other writers prominent in the subgenre of military science fiction include John Ringo (a military advisor to Fox News, with four years in the Army Airborne including service in Operation Urgent Fury and Desert Storm), Elizabeth Moon (USMC 1968–71, 1st lieutenant), Robert Buettner (Army Intelligence captain), and Michael Z. Williamson (ex–USAF, later a U.S. Army staff sergeant on active reserve). Several others have no military experience, including Lois McMaster Bujold, Larry Niven, David Weber (a former war-game designer), and Eric Flint (an anti–Vietnam war activist). All of these except for Buettner are published by Baen Books, which was founded by Jim Baen (who joined the Army at 17 before starting college on the G.I. Bill); while not the only publishers of military science fiction, they are readily identified with it, actively target bookshops on or near military bases in their marketing campaigns, and donate books to the U.S. Navy.[75]

Franklin's use of the word "mercenaries" is worth noting here, particularly in the light of the increasing use of "private security contractors" in the Iraq War and Afghanistan, and the negative image caused by incidents such as employees of the frequently renamed Blackwater being convicted of the murders of Iraqi civilians in Nisour Square. Both Pournelle and Drake have written series of books about interstellar mercenaries: Pournelle's "Janissaries" with Roland J. Green and his "Falkenberg's Legion" series, and Drake's "Hammer's Slammers." Bujold's Miles Vorkosigan, in his other identity as Admiral Naismith, commands a team of mercenaries used by his government's intelligence service when plausible deniability is required. Moon's Kylara Vatta and Herrano Serris's respective stories begin with their being forced out of military service by corrupt superiors and finding employment on privately owned spaceships.

Of course, not all of the protagonists in military science fiction are mercenaries: in series published by Baen, Bujold's Miles Vorkosigan, Weber's Honor Harrington and Moon's Esmay Suiza are career soldiers, as is Buettner's Jason Wander, while the protagonists in many of Ringo's near-future novels include Navy SEALs, Marines, Special Forces soldiers, and others serving in the U.S. military.

Most of these characters, though, come from political systems very different from the USA's, and their enemies are no longer thinly disguised Russians. Bujold's Miles Vorkosigan, in fact, is raised in a largely Russian culture of serfs and aristocrats, though his mother comes from an ultra-liberal democracy on another planet.[76] Moon's Esmay Suiza must rescue a fellow crew-member from the "New Texas Godfearing Militia," which enslaves women, gang-rapes and impregnates them, and renders them mute.[77] What Pournelle describes as "the attractions of a properly run military outfit"[78] are, at least according these stories, clearly not restricted to serving in the U.S. military.

◆ ◆ ◆

That the U.S. military sees Marvel's super-soldier and other heroes as useful is demonstrated by the frequent appearance of actors playing these characters at military bases (including, rather alarmingly, the biological and chemical weapon labs of Fort Detrick) and VA hospitals,[79] and in a photo session with Defense Secretary Donald Rumsfeld as part of a Department of Defense program called "America Supports You."[80]

So it must have been disturbing to the DoD when critic Michael Medved branded Captain America a traitor for not offering "a word of rebuttal to the pro-terrorist tirade"[81] delivered by (fictional) terrorist Al-Tariq in

Captain America: The New Deal (2003). Al-Tariq has come to Centreville, a (fictional) U.S. town whose main industry is manufacturing land mines, and accuses Americans of being terrorists. Medved accused Marvel of "making one-sided, damning references to controversial elements of American foreign policy" in an essay much quoted on right-wing websites, which begins:

> As if Defense Department officials didn't face enough challenges in and around Iraq, they must now prepare for battle without a celebrated component of past victories. Captain America, the patriotic superhero whose comic-book exploits inspired the nation in World War II, now feels uncertain about the nation's cause....[82]

and concludes:

> We might expect such blame–America logic from Hollywood activists, academic apologists, or the angry protesters who regularly fill the streets of European capitals (and many major American cities). When such sentiments turn up, however, hidden within star-spangled, nostalgic packaging of comic books aimed at kids, we need to confront the deep cultural malaise afflicting the nation on the eve of war.[83]

While the idea that the Defense Department might consider Captain America's lack of support for the invasion of Iraq a "challenge" may seem ludicrous, it should be remembered that the character was first created as a response to a request from Congress to "publishing media to encourage those literary themes that were consistent with *the government's* position on the war."[84]

But that was another war, and many in the USA of 2003 would disagree as to the nature of Medved's "deep cultural malaise afflicting the nation." As Brancatelli points out in his history of the character:

> Steve Rogers became a spy, then a cop, then a drifter, and finally a neurotic introvert who considered himself an anachronism ... and, in the strangest quirk, the 1950s Captain America was revealed as a reactionary fraud....
>
> Over the years, Captain America has always mirrored the American psyche: in the 1940s, he was the super-patriot; in the 1950s, he was the reactionary; today he is the unsure giant. He *is* America.[85]

Or maybe that should be he *was* America, because in 2007, Marvel comics killed Captain America not once but twice, in different storylines. In *Captain America: The Chosen*, David Morrell (author of *First Blood*) depicts World War II veteran Captain America as slowly dying, but manifesting in spirit form to lend assistance to a U.S. soldier serving in Afghanistan and trapped by a cave-in.[86] In the series *The Civil War*, Captain America is assassinated after taking an antigovernment stance in response to a superhero registration act.

In this story, written by Ed Brubaker, Captain America is shot while surrendering to pro-registration Tony Stark, aka Iron Man, who had briefly served as Secretary of Defense in 2004 and pushed for the development and use of more nonlethal weapons by the military (the military's response to this policy was to activate all of Stark's previous Iron Man suits and send them to Washington to disrupt Stark's Senate confirmation hearing).[87]

One of Captain America's allies in this dispute had been the Punisher, who had first appeared in *The Amazing Spider-man #129* in April 1974 as a villain, but would not acquire an origin story until years later. A perpetually gun-toting ex–Marine, a "born soldier" who received "two Bronze Stars, two Silver Stars and four Purple Hearts for his exemplary service in Vietnam"[88] and "positively relishes his role as an executioner,"[89] he wears a black costume with a huge death's-head motif, the teeth of the skull forming part of his cartridge belt. Daniels, in 1991, described him as "a symptom of our times, or perhaps a commentary on how we see ourselves today. Captain America came wrapped in Old Glory, but The Punisher's costume appears to be made out of a pirate's flag."[90] This echoes Mark Twain's suggestion, when he was vice-president of the Anti-Imperialist League during the Philippine War, that when the U.S. embarked on a war of conquest and asked its soldiers to "do bandit's work under a flag which bandits have been accustomed to fear, not to follow," it should disguise the soldiers and redesign its flag "with the white stripes painted black and the stars replaced by the skull and cross-bones."[91]

After Captain America's assassination in the *Civil War* storyline, the Punisher takes Captain America's discarded mask and keeps it for himself. *Punisher War Journal Volume 2* shows the Punisher wearing a new costume, with the stars from Captain America's costume as well as the skull from his own ... which in the light of Brancatelli's and Daniels's comments, suggests that the image of the American super-soldier, in the time of the Iraq War, had become much darker.[92]

Ironically, particularly in the light of Franklin's suggestion that Americans idea of their military prowess is profoundly influenced by "fantasies of technowonders and of superheroes,"[93] a platoon in the U.S. 173rd Airborne which had adopted the Punisher's skull emblem as their own was overrun by Afghani insurgents in July 2008.[94] The platoon's "ammunition stockpile was hit by rocket-propelled grenade, igniting a stack of 120-millimeter mortar rounds—and the resulting fireball flung the unit's antitank missiles into the command post"[95]—in short, their own weapons were turned against them, in a firefight described as "the new template for how not to win in Afghanistan."[96]

♦ ♦ ♦

Like the Vietnam War before it, the Iraq War divided the science fiction writing community into Jeffersonian and Hamiltonian camps. The arguments raged briefly but intensely in SFWA's members-only magazine *Forum* in 2003–2004, with some speaking against the war, some for, some praising SFWA for "not jumping on a bandwagon of either type," a few calls for resignations, and a great many gratuitous insults being thrown around—"abhorrent turd" and "doddering expatriate" being two of the more memorable.[97]

Sam J. Lundwall resigned as Overseas Regional Director of SFWA because he couldn't get the organization to issue a statement of opposition to the war in Iraq.[98] To date, 128 writers have since signed Michael Swanwick's on-line statement against the war—including Harry Harrison and Ursula LeGuin, both signatories to the letter opposing the war in Vietnam, as well as Fred Pohl, who had published it, and Joe Haldeman,[99] who marched in protests against both the 1991 and 2003 invasions of Iraq.[100]

On the other side, Jerry Pournelle (who signed the letter supporting the continuation of the Vietnam War), while describing the Iraq campaign as a debacle[101] and admitting, "Perhaps we should never have gone in," called for the U.S. military to "kill or capture [enemy] forces before they can reorganize and fight again."[102] John Ringo similarly has called for the use of "overwhelming force."[103] And Orson Scott Card has become a strident supporter of the war and the military, saying in 2003: "War is a terrible thing, and woe to the nation that ever gets a taste for it. But when there is no rational, moral choice but to go to war, how fortunate the nation whose military forces have such leadership as ours."[104]

In his novel *Empire* (2006), conceived as the background for the computer game *Shadow Complex* (written by Peter David), one of the heroes, Special Ops soldier Major Malich, argues that other countries "respect us now because we have a dangerous military. They adopt our culture because we're rich. If we were poor and unarmed, they'd peel off American culture like a snake shedding its skin."[105] To his surprise, his professor, NSA Consultant Averill Torrent, agrees, saying, "Only a fool thinks the turns of history can be measured by any other standard other than which wars were fought, and who won them."[106]

Malich regards the course he is taking at Princeton University as "a Ph.D. in the rhetoric and beliefs of the insane Left ... being embedded with the enemy as surely as when he was on a deep Special Ops assignment."[107] He tells Torrent, "The U.S. Army is absolutely dominated by red-state ideals. There are some blue-staters, yes, of course. But you don't join the military, as a general rule, unless you share much of the red-state ideology."

Torrent asks, "What if the White House were in the control of the blue-staters?... What if the President ordered American troops to fire on American citizens who fought for red-state ideals?" Malich replies, "We obey the President, sir."[108] After the president, vice-president, Secretary of Defense and chairman of the Joint Chiefs are all assassinated on the same day, in a scenario Malich had envisaged, some accuse Malich of being part of a coup proposed by right-wing Army General Alton (who suffers from "generalitis, the inflammation of the ego that came from having everybody salute you and say yessir all the time."[109]) Alton has "succeeded in retiring most of the top officers who would oppose us. All of the stateside forces of any size are already under our control."[110] When Malich's aide, Captain Coleman, argues that Alton may have been manipulated by the conspirators who assassinated the president, "so they'd have an excuse to go to war to save the country from you," Alton counters, "So what? We've got all the guns."[111]

The House Majority Leader, a Mormon Republican from Idaho, takes over the presidency, and Malich and Coleman talk him out of going along with Alton's plan. The army remains loyal to the president, but the "Progressive Restoration" takes over cities with "blue-state" ideals, policing New York with walking tanks and robots created by left-wing billionaire Aldo Verus, and Malich and Coleman are assigned to prove that the assassination was the result of a left-wing conspiracy rather than a right-wing one. They succeed in doing this, and Torrent, proclaiming himself a moderate, is nominated by both the Democratic and Republican parties and becomes the next president (apparently unopposed)—which Card suggests is actually a *worse* outcome than the current divide between America's left and right.

Looking back at science fiction writers' differing views on American wars after 1945, and even on increases in military spending on projects such as SDI viewed as an alternative to diplomacy and treaties, there have been no wars or significant military interventions in nearly seven decades that have not caused some dissent among America's science fiction writers. It is conceivable that a war could break out against an enemy so horrific that it united the science fiction writing community, even its most pacifistic members, to support it as they did in World War II, but I consider this unlikely in the foreseeable future. It is also possible that America might become embroiled in a war that united all American science fiction writers *against* it—but the evidence, particularly the case of the Vietnam and Iraq wars, suggests that this is less likely still, almost as unlikely as the scenario in *Empire*. And while I will not sing hymns to "the everlasting glory of the infantry," neither do I expect to see a day when Americans "study war no more." There may be less war and more study, and casualty rates may continue to fall as boots on the ground are increasingly replaced by the mechanized legs, wheels, treads and wings of smarter (i.e., more autonomous, robot-like rather than remotely controlled) machines ... but history suggests that while U.S. military spending and enlistment may fluctuate, for the foreseeable future, the U.S. will retain enough military personnel and weaponry (some of it inspired by science fiction) to always present a "credible threat of force"[112] with its ability to deliver "gleaming weaponry and beautiful explosions."

It seems most probable, therefore, that at least some American science fiction writers will cheerfully continue to aid and promote the U.S. military; some will do so unintentionally; and others will use the genre and their status to criticize its actions and its costs.

◆ ◆ ◆

François Truffaut once said that because even gruesome movies make war seem exciting, there's no such thing as an antiwar war movie.[113] John Scalzi's review of *Starship Troopers* goes further, describing the battle scenes as "marvelously violent, action-packed and actually arousing."[114] Spielberg has claimed the reverse, that "every war movie, good or bad, is an antiwar movie."[115] A more nuanced, and probably accurate, answer came from Anthony Swofford in *Jarhead*:

> But actually, Vietnam war films are all pro-war, no matter what the supposed message, what Kubrick or Coppola or Stone intended. Mr. and Mrs. Johnson in Omaha or San Francisco or Manhattan will watch the films and weep and decide once and for all that war is inhumane and terrible, and they will tell their friends at church and their family this, but Corporal Johnson at Camp Pendleton and Sergeant Johnson at Travis Air Force Base and Seaman Johnson at Coronado Naval Station and Spec 4 Johnson at Fort Bragg and Lance Corporal Swofford at Twentynine Palms Marine Corps Base watch the same films and are excited by them, because the magic brutality of the films celebrates the terrible and despicable beauty of their fighting skills.[116]

Unfortunately, the evidence would seem to support Swofford, if not Truffaut. If Spielberg was correct, it's difficult to imagine why the Pentagon would give so much expensive support to Hollywood to make films such as *Transformers: Revenge of the Fallen* and *Battleship* and TV shows such as *JAG* or *Stargate SG-1*, or produce its own video games, or recruit in theater foyers (I've heard that this was even done in some theaters showing *Starship Troopers*, though I've been unable to find a reference to confirm this). There would be no need for terms such as "military-entertainment complex" or "militainment."

Several science fiction stories have addressed this idea of war as entertainment, including Robert Asprin's *The Cold Cash War*[117] (first published in the same issue of *Analog* as "Ender's Game"), Mack Reynolds's "Mercenary,"[118] George Alec Effinger's "Curtains,"[119] and Dan Simmons's "E-Ticket to 'Namland."[120] In John Varley's *Titan* (1979), the "goddess" Gaea is inspired by television signals from Earth to hold a war: "You people seemed to like them so much, holding one every few years, that I thought I'd give them a try."[121]

Science fiction, despite its expense, has a particular appeal to makers of pro-war entertainments: as well as "gleaming weaponry and beautiful explosions" and power-fantasy superheroes, it can offer any number of possible alien races as "faceless gunfodder," purely hypothetical enemies whose possible existence nonetheless requires eternal vigilance and the potential for the everlasting glory of the infantry.

◆ ◆ ◆

As literary science fiction loses market share and shelf space to epic fantasy, will we see more weapons named after fantasy icons such as dragons and magical swords?

Considering the success of *The Lord of the Rings* and the TV series *Game of Thrones* and the prospect of yet more fantasy films and series, this is certainly possible. Several reviews and newspaper editorials of the Peter Jackson films have tried to explain their popularity in terms of the "War on Terror," and Senator Rick Santorum, a supporter of the Iraq war, compared them in a campaign speech in 2006: "As the hobbits are going up Mount Doom, the Eye of Mordor is being drawn somewhere else.... It's being drawn to Iraq and it's not being drawn to the U.S. You know what? I want to keep it on Iraq. I don't want the Eye to come back here to the United States."[122] The proposed replacement for the Paladin[123] howitzer was named Crusader,[124] after another armored medieval warrior; military payloads are launched on Minotaur rockets[125]; laser weapon programs are named Excalibur[126]; and soldiers are buying DragonSkin body armor.[127] Nostalgia sells well in the USA, particularly among the conservatives who are more likely to support military action.

However, the U.S. military is unlikely to reduce its dependency on superior technology—quite the reverse—and Tolkienesque fantasy is, as Jameson points out, "technically reactionary."[128] No matter how glamorous the U.S. makes military service, it will not be able to defeat all of its opponents by numerical superiority in manpower alone, nor in the willingness to accept casualties. Increasingly, it is likely to depend on its superior mobility and firepower, as well as technology such as lasers and computers for more accurate pinpointing of targets. To reduce civilian casualties and friendly fire incidents, it is also sponsoring the development of nonlethal weapons and robot-like remotes (the last two combined at the Pentagon's behest by iRobot.com and TASER International).[129] Because of this dependency, the U.S. military is almost certain to continue to draw on science fiction as a source of "the kinds of narrative an audience will accept,"[130] if only because its plans for the "Future Force Warrior" is more likely to resemble Iron Man[131] or a *Star Wars* stormtrooper, with the high-tech skills of a Captain Kirk or Han Solo, rather than, say, Conan the Barbarian, Aragorn or Gandalf. Or even John Wayne.

Appendix A
Science Fiction Writers Who Served in the U.S. Military, World War II to Vietnam

WORLD WAR II

Isaac Asimov, Army 1945–1946, corporal
Lloyd Biggle Jr., Army 1943–1946, sergeant
James Blish, Army Medical Corps 1942–1944
John Boyd, Navy 1940–1945, lt. commander
F.M. Busby, National Guard 1930–1940, Army 1940–1941, 1943–1945
Louis Charbonneau, Army Air Force 1943–1946, staff sergeant
Gene L. Coon, USMC 1942–1946, 1950–52
Alfred Coppell, Army Air Force 1942–1945, 1st lieutenant
Avram Davidson, Navy 1942–1946
Chandler Davis, Naval Reserve 1944–1946
Gordon R. Dickson, Army 1943–1946
Philip José Farmer, Army Air Force 1941–1942
Daniel Galouye, Navy pilot 1941–1946, Naval reserve, lieutenant
Randall Garrett, USMC, corporal
Horace Gold, combat engineer 1944–1946
James Gunn, Naval Reserve 1943–1946
Cyril Kornbluth, infantry, Bronze Star
Henry Kuttner, Army Medical Corps
R.A. Lafferty, Army 1942–1946, staff sergeant
Stirling E. Lanier, Army, World War II and Korea
Keith Laumer, Army 1943–1945, corporal; Air Force 1952–1956, 1959–1965, captain
Paul Linebarger (Cordwainer Smith), Army Intelligence; helped found the Office of War Information, where Pat Frank, Will Jenkins (Murray Leinster) and Reginald Bretnor worked as writers

Richard Matheson, 87th Infantry
Walter M. Miller, Army Air Force 1942–1945
Kris Neville, Army Signal Corps
Edgar Pangborn, Army Medical Corps 1942–1945
Fred Pohl, Army Air Corps 1943–1945, sergeant
Mack Reynolds, Army Transportation Corps
Frank M. Robinson, Navy radar technician 1944–1945, 1950–1951
Gene Roddenberry, Army Air Corps 1941–1946, Distinguished Flying Cross, Air Medal
William Rotsler, Army 1944–1945
Hilbert Schenk, Navy electronics technician 1944–1946
Thomas N. Scortia, infantry 1944–1946, chemical corps 1951–1953
Hank Searls, Navy 1941–1954, lieutenant commander
Rod Serling, 11th Airborne, 1943–1946
E.E. "Doc" Smith, Army 1941–1945, served in an explosives arsenal
George H. Smith, Navy 1942–1945
George O. Smith, editorial engineer, National Defense Research Council 1944–1945
Jerry Sohl, Army Air Corps 1942–1945, sergeant
George R. Stewart, Navy civilian technician 1944
Harry Stubbs (Hal Clement), bomber pilot 8th Air Force World War II, 35 combat missions, then Air Force Reserve, lieutenant colonel 1953–1976
Stephen Tall, OSS intelligence officer 1945–1945, captain
William Tenn, Army
Walter Tevis, Navy 1945
Ted Thomas, Army 1943–1946, 1st lieutenant
Kurt Vonnegut, Infantry scout 1942–1945
John A. Williams, Navy 1943–1946
Jack Williamson, Army weather forecaster 1942–1945, staff sergeant
Richard Wilson, Signal Corps and Air Force 1942–1946

1946–1950

Martin Caidin, USAF 1947–1950, sergeant, consultant to New York State Civil Defense Commission 1950–1962, Air Force Missile Test Center Cape Canaveral 1955
Zach Hughes, 82nd Airborne 1946–1948
Alan E. Nourse, Navy 1946–1948, hospitalman 3rd class
Doris Piserchia, Army 1950–1954, lieutenant
Robert Sheckley, Army 1946–1948
Robert F. Young, Army

Korea

Lin Carter, Army Infantry 1951–1953
Dean Ing, Air Force 1951–1955, Airman 1st Class
Jerry Pournelle, Army 1950–1952
Fred Saberhagen, Air Force 1951–1955
Gene Wolfe Army 1952–1954

1954–1964

Piers Anthony, Army 1957–1959
Harlan Ellison, Army 1957–1959, saved from court-martial by Joe Hensley (hospital corpsman, Navy 1944–1946)
Robert Forward, Air Force 1954–1956, captain
Richard Lupoff, Army Adjutant General's Corps 1956–1958, 1st lieutenant
Jack McDevitt, Navy 1958–1962
Richard C. Meredith, Army 1957–1960, 1962
John Morressy, Army 1953–1955
Alexei Panshin, Army 1960–1962
Tom Purdom, Army Medical Corps 1959–1961
Roger Zelazny, Ohio National Guard 1960–1963, Army Reserve 1963–1966

Vietnam

Robert Asprin, Army 1965–1966
Jack L. Chalker, USAF 135th Air Commando Group 1968–1971, Maryland Air National Guard 1968–1969, staff sergeant
Brian Daley, Army 1965–1969, tours in Vietnam and West Berlin
Gardner Dozois, military journalist 1966–1969
David Drake, Army 1969–1971, interrogator
Alan Dean Foster, Army Reserve 1969–1975
M.A. Foster, Air Force 1957–1962, 1965–1976, captain (Russian linguist, Intelligence, Strategic Missiles, Intercept Weapons Director)
Joe Haldeman, drafted 1967, Army Combat Engineer 1968–1969, Purple Heart
George R.R. Martin, conscientious objector, alternative service with VISTA 1972–1974
Elizabeth Moon, USMC 1968–1971 (at HQMC)
Warren Norwood, Army 1966–1969
Elizabeth Ann Scarborough, Army nurse
Howard Waldrop, Army information specialist 1970–1972
Gary K. Wolf, Air Force 1963–1969, major

Appendix B
From Jeep to JEDI: SF Influences on Military Terminology

It must be admitted that it is sometimes merely a coincidence that the same word or acronym occurs both in U.S. military parlance and in science fictional entertainments—for example, that the Director of Naval Intelligence and a popular video game console are both named Sega; that "Thor" and "Vigilante" were the names both of American comic-book superheroes and American nuclear weapons at roughly the same time; that the 1994 SF movie *Stargate* shares its name with a 1953 Defense Intelligence Agency ESP experiment; or that U.S. Navy ordnance handlers and *Star Trek*'s expendable cannon-fodder are both known as "red shirts."

Because there are only twenty-six letters in the Anglophone alphabet, and there is generally a preference for acronyms and neologisms that are easily pronounced and memorable, the same words can arise independently in both dialects. Furthermore, the choice of names for U.S. military hardware and projects is often eccentric—weapons projects have been named "Fat Man" after Sidney Greenstreet's character in *The Maltese Falcon* and "Snark" after Lewis Carroll's imaginary creature, as well as a wide range of birds, fish, figures from Greek mythology, and Native American tribes.

The 193rd Special Operations Group's Commando Solo, a Hercules modified for "information operations, psychological operations and civil affairs broadcasts," may sound suspiciously like "Commander Solo," the rank and name of Harrison Ford's character in *The Empire Strikes Back* (1980), but the name was only changed from "Volant Solo" in 1990, and the group has been using the "Solo" name since flying the "Coronet Solo" on similar missions in 1967. (The name doesn't describe the eleven-man crew, but may be a reference to the aircraft's uniqueness or to Napoleon Solo, a spy from the TV series *The Man from U.N.C.L.E.* [1964–1968].)

There are, however, several cases where the military has obviously borrowed from science fiction, including the following:

Military Hardware	Year	Science Fiction Source	Year
Jeep (General Purpose Transport)	1939	Popeye (creature from 4th dimension)[1]	1937
Mighty Mouse (2.75[qm] air-to-airrocket)[2]	1950	Mighty Mouse	1942
Superman (nuclear weapons project)	1952	Superman	1938–present
Blue Beetle T-63 training "shape" (dummy nuclear weapon)	1954	Blue Beetle (inventor/crimefighter, DC Comics)	1939
"Star Wars" missile defense	1983–present	Star Wars	1977–present
Tier III Minus Dark Star reconnaissance drone[3]	1995	Dark Star	1974
F-14 Viper (fighter plane, also known as Fighting Falcon)[4]	1978	Battlestar Galactica	1978
X-Wing (Sikorsky S-72 experimental aircraft)[5]	1983	Star Wars	
Predator (unmanned aerial vehicle)	1990	Predator	1987–2010
F-22 Raptor	1998	Jurassic Park (abbreviation of "velociraptor," cloned dinosaur)	1997–2002
JEDI (Joint Expeditionary Digital Information)[6]	2002	Star Wars	1997–present
Operation Red Dawn[7]	2003	Red Dawn	1984
PHaSR (Personnel Halting and Stimulation Response) energy weapon[8]	2005	Star Trek's phaser	1965–present
Counter RocketArtillery Mortar, aka R2D2[9]	2004	Star Wars	1977–present
Aurora GoldenEye UAV[10]	2003	GoldenEye	1995
HULC (Human Universal Load Carrier) powered exoskeleton[11]	2009	The Incredible Hulk	1962–present
Transformer (VTOL ground transport)[12]	2009	Transformers	1986–present
Avatar Project[13]	2012	Avatar	2010

Appendix C
The Vietnam War Advertisements, 1968

An advertising campaign was organized by Judith Merril, who had unsuccessfully campaigned to have the Science Fiction Writers of America protest against the war (Franklin, *Vietnam* 146). Saying "We oppose the participation of the United States in the War in Vietnam," it was published in *Fantasy and Science Fiction* (March 1968) and *Galaxy Science Fiction* (June 1968) magazines, and signed by Forrest J Ackerman, Isaac Asimov, Peter S. Beagle, Jerome Bixby, James Blish, Anthony Boucher, Lyla G. Boyd, Ray Bradbury, Terry Carr, J. Clem, Ed M. Clinton, Theodore Cogswell, Arthur Jean Cox, Allan Danzig, John DeCles, Miriam Allen deFord, Samuel R. Delany, Lester del Rey, Philip K. Dick, Thomas M. Disch, Sonya Dorman, Larry Eisenberg, Harlan Ellison, Phillip José Farmer, David E. Fisher, Ron Goulart, Harry Harrison, H. Daniel Keyes, Virginia Kidd, Damon Knight, Allen Lang, March Laumer, Ursula K. Le Guin, Fritz Leiber, Irwin Lewis, Robert A.W. Lowndes, Katherine Maclean, Barry Malzberg, Robert E. Margroff, Anne Marple, Ardrey Marshall, Bruce McAllister, Judith Merril, Robert P. Mills, Howard L. Morris, Kris Neville, Alexei Panshin, Emil Petaja, J.R. Pierce, Arthur Porges, Mack Reynolds, Gene Roddenberry, Joanna Russ, James Sallis, William Sambrot, Hans Stefan Santesson, J.W. Schutz, Robin Scott, Larry T. Shaw, John Shepley, T.L. Sherred, Robert Silverberg, Henry Slesar, Jerry Sohl, Norman Spinrad, Margaret St. Clair, Jacob Transvue, Thurlow Weed, Kate Wilhelm, Richard Wilson and Donald A. Wollheim.

On hearing that these ads would be posted, Robert Heinlein contacted Jack Williamson, and organized a group of 68 writers willing to sign an advertisement proclaiming, "We the undersigned believe the United States must remain in Vietnam to fulfill its responsibilities to the people of that country." The undersigned were Karen and Poul Anderson,

Harry Bates, Lloyd M. Biggle, J.F. Bone, Leigh Brackett, Marion Zimmer Bradley, Maria Brand, Reginald Bretnor, Fredric Brown, Doris Pitkin Buck, William R. Burkett, Jr., F.M. Busby, John W. Campbell, Hal Clement, Compton Crook, Hank Davis, L. Sprague de Camp, Charles V. de Vet, William B. Ellern, Richard H. Eney, T.R. Fehrenbach, R.C. Fitzpatrick, Raymond Gallun, Daniel Galouye, Robert M. Green, Jr., Frances T. Hall, Edmond Hamilton, Robert Heinlein, Joe L. Hensley, Paul G. Herkart, Dean C. Ing, Jay Kay Klein, David A. Kyle, R.A. Lafferty, Robert J. Lemon, C.C. MacApp, Robert Mason, D.M. Melton, Norman Metcalf, P. Schuyler Miller, Sam Moskowitz, John Myers Myers, Larry Niven, Alan E. Nourse, Gerold W. Page, Stuart Palmer, Rachel Cosgrave Payes, Lawrence A. Perkins, Jerry Pournelle, Joe Poyer, E. Hoffman Price, George W. Price, Alva Rogers, Fred Saberhagen, George O. Smith, W.E. Sprague, G. Harry Stine, Dwight V. Swain, Thomas Burnett Swann, Albert Teichner, Theodore L. Thomas, Rena M. Vale, Jack Vance, Harl Vincent, Don Walsh Jr., Robert Moore Williams, Jack Williamson, Rosco E. Wright and Karl Wurf.

Appendix D
Science Fiction Films Made with the Assistance of the Pentagon (to 2013)

Condensed from Freedom of Information Act Response FOA 13-F-0135, from Michael Bowers, Office of the Secretary of Defense and Joint Staff FOIA Request Service Center, to Dr. Steven Underhill, Marshall University. https://www.academia.edu/4460251/Complete_List_of_Commercial_Films_Produced_with_Assistance_from_the_Pentagon

Armageddon (1998)
Battle Los Angeles (2011)
Battleship (2012)
Contact (1997)
The Core (2003)
The Day After Tomorrow (2004)
The Day the Earth Stood Still (1951 And 2008)
Deep Impact (1998)
The Final Countdown (1980)
Firefox (1982)
Goldeneye (1995)
I Am Legend (2007)
Invaders from Mars (1986)
Invasion USA (1985)
Iron Man (2008)
Iron Man 2 (2010)
Jurassic Park III (2001)
King Kong (1976) (According to Suid, the Navy turned down a request for the use of its planes for the 1933 *King Kong*, but the

studio paid four Naval aviators to "go and jazz the Empire State Building."[1])
Mac and Me (1988)
Red Dawn (1984)
Robojox (Aka *Robot Jox*) (1989)
The Rocketeer (1991)
Sphere (1998)
Star Trek IV (1986)
The Swarm (1978)
Tomorrow Never Dies (1997)
Transformers (2007)
Transformers: Dark of the Moon (2011)
Transformers: Revenge of the Fallen (2009)

Chapter Notes

Introduction

1. Aldiss, Brian, and David Wingrove. *Trillion Year Spree: The History of Science Fiction* (London: Victor Gollancz, 1986), pp. 13–14.
2. Campbell, John W. *The Astounding Science Fiction Anthology* (New York: Simon & Schuster, 1952), p. xv.
3. Disch, Thomas M. *The Dreams Our Stuff Is Made Of* (New York: Free Press, 1998), p. 15.
4. Clute, John, and Peter Nicholls. *The Encyclopedia of Science Fiction*. 2nd Edition (London: Orbit, 1993, 1999), p. 314.
5. Eschbach, Lloyd Arthur. *Of Worlds Beyond: The Science of Science Fiction Writing* (Chicago: Advent, 1971), p. 17.
6. Bradbury, Ray. "G.B.S.: Refurbishing the Tin Woodman: Science Fiction with a Heart, a Brain and the Nerve!" *Shaw* 17 (1997): pp. 11–17. 1 October 2011. http://www.jstor.org/pss/40681460 p. 12.
7. *Ibid.*, pp. 12–13.
8. Clute, John, and Peter Nicholls. *The Encyclopedia of Science Fiction*. 2nd Edition (London: Orbit, 1993, 1999), p. 314.
9. Gannon, Charles E. *Rumors of War and Infernal Machines: Technomilitary Agenda-Setting in American and British Speculative Fiction* (Liverpool: Liverpool University Press, 2003), p. 119.
10. Franklin, H. Bruce. *Vietnam and Other American Fantasies* (Amherst, Mass: University of Massachusetts Press, 2000), p. 151.
11. Franklin, H. Bruce. *War Stars: The Superweapon and the American Imagination* (Oxford: Oxford University Press, 1988), p. 20.
12. *Ibid.*, p. 22.
13. Eagleton, Terry. *Criticism & Ideology* (London: Verso, 1986), p. 55.
14. Aldiss, Brian, and David Wingrove. *Trillion Year Spree: The History of Science Fiction* (London: Victor Gollancz, 1986), p. 14.
15. Wiseman, John. *SAS Survival Handbook* (London: HarperCollins, 2003), p. 24.
16. *New York Times*, online edition, 17 June 2004 to 27 June 2004.
17. *New York Times*, online edition, 2 March 2002.
18. *New York Times*, online edition, 4 October 2002.
19. *New York Times*, online edition, 25 June 2003.
20. Barr, Marleen S., ed. *Envisioning the Future: Science Fiction and the Next Millennium* (Middletown CT: Wesleyan University Press, 2003), p. xv.
21. *New York Times*, online edition: 30 July 2003, 16 January 2004, 5 February 2004, 6 February 2004, 23 May 2004, 10 February 2006, 10 May 2006, 27 January 2007; News.com, 10 November 2003; Spacedaily.com, 14 February 2003, 22 February 2003; *Washington Post*, online edition, 23 December 2003.
22. *New York Times*, online edition, 6 August 2002; 15 August 2006.
23. *New York Times*, online edition, 25 June 2003, 35.
24. *New York Times*, online edition, 21 November 2004, 36.
25. Sandalow, Marc. "Cheney says dissent on war helps the enemy." SFGate Politics Blog, October 24, 2006. http://sfgate.com/cgi-bin/blogs/sfgate/detail?blogid=14&entry_id=10170
26. politicalhumor.about.com, January 10, 2007.
27. Anderson, Scott. "'It's What I Do,' by Lynsey Addario." Boot, Max. "'Right of Boom,' by Benjamin E. Schwartz." Sunday Book Review, *New York Times*, February 4, 2015. http://www.nytimes.com/2015/02/08/books/review/its-what-i-do-by-lynsey-addario.html?emc=edit_bk_20150206&nl=books&nlid=25553262&_r=0.
28. Franklin, H. Bruce. *War Stars: The Superweapon and the American Imagination* (Oxford: Oxford University Press, 1988), pp. 9–10.
29. Jackson, Patrick Thaddeus, and Daniel H. Nexon. "Representation is Futile?: American Anti-Collectivism and the Borg." *To Seek*

Out New Worlds: Exploring Links Between Science Fiction and World Politics. Ed. Jutta Weldes (New York: Palgrave Macmillan, 2003), p. 144.
30. Graham, Bradley. "Missile Defense Failing to Launch as Voting Issue." *Washington Post*, July 28, 1996, A06.
31. Van Creveld, Martin. *Technology and War: From 2000 B.C. to the Present*. 1989 (New York: Free Press, 1991), p. 74.
32. http://www.thetimes.co.uk/tto/news/world/article1970726.ece.
33. Van Creveld, Martin. *Technology and War: From 2000 B.C. to the Present* (New York: Free Press, 1991), pp. 74–75.
34. *Ibid.*
35. Haldeman, Joe. *1968* (London: Hodder and Stoughton, 1995), p. 25.
36. *Star Wars: Episode IV, A New Hope*. Written by George Lucas. Dir. George Lucas. Cast: Mark Hamill, Carrie Fisher, Harrison Ford, Peter Cushing, Alec Guinness. Twentieth Century Fox, 1977.
37. *Dr. Strangelove, or: How I Learned to Stop Worrying and Love the Bomb*. Screenplay by Peter George, Stanley Kubrick and Terry Southern, from the novel *Two Hours to Doom* by Peter George. Dir. Stanley Kubrick. Cast: Peter Sellers, George C. Scott, Sterling Hayden, Keenan Wynn, Slim Pickens. Columbia Pictures, 1964.
38. Franklin, H. Bruce. *Vietnam and Other American Fantasies* (Amherst, Mass: University of Massachusetts Press, 2000), p. 151.
39. Jameson, Frederic. *Archaeologies of the Future: The Desire Called Utopia and Other Science Fictions* (London: Versu, 2005), p. 93.
40. Jackson, Patrick Thaddeus, and Daniel H. Nexon. "Representation is Futile?: American Anti-Collectivism and the Borg." *To Seek Out New Worlds: Exploring Links Between Science Fiction and World Politics*. Ed. Jutta Weldes (New York: Palgrave Macmillan, 2003), p. 144.
41. Disch, Thomas M. *The Dreams Our Stuff Is Made Of* (New York: Free Press, 1998), p. 51.
42. Poe, Edgar Allan. "The Man That Was Used Up: A Tale of the Late Bugaboo and Kickapoo Campaigns." *The Unabridged Edgar Allan Poe* (Philadelphia: Running Press, 1983), p. 529.
43. Jones, Terry. *Chaucer's Knight: Portrait of a Medieval Mercenary* (London: Methuen, 1994).
44. Franklin, H. Bruce. *War Stars: The Superweapon and the American Imagination* (Oxford: Oxford University Press, 1988), p. 22.
45. Aldiss, Brian, and David Wingrove. *Trillion Year Spree: The History of Science Fiction* (London: Victor Gollancz, 1986), p. 18.
46. Disch, Thomas M. *The Dreams Our Stuff Is Made Of* (New York: Free Press, 1998), p. 32.
47. Jameson, Frederic. *Archaeologies of the Future: The Desire Called Utopia and Other Science Fictions* (London: Versu, 2005), p. 93.
48. Suvin, Darko. "Of Starship Troopers and Refuseniks: War and Militarism in U.S. Science Fiction, Part 2." *Extrapolation* 48, No. 1, p. 9.
49. Schama, Simon. *The American Future: A History from the Founding Fathers to Barack Obama* (London: Vintage Books, 2009), p. 47.
50. *Ibid.*, p. 48.

Chapter 1

1. Disch, Thomas M. *The Dreams Our Stuff Is Made Of* (New York: Free Press, 1998), p. 78.
2. Aaronovitch, David. "Eventually, we will all hate Obama too." timesonline.co.uk, 22 July 2008. http://www.timesonline.co.uk/tol/comment/columnists/david_aaronovitch/article4374704.ece?source=cmailer.
3. Derleth, August, and Donald Wandrei, eds. *Selected Letters*, Volume 2 (Sauk City, WI: Arkham House, 1968), p. 37.
4. Clute, John, and Peter Nicholls. *The Encyclopedia of Science Fiction*. 2nd Edition (London: Orbit, 1993, 1999), p. 368.
5. Slotkin, Richard. *Gunfighter Nation: The Myth of the Frontier in Twentieth-Century America* (Norman: University of Oklahoma Press, 1992), p. 10.
6. Wills, Garry. *John Wayne's America: The Politics of Celebrity* (New York: Simon & Schuster, 1997), p. 302.
7. *Ibid.*, p. 313.
8. Slotkin, Richard. *Gunfighter Nation: The Myth of the Frontier in Twentieth-Century America* (Norman: University of Oklahoma Press, 1992), p. 231.
9. Bourke, Joanna. *An Intimate History of Killing: Face-to-Face Killing in Twentieth-Century Warfare*. (London: Granta Books, 1999), p. 13.
10. ABC News, 23 March 2003.
11. Mills, Jane. *The Money Shot: Cinema, Sin and Censorship* (Annandale, NSW: Pluto Press Australia, 2000), p. 39.
12. Bourke, Joanna. *An Intimate History of Killing: Face-to-Face Killing in Twentieth-Century Warfare*. (London: Granta Books, 1999), pp. 25–26.
13. Urbandictionary.com
14. Slotkin, Richard. *Gunfighter Nation: The Myth of the Frontier in Twentieth-Century*

America. (New York: University of Oklahoma Press, 1992), p. 10.
 15. Wills, Garry. *John Wayne's America: The Politics of Celebrity* (New York: Simon & Schuster, 1997), p. 302.
 16. Slotkin, Richard. *Gunfighter Nation: The Myth of the Frontier in Twentieth-Century America* (Norman: University of Oklahoma Press, 1992), p. 272.
 17. Brookings. "The Davy Crockett." http://www.brookings.edu/about/projects/archive/nucweapons/davyc
 18. Slotkin, Richard. *Gunfighter Nation: The Myth of the Frontier in Twentieth-Century America* (Norman: University of Oklahoma Press, 1992), p. 380.
 19. Franklin, H. Bruce. *Vietnam and Other American Fantasies* (Amherst: University of Massachusetts Press, 2000), p. 14.
 20. Wills, Garry. *John Wayne's America: The Politics of Celebrity* (New York: Simon & Schuster, 1997), p. 302.
 21. McKee, Robert. *Story: Substance, Structure, Style and the Principles of Screenwriting* (London: Methuen, 1998, 1999), p. 93.
 22. Lucas, George. "The Wizard of *Star Wars*." Interview by Paul Scanlon, *Rolling Stone*, 25 August 1977. http://www.rollingstone.com/movies/news/the-wizard-of-star-wars-20120504?page=6.
 23. "Cowboys and Europeans." *Wall Street Journal*, 24 May 2002. http://online.wsj.com/news/articles/SB1022194791143464520.
 24. Sardar, Ziauddin, and Merryl Wyn Davies. *Why Do People Hate America?* (Crows Nest, NSW: Allen & Unwin, 2002), p. 171.
 25. Slotkin, Richard. *Gunfighter Nation: The Myth of the Frontier in Twentieth-Century America* (Norman: University of Oklahoma Press, 1992), pp. 194–207.
 26. Fenton, Robert W. *Edgar Rice Burroughs and Tarzan: A Biography of the Author and His Creation* (Jefferson, NC: McFarland, 2003), pp. 24–26.
 27. Slotkin, Richard. *Gunfighter Nation: The Myth of the Frontier in Twentieth-Century America* (Norman: University of Oklahoma Press, 1992), p. 204.
 28. *Ibid.*, pp. 635–636; Turner, Barnard E., *Cultural Tropes of the Contemporary American West* (Lewiston, NY: Edwin Mellen, 2005); Abbott, Carl. *Frontiers Past and Future: Science Fiction and the American West* (Lawrence: University of Kansas Press, 2006).
 29. Clute, John, and Peter Nicholls. *The Encyclopedia of Science Fiction*. 2nd Edition (London: Orbit, 1993, 1999), p. 120.
 30. Markstein, Don. *Don Markstein's Toonopedia*. 1 March 2005. http://www.toonopedia.com/buckrog.htm.

 31. Williams, Lorraine D., ed. *Buck Rogers: The First 60 Years in the 25th Century*. (Lake Geneva, WI: TSR, 1988), pp. 62–66.
 32. Briley, Ron. "Gene Autry and *The Phantom Empire*: The Cowboy in the Wired West of the Future." *Journal of Texas Music History* 10, No. 1 (2010): Art. 5.
 33. Heinlein, Robert A. "Shooting *Destination Moon*." 1950. In *Focus on the Science Fiction Film*. Ed. William Johnson (New Jersey: Prentice-Hall, 1972); pp. 52–65.
 34. Hill, Douglas. "Major Themes." From *Encyclopedia of Science Fiction*. Ed. Robert Holdstock (London: Octopus Books, 1978), p. 33.
 35. Harrison, Harry. *Great Balls of Fire: A History of Sex in Science Fiction Illustration* (London: Big O, 1977), pp. 57–58.
 36. *Galaxy Science Fiction*, October 1950. Rear cover.
 37. Benton, Mike. *Science Fiction Comics* (Dallas: Taylor, 1992), p. 29.
 38. Piper, H. Beam, and John McGuire, *Lone Star Planet*. 1958 (New York: Ace Books, 1979).
 39. Bozarth, G. Richard. "Bat Durston, Space Marshall." *Isaac Asimov's Science Fiction Magazine*, September–October 1978.
 40. Anthony, Piers. *Bearing an Hourglass* (New York: Del Rey/Ballantine, 1984).
 41. Whitfield, Stephen E. *The Making of Star Trek* (New York: Ballantine, 1968), p. 22.
 42. Richards, Thomas. *The Meaning of Star Trek* (New York: Doubleday, 1997), p. 5.
 43. *Moon Zero Two*. Screenplay by Michael Carreras, from an original story by Gavin Lyall, Frank Hardman and Mark Davison. Dir. Roy Ward Baker. Cast: James Olson, Catherine Schell. Warner Brothers/Seven Arts, 1969.
 44. Jenkins, Garry. *Empire Building: The Remarkable Real Life Story of Star Wars* (London: Simon & Schuster, 1997), p. 63.
 45. Slotkin, Richard. *Gunfighter Nation: The Myth of the Frontier in Twentieth-Century America* (Norman: University of Oklahoma Press, 1992), p. 635.
 46. Lucas, George. "The Wizard of *Star Wars*." Interview by Paul Scanlon, *Rolling Stone*, 25 August 1977. http://www.rollingstone.com/movies/news/the-wizard-of-star-wars-20120504?page=6.
 47. "West of Mars." *Lost in Space*. Script by Michael Fessier. Dir. Nathan Juran. Irwin Allen Productions, 1966; *Galaxina*. Screenplay by William Sachs. Dir. William Sachs. Cast: Dorothy Stratten, Avery Schreiber. Marimark Productions, 1980.
 48. "The Lost Warrior." *Battlestar Galactica*. Script by Donald P. Bellisario, story by

Herman Groves. Dir. Rod Holcomb. Universal TV, 1978; "The Magnificent Warriors." *Battlestar Galactica*. Script by Glen A. Larson. Dir. Christian Nyby II. Universal TV, 1978.

49. *Battle Beyond the Stars*. Written by John Sayles and Ann Dyer. Dir. Jimmy T. Murakami. Exec. Prod. Roger Corman. Cast: Richard Thomas, Robert Vaughan, Sam Jaffe, Sybil Danning. New World Pictures, 1980.

50. *Outland*. Written by Peter Hyams. Dir. Peter Hyams. Cast: Sean Connery, Peter Boyle. Ladd Company, 1981.

51. "Stardust." *Space: Above and Beyond*. Written by Howard Grigsby. Dir. Jesus Salvador Trevino. Fox, 1995.

52. "Spirits." *Stargate SG-1*. Written by Tor Alexander Valenza. Dir. Martin Wood. MGM, 1977.

53. "Here's How it Was: The Making of *Firefly*"; Erisman, Fred. "*Stagecoach* in Space: The Legacy of *Firefly*." *Extrapolation* 47, No. 2, pp. 249–258.

54. *Serenity*. Written by Joss Whedon. Dir. Joss Whedon. Cast: Nathan Fillion, Gina Torres, Adam Baldwin. Universal Pictures, 2005.

55. *Cowboys and Aliens*. Dir. Jon Favreau. Screenplay by Roberto Orci, Cast: Alex Kurtzman, Damon Lindelof, Mark Fergus and Hawk Ostby. Dreamworks, 2011.

56. *Westworld*. Written by Michael Crichton. Dir. Michael Crichton. Cast: Yul Brynner, Richard Benjamin. MGM, 1973.

57. *Timerider: The Adventure of Lyle Swann*. Written by William Dear and Michael Nesmith. Dir. William Dear. Cast: Fred Ward, Peter Coyote. Zoomo Productions, 1982; *Back to the Future Part III*. Screenplay by Bob Gale, story by Bob Gale and Robert Zemeckis. Dir. Robert Zemeckis. Cast: Michael J. Fox, Christopher Lloyd, Mary Steenburgen. Universal Pictures, 1990; *Timecop*. Screenplay by Mark Verheiden, story by Mike Richardson and Mark Verheiden, based on their comic series. Cast: Jean-Claude Van Damme, Mia Sara. Largo Entertainment, 1994.

58. Wills, Garry. *John Wayne's America: The Politics of Celebrity* (New York: Simon & Schuster, 1997), p. 302.

Chapter 2

1. Quoted in Darnall, Steve. "America's Uncle: a brief, unofficial, largely apolitical treatise detailing the creation and evolution of UNCLE SAM." *Uncle Sam* (New York: DC Comics, 1998), p. 2.

2. Williams, Lorraine D., ed. *Buck Rogers: The First 60 Years in the 25th Century*. (Lake Geneva, WI: TSR, 1988), p. 49.

3. Nowlan, Phillip Francis. "Armageddon 2419 A.D." *Amazing Stories*, August 1928.

4. Aldrin, Buzz. "Mr. President, Will You Lead us to Greatness in Space?" *Huffington Post*, 21 October 2009, 23 October 2009. http://www.huffingtonpost.com/buzz-aldrin/mr-president-will-you-lea_b_328975.html.

5. Gannon, Charles E. *Rumors of War and Infernal Machines: Technomilitary Agenda-Setting in American and British Speculative Fiction* (Liverpool: Liverpool University Press, 2003), p. 125.

6. Williams, Lorraine D., ed. *Buck Rogers: The First 60 Years in the 25th Century*. (Lake Geneva, WI: TSR, 1988); p. 49.

7. "The Shadow: A Short Radio History." http://www.old-time.com/sights/shadow.html.

8. "Doc Savage." *The Pulp.Net*. http://www.thepulp.net/the-links/docsavage/.

9. "The Phantom." http://www.toonopedia.com/phantom.htm.

10. "Alley Oop." *Don Markstein's Toonopedia*. http://www.toonopedia.com/oop.htm.

11. Gray, Harold. *Complete Little Orphan Annie*, Volume 6 (San Diego: IDW, 1991).

12. "Eugene the Jeep." http://popeye.wikia.com/wiki/Eugene_the_Jeep.

13. Wright, Bradford W. *Comic Book Nation: The Transformation of Youth Culture in America* (Baltimore: Johns Hopkins University Press, 2001), p. 4.

14. Daniels, Les. *Marvel: Five Decades of the World's Greatest Comics* (London: Virgin, 1991), p. 17.

15. Jones, Gerard. *Men of Tomorrow: Geeks, Gangsters and the Birth of the Comic Book* (New York: Basic Books, 2004), p. 102.

16. Holmsten, Brian, and Lubertozzi, Alex, eds. *The Complete War of the Worlds* (Naperville, IL: Sourcebooks, 2001), p. 13.

17. *Ibid.*, p. 16.

18. *Ibid.*, p. 8.

19. *New York Times*, October 31, 1938.

20. Franklin, H. Bruce. *War Stars: The Superweapon and the American Imagination* (Oxford: Oxford University Press, 1988), p. 31.

21. Hand, Richard. *Terror on the Air: Horror Radio in America, 1931–1952* (Jefferson, NC: McFarland, 2006), p. 7.

22. Miller, John Jackson. "Million-dollar Action #1 copy was once one-in-200,000." *The Comics Chronicles*, 22 February 2010, 30 September 2011. http://blog.comichron.com/2010/02/million-dollar-action-1-copy-was-once.html.

23. "The Press: Superman's Dilemma." *Time Magazine*, April 13, 1942. 1 October 2011. http://www.time.com/time/magazine/article/0,9171,766523,00.html.

24. Wright, Bradford W. *Comic Book Nation:*

The Transformation of Youth Culture in America (Baltimore: Johns Hopkins University Press, 2001), p. 11.
25. Daniels, Les. *Marvel: Five Decades of the World's Greatest Comics* (London: Virgin, 1991), p. 21.
26. *Ibid.*, p. 27.
27. Wright, Bradford W. *Comic Book Nation: The Transformation of Youth Culture in America* (Baltimore: Johns Hopkins University Press, 2001), p. 39.
28. Darnall, Steve. "America's Uncle: a brief, unofficial, largely apolitical treatise detailing the creation and evolution of UNCLE SAM." *Uncle Sam* (New York: DC Comics, 1998), p. 2.
29. Asimov, Isaac. *In Memory Yet Green: The Autobiography of Isaac Asimov, 1920–1954* (New York: Avon Books, 1979, 1980), p. 183.
30. *Ibid.*, p. 340.
31. *Ibid.*, p. 341.
32. *Ibid.*, p. 342.
33. Asimov, Isaac. *The Early Asimov* (New York: Doubleday, 1972), p. 90.
34. *Ibid.*, p. 93.
35. Daniels, Les. *Marvel: Five Decades of the World's Greatest Comics* (London: Virgin, 1991), p. 23.
36. *Amazing Stories*, May 1939. http://www.isfdb.org/cgi-bin/pl.cgi?56541.
37. *Amazing Stories*, August 1939. http://www.isfdb.org/cgi-bin/pl.cgi?56234.
38. *Amazing Stories*, November 1939. http://www.isfdb.org/cgi-bin/pl.cgi?56588.
39. *Amazing Stories*, December 1939. http://www.isfdb.org/cgi-bin/pl.cgi?56278.
40. Miller, Ron. *The Dream Machines: An Illustrated History of the Spaceship in Art, Science and Literature* (Malabar, FL: Krieger Publishing, 1993), p. 284.
41. Franklin, H. Bruce, ed. *Countdown to Midnight* (New York: DAW Books, 1984), p. 14.
42. Franklin, H. Bruce. *War Stars: The Superweapon and the American Imagination* (Oxford: Oxford University Press, 1988), pp. 138–142; Rosenfeld, Gavriel David. *The World Hitler Never Made: Alternate History and the Memory of Nazism* (Cambridge: Cambridge University Press, 2005), pp. 97–100.
43. Franklin, H. Bruce. *War Stars: The Superweapon and the American Imagination* (Oxford: Oxford University Press, 1988), p. 138.
44. Rosenfeld, Gavriel David. *The World Hitler Never Made: Alternate History and the Memory of Nazism* (Cambridge: Cambridge University Press, 2005), p. 100.
45. Crawford, Hubert H. *Crawford's Encyclopedia of Comic Books* (New York: Jonathan David, 1978), p. 341.
46. Daniels, Les. *Marvel: Five Decades of the World's Greatest Comics* (London: Virgin, 1991), p. 37.
47. Asimov, Isaac. *The Early Asimov* (New York: Doubleday, 1972), pp. 261–262.
48. Jones, Gerard. *Men of Tomorrow: Geeks, Gangsters and the Birth of the Comic Book* (New York: Basic Books, 2004), p. 102.
49. Heinlein, Robert A. "Solution Unsatisfactory." 1940. *Expanded Universe* (New York: Ace Science Fiction Books, 1980, 1983), p. 97, p. 130.
50. *Ibid.*, p. 125.
51. *Ibid.*, p. 110.
52. *Ibid.*, p. 127.
53. *Ibid.*, p. 144.
54. *Ibid.*, p. 128.
55. *Ibid.*, p. 144.
56. Asimov, Isaac. *I, Asimov: A Memoir* (New York: Doubleday, 1994), p. 78.
57. Heinlein, Robert A. "Solution Unsatisfactory." 1940. *Expanded Universe* (New York: Ace Science Fiction Books, 1983), p. 144.
58. *Ibid.*, p. 139.
59. *Ibid.*, p. 144.
60. *Ibid.*, p. 141.
61. Heinlein, Robert A. *The Day After Tomorrow*. 1941 (London: New English Library, 1972).
62. Crawford, Hubert H. *Crawford's Encyclopedia of Comic Books* (New York: Jonathan David, 1978), p. 341.
63. Daniels, Les. *Marvel: Five Decades of the World's Greatest Comics* (London: Virgin, 1991), p. 77.
64. Simon and Kirby, in Daniels. p. 39.
65. Daniels, Les. *Marvel: Five Decades of the World's Greatest Comics* (London: Virgin, 1991), p. 37.
66. Wright, Bradford W. *Comic Book Nation: The Transformation of Youth Culture in America* (Baltimore: Johns Hopkins University Press, 2001), p. 43.
67. Daniels, Les. *Marvel: Five Decades of the World's Greatest Comics* (London: Virgin, 1991), p. 37.
68. Wright, Bradford W. *Comic Book Nation: the transformation of youth culture in America* (Baltimore: Johns Hopkins University Press, 2001), p. 43.
69. Puszt, Matthew J. *Comic Book Culture: Fanboys and True Believers* (Jackson: University Press of Mississippi, 1999), p. 29.
70. *Ibid.*

Chapter 3

1. Aldiss, Brian, and David Wingrove. *Trillion Year Spree: The History of Science Fiction* (London: Victor Gollancz, 1986), pp. 47–48.

2. Heinlein, Robert A. "The Last Days of the United States." 1947. *Expanded Universe* (New York: Ace Science Fiction Books, 1980, 1983), p. 152.

3. Wright, Bradford W. *Comic Book Nation: The Transformation of Youth Culture in America* (Baltimore: Johns Hopkins University Press, 2001), p. 31.

4. "The Press: Superman's Dilemma." *Time Magazine*, April 13, 1942. 1 October 2011. http://www.time.com/time/magazine/article/0,9171,766523,00.html.

5. Lowther, George. *The Adventures of Superman* (Bedford, MA: Applewood Books, 1995), p. xv.

6. Sabin, Roger. *Adult Comics: An Introduction* (London: Routledge, 1993), p. 146.

7. Ibid., pp. 147–148.

8. Valant, Gary M.; *Vintage Aircraft Nose Art* (Osceola, NE: Motorbooks International, 1987).

9. http://www.homeofheroes.com/.

10. Quoted in Daniels, Les. *Marvel: Five Decades of the World's Greatest Comics* (London: Virgin, 1991), p. 40.

11. Ibid.

12. Steranko, James. *The Steranko History of Comics* (Reading, PA: Supergraphics, 1970).

13. Wright, Bradford W. *Comic Book Nation: The Transformation of Youth Culture in America* (Baltimore: Johns Hopkins University Press, 2001), p. 43.

14. Jones, Gerard. *Men of Tomorrow: Geeks, Gangsters and the Birth of the Comic Book* (New York: Basic Books, 2004), p. 214.

15. McGrath, John J. *The Other End of the Spear: The Tooth to Tail Ratio (T3R) in Modern Military Operations* (Fort Leavenworth: Combat Studies Institute Press, 2007), pp. 73–74.

16. "The Ghost Front." *The War*. Script by Geoffrey C. Ward. Dir. Ken Burns. Florentine Films, 2007.

17. U.S. War Department. *Order of Battle of the United States Land Forces in the World War, American Expeditionary Forces: General Headquarters, Armies, Army Corps, Services of Supply, Separate Forces*, Volume 1, 8.

18. McGrath, John J. *The Other End of the Spear: The Tooth to Tail Ratio (T3R) in Modern Military Operations* (Fort Leavenworth: Combat Studies Institute Press, 2007), pp. 73–74.

19. Jones, Gerard. *Men of Tomorrow: Geeks, Gangsters and the Birth of the Comic Book* (New York: Basic Books, 2004), p. 214.

20. Bull, Stephen. *World War II Infantry Tactics: Squad and Platoon* (Oxford: Osprey, 2004).

21. Marshall Cavendish Corporation. *History of World War II*, Volume 3: *Victory and Aftermath* (New York: Marshall Cavendish, 2005).

22. Jones, Gerard. *Men of Tomorrow: Geeks, Gangsters and the Birth of the Comic Book* (New York: Basic Books, 2004), p. 214.

23. Daniels, Les. *Marvel: Five Decades of the World's Greatest Comics* (London: Virgin, 1991), pp. 52–54.

24. Jones, Gerard. *Men of Tomorrow: Geeks, Gangsters and the Birth of the Comic Book* (New York: Basic Books, 2004), p. 214.

25. NavSource Online: Service Ship Photo Archive. 26 September 2008. 27 January 2009. http://www.navsource.org/archives/09/46/46103.htm.

26. Asimov, Isaac. *I, Asimov: A Memoir* (New York: Doubleday, 1994), p. 76.

27. Disch, Thomas M. *The Dreams Our Stuff Is Made Of* (New York: Free Press, 1998), p. 165.

28. Asimov, Isaac. *In Memory Yet Green: The Autobiography of Isaac Asimov, 1920–1954* (New York: Avon Books, 1980), p. 337.

29. Ibid., pp. 79–80.

30. Ibid., pp. 401.

31. Ibid., p. 125.

32. Ibid., p. 377.

33. Ibid., p. 461.

34. Pohl, Fred. *The Way the Future Was: A Memoir* (New York: Del Rey Books, 1978), p. 135.

35. Ibid., pp. 137–138.

36. Ibid., p. 137.

37. Ibid., p. 138.

38. Ibid.

39. Ibid., p. 140.

40. Ibid., p. 148.

41. Miller, Russell. *Bare-Faced Messiah: The True Story of L. Ron Hubbard* (London: Michael Joseph, 1987), pp. 95–111.

42. Heinlein, Robert A. "Agape and Eros: The Art of Theodore Sturgeon." Foreword to Sturgeon, Theodore. *Godbody* (New York: Donald I. Fine, 1986), p. 9.

43. Ibid., p. 11.

44. Weller, Sam. *The Bradbury Chronicles: The Life of Ray Bradbury* (New York: HarperCollins, 2005), p. 115.

45. Ibid., p. 106.

46. Ibid., p. 12.

47. Heinlein, Robert A. "Agape and Eros: The Art of Theodore Sturgeon." Foreword to Sturgeon, Theodore. *Godbody* (New York: Donald I. Fine, Inc., 1986), p. 9.

48. Asimov, Isaac. *In Memory Yet Green: The Autobiography of Isaac Asimov, 1920–1954* (New York: Avon Books, 1980), p. 388.

49. Miller, Russell. *Bare-Faced Messiah: The True Story of L. Ron Hubbard* (London: Michael Joseph, 1987), p. 108.

50. Silverberg, Robert. "Reflections: The Cleve Cartmill Affair." 2003. *Asimov's Science Fiction*. 21 March 2007. http://www.asimovs.com/_issue_0310/ref.shtml.
51. Franklin, H. Bruce, ed. *Countdown to Midnight* (New York: DAW Books, 1984), p. 15.
52. Seed, David. *American Science Fiction and the Cold War* (Edinburgh: Edinburgh University Press, 1999), p. 15.
53. Franklin, H. Bruce. *War Stars: The Superweapon and the American Imagination* (Oxford: Oxford University Press, 1988), p. 147.
54. Silverberg, Robert. "Reflections: The Cleve Cartmill Affair." 2003. *Asimov's Science Fiction*. 21 March 2007. http://www.asimovs.com/_issue_0310/ref.shtml.
55. *Ibid.*
56. *Ibid.*
57. *Ibid.*
58. *Ibid.*
59. Brians, Paul. "Nuclear Holocausts: Atomic War in Fiction." 15 March 2007. http://www.wsu.edu:8080/~brians/nuclear/1chap.htm.
60. Franklin, H. Bruce. *War Stars: The Superweapon and the American Imagination* (Oxford: Oxford University Press, 1988), p. 183.
61. Haldeman, Joe. *Old Twentieth* (New York: Ace Books, 2005), p. 134.
62. De Camp, L. Sprague. "Retrospective." 1988. *Requiem*. Ed. Kondi Yojo (New York: Tor Books, 1992), p. 292.
63. Asimov, Isaac. *In Memory Yet Green: The Autobiography of Isaac Asimov, 1920–1954* (New York: Avon Books, 1980), p. 118.

Chapter 4

1. "National Affairs: LEAST ABHORRENT CHOICE." *Time Magazine*, February 3, 1947. 1 October 2011. http://www.time.com/time/magazine/article/0,9171,886289,00.html.
2. *Ibid.*
3. Boyer, Paul. *By the Bomb's Early Light: American Thoughts and Culture at the Dawn of the Atomic Age* (Chapel Hill, NC: University of North Carolina, 1994), p. 257.
4. Wells, Herbert George. *The Last War: A World Set Free*. 1914 (Lincoln, NE: Bison Books, 2001).
5. *Things to Come*. Screenplay by H.G. Wells, adapted from his novel *The Shape of Things to Come*. Dir. William Cameron Menzies. Prod. Alexander Korda. Cast: Ralph Richardson, Raymond Massey, Edward Chapman, Cedric Hardwicke. London Film Productions, 1936.

6. Gannon, Charles E. *Rumors of War and Infernal Machines: Technomilitary Agenda-Setting in American and British Speculative Fiction* (Liverpool: Liverpool University Press, 2003), p. 112.
7. Heinlein, Robert A. *Expanded Universe* (New York: Ace Science Fiction Books, 1983), p. 276.
8. *Ibid.*, p. 145.
9. *Ibid.*, p. 146.
10. *Ibid.*
11. Heinlein, Robert A. "The Last Days of the United States." 1947. *Expanded Universe* (New York: Ace Science Fiction Books, 1983), p. 150.
12. *Ibid.*, p. 151.
13. *Ibid.*, p. 154.
14. *Ibid.*, p. 155.
15. *Ibid.*, p. 156.
16. *Ibid.*
17. *Ibid.*, p. 162.
18. Franklin, H. Bruce. *War Stars: The Superweapon and the American Imagination* (Oxford: Oxford University Press, 1988), p. 160.
19. *Ibid.*, p. 161.
20. Brians, Paul. "Nuclear Holocausts: Atomic War in Fiction." 15 March 2007. http://www.wsu.edu:8080/~brians/nuclear/1chap.htm.
21. Davis, Chandler. "To Still the Drums." 1946. *Countdown to Midnight*. Ed. H. Bruce Franklin (New York: DAW Books, 1984), p. 31.
22. Sturgeon, Theodore. "Thunder and Roses." 1947. *Thunder and Roses* (Berkeley: North Atlantic Books, 1997), pp. 125–149.
23. Neville, Kris. "Cold War." 1949. In Lewis, Tony, ed. *The Best of Astounding* (New York: Baronet, 1978).
24. Heinlein, Robert A. "The Long Watch." 1948. *The Green Hills of Earth* (New York: New American Library, 1951), p. 40.
25. *Ibid.*, p. 41.
26. *Ibid.*, p. 42.
27. *Ibid.*, p. 41.
28. Daniels, Les. *Marvel: Five Decades of the World's Greatest Comics* (London: Virgin, 1991), p. 54.
29. *Ibid.*, p. 55.
30. *Ibid.*
31. Miller, Ron. *The Dream Machines: An Illustrated History of the Spaceship in Art, Science and Literature* (Malabar, FL: Krieger, 1993), p. 289.
32. *Ibid.*, p. 292.

Chapter 5

1. *The Thing from Another World*. Screenplay by Charles Lederer, Howard Hawks and

Ben Hecht; adapted from "Who Goes There" by John W. Campbell. Dir. Christian Nyby. Prod. Howard Hawkes. Cast: Kenneth Tobey, Robert Cornthwaite, Douglas Spencer, James Arness. Winchester Pictures Corporation, 1951.

2. Prokosch, Eric. *The Technology of Killing: A Military and Political History of Antipersonnel Weapons* (London: Zed Books Ltd, 1995), p. 16.

3. Aldiss, Brian. "A Brief History." *The Science Fiction Source Book*. Ed. David Wingrove (Essex: Longman Group Limited, 1984), p. 17.

4. Clute, John. *Science Fiction: The Illustrated Encyclopaedia* (Surry Hills, NSW: Dorling Kindersley, 1995).

5. Lucanio, Patrick. *Them or Us: Archetypal Interpretations of Fifties Alien Invasion Films* (Bloomington: Indiana University Press, 1988), p. 1.

6. Wingrove, David, ed. *Science Fiction Film Source Book* (London: Longman Group, 1985), p. 314.

7. *Destination Moon*. Screenplay by Rip Van Ronkel, James O'Hanlon and Robert A. Heinlein, from novel *Rocketship Galileo* by Robert A. Heinlein. Dir. Irving Pichel. George Pal Productions, 1950.

8. *Ibid.*
9. *Ibid.*
10. *Ibid.*

11. Heinlein, Robert A. *Rocketship Galileo*. 1947 (London: New English Library, 1973).

12. Miller, Ron. *The Dream Machines: An Illustrated History of the Spaceship in Art, Science and Literature* (Malabar, FL: Krieger, 1993), p. 408.

13. Waldrop, Howard. "You Are What You See. 2. Do We Eat Lunch, or Do We Go to the Moon?" *The Infinite Matrix*, 6 January 2006, 3 January 2007. http://www.infinitematrix.net/columns/waldrop/waldrop22.html.

14. *Rocketship X-M*. Screenplay by Dalton Trumbo, Kurt Neumann and Orville Hampton. Dir. Kurt Neumann. Lippert Pictures, 1950.

15. *Ibid.*

16. Schama, Simon. *The American Future: A History from the Founding Fathers to Barack Obama* (London: Vintage Books, 2009), p. 47.

17. *Ibid.*, p. 49.

18. King, Stephen. *Danse Macabre* (London: Macdonald Futura, 1981), p. 145.

19. *Ibid.*
20. *Ibid.*, p. 147.

21. Lederer, Charles. *The Thing from Another World*. Early draft screenplay, 29 August 1950. 3 April 2007. http://www.scifiscripts.com/scripts/ThingFromAnotherWorld.txt.

22. *Ibid.*

23. King, Stephen. *Danse Macabre* (London: Macdonald Futura, 1981), p. 151.

24. Evans, Joyce A. *Celluloid Mushroom Clouds: Hollywood and the Atomic Bomb* (Boulder, CO: Westview Press, 1998), p. 179.

25. Jancovich, Mark. *Rational Fears: American Horror in the 1950s* (New York: Manchester University Press, 1996), p. 35.

26. *Ibid.*, p. 36.

27. King, Stephen. *Danse Macabre* (London: Macdonald Futura, 1981), p. 146.

28. Strick, Phillip. *Science Fiction Movies* (London: Octopus Books, 1976), p. 22.

29. imdb.com.

30. *Invasion USA*. Screenplay by Robert Smith, story by Robert Smith and Frank Spencer. Dir. Alfred E. Green. Columbia Pictures, 1952.

31. *The Day the Earth Stood Still*. Dir. Robert Wise. Screenplay by Edmund H. North, from "Farewell to the Master" by Harry Bates. Cast: Michael Rennie, Patricia Neal, Hugh Marlowe, Sam Jaffe, Billy Gray, Lock Martin. Twentieth Century Fox, 1951.

32. Wise, Robert. Commentary on DVD. *The Day the Earth Stood Still*

33. *Ibid.*

34. Phillips, Kendall R. *Projected Fears: Horror Films and American Culture* (Westport CT: Praeger, 2005), p. 44.

35. *The Day the Earth Stood Still*. Dir. Robert Wise. Screenplay by Edmund H. North, from "Farewell to the Master" by Harry Bates. Cast: Michael Rennie, Patricia Neal, Hugh Marlowe, Sam Jaffe, Billy Gray, Lock Martin. Twentieth Century Fox, 1951.

36. *Ibid.*
37. *Ibid.*
38. *Ibid.*
39. *Ibid.*
40. *Ibid.*

41. Meyer, Nicholas. Commentary on DVD. *The Day the Earth Stood Still*.

42. Wise, Robert. Commentary on DVD. *The Day the Earth Stood Still*.

43. *Ibid.*

44. Cannon, Lou. *President Reagan: The Role of a Lifetime* (New York: Simon & Schuster, 1991), p. 60.

45. Schelde, Per. *Androids, Humanoids, and Other Science Fiction Monsters: Science and Soul in Science Fiction Films* (New York: New York University Press, 1993), p. 94.

46. Franklin, H. Bruce. *War Stars: The Superweapon and the American Imagination* (Oxford: Oxford University Press, 1988), p. 182.

47. *Invaders from Mars*. Screenplay by Richard Blake. Dir. William Cameron Menzies. 20th Century Fox, 1953.

48. *Earth vs. the Flying Saucers*. Screen story by Curt Siodmak, suggested by *Flying Saucers from Outer Space* by Major Donald E. Keyhoe. Dir. Fred F. Sears. Cast: Hugh Marlowe. Clover Productions, 1956.
49. *The Amazing Colossal Man*. Screenplay by Max Hanna and Bert I. Gordon. Dir. Bert I. Gordon. American International Pictures, 1957; *Them!* Screenplay by Russell Hughes and Ted Sherdeman from a story by George Worthing Yates. Dir. Gordon Douglas. Cast: James Whitmore, James Arness, Edmund Gwenn, Joan Weldon. Warner Brothers Pictures, 1954; *Invisible Invaders*. Written by Samuel Newman. Dir. Edward L. Cahn. Cast: John Agar. United Artists, 1959; *The Beast From 20,000 Fathoms*. Screenplay by Lou Morheim and Fred Freiberger. Story by Ray Bradbury. Dir. Eugene Lourie. Perf. Paul Hubschmid, Kenneth Tobey, Lee Van Cleef. Animation effects by Ray Harryhausen. Warner Bros, 1953.
50. *Tarantula*. Screenplay by Robert M. Fresco and Martin Berkeley; story by Jack Arnold and Robert M. Fresco. Dir. Jack Arnold. Perf. John Agar, Leo G. Carroll. Universal Pictures, 1955; *Gog*. Screenplay by Tom Taggart, story by Ivan Tors. Dir. Herbert L. Strock. United Artists, 1954.
51. *It Came From Beneath the Sea*. Screenplay by George Worthing Yates and Hal Smith, story by George Worthing Yates. Dir. Robert Gordon. Cast: Kenneth Tobey, Faith Domergue. Visual effects by Ray Harryhausen. Columbia Pictures, 1955; *The Monster that Challenged the World*. Written by David Duncan and Pat Fielder. Dir. Arnold Laven. United Artists, 1957; *The Atomic Submarine*. Written by Orville H. Hampton. Dir. Spencer Gordon Bennett. Allied Artists Pictures, 1959.
52. *The Deadly Mantis*. Screenplay by Martin Berkeley, story by William Alland. Dir. Nathan Juran. Universal Pictures, 1957.
53. Imdb.com.
54. *Invasion USA*. Screenplay by Robert Smith, story by Robert Smith and Franz Schulz. Dir. Alfred E. Green. American Pictures, 1952.
55. *The War of the Worlds*. Screenplay by Barre Lyndon, from the novel by H.G. Wells. Dir Byron Haskin. Prod. George Pal. Cast: Gene Barry, Robert Cornthwaite. Paramount, 1953.
56. *Forbidden Planet*. Screenplay by Cyril Hume, based on a story by Irving Block and Allen Adler. Dir. Fred McLeod Wilcox. Cast: Leslie Nielsen, Walter Pidgeon, Anne Francis, Warren Stevens. MGM, 1956,
57. *This Island Earth*. Screenplay by Franklin Coen and Edward G. O'Callaghan, from the story "The Alien Machine" by Raymond F. Jones. Dir. Joseph M. Newman and Jack Arnold. Cast: Jeff Morrow, Faith Domergue, Rex Reason, Russell Johnson. Universal Pictures, 1955.
58. Clary, David. *Before and After Roswell: The Flying Saucer in America, 1947–1999* (Bloomington IN: Xlibris, 2000), p. 57.
59. *Earth vs. the Flying Saucers*. Screen story by Curt Siodmak, suggested by *Flying Saucers from Outer Space* by Major Donald E. Keyhoe. Dir. Fred F. Sears. Cast: Hugh Marlowe. Clover Productions, 1956.
60. *Ibid.*
61. Tucker, Wilson. *The Long Loud Silence* (London: Coronet, 1952, 1980).
62. Knight, Damon. *In Search of Wonder* (Chicago: Advent, 1968), pp. 178–180.
63. Dick, Philip K., "Pessimism in Science Fiction" (1955) in *The Shifting Realities of Philip K. Dick* (New York: Pantheon Books, 1995), p. 54.
64. Bradbury, Ray. "There Will Come Soft Rains" (1950). *The Silver Locusts* (London: Corgi Books, 1972), pp. 166–171.
65. The Internet Science Fiction Database. http://www.isfdb.org/cgi-bin/pl.cgi? 310539.
66. Asimov, Isaac. *The Currents of Space*. 1952 (London: Panther Books, 1973).
67. Asimov, Isaac. "The Gentle Vultures" 1957. *Nine Tomorrows* (London: Pan Science Fiction, 1976), pp. 133–151.
68. Asimov, Isaac. "Spell My Name with an S" 1958. *Nine Tomorrow* (London: Pan Science Fiction, 1976), pp. 171–188.
69. Miller, Walter M. *A Canticle for Leibowitz*. 1959 (London: Corgi, 1975).
70. *Invasion USA*. Screenplay by Robert Smith, story by Robert Smith and Frank Spencer. Dir. Alfred E. Green. Columbia Pictures, 1952.
71. *King Dinosaur*. Screenplay by Tom Gries, based on an original story by Bert I. Gordon and Al Zimbalist. Dir. Bert I. Gordon. Lippert Pictures, 1955.
72. *Invasion USA*. Screenplay by Robert Smith, story by Robert Smith and Frank Spencer. Dir. Alfred E. Green. Columbia Pictures, 1952; *Rocket Attack U.S.A.* Written by Barry Mahon. Dir. Barry Mahon. Exploit Films, 1961.
73. *Five*. Written by Arch Oboler and James Weldon Johnson. Dir. Arch Oboler. Columbia Pictures, 1951; *Teenage Caveman*. Screenplay by R. Wright Campbell. Dir. Roger Corman. Cast: Robert Vaughn. American International Pictures, 1957; *On the Beach*. Screenplay by John Paxton, from the novel by Nevil Shute. Dir. Stanley Kramer. Cast: Gregory Peck, Ava Gardner, Fred Astaire. Stanley Kramer Productions, 1959.

74. *On the Beach*. Screenplay by John Paxton, from the novel by Nevil Shute. Dir. Stanley Kramer. Cast: Gregory Peck, Ava Gardner, Fred Astaire. Stanley Kramer Productions, 1959.

75. Gannon, Charles E. *Rumors of War and Infernal Machines: Technomilitary Agenda-Setting in American and British Speculative Fiction* (Liverpool: Liverpool University Press, 2003), p. 134.

76. *Panic in Year Zero!* Screenplay by Jay Simms and John Morton, story by John Morton, based on *Lot* and *Lot's Daughter* by Ward Moore. Dir. Ray Milland. Cast: Ray Milland. American International Pictures, 1962.

77. *The Amazing Colossal Man*. Screenplay by Max Hanna and Bert I. Gordon. Dir. Bert I. Gordon. American International Pictures, 1957; *The Monster that Challenged the World*. Written by David Duncan and Pat Fielder. Dir. Arnold Laven. United Artists, 1957; *Them!* Screenplay by Russell Hughes and Ted Sherdeman from a story by George Worthing Yates. Dir. Gordon Douglas. Cast: James Whitmore, James Arness, Edmund Gwenn, Joan Weldon. Warner Brothers Pictures, 1954; *The Beast From 20,000 Fathoms*. Screenplay by Lou Morheim and Fred Freiberger. Story by Ray Bradbury. Dir. Eugene Lourie. Cast: Paul Hubschmid, Kenneth Tobey, Lee Van Cleef. Animation effects by Ray Harryhausen. Warner Bros, 1953; *It Came From Beneath the Sea*. Screenplay by George Worthing Yates and Hal Smith, story by George Worthing Yates. Dir. Robert Gordon. Cast: Kenneth Tobey, Faith Domergue. Visual effects by Ray Harryhausen. Columbia Pictures, 1955; *The Incredible Shrinking Man*. Written by Richard Matheson. Dir. Jack Arnold. Universal Pictures, 1957; *The Beast of Yucca Flats*. Written by Coleman Francis. Dir. Coleman Francis. Cast: Tor Johnson, Douglas Mellor, Barbara Francis, Ronald Francis, Alan Francis, Coleman Francis. Cinema Associates, 1961.

78. *It Came From Beneath the Sea*. Screenplay by George Worthing Yates and Hal Smith, story by George Worthing Yates. Dir. Robert Gordon. Cast: Kenneth Tobey, Faith Domergue. Visual effects by Ray Harryhausen. Columbia Pictures, 1955.

79. Bradbury, Ray. "Embroidery" 1951. Bradbury, Ray. *The Golden Apples of the Sun* (London: Corgi Books, 1953, 1973), pp. 73–76.

80. Asimov, Isaac. "Hell-Fire" (1956) Asimov, Isaac. *Earth is Room Enough* (London: Panther Books, 1976), pp. 117–118.

81. Asimov, Isaac. "Silly Asses" (1958) in Asimov, Isaac. *Buy Jupiter!* (London: Panther, 1976), pp. 142–146.

82. *Them!* Screenplay by Russell Hughes and Ted Sherdeman from a story by George Worthing Yates. Dir. Gordon Douglas. Cast: James Whitmore, James Arness, Edmund Gwenn, Joan Weldon. Warner Brothers Pictures, 1954.

83. *The Space Children*. Screenplay by Bernard C. Schoenfeld, story by Tom Filer. Dir. Jack Arnold. Paramount Pictures, 1958.

84. *Plan 9 From Outer Space*. Screenplay by Edward D. Wood Jr. Dir. Edward D. Wood Jr. Cast: Gregory Walcott, Tom Keene, Dudley Manlove. Reynolds Pictures, 1959.

85. Evans, Joyce A. *Celluloid Mushroom Clouds: Hollywood and the Atomic Bomb* (Boulder, CO: Westview Press, 1998), p. 179.

86. Zicree, Marc Scott. *The Twilight Zone Companion* (New York: Bantam Books, 1982), p. 136.

87. "*King Nine* Will Not Return." *The Twilight Zone*. Written by Rod Serling. Dir. Buzz Kulik. Cast: Bob Cummings. CBS, 1960.

88. "The Thirty-Fathom Grave" *The Twilight Zone*. Written by Rod Serling. Dir. Perry Lafferty. Cast: Mike Kellin, Simon Oakland, Bill Bixby. CBS, 1963.

89. Zicree, Marc Scott. *The Twilight Zone Companion* (New York: Bantam Books, 1982), p. 4.

90. *Ibid.*, p. 26.

91. "Where Is Everybody?" *The Twilight Zone*. Written by Rod Serling. Dir. Robert Stevens. Cast: Earl Holliman. CBS, 1959.

92. "The Purple Testament." *The Twilight Zone*. Written by Rod Serling. Dir. Richard L. Bare. Cast: William Reynolds, Dick York. CBS, 1960.

93. "A Quality of Mercy." *The Twilight Zone*. Written by Rod Serling, based on an idea by Sam Rolfe. Dir. Buzz Kulik. Cast: Dean Stockwell, Albert Salmi, Jerry Fujikawa, Dale Ishimoto, Leonard Nimoy, Michael Pataki. CBS, 1961.

94. Zicree, Marc Scott. *The Twilight Zone Companion* (New York: Bantam Books, 1982), p. 4.

95. "Two." *The Twilight Zone*. Written and directed by Montgomery Pittman. Cast: Charles Bronson, Elizabeth Montgomery. CBS, 1961.

96. Zicree, Marc Scott. *The Twilight Zone Companion* (New York: Bantam Books, 1982), p. 423.

97. "The Encounter." *The Twilight Zone*. Written by Martin M. Goldsmith. Dir. Robert Butler. Cast: Neville Brand, George Takei. CBS, 1964.

98. Takei, George. "George Takei Discusses *The Twilight Zone*." https://www.youtube.com/watch?v=bA-9iIsAcI0.

99. "I Shot An Arrow Into The Air." *The*

Twilight Zone. Written by Rod Serling, based on an idea by Madelon Champion. Dir. Stuart Rosenberg. CBS, 1960.
100. "The 7th is Full of Phantoms." *The Twilight Zone.* Written by Rod Serling. Dir. Alan Crosland Jr. CBS, 1963.
101. "In Praise of Pip." *The Twilight Zone.* Written by Rod Serling. Dir. Bert Granet. Cast: Jack Klugman, Billy Mumy, Bob Diamond. CBS, 1963.
102. "The Last Flight." *The Twilight Zone.* Written by Richard Matheson. Dir. William Claxton. Cast: Kenneth Haigh. CBS, 1960.
103. Wright, Bradford W. *Comic Book Nation: The Transformation of Youth Culture in America* (Baltimore: Johns Hopkins University Press, 2001), p. 111.
104. Nolan, Michelle. "Collecting the Marvel Family Horror Stories." *Nolan's Niche*, CGC Comics (2008). http://www.cgccomics.com/news/enews/2008/November/article3.asp.
105. Wright, Bradford W. *Comic Book Nation: The Transformation of Youth Culture in America* (Baltimore: Johns Hopkins University Press, 2001), p. 155.
106. Daniels, Les. *Marvel: Five Decades of the World's Greatest Comics* (London: Virgin, 1991), p. 66.
107. Jones, Gerard. *Men of Tomorrow: Geeks, Gangsters and the Birth of the Comic Book* (New York: Basic Books, 2004), p. 257.
108. Ibid.
109. Wright, Bradford W. *Comic Book Nation: The Transformation of Youth Culture in America.* (Baltimore: Johns Hopkins University Press, 2001), p. 112.
110. Marvel Database. "Captain America Comics Vol. 1, No. 77." http://marvel.wikia.com/Captain_America_Comics_Vol_1_77.
111. Lehto, Steve. *The Great American Jet Pack: The Quest for the Individual Lift Device* (Chicago: Chicago Review Press, 2013), p. 17.
112. Ibid., p. 24.
113. Ibid., pp. 24–26.
114. Ibid., p. 29.
115. Ibid., p. 80.
116. Ibid., pp. 91–92.
117. *The Day the Earth Stood Still.* Dir. Robert Wise. Screenplay by Edmund H. North, from "Farewell to the Master" by Harry Bates. Cast: Michael Rennie, Patricia Neal, Hugh Marlowe, Sam Jaffe, Billy Gray, Lock Martin. Twentieth Century–Fox, 1951.
118. Carosso, Andrea. *Cold War Narratives: American Culture in the 1950s* (Bern: Peter Lang AG, 2012), p. 24.
119. *Historical Tables: Budget of the United States Government, Fiscal Year 2009.* www.whitehouse.gov/omb/budget/fy2009/pdf/hist.pdf 1 October 2011, pp. 48–50.
120. Jameson, Frederic. *Archaeologies of the Future: The Desire Called Utopia and Other Science Fictions* (London: Versu, 2005), p. 93.
121. Kornbluth, Cyril M. "The Adventurer." 1953. Kornbluth, Cyril M. *The Best of C.M. Kornbluth* (New York: Ballantine Books, 1976), pp. 23–28.
122. Dick, Philip K. "The Defenders." 1953. Dick, Philip K. *Beyond Lies the Wub: Volume One of the Collected Short Stories* (London: Gollancz, 1999), p. 86.
123. Bradbury, Ray. "A Piece of Wood." 1952. Bradbury, Ray. *Long After Midnight* (New York: Bantam Books, 1975), p. 49.
124. Ibid., p. 53.
125. Clarke, Arthur C. *Childhood's End.* 1953 (London: Pan Books, 1973), p. 97.
126. Pohl, Frederik. "The Wizard of Pung's Corners." 1958. Pohl, Frederick. *The Frederik Pohl Omnibus* (St. Albans: Panther, 1973), pp. 236–264.
127. Heinlein, Robert A. *Starship Troopers* (New York: Ace Books, 1959, 1987), p. 24.
128. Panshin, Alexei. *Heinlein in Dimension: A Critical Analysis* (Chicago: Advent, 1968), p. 97.
129. Vonnegut, Kurt. *Player Piano* (New York: The Dial Press, 1952, 1999), p. 66.
130. Ibid., p. 68.
131. Heinlein, Robert A. *Starship Troopers* (New York: Ace Books, 1959, 1987), p. 131.
132. Heinlein, Robert A. *Expanded Universe* (New York: Ace Science Fiction Books, 1980, 1983), p. 398.
133. Heinlein, Robert A. *Between Planets* (New York: Ace Books, 1951), p. 135.
134. Ibid., p. 156.
135. Ibid., p. 144.
136. Ibid., pp. 172–173.
137. Ibid., p. 177.
138. Ibid., p. 14.
139. Ibid., p. 145.
140. Heinlein, Robert A. *Expanded Universe* (New York: Ace Science Fiction Books, 1983), p. 393.
141. Asimov, Isaac. *In Joy Still Felt: The Autobiography of Isaac Asimov, 1954–1978* (New York: Avon Books, 1981), p. 10.
142. Heinlein, Robert A. *Expanded Universe* (New York: Ace Science Fiction Books, 1983), p. 398.
143. Ibid.
144. Ibid.
145. Kavenay, Roz. *From Alien to the Matrix: Reading Science Fiction Film* (London: I.B. Tauris, 2005), p. 19.
146. Heinlein, Robert A. *Starship Troopers* (New York: Ace Books, 1959, 1987), p. 152.
147. Ibid., p. 153.
148. Quoted in Panshin, Alexei. *The Abyss*

Notes. Chapter 5

of Wonder. 2 April 2007. http://www.enter.net/~torve/contents.htm.

149. Quoted in Panshin, Alexei. *The Abyss of Wonder.* 2 April 2007. http://www.enter.net/~torve/contents.htm.

150. Panshin, Alexei. *Heinlein in Dimension: A Critical Analysis* (Chicago: Advent, 1968), p. 94.

151. *Ibid.*, p. 96.

152. Franklin, H. Bruce. *Robert A. Heinlein: America as Science Fiction* (New York: Oxford University Press, 1980), p. 111.

153. Spinrad, Norman. *Science fiction in the Real World* (Carbondale: Southern Illinois University Press, 1990), p. 144.

154. Blish, James, quoted in Panshin, Alexei. *The Abyss of Wonder.* 2 April 2007. http://www.enter.net/~torve/contents.htm.

155. Heinlein, Robert A. *Starship Troopers.* 1959 (New York: Ace Books, 1987), p. 208.

156. *Ibid.*, page v.

157. *Ibid.*, p. 70.

158. *Ibid.*, p. 56.

159. *Ibid.*, p. 83.

160. *Ibid.*, p. 82.

161. *Ibid.*, p. 189.

162. http://web.archive.org/web/20060222120250/http://www.marines.mil/almars/almar2000.nsf/0/91c8a9b3b9a2b59785256a55005e129d?OpenDocument; http://web.archive.org/web/20051219025149/http://www.lejeune.usmc.mil/2dmardiv/26/three.html.

163. http://www.navyreading.navy.mil/CMSPages/.

164. Heinlein, Robert A. *Starship Troopers.* 1959 (New York: Ace Books, 1987), p. 9.

165. Weinberger, Sharon. *Imaginary Weapons: A Journey through the Pentagon's Scientific Underworld* (New York: Nation Books, 2006).

166. Heinlein, Robert A. *Starship Troopers.* 1959 (New York: Ace Books, 1987), p. 11.

167. *Ibid.*, p. 135.

168. "Robust Nuclear Earth Penetrator." GlobalSecurity.org. http://www.globalsecurity.org/wmd/systems/rnep.htm.

169. Beckhusen, Robert. "Smile! U.S. Troops cover up with new "Facial Armor." Wired.com. http://www.wired.com/2012/05/face-shields/.

170. Weinberger, Sharon. "Iron Man to Batman: The Future of Soldier Suits." BBC Future 21 January 2013. http://www.bbc.com/future/story/20130121-batman-meets-ironman-in-combat.

171. Durant, Michael J. with Steven Hartov. *In the Company of Heroes* (New York: G.P. Putnam Sons, 2003).

172. Franklin, H. Bruce. *Robert A. Heinlein: America as Science Fiction* (New York: Oxford University Press, 1980), p. 111.

173. *Ibid.*, p. 116.

174. *Ibid.*, p. 117.

175. Heinlein, Robert A. *Expanded Universe* (New York: Ace Science Fiction Books, 1983), p. 397.

176. Heinlein, Robert A. *Starship Troopers.* 1959 (New York: Ace Books, 1987), p. 109.

177. Heinlein, Robert A. *Expanded Universe* (New York: Ace Science Fiction Books, 1983), p. 397.

178. Gifford, James. "The Nature of Federal Service in Robert A. Heinlein's *Starship Troopers.*" 12 March 2007. http://www.nitrosyncretic.com/rah/ftp/fedrlsvc.pdf p 11.

179. Heinlein, Robert A. *Expanded Universe* (New York: Ace Science Fiction Books, 1983), p. 397.

180. Heinlein, Robert A. *Starship Troopers.* 1959 (New York: Ace Books, 1987), p. 137.

181. Heinlein, Robert A. *Expanded Universe* (New York: Ace Science Fiction Books, 1983), p. 397.

182. Heinlein, Robert A. *Starship Troopers.* 1959 (New York: Ace Books, 1987), p. 29.

183. *Ibid.*, p. 30.

184. *Ibid.*, p. 162.

185. Farmer, Philip José, quoted in Panshin, Alexei. *The Abyss of Wonder.* 2 April 2007. http://www.enter.net/~torve/contents.htm.

186. Heinlein, Robert A. *Starship Troopers.* 1959 (New York: Ace Books, 1987), p. 180.

187. *Ibid.*, p. 182.

188. *Ibid.*, p. 163.

189. Vonnegut, Kurt. *Player Piano.* 1952 (New York: Dial Press, 1999), p. 66.

190. Heinlein, Robert A. *Expanded Universe* (New York: Ace Science Fiction Books, 1983), p. 396.

191. Heinlein, Robert A. *Starship Troopers.* 1959 (New York: Ace Books, 1987), p. 126.

192. *Ibid.*, p. 184.

193. *Ibid.*, p. 176.

194. *Ibid.*, p. 36.

195. Aldiss, Brian W. "Heinlein's Starship Troopers." 2 March 2007. http://www.enter.net/~torve/critics/PITFCS/141aldiss.html.

196. Heinlein, Robert A. *Starship Troopers.* 1959 (New York: Ace Books, 1987), p. 109.

197. *Ibid.*, p. 184.

198. *Ibid.*, p. 181.

199. Panshin, Alexei. *Heinlein in Dimension: A Critical Analysis* (Chicago: Advent Publishing, 1968), p. 96.

200. *Ibid.*, p. 91.

201. Heinlein, Robert A. *Starship Troopers.* 1959 (New York: Ace Books, 1987), p. 26.

202. *Ibid.*, p. 184.

203. *Ibid.*, p. 208.

204. The Science Fiction and Fantasy Research Database. http://sffrd.library.tamu.edu/about/.

205. Franklin, H. Bruce. *Robert A. Heinlein: America as Science Fiction* (New York: Oxford University Press, 1980), p. 110.
206. Heinlein, Robert A. *Expanded Universe* (New York: Ace Science Fiction Books, 1983), p. 396.
207. Rosenbaum, Jonathan. *Movie Wars: How Hollywood and the Media Conspire to Limit What Films We Can See* (Chicago: A Capella Books, 2000).
208. Heinlein, Robert A. *Starship Troopers.* 1959 (New York: Ace Books, 1987), p. 178, p. 223.
209. *Ibid.*, p. 182.
210. *Ibid.*, p. 125.
211. *Ibid.*, p. 186.
212. *Ibid.*, p. 24.
213. *Ibid.*, p. 118.
214. *Ibid.*, p. 262.
215. *Ibid.*, p. 100.
216. *Ibid.*, p. 178.
217. Panshin, Alexei. *Heinlein in Dimension: A Critical Analysis* (Chicago: Advent Publishing, 1968), p. 97.

Chapter 6

1. Orwell, George. *Nineteen Eighty-Four.* 1949 (Harmondsworth, UK: Penguin Books, 1980), p. 155.
2. Harrison, Harry. "Commando Raid." 1970. Ed. Joe Haldeman. *Study War No More* (New York: Avon Books, 1977), p. 122.
3. Moore, Alan. *Watchmen* (New York: DC Comics, 1986, 1987), Chapter 4, p. 19.
4. Haldeman, Joe. *1968* (London: Hodder and Stoughton, 1995), p. 31.
5. Drake, David. "Afterword: We Happy Few." *The Tank Lords* (New York: Baen Books, 1986, 1997), p. 390.
6. Evans, Joyce A. *Celluloid Mushroom Clouds: Hollywood and the Atomic Bomb* (Boulder, CO: Westview Press, 1998), Appendix.
7. *Panic in Year Zero!* Screenplay by Jay Simms and John Morton, story by John Morton, based on *Lot* and *Lot's Daughter* by Ward Moore. Dir. Ray Milland. Cast: Ray Milland. American International Pictures, 1962.
8. Burdick, Eugene, and Harvey Wheeler. *Fail-Safe*. 1962 (New York: Dell, 1987), p. 267.
9. *Ibid.*, p. 86.
10. *Ibid.*, p. 154.
11. *Ibid.*, p. 278.
12. *Ibid.*, p. 279.
13. Strick, Phillip. *Science Fiction Movies* (London: Octopus Books, 1976), p. 92.
14. Robb, David L. *Operation Hollywood: How the Pentagon Shapes and Censors the Movies* (Amherst, NY: Prometheus Books, 2004), p. 118.
15. *Inside the Making of "Dr. Strangelove."* Screenplay by Lee Pfeiffer. Dir. David Naylor. Columbia Pictures, 2000.
16. *Ibid.*
17. *Dr. Strangelove, or: How I Learned to Stop Worrying and Love the Bomb.* Screenplay by Peter George, Stanley Kubrick and Terry Southern, from the novel *Two Hours to Doom* by Peter George. Dir. Stanley Kubrick. Cast: Peter Sellers, George C. Scott, Sterling Hayden, Keenan Wynn, Slim Pickens. Columbia Pictures, 1964.
18. Walker, Alexander. *Stanley Kubrick Directs* (Aylesbury, UK: Abacus, 1973), p. 160.
19. *Dr. Strangelove, or: How I Learned to Stop Worrying and Love the Bomb.* Screenplay by Peter George, Stanley Kubrick and Terry Southern, from the novel *Two Hours to Doom* by Peter George. Dir. Stanley Kubrick. Cast: Peter Sellers, George C. Scott, Sterling Hayden, Keenan Wynn, Slim Pickens. Columbia Pictures, 1964.
20. Walker, Alexander. *Stanley Kubrick Directs* (Aylesbury, UK: Abacus, 1973), p. 172.
21. *Dr. Strangelove, or: How I Learned to Stop Worrying and Love the Bomb.* Screenplay by Peter George, Stanley Kubrick and Terry Southern, from the novel *Two Hours to Doom* by Peter George. Dir. Stanley Kubrick. Cast: Peter Sellers, George C. Scott, Sterling Hayden, Keenan Wynn, Slim Pickens. Columbia Pictures, 1964.
22. *Ibid.*
23. Heinlein, Robert A. *Starship Troopers.* 1959 (New York: Ace Books, 1987), p. 141.
24. *Dr. Strangelove, or: How I Learned to Stop Worrying and Love the Bomb.* Screenplay by Peter George, Stanley Kubrick and Terry Southern, from the novel *Two Hours to Doom* by Peter George. Dir. Stanley Kubrick. Cast: Peter Sellers, George C. Scott, Sterling Hayden, Keenan Wynn, Slim Pickens. Columbia Pictures, 1964.
25. *Seven Days in May.* Screenplay by Rod Serling, based on the novel by Fletcher Knebel and Charles W. Bailey II. Dir. John Frankenheimer. Cast: Kirk Douglas, Burt Lancaster. Paramount Pictures, 1964.
26. Seed, David. *American Science Fiction and the Cold War* (Edinburgh: Edinburgh University Press, 1999), p. 148.
27. Schlesinger, Arthur M. *Robert Kennedy and his Times.* 1978 (Boston: Mariner Books, 2002), p. 450.
28. Crowther, Bosley. "Seven Days in May (1964)." *New York Times.* http://www.nytimes.com/movies/movie/43837/Seven-Days-in-May/overview.

29. Schlesinger, Arthur M. *Robert Kennedy and his Times*. 1978 (Boston: Mariner Books, 2002), p. 450.
30. *Seven Days in May* (1964). Trivia. http://www.imdb.com/title/tt0058576/trivia.
31. Schlesinger, Arthur M. *Robert Kennedy and his Times*. 1978 (Boston: Mariner Books, 2002), p. 29.
32. *Seven Days in May* (1964). Trivia. http://www.imdb.com/title/tt0058576/trivia
33. Heinlein, Robert A. *Glory Road* (New York: Berkeley, 1963), p. 11.
34. *Ibid.*, p. 15.
35. *Ibid.*
36. *Ibid.*, p. 16.
37. *Ibid.*, p. 17.
38. *Ibid.*, p. 25.
39. *Ibid.*, p. 27.
40. *Ibid.*
41. *Ibid.*, p. 16.
42. *Ibid.*, pp. 284–285.
43. *Ibid.*, p. 285.
44. Franklin, H. Bruce. *Vietnam and Other American Fantasies* (Amherst, MA: University of Massachusetts Press, 2000), pp. 105–106.
45. Heinlein, Robert A. *Expanded Universe* (New York: Ace Science Fiction Books, 1983), p. 398.
46. Samuelson, David N. "Frontiers of the Future: Heinlein's Future History Stories." Olander, Joseph D. and Martin Harry Greenberg, eds. *Robert A. Heinlein* (Edinburgh: Paul Harris Publishing, 1978), p. 53.
47. Heinlein, Robert A. Afterword to *Glory Road* (New York: Berkeley, 1963), p. 316.
48. Heinlein, Robert A. *Glory Road* (New York: Berkeley, 1963), p. 288.
49. Heinlein, Robert A. *Between Planets* (New York: Ace Books, 1951), pp. 172–173.
50. Heinlein, Robert A. *Glory Road* (New York: Berkeley, 1963), p. 287.
51. *Ibid.*
52. Lee, Stan. *Tales of Suspense* #39 (New York: Marvel, 1963), p. 4.
53. Haldeman, Joe. *1968* (London: Hodder and Stoughton, 1995), p. 41.
54. Lee, Stan. *Tales of Suspense* #39 (New York: Marvel, 1963), p. 4.
55. *Ibid.*, p. 11.
56. Lee, Stan. *Tales of Suspense* #70 (New York: Marvel, 1965), p. 6.
57. Lee, Stan. *Tales of Suspense* #73 (New York: Marvel, 1965), p. 11.
58. Lee, Stan. *Tales of Suspense* #84 (New York: Marvel, 1966), p. 11.
59. Lee, Stan. *Tales to Astonish* #82 (New York: Marvel, 1966), p. 12.
60. *Ibid.*, p. 2.
61. Lee, Stan. *Tales of Suspense* #59 (New York: Marvel, 1964).
62. Quoted in Lee, Stan. *Tales of Suspense* #64 (New York: Marvel, 1965), p. 11.
63. Lee, Stan. *Tales of Suspense* #63 (New York: Marvel, 1965), p. 3.
64. *Ibid.*, p. 4.
65. Lee, Stan. *Tales of Suspense* #65 (New York: Marvel, 1965), p. 2.
66. Lee, Stan. *Tales of Suspense* #71 (New York: Marvel, 1965), p. 11.
67. Lee, Stan. *Tales of Suspense* #72 (New York: Marvel, 1965), p. 11.
68. Lee, Stan. *Tales of Suspense* #92 (New York: Marvel, 1967), p. 3.
69. Lee, Stan. *Tales of Suspense* #96 (New York: Marvel, 1967), p. 11.
70. Lee, Stan. *Tales of Suspense* #97 (New York: Marvel, 1967), p. 13.
71. Lee, Stan. *Journey into Mystery* #117 (New York: Marvel, 1965), p. 13.
72. *Ibid.*
73. Wright, Bradford W. *Comic Book Nation: The Transformation of Youth Culture in America* (Baltimore: Johns Hopkins University Press, 2001), p. 240.
74. Kanigher, Robert. *Superman* #216 (New York: DC Comics, 1969).
75. Harrison, Harry. "An Evening with Harry Harrison." 25 May 2007. http://www.octocon.com/1997/hharrison.htm.
76. Harrison, Harry. *Bill, the Galactic Hero*. 1965 (New York: Avon Books, 1979), p. 3.
77. Spinrad, Norman. *Science fiction in the Real World* (Carbondale: Southern Illinois University Press, 1990), p. 143.
78. Harrison, Harry. *Bill, the Galactic Hero*. 1965 (New York: Avon Books, 1979), p. 163.
79. *Ibid.*, p. 185.
80. Harrison, Harry. "The Beginning of the Affair." *Hell's Cartographers*. Aldiss, Brian W. and Harry Harrison, eds. (SF Horizons, 1975), p. 78.
81. Harrison, Harry. Quoted in Platt, Charles. *Dream Makers: Science Fiction Writers at Work* (London: Xanadu, 1987), p. 225.
82. "The Inheritors." *The Outer Limits*. Teleplay by Seeleg Lester and Sam Neuman, story by Ed Adamson, Seeleg Lester and Sam Neuman. Dir. James Goldstone. Cast: Robert Duvall, Steve Ihnat, James Shigeta. ABC, 1964.
83. Holcomb, David C. "The Inheritors." *The Fashion of Dreaming: A Critical Guide to The Outer Limits*. http://home.earthlink.net/~markholcomb/ol/ol_inheritors.html.
84. "The Human Factor." *The Outer Limits*. Written by David Duncan. Dir. Abner Biberman. Cast: Gary Merrill, Harry Guardino, Sally Kellerman. ABC, 1963.
85. "The Zanti Misfits." *The Outer Limits*. Written by Joseph Stefano. Dir. Leonard Horn.

Cast: Michael Tolan, Robert F. Simon, Olive Deering, Bruce Dern. ABC, 1963.

86. "Nightmare." *The Outer Limits*. Written by Joseph Stefano. Dir. Leonard Horn. Cast: Michael Tolan, Robert F. Simon, Olive Deering, Bruce Dern. ABC, 1963.

87. "The Condemned." *Voyage to the Bottom of the Sea*. Written by William Read Woodfield. Dir. Leonard Horn. Cast: Richard Basehart, David Hedison, J.D. Cannon. ABC, 1965.

88. "The Sky Is Falling." *Voyage to the Bottom of the Sea*. Written by Don Brinkley. Dir. Leonard Horn. Cast: Richard Basehart, David Hedison, Charles McGraw. ABC, 1964.

89. "The Mist of Silence." *Voyage to the Bottom of the Sea*. Written by John McGreevey. Dir. Leonard Horn. Cast: Richard Basehart, David Hedison. ABC, 1964.

90. "Long Live the King." *Voyage to the Bottom of the Sea*. Written by Raphael Hayes. Dir. Laslo Benedek. Cast: Richard Basehart, David Hedison. ABC, 1964.

91. "Doomsday." *Voyage to the Bottom of the Sea*. Written by William Read Woodfield. Dir. James Goldstone. Cast: Richard Basehart, David Hedison, Donald Harron, Paul Carr. ABC, 1964.

92. Grossman, Dave. *On Killing: The Psychological Cost of Learning to Kill in War and Society* (Boston: Little, Brown, 1996).

93. "The Reluctant Stowaway." *Lost in Space*. Written by Shimon Wincelberg. Dir. Anton Leader. Cast: Billy Mumy, Bob May, Guy Williams, Mark Goddard, June Lockhart, Jonathan Harris. ABC, 1964.

94. "Doomsday Minus One." *The Invaders*. Written by Louis Vittes. Dir. Paul Wendkos. Cast: Roy Thinnes, William Windon, Andrew Duggan. ABC, 1967.

95. *Ibid.*

96. "Quantity: Unknown." *The Invaders*. Teleplay by Don Brinkley; story by Clyde Ware. Dir. Sutton Roley. Cast: Roy Thinnes, James Whitmore. ABC, 1967.

97. "The Innocent." *The Invaders*. Teleplay by John W. Bloch; story by John W. Bloch, Norman Klenman and Bernard Rothman. Dir. Sutton Roley. Cast: Roy Thinnes, Michael Rennie, Dabney Coleman, William Smithers, Paul Carr. ABC, 1967.

98. "Condition: Red." *The Invaders*. Written by Laurence Heath. Dir. Sutton Roley. Cast: Roy Thinnes, Michael Rennie, Dabney Coleman, William Smithers, Paul Carr. ABC, 1967.

99. "Dark Outpost." *The Invaders*. Written by Jerry Sohl. Dir. George McCowan. Cast: Roy Thinnes, Andrew Prine, Whit Bissell. ABC, 1967.

100. "The Peacemaker." *The Invaders*. Written by David W. Rintels. Dir. Robert Day. Cast: Roy Thinnes, James Daly, Lin McCarthy. ABC, 1968.

101. Franklin, H. Bruce. "Star Trek in the Vietnam Era." *Science Fiction Studies* 21(1) 24–34. March 1994, p. 24.

102. Suvin, Darko. "Of Starship Troopers and Refuseniks: War and Militarism in U.S. Science Fiction, Part 2." *Extrapolation* 48, No. 1, p. 12.

103. Wortland, Rick. "Captain Kirk: Cold Warrior." *Journal of Popular Film and Television* 16 (Fall 1988): 109–117; Snyder, J. William. "*Star Trek*: A Phenomenon and Social Statement on the 1960s." 25 June 2007. http://www.ibiblio.org/jwsnyder/wisdom/trek.html; Gerrold, David. *The World of Star Trek*. New York: Ballantine Books, 1979.

104. Gerrold, David. *The World of Star Trek* (New York: Ballantine Books, 1979), p. 159.

105. Wortland, Rick. "Captain Kirk: Cold Warrior." *Journal of Popular Film and Television* 16 (Fall 1988): 109–117.

106. Franklin, H. Bruce. "Star Trek in the Vietnam Era." *Science Fiction Studies* 21(1) 24–34. March 1994, p. 24.

107. *Ibid.*, p. 40.

108. "The Omega Glory." *Star Trek*. Written by Gene Roddenberry. Dir. Vincent McEveety. NBC, 1968.

109. "A Private Little War." *Star Trek*. Script by Gene Roddenberry from a story by Judd Crucis. Dir. Marc Daniels. NBC, 1968.

110. Asherman, Allan. *The Star Trek Compendium* (Bath: Star Books, 1983), p. 128.

111. Franklin, H. Bruce. *Vietnam and Other American Fantasies* (Amherst, MA: University of Massachusetts Press, 2000), p. 141.

112. *Ibid.*

113. *Ibid.*

114. *Star Trek VI: The Undiscovered Country*. Screenplay by Nicholas Meyer and Denny Martin Flinn, from a story by Leonard Nimoy, Lawrence Konner and Mark Rosenthal. Dir. Nicholas Meyer. Paramount Pictures, 1991.

115. "Errand of Mercy." *Star Trek*. Script by Gene L. Coon. Dir. John Newland. NBC, 1967.

116. "Operation: Annihilate!" *Star Trek*. Script by Stephen W. Carabatsos. Dir. Herschel Daugherty. NBC, 1967.

117. Canady, John E. Jr., and John L. Allen, Jr. "Illumination from Space from Orbiting Solar-Reflector Spacecraft." *NASA Technical Paper 2065*, 1982.

118. "Operation—Annihilate!" in Blish, James. *Star Trek 2* (London: Corgi, 1972).

119. "Filming Locations." *Memory Alpha*.

http://en.memory-alpha.org/wiki/Filming_locations.
120. "Friday's Child." *Star Trek*. Script by Dorothy C. Fontana. Dir. Joseph Pevney. NBC, 1967.
121. "The Trouble with Tribbles." *Star Trek*. Script by David Gerrold. Dir. Joseph Pevney. NBC, 1967.
122. "Day of the Dove." *Star Trek*. Script by Jerome Bixby. Dir. Marvin Chomsky. NBC, 1967.
123. "Day of the Dove." *Memory Alpha*. http://en.memory-alpha.org/wiki/Day_of_the_Dove.
124. "A Taste of Armageddon." *Star Trek*. Script by Gene Coon and Robert Hamner. Dir. Joseph Pevney. NBC, 1967.
125. "Day of the Dove." *Star Trek*. Script by Jerome Bixby. Dir. Marvin Chomsky. NBC, 1967.
126. "Errand of Mercy." *Star Trek*. Script by Gene L. Coon. Dir. John Newland. NBC, 1967.
127. "Mirror, Mirror." *Star Trek*. Script by Jerome Bixby. Dir. Marc Daniels. NBC, 1967.
128. Whitfield, Stephen E. *The Making of Star Trek* (New York: Ballantine Books, 1968), p. 165.
129. *Ibid.*, p. 171.
130. *Ibid.*
131. *Ibid.*, p. 177.
132. *Ibid.*, p. 326.
133. *Ibid.*
134. White, Matthew, & Jaffer Ali. *The Official Prisoner Companion* (New York: Warner Books, 1998), p. 84, p. 148.
135. Gerrold, David. *The Trouble with Tribbles* (Toronto: Del Rey, 1973), p. 155.
136. "The Ultimate Computer." *Star Trek*. Teleplay by Dorothy C. Fontana, from a story by Laurence N. Wolf. Dir. John Meredith Lucas. NBC 1968; "The Menagerie." *Star Trek*. Written by Gene Roddenberry. Dirs. Marc Daniels and Robert Butler. NBC 1966; "Amok Time." *Star Trek*. Written by Theodore Sturgeon. Dir. Joseph Pevney. NBC 1967; "The Deadly Years" *Star Trek*. Written by David P. Harmon. Dir. Joseph Pevney. NBC 1967; "The Doomsday Machine." *Star Trek*. Written by Norman Spinrad. Dir. Marc Daniels. NBC 1967; "Court Martial." *Star Trek*. Teleplay by Don M. Mankiewicz and Steven W. Carabatsos, story by Don M. Mankiewicz. Dir Marc Daniels. NBC 1967; "Bread and Circuses." *Star Trek*. Written by Gene Roddenberry and Gene L. Coon. Dir. Ralph Senensky. NBC 1968; "The Omega Glory." *Star Trek*. Written by Gene Roddenberry. Dir, Vincent McEveety. NBC 1968.
137. "Conspiracy." *Star Trek: The Next Generation*. Story by Robert Sabaroff, teleplay by Tracy Torme. Dir. Cliff Bole. Paramount Domestic Television, 1988; Nemecek, Larry. *Star Trek: The Next Generation Companion* (New York: Pocket Books, 2003); Thill, Scott. "The Best and Worst of *Star Trek: The Next Generation*'s Sci-Fi Optimism." Wired 25 September 2012. http://www.wired.com/2012/09/star-trek-next-generation-best-worst/?pid=8125&viewall=true.
138. Sackett, Susan. *Letters to Star Trek* (New York: Ballantine Books, 1977), pp. 108–109.
139. Gannon, Charles E. *Rumors of War And Infernal Machines: Technomilitary Agenda-Setting In American And British Speculative Fiction* (Liverpool: Liverpool University Press, 2003), pp. 187–188.
140. Franklin, H. Bruce. "*Star Trek* in the Vietnam Era." *Science Fiction Studies* 21(1) 24–34 (March 1994): p. 146.
141. *Ibid.*, p. 152.
142. *Ibid.*, p. 153.
143. Jameson, Frederic. *Archaeologies of the Future: The Desire Called Utopia and Other Science Fictions* (London: Versu, 2005), p. 93.
144. Anders, Charlie Jane. "R.I.P. Harry Harrison, creator of the Stainless Steel Rat, Bill the Galactic Hero, and Soylent Green." io9.com, 15 August 2012. http://io9.com/5934884/rip-harry-harrison-creator-of-the-stainless-steel-rat-bill-the-galactic-hero-and-soylent-green.
145. Pederson, Jay P., ed. *St James Guide to Science Fiction Writers* (New York: St James Press, 1996), p. 543.
146. Greenberg, Martin H., ed. *Fantastic Lives: Autobiographical Essays by Notable Science Fiction Writers* (Carbondale: Southern Illinois University Press, 1981), p. 69.
147. Clute, John, and Peter Nicholls. *The Encyclopedia of Science Fiction*. 2nd Edition (London: Orbit, 1993, 1999), p. 298.
148. Pournelle, Jerry. Interview by Charles Platt. *Dream Makers: Science Fiction Writers at Work* (London: Xanadu, 1987), p. 3.
149. *Ibid.*, p. 7.
150. Pohl, Fred. *The Way the Future Was: A Memoir* (New York: Del Rey Books, 1978), p. 149.
151. Davin, Eric Leif. *Fight the Power: A Memoir of the Sixties* (Pittsburgh: DavinBooks, 2009), p. 278.
152. Herr, Michael. *Dispatches*. 1977 (London: Pan Books, 1978), p. 161.
153. Asimov, Isaac. *In Joy Still Felt: The Autobiography of Isaac Asimov, 1954–1978* (New York: Avon Books, 1981), p. 358.
154. LeGuin, Ursula K. "Introduction to *The Word for World is Forest*." In *The Language*

of the Night: Essays on Fantasy and Science Fiction (New York: Berkley, 1982), p. 141.
155. *Ibid.*
156. *Ibid.*, p. 142.
157. *Ibid.*
158. Spinrad, Norman. *The Star-Spangled Future* (New York: Ace Books, 1979), p. 6.
159. Harrison, Harry. "The Beginning of the Affair." *Hell's Cartographers.* Eds. Brian W. Aldiss and Harry Harrison (Birkenhead: SF Horizons, 1975), p. 94.
160. Lynch, Richard. "New Frontiers." 25 May 2007. http://jophan.org/1960s/chapter1.htm.
161. Ellison, Harlan. *The Other Glass Teat.* 1972 (New York: Ace Books, 1983), pp. 74–75.
162. *Ibid.*, p. 78.
163. *Punishment Park.* Written and directed by Peter Watkins. Cast: Carmen Argenziano, Jim Bohan, Katherine Quittner, Stan Armsted, Mark Keats, Jim Churchill. Sherpix, 1971.
164. Wright, Bradford W. *Comic Book Nation: The Transformation of Youth Culture in America* (Baltimore: Johns Hopkins University Press, 2001), p. 241.
165. Lee, Stan. *Origins of Marvel Comics* (New York: Marvel, 1997), p. 81.
166. Englehart, Steve. *Captain America and the Falcon* #175 (New York: Marvel, 1974), p. 11.
167. Englehart, Steve. *Captain America and the Falcon* #176 (New York: Marvel, 1974), p. 27.
168. *Ibid.*, p. 31.
169. Quoted in *Captain America and the Falcon* #180 (New York: Marvel, 1974).
170. Englehart, Steve. *Captain America* #183 (New York: Marvel, 1975).
171. Wright, Bradford W. *Comic Book Nation: The Transformation of Youth Culture in America* (Baltimore: Johns Hopkins University Press, 2001), p. 243.
172. *Ibid.*
173. Spinrad, Norman. *Science fiction in the Real World* (Carbondale: Southern Illinois University Press, 1990), p. 145.
174. Spinrad, Norman. *The Men in the Jungle.* 1967 (Glasgow: Grafton, 1989).
175. Spinrad, Norman. "Heirloom." 1972. *No Direction Home* (Glasgow: William Collins & Sons, 1977), p. 24.
176. Spinrad, Norman. "The Conspiracy." 1969. *No Direction Home* (Glasgow: William Collins & Sons, 1977), p. 54.
177. Spinrad. "The Big Flash." 1969. *No Direction Home* (Glasgow: William Collins & Sons, 1977), p. 52.
178. Dick, Philip K. *The Penultimate Truth.* 1964 (London: Gollancz, 2005), p. 131.

179. Harrison, Harry. "Commando Raid." 1970. Ed. Joe Haldeman. *Study War No More* (New York: Avon Books, 1977), pp. 122–123.
180. Franklin, H. Bruce. *Vietnam and Other American Fantasies* (Amherst, MA: University of Massachusetts Press, 2000), p. 162.
181. Wilhelm, Kate. "The Village." 1973. Ed. Thomas Disch. *Bad Moon Rising* (London: Hutchinson of London, 1974), p. 158.
182. Ellison, Harlan. "Basilisk." 1972. Ed. Joe Haldeman. *Study War No More* (New York: Avon Books, 1977), pp. 7–26.
183. Silverberg, Robert. "Caught in the Organ Draft." 1972. *Unfamiliar Territory* (London: Coronet, 1977).
184. Blish, James. *The Day After Judgement.* 1972 (Middlesex: Penguin Books, 1974), p. 95.
185. Bachman, Richard. *The Long Walk* (Bergenfield, NJ: New American Library, 1979).
186. Robinson, Spider. "Unnatural Causes." 1975. *Callahan's Crosstime Saloon* (New York: Tor Books, 1999), p. 171.
187. *Ibid.*, p. 172.
188. *Ibid.*, p. 173.
189. Franklin, H. Bruce. *Vietnam and Other American Fantasies* (Amherst, MA: University of Massachusetts Press, 2000), p. 158.
190. Poyer, Joe. "Challenge: The Insurgent vs. The Counterinsurgent." *Analog Science Fiction—Science Fact*, September 1966.
191. Franklin, H. Bruce. *Vietnam and Other American Fantasies* (Amherst, MA: University of Massachusetts Press, 2000), p. 157.
192. Poyer, Joe. "Null Zone." *Analog Science Fiction—Science Fact*, June 1968.
193. Ellison, Harlan. "In Which the Imp of Delight Tries to Make the World Smile." 1973. *The Harlan Ellison Hornbook* (New York: Penzler Books, 1990), p. 173.
194. Haldeman, Joe, Interview by Charles Platt. *Dream Makers: Science Fiction Writers at Work* (London: Xanadu, 1987), p. 123.
195. *Ibid.*
196. *Ibid.*, p. 124.
197. Haldeman, Joe. "Robert A. Heinlein and Us." Ed. Yoji Kondo. *Requiem* (New York: Tor Books, 1994), p. 353.
198. Haldeman, Joe. *The Forever War.* 1974 (London: Orbit Books, 1976), p. 3.
199. Haldeman, Joe. Speech, "Con with the Wind," New Zealand National Science Fiction Convention, 1–3 June 2002.
200. Haldeman, Joe, Interview by Charles Platt. *Dream Makers: Science Fiction Writers at Work* (London: Xanadu, 1987), p. 125.
201. Blish, James, quoted in Panshin, Alexei. *The Abyss of Wonder.* 2 April 2007. http://www.enter.net/~torve/contents.htm.
202. Haldeman, Joe. "The Forever Awarded."

Interview by Geoff. 2002. 4 July 2007. http://www.spacedoutinc.org/DU-12/Haldeman.html.
203. Haldeman, Joe. *The Forever War*. 1974 (London: Orbit Books, 1976).
204. *Ibid.*, p. 191.
205. *Ibid.*, p. 232.
206. *Ibid.*
207. Robinson, Spider. "Robert." Ed. Yoji Kondo. *Requiem* (New York: Tor Books, 1994), p. 404.
208. Haldeman, Joe, interview by Charles Platt. *Dream Makers: Science Fiction Writers at Work* (London: Xanadu, 1987), p. 125.
209. Heinlein, Robert A. "Guest of Honor Speech at the at the 34th World Science Fiction Convention—Kansas City 1976." Ed. Yoji Kondo, Yoji (ed.). *Requiem*. (New York: Tor Books, 1994), p. 278.
210. *Ibid.*
211. Franklin, H. Bruce. *Vietnam and Other American Fantasies* (Amherst, MA: University of Massachusetts Press, 2000), p. 152.
212. Jenkins, Garry. *Empire Building: The Remarkable Real Life Story of Star Wars* (New York: Simon & Schuster), 1998, p. 188.

Chapter 7

1. Quoted in Rhodes, Richard. *Arsenals of Folly: The Making of the Nuclear Arms Race* (London: Simon & Schuster UK, 2007), p. 207.
2. Quoted in Broad, William J. *Star Warriors—The Weaponry of Space: Reagan's Young Scientists* (New York: Simon & Schuster, 1985), pp. 109–110.
3. Powers, Thomas. *Intelligence Wars: American Secret History from Hitler to Al-Qaeda* (New York: New York Review Books, 2002), pp. 332–334.
4. Benford, Greg. "Old Legends." In *New Legends*. Ed. Greg Bear (Sydney: Random House, 1995), p. 303; Clarke, Arthur C. *Greetings, Carbon-Based Bipeds! A vision of the 20th Century as it Happened* (London: Voyager, 1999), p. 425.
5. Bova, Ben. *Assured Survival: Putting the Star Wars Defense in Perspective* (Boston: Houghton Mifflin, 1984), p. 186.
6. Macksey, Kenneth. *Technology in War: The Impact of Science on Weapon Development and Modern Battle* (London: Arms and Armour Press, 1986), p. 120.
7. Serviss, Garrett P. *Edison's Conquest of Mars*. 1898 (Los Angeles: Carcosa House, 1947). http://www.gutenberg.org/files/21670/21670-h/21670-h.htm#CHAPTER_TWO.
8. Fanning, William J. "The Historical Death Ray and Science Fiction in the 1920s and 1930s." *Science Fiction Studies* 111, No. 37, Part 2 (July 2010): p. 258; Prucher, Jeff. *Brave New Words: The Oxford Dictionary of Science Fiction* (Oxford: Oxford University Press, 2007).
9. Fanning, William J. "The Historical Death Ray and Science Fiction in the 1920s and 1930s." *Science Fiction Studies* 111, No. 37, Part 2 (July 2010): p. 254.
10. *Ibid.*, pp. 254–255.
11. *Ibid.*, p. 255.
12. *Ibid.*
13. *Ibid.*, p. 256.
14. *Ibid.*, pp. 257–260.
15. "TESLA, AT 78, BARES NEW 'DEATH BEAM.'" *New York Times*, 11 July 1934, p. 18.
16. Fanning, William J. "The Historical Death Ray and Science Fiction in the 1920s and 1930s." *Science Fiction Studies* 111, No. 37, Part 2 (July 2010): p. 257.
17. Macksey, Kenneth. *Technology in War: The Impact of Science on Weapon Development and Modern Battle* (London: Arms and Armour Press, 1986), p. 120.
18. Herken, Gregg. *Brotherhood of the Bomb: The Tangled Lives and Loyalties of Robert Oppenheimer, Ernest Lawrence, and Edward Teller* (New York: Henry Holt, 2002), p. 76.
19. Fanning, William J. "The Historical Death Ray and Science Fiction in the 1920s and 1930s." *Science Fiction Studies* 111, No. 37, Part 2 (July 2010): p. 257.
20. Berkowitz, Bruce. *The New Face of War* (New York: Simon & Schuster, 2003), p. 25.
21. Fanning, William J. "The Historical Death Ray and Science Fiction in the 1920s and 1930s." *Science Fiction Studies* 111, No. 37, Part 2 (July 2010): pp. 257–258.
22. *Murder in the Air*. Screenplay by Raymond L. Schrock. Dir. Lewis Seiler. Cast: Ronald Reagan. Warner Bros. Pictures, 1940.
23. Herken, Gregg. *Brotherhood of the Bomb: The Tangled Lives and Loyalties of Robert Oppenheimer, Ernest Lawrence, and Edward Teller* (New York: Henry Holt, 2002), p. 344.
24. "Missile Wars" *Frontline*. Written and produced by Sherry Jones, Public Broadcasting Service, 2002.
25. Fanning, William J. "The Historical Death Ray and Science Fiction in the 1920s and 1930s." *Science Fiction Studies* 111, No. 37, Part 2 (July 2010): p. 258.
26. Franklin, H. Bruce. *War Stars: The Superweapon and the American Imagination* (Oxford: Oxford University Press, 1988), p. 157.
27. *Ibid.*

28. Heinlein, Robert A. "The Last Days of the United States." 1947. *Expanded Universe* (New York: Ace Science Fiction Books, 1983), p. 155.
29. Ibid., pp. 155–156.
30. Bova, Ben. *Assured Survival: Putting the Star Wars Defense in Perspective* (Boston: Houghton Mifflin, 1984), p. 31.
31. Ibid.
32. Ibid.
33. Quoted in Lee, Stan. *Tales of Suspense* #66 (New York: Marvel, 1965).
34. Ibid.
35. Bova, Ben. *Assured Survival: Putting the Star Wars Defense in Perspective* (Boston: Houghton Mifflin, 1984), pp. 34–35.
36. Bova, Ben. *Millennium.* 1977 (Glasgow: Orbit, 1978).
37. Rhodes, Richard. *Arsenals of Folly: The Making of the Nuclear Arms Race* (London: Simon & Schuster UK, 2007), p. 207.
38. Bova, Ben. *Assured Survival: Putting the Star Wars Defense in Perspective* (Boston: Houghton Mifflin, 1984), p. 149.
39. Kegley, Charles W. Jr., and Wittkopf, Eugene R., eds. *The Nuclear Reader: Strategy, Weapons, War* (New York: St. Martin's Press, 1985), p. 215.
40. Seed, David. *American Science Fiction and the Cold War* (Edinburgh: Edinburgh University Press, 1999), pp. 189–190.
41. Ibid., p. 96.
42. Sohl, Jerry. *Point Ultimate* (New York: Rineheart, 1955), p. 8.
43. Scheer, Robert. *With Enough Shovels: Reagan, Bush, and Nuclear War* (New York: Random House, 1982).
44. American Studies Web Resources. 5 November 2009. http://www.colorado.edu/AmStudies/lewis/2010/nuclear.htm.
45. Bova, Ben. *Millennium.* 1977 (Glasgow: Orbit, 1978).
46. Bova, Ben. *Colony.* 1978 (New York: Eos, 1999).
47. Robinson, Spider. *Lady Slings the Booze* (New York: Baen Books, 2002).
48. Clarke, Arthur C. "Loophole." 1946. *The Collected Stories* (London: Gollancz, 2003), pp. 29–34; Wylie, Phillip. *The Smuggled Atom Bomb* (New York: Avon, 1956); Collins, Larry, and Dominique LaPierre. *The Fifth Horseman* (New York: Avon, 1980); Turtledove, Harry. *Worldwar: Upsetting the Balance* (New York: Ballantine Del Rey, 1996).
49. Herken, Gregg. *Brotherhood of the Bomb: The Tangled Lives and Loyalties of Robert Oppenheimer, Ernest Lawrence, and Edward Teller* (New York: Henry Holt, 2002), p. 204.
50. Clarke, Arthur C. *Greetings, Carbon-Based Bipeds! A Vision of the 20th Century as it Happened* (London: Voyager, 1999), p. 425.
51. Jenkins, Garry. *Empire Building: The Remarkable Real Life Story of Star Wars* (New York: Simon & Schuster, 1998), p. 153.
52. Ibid., p. 188.
53. *Damnation Alley.* Screenplay by Lukas Heller and Alan Sharp. Dir. Jack Smight. Cast: Jan-Michael Vincent, George Peppard, Paul Winfield, Dominique Sanda, Jackie Earl Haley. 20th Century–Fox, 1977.
54. "Damnation Alley (Film)." *World Public Library.* http://netlibrary.net/articles/Damnation_Alley_%28film%29.
55. King, Stephen. *Danse Macabre* (London: Macdonald Futura, 1981), p. 151.
56. *Alien.* Written by Dan O'Bannon and Ronald Shusett. Dir. Ridley Scott. Cast: Sigourney Weaver, Ian Holm, John Hurt. Twentieth Century–Fox, 1979; *Battlestar Galactica.* Created by Glen A. Larson. American Broadcasting Company (ABC) 1978–1979; *Invasion of the Body Snatchers.* Screenplay by W. D. Richter, from the novel by Jack Finney. Dir. Philip Kaufman. Cast: Donald Sutherland, Brooke Adams, Jeff Goldblum, Leonard Nimoy. United Artists, 1978; *Buck Rogers in the 25th Century.* Screenplay by Glen A. Larson and Leslie Stevens. Dir. Daniel Haller. Universal Pictures, 1979.
57. *Battle Beyond the Stars.* Written by John Sayles and Ann Dyer. Dir. Jimmy T. Murakami. Exec. Prod. Roger Corman. Cast: Richard Thomas, Robert Vaughan, Sam Jaffe, Sybil Danning. New World Pictures, 1980.
58. *Starship Invasions.* Written and directed by Ed Hunt. Cast: Robert Vaughn, Christopher Lee. Warner Brothers Pictures, 1977; *Laserblast.* Screenplay by Frank Ray Perilli and Fran Schacht. Dir. Michael Rae. Selected Pictures, 1978; *Superman: The Movie.* Screenplay by Mario Puzo, David Newman, Leslie Newman and Robert Benton. Superman created by Jerry Siegel and Joe Schuster. Dir. Richard Donner. Warner Bros, 1978; *Superman II.* Screenplay by Mario Puzo, David Newman, Leslie Newman and Robert Benton. Superman created by Jerry Siegel and Joe Schuster. Dirs. Richard Lester, Richard Donner. Warner Bros, 1980; *Star Trek: The Motion Picture.* Written by Alan Dean Foster, Harold Livingstone, Gene Roddenberry. Dir. Robert Wise. Paramount Pictures, 1979.
59. Taylor, Chris. *How Star Wars Conquered the Universe* (London: Head of Zeus Ltd, 2014), p. 50.
60. Ibid., p. 51.
61. Ibid., p. 88.
62. Ibid., p. ix.
63. Ibid., p. 79.

64. Ibid., p. 88.
65. Lucas, George. "The Wizard of Star Wars." Interview by Paul Scanlon, Rolling Stone, 25 August 1977. http://www.rollingstone.com/movies/news/the-wizard-of-star-wars-20120504?page=6.
66. Ibid.
67. Taylor, Chris. How Star Wars Conquered the Universe (London: Head of Zeus Ltd, 2014), p. 236.
68. http://www.nasa.gov/mission_pages/shuttle/shuttlemissions/index.html.
69. Raymond, Eric S. "A Political History of SF." 9 February 2007. 8 July 2007. http://www.catb.org/~esr/writings/sf-history.html.
70. Cannon, Lou. President Reagan: The Role of a Lifetime (New York: Simon & Schuster, 1991), p. 60.
71. WarGames. Screenplay by Lawrence Lasker and Walter F. Parkes. Dir. John Badham. Cast: Matthew Broderick, Ally Sheedy, John Wood. MGM 1983.
72. Novak, Matt. "The Computer Simulation That Almost Started World War III." Gizmodo Australia, 18 February 2015. http://www.gizmodo.com.au/2015/02/the-computer-simulation-that-almost-started-world-war-iii/.
73. Gannon, Charles E. Rumors of War and Infernal Machines: Technomilitary Agenda-Setting in American and British Speculative Fiction (Liverpool: Liverpool University Press, 2003), p. 135.
74. Cannon, Lou. President Reagan: The Role of a Lifetime (New York: Simon & Schuster, 1991), p. 60.
75. Ibid., p. 127.
76. Gray, Chris Hables. ""There Will Be War!": Future War Fantasies and Militaristic Science Fiction in the 1980s." Science Fiction Studies 64, November 1994. 1 March 2004. http://www.depauw.edu/sfs/backissues/64/gray.htm.
77. Spinrad, Norman. "Too High the Moon." Le Monde diplomatique, July 1999. 27 February 2004. http://mondediplo.com/1999/07/14star.
78. Inside the Making of "Dr. Strangelove." Screenplay by Lee Pfeiffer. Dir. David Naylor. Columbia Pictures, 2000.
79. FitzGerald, Frances. Way Out There in the Blue: Reagan, Star Wars and the End of the Cold War (New York: Simon & Schuster, 2000), p. 23.
80. "Star Wars Dreams." BBC Four Storyville. Written and directed by Leslie Woodhead. BBC, 2003.
81. Clarke, Arthur C. Greetings, Carbon-Based Bipeds! A Vision of the 20th Century as it Happened (London: Voyager, 1999), p. 98.

82. Reagan Library Website. http://www.reagan.utexas.edu/speeches.htm.
83. Broad, William J. Star Warriors—The Weaponry of Space: Reagan's Young Scientists (New York: Simon & Schuster, 1985), p. 114.
84. Reiss, Edward. The Strategic Defense Initiative (Wiltshire, UK: Cambridge University Press, 1992), p. 42.
85. "Star Wars Dreams." BBC Four Storyville. Written and directed by Leslie Woodhead. BBC, 2003.
86. Kramer, Peter. "Star Wars." 2000. In The Movies as History: Visions of the Twentieth Century. Ed. David Ellwood (Gloucestershire: Sutton, 2000), p. 5.
87. Ibid.
88. Rucker, Rudy. "PAC-Man." The 57th Franz Kafka (New York: Ace Books, 1983), p. 243.
89. Titelman, Carol, ed. The Art of Star Wars (New York: Ballantine Books, 1979).
90. Broad, William J. Star Warriors—The Weaponry of Space: Reagan's Young Scientists (New York: Simon & Schuster, 1985), p. 121.
91. Hagelstein, Peter, quoted in Broad, William J. Star Warriors—The Weaponry of Space: Reagan's Young Scientists (New York: Simon & Schuster, 1985), pp. 109–110.
92. Ibid., p. 106.
93. Rhodes, Richard. Arsenals of Folly: The Making of the Nuclear Arms Race (London: Simon & Schuster UK, 2007), pp. 261–266.
94. Aspin, Les. Department of Defense News Briefing, Thursday May 13, 1993.
95. Isaacs, John. "Star Wars: Play it again, Bob." The Bulletin of Atomic Scientists, May/June 1996.
96. Crowley, Michael. "Son of Star Wars." Boston Phoenix, December 7, 1998, 22 October 2009. http://weeklywire.com/ww/12-07-98/boston_feature_1.html.
97. Lipton, Eric. "Insiders Projects Drained Missile-Defense Millions." New York Times, 11 October 2008. 18 September 2009. http://www.nytimes.com/2008/10/12/washington/12missile.html?_r=2&oref=slogin&oref=slogin.
98. Ibid.
99. Pournelle, Jerry, and Larry Niven. Interview with Geoffrey Landis. 15 February 2004 http://home.earthlink.net/~geoffreylandis/NPinterview.html.
100. Niven, Larry. "Known Space" FAQ. 2 March 2004. http://www.larryniven.org/reviews/h_summaries.htm.
101. Pournelle, Jerry, and Larry Niven. Interview with Geoffrey Landis. 15 February 2004. http://home.earthlink.net/~geoffreylandis/NPinterview.html.
102. Gannon, Charles E. Rumors of War

And Infernal Machines: Technomilitary Agenda-Setting In American And British Speculative Fiction (Liverpool: Liverpool University Press, 2003), p. 202.
103. Benford, Greg. "Old Legends." In *New Legends*. Ed. Greg Bear (Sydney: Random House, 1995), pp. 301-302.
104. Clarke, Arthur C. *Astounding Days* (London: Victor Gollancz, 1989), p. 162.
105. Marx, György. "The Martians' vision of the future." 23rd Symposium of the International Committee for the History of Technology, Budapest, 8-9 August 1996. 5 February 2004. http://www.neumann-haz.hu/muvek/tudtor/tudosl/ martians.stm.
106. Broad, William J. *Star Warriors—The Weaponry of Space: Reagan's Young Scientists* (New York: Simon & Schuster, 1985), p. 104.
107. Benford, Greg. "Old Legends." In *New Legends*. Ed. Greg Bear (Sydney: Random House, 1995), 304-305.
108. Spinrad, Norman. "Too High the Moon." *Le Monde diplomatique*, July 1999. 27 February 2004. http://mondediplo.com/1999/07/14star.
109. Seed, David. *American Science Fiction and the Cold War* (Edinburgh: Edinburgh University Press, 1999), p. 190.
110. Benford, Greg. "Old Legends." In *New Legends*. Ed. Greg Bear (Sydney: Random House, 1995), pp. 303-304.
111. Heinlein, Robert A. "The Last Days of the United States." 1947. *Expanded Universe*. 1980 (New York: Ace Science Fiction Books, 1983), p. 155.
112. Clarke, Arthur C. *Greetings, Carbon-Based Bipeds! A Vision of the 20th Century as it Happened* (London: Voyager, 1999), p. 424.
113. Sawyer, Robert. "Author has Harsh Words for Star Wars Plan." *Toronto Star*, 18 August 1985. 2 September 2004. http://www.sfwriter.com/asimov2.htm.
114. *Ibid.*
115. *Ibid.*
116. *Ibid.*
117. Spinrad, Norman. "Too High the Moon." *Le Monde diplomatique*, July 1999. 27 February 2004. http://mondediplo.com/1999/07/14star.
118. Clarke, Arthur C. *Greetings, Carbon-Based Bipeds! A Vision of the 20th Century as it Happened* (London: Voyager, 1999), p. 527.
119. Bova, Ben. *Assured Survival: Putting the Star Wars Defense in Perspective* (Boston: Houghton Mifflin, 1984), p. 142.
120. Reiss, Edward. *The Strategic Defense Initiative* (Wiltshire, UK: Cambridge University Press, 1992), p. 42.
121. Reagan, Ronald. Interview in *Newsweek*, March 18, 1985.

122. Hernandez, Raymond. "Questions Arise About Resume of Challenger to Clinton." *New York Times*, March 23, 2006. http://www.nytimes.com/2006/03/23/nyregion/23kt.html?pagewanted=print&_r=0.
123. Pournelle, Jerry, and Larry Niven. Interview with Geoffrey Landis. 15 February 2004. http://home.earthlink.net/~geoffreylandis/NPinterview.html.
124. Pournelle, Jerry. "Le Monde, SDI, Space, and The Council." CHAOS MANOR debates. April 19, 2000. 2 March 2004. http://www.jerrypournelle.com/debates/nasa-sdi.html.
125. Spinrad, Norman. "Too High the Moon." *Le Monde diplomatique*, July 1999. 27 February 2004. http://mondediplo.com/1999/07/14star.
126. Pournelle, Jerry. "Le Monde, SDI, Space, and The Council." CHAOS MANOR debates. April 19, 2000. 2 March 2004. http://www.jerrypournelle.com/debates/nasa-sdi.html.
127. *Ibid.*
128. *Ibid.*
129. Bova, Ben. *Assured Survival: Putting the Star Wars Defense in Perspective* (Boston: Houghton Mifflin, 1984), p. 321.
130. *Ibid.*, p. 280.
131. *RoboCop*. Screenplay by Edward Neumeier and Michael Miner. Dir. Paul Verhoeven. Orion, 1987.
132. Brin, David. *The Postman* (Reading: Bantam, 1987).
133. Heinlein, Robert A. "The Last Days of the United States." 1947. *Expanded Universe*. 1980 (New York: Ace Science Fiction Books, 1983), pp. 155-156.
134. Clarke, Arthur C. *Greetings, Carbon-Based Bipeds! A Vision of the 20th Century as it Happened* (London: Voyager, 1999), p. 423.
135. *Ibid.*, p. 424.
136. Franklin, H. Bruce. *War Stars: The Superweapon and the American Imagination* (Oxford: Oxford University Press, 1988), p. 157.
137. *Ibid.*
138. Spinrad, Norman. "Too High the Moon." *Le Monde diplomatique*, July 1999. 27 February 2004. http://mondediplo.com/1999/07/14star.
139. Seed, David. *American Science Fiction and the Cold War* (Edinburgh: Edinburgh University Press, 1999), p. 190.
140. Lipton, Eric. "Insiders Projects Drained Missile-Defense Millions." *New York Times*, 11 October 2008. http://www.nytimes.com/2008/10/12/washington/12missile.html?_r=2&oref=slogin&oref=slogin.
141. Clarke, Arthur C. *Greetings, Carbon-Based Bipeds! A Vision of the 20th Century as it Happened* (London: Voyager, 1999), p. 425.

142. Ibid.
143. Powers, Thomas. *Intelligence Wars: American Secret History from Hitler to Al-Qaeda*. (New York: New York Review Books, 2002), p. 332–334; Benford, Greg. "Old Legends." In *New Legends*. Ed. Greg Bear (Sydney: Random House, 1995), p. 305.
144. Powers, Thomas. *Intelligence Wars: American Secret History from Hitler to Al-Qaeda* (New York: New York Review Books, 2002), p. 333–334; FitzGerald, Frances. *Way Out There in the Blue: Reagan, Star Wars and the End of the Cold War* (New York: Simon & Schuster, 2000), p. 560.
145. Hoffman, David. "Cold War hotted up when sabotaged Soviet pipeline went off with a bang." *Sydney Morning Herald*, 28 February 2004. 18 September 2009. http://www.smh.com.au/articles/2004/02/27/1077676970856.html?from=storyrhs.
146. Wright, Bradford W. *Comic Book Nation: The Transformation of Youth Culture in America* (Baltimore: Johns Hopkins University Press, 2001), p. 293.
147. "The Corbomite Maneuver." *Star Trek*. Script by Jerry Sohl. Dir. Joseph Sargent. NBC, 1965.
148. *The Rise and Rise of Michael Rimmer*. Screenplay by Peter Cook, John Cleese, Graham Chapman and Kevin Billington. Dir. Kevin Billington. Cast: Peter Cook, Denholm Elliott, Harold Pinter, John Cleese. Warner Brothers, 1970.
149. Niven, Larry. *Convergent Series* (New York: Ballantine, 1979).
150. Franklin, H. Bruce. *War Stars: The Superweapon and the American Imagination* (Oxford: Oxford University Press, 1988), p. 202.
151. FitzGerald, Frances. *Way Out There in the Blue: Reagan, Star Wars and the End of the Cold War* (New York: Simon & Schuster, 2000), p. 24.
152. Scheer, Robert. *With Enough Shovels: Reagan, Bush, and Nuclear War* (New York: Random House, 1982), p. 260.
153. Keyworth, George A. "The Case for Strategic Defense: An Option for a World Disarmed," 1984, in Haley, P. Edward and Jack Merritt, *Strategic Defense Initiative: Folly or Future?* (Boulder, CO: Westview Press, 1986).
154. Clarke, Arthur C. *Greetings, Carbon-Based Bipeds! A Vision of the 20th Century as it Happened* (London: Voyager, 1999), p. 423.
155. Taylor, Chris. *How Star Wars Conquered the Universe* (London: Head of Zeus Ltd, 2014), p. 104.
156. Kramer, Peter. "Star Wars." 2000. In *The Movies as History: Visions of the Twentieth Century*. Ed. David Ellwood (Gloucestershire: Sutton, 2000), p. 5.
157. Jackson, Patrick Thaddeus, and Daniel H. Nexon. "Representation is Futile?: American Anti-Collectivism and the Borg." In *To Seek Out New Worlds: Exploring Links Between Science Fiction and World Politics*. Ed. Jutta Weldes (New York: Palgrave Macmillan, 2003), p. 144.
158. "Star Wars Dreams." *BBC Four Storyville*. Written and directed by Leslie Woodhead. BBC, 2003.
159. Graham, Bradley. "Missile Defense Failing to Launch as Voting Issue." *Washington Post*, July 28, 1996. A06.
160. FitzGerald, Frances. *Way Out There in the Blue: Reagan, Star Wars and the End of the Cold War* (New York: Simon & Schuster, 2000), p. 499.
161. Quoted in Rhodes, Richard. *Arsenals of Folly: The Making of the Nuclear Arms Race* (London: Simon & Schuster UK, 2007), p. 230.
162. Ibid., pp. 261–263.
163. FitzGerald, Frances. *Way Out There in the Blue: Reagan, Star Wars and the End of the Cold War* (New York: Simon & Schuster, 2000), p. 480.
164. Ibid., p. 562.
165. Marks, Paul, and Ian Sample. "Recognizing Friend from Foe." *New Scientist* 2389: 5 April 2003.
166. "THREATS AND RESPONSES; Excerpts from Testimony by Clinton and Bush Officials to the Sept. 11 Commission." *New York Times* March 24, 2004, Late Edition Final. A14.
167. "StarWars.com Databank." 2 March 2004. http://www.starwars.com/vault/databank/.
168. Rhodes, Richard. *Arsenals of Folly: The Making of the Nuclear Arms Race* (London: Simon & Schuster UK, 2007), p. 211.
169. http://originalvidjunkie.blogspot.com.au/2011/07/never-got-made-files-66-cannons-captain.html?zx=f417fbd91e2a9fc.
170. Gruenwald, Matt. *Captain America* #344 (New York: Marvel, 1988).

Chapter 8

1. Millar, Marc. *The Ultimates*, Vol. 1: *Super-Human* (New York: Marvel Comics Group, 2002), Chapter 2, p. 5.
2. Clarke, Arthur C. *Greetings, Carbon-Based Bipeds! A Vision of the 20th Century as it Happened* (London: Voyager, 1999), p. 180.
3. Card, Orson Scott. "Cross-Fertilization or Coincidence? Science fiction and videogames." In *Reading Science Fiction*. Eds. Gunn, James, Marleen S. Barr and Matthew

Candelaria (Basingstoke: Palgrave Macmillan, 2009), p. 100.

4. Weinberger, Sharon. *Imaginary Weapons: A Journey through the Pentagon's Scientific Underworld* (New York: Nation Books, 2006), p. 3.

5. Ronson, Jon. *The Men Who Stare at Goats* (London: Picador, 2004), pp. 13–14.

6. Gizmodo.com. "DARPA Binoculars Will Give Soldiers a Spidey Sense." 15 July 2007. http://gizmodo.com/gadgets/gadgets/darpa-binoculars-will-give-soldiers-a-spidey-sense-251934.php.

7. Walker, James, Lewis Bernstein and Sharon Lang. *Seize the High Ground: The Army in Space and Missile Defense* (Washington, DC: Center of Military History, 2003), p. 12.

8. Dryden Flight Research Center. http://www.dfrc.nasa.gov/Gallery/Photo/X-Wing/HTML/EC86-33555-2.html.

9. Hersch, Seymour M. *Chain of Command: The Road from 9/11 to Abu Ghraib* (New York: HarperCollins, 2004), p. 177.

10. Vanhastel, Stefaan. "F-16. net." 17 Jul 2007. http://www.f-16.net/articles_ article10.html?module=pagesetter&func=viewpub&tid=2&pid=27.

11. Shaban, Hamza. "Playing War: How the Military Uses Video Games." *The Atlantic*, 10 October 2013. http://www.theatlantic.com/technology/archive/2013/10/playing-war-how-the-military-uses-video-games/280486/; Walker, James, Lewis Bernstein and Sharon Lang. *Seize the High Ground: The Army in Space and Missile Defense* (Washington, DC: Center of Military History, 2003), p. 12.

12. Graetz, J.M. "Home Computer Games: The Origin of *Spacewar*!" 10 July 2007. http://www.atarimagazines.com/cva/v1n1/spacewar.php.

13. Markowitz, Maury. "Spacewar." 10 July 2007. http://www3.sympatico.ca/maury/games/space/spacewar.html.

14. Franklin, H. Bruce. *Vietnam and Other American Fantasies* (Amherst, MA: University of Massachusetts Press, 2000), pp. 148–149.

15. Card, Orson Scott. "OSC Answers Questions." http://www.hatrack.com/research/questions/q0029.shtml.

16. Spinrad, Norman. *Science fiction in the Real World* (Carbondale: Southern Illinois University Press, 1990), p. 27.

17. Ibid., p. 144.

18. Card, Orson Scott. *Ender's Game*. 1985 (London: Arrow Books, 1986), pp. 11–12.

19. Spinrad, Norman. *Science Fiction in the Real World* (Carbondale: Southern Illinois University Press, 1990), p. 26.

20. Ibid., p. 28.

21. Card, Orson Scott. *Ender's Game*. 1985 (London: Arrow Books, 1986), p. 331.

22. Ibid.

23. Card, Orson Scott. "Cross-Fertilization or Coincidence? Science fiction and videogames." In *Reading Science Fiction*. Eds. Gunn, James, Marleen S. Barr and Matthew Candelaria (Basingstoke: Palgrave Macmillan, 2009), p. 97.

24. Grossman, Dave. *On Killing: The Psychological Cost of Learning to Kill in War and Society* (Boston: Little, Brown, 1996), p. 288.

25. Ibid., p. 289.

26. Spinrad, Norman. *Science Fiction in the Real World* (Carbondale: Southern Illinois University Press, 1990), p. 25.

27. Ibid.

28. Card, Orson Scott. *Ender's Game*. 1985 (London: Arrow Books, 1986), p. 339.

29. "News about Ender's Game: The Movie." 14 March 2005. 10 July 2007. http://www.frescopictures.com/movies/ender/endersgame_update.html.

30. Clarke, Arthur C. *Greetings, Carbon-Based Bipeds! A Vision of the 20th Century as it Happened* (London: Voyager, 1999), p. 99.

31. *The Panama Deception*. Written by David Kasper. Dir. Barbara Trent. Empowerment Project, 1992.

32. Burns, Ken. "The Painful, Essential Images of War." *New York Times*, 27 January 1991. http://www.nytimes.com/1991/01/27/arts/the-painful-essential-images-of-war.html?src=pm&pagewanted=1&pagewanted=all.

33. Klein, Naomi. "The End of Video Game Wars." 13 September 2001. 11 July 2007. http://www.alternet.org/story/11503/.

34. DeGhett, Torie Rose. "The War Photo No One Would Publish." *The Atlantic*, 8 August 2014. http://www.theatlantic.com/features/archive/2014/08/the-war-photo-no-one-would-publish/375762/.

35. Goode, Laurie. http://starwarsinterviews1.blogspot.com.au/2010/05/laurie-goode-interview-saurin.html.

36. Card, Orson Scott. "Cross-Fertilization or Coincidence? Science fiction and videogames." In *Reading Science Fiction*. Eds. Gunn, James, Marleen S. Barr and Matthew Candelaria (Basingstoke: Palgrave Macmillan, 2009), p. 99.

37. "Tomohiro Nishikado" *Giant Bomb*. http://www.giantbomb.com/tomohiro-nishikado/3040-55262/.

38. Parkin, Simon. "The Space Invader." *New Yorker*, 17 October 2013. http://www.newyorker.com/tech/elements/the-space-invader.

39. Platoni, K. "The Pentagon goes to the video arcade." *Progressive* (July 1999) 63:27. 13

July 2007. http://findarticles.com/p/articles/mi_m1295/is_7_63/ai_54968180/pg_5 p 2.

40. Rotberg, Ed. Interview with James Hague. *Halcyon Days*. http://www.dadgum.com/halcyon/BOOK/ROTBERG.HTM.

41. Rubens, Alex. "The Creation of Missile Command and the Haunting of its Creator, Dave Theurer." *Polygon*, 15 August 2013. http://www.polygon.com/features/2013/8/15/4528228/missile-command-dave-theurer.

42. "Video Games Under Fire." *The Multinational Monitor*, December 1982. 13 July 2007. http://multinationalmonitor.org/hyper/issues/1982/12/games.html.

43. Reagan, Ronald. *Notable Quotes*. http://www.notable-quotes.com/r/reagan_ronald.html.

44. Riddell, Rob. "Doom Goes to War." *Wired* 5.04, April 1997. http://archive.wired.com/wired/archive/5.04/ff_doom.html.

45. "America's Army (Die Jugend Marschiert)." Propagandhi lyrics. http://www.plyrics.com/lyrics/propagandhi/americasarmydiejugendmarschiert.html.

46. Graham, Marty. "Army Game Proves U.S. Can't Lose." Wired.com. 27 November 2006. http://archive.wired.com/science/discoveries/news/2006/11/72156.

47. Marchetti, Nino. "Video game gives soldiers better skills to handle bomb-sniffing dogs." *Gizmag*, 10 November 2014. http://gizmag.com/rover-dog-ied-finder/34674/.

48. Johnson, Ben. "Using virtual reality video games to treat PTSD." *Marketplace*, 5 December 2013. http://www.marketplace.org/topics/tech/mind-games-mental-health-and-virtual-reality/using-virtual-reality-video-games-treat.

49. Bangert, Christoph. "G.I.'s Deployed in Iraq Desert with Lots of American Stuff." NYTimes.com. 13 August 2005.

50. *Ibid*.

51. "DOD Stops Plan to Send Christian Video Game to Troops in Iraq." *ABC News*. 15 August 2007. 18 September 2009. http://blogs.abcnews.com/theblotter/2007/08/dod-stops-plan-.html.

52. Novak, Matt. "The Computer Simulation That Almost Started World War III." *Gizmodo Australia*, 18 February 2015. http://www.gizmodo.com.au/2015/02/the-computer-simulation-that-almost-started-world-war-iii/.

53. *Ibid*.

54. *WarGames*. Screenplay by Lawrence Lasker and Walter F. Parkes. Dir. John Badham. Cast: Matthew Broderick, Ally Sheedy, John Wood. MGM 1983.

55. *The Terminator*. Written by James Cameron and Gale Ann Hurd. Dir. James Cameron. Cast: Arnold Schwarzenegger, Linda Hamilton, Michael Biehn. Orion Pictures, 1984.

56. Clarke, Arthur C. "Superiority." 1951. *The Collected Stories* (London: Gollancz, 2000).

57. Vonnegut, Kurt. *Cat's Cradle*. 1963 (London: Penguin, 1965).

58. "The Ultimate Computer." *Star Trek*. Teleplay by D.C. Fontana. Story by Lawrence N. Wolfe. Dir. John Meredyth Lucas. NBC, 1966.

59. *Colossus: The Forbin Project*. Screenplay by James Bridges. Novel by D.F. Jones. Dir. Joseph Sargent. Universal Pictures, 1970.

60. *Futureworld*. Written by Mayo Simon and George Schenk. Dir. Richard T. Heffron. American International, 1976.

61. *Dark Star*. Original story and screenplay by Dan O'Bannon and John Carpenter. Dir. John Carpenter. Cast: Brian Narelle, Dan O'Bannon. Jack H. Harris Enterprises, 1974.

62. *The Andromeda Strain*. Screenplay by Nelson Giddings, based on the novel by Michael Crichton. Dir. Robert Wise. Cast: Arthur Hill, Kate Reid, James Olson. Universal Pictures, 1971.

63. Haldeman, Joe. *The Forever War*. 1974 (London: Orbit Books, 1976), p. 35.

64. Haldeman, Joe. *Forever Peace*. 1997 (New York: Ace Science Fiction, 1998), p. 12.

65. *RoboCop*. Screenplay by Edward Neumeier and Michael Miner. Dir. Paul Verhoeven. Orion, 1987.

66. Haldeman, Joe. "War—Past, Present and Future." Speech at Cosmopolis, September 2004. http://www.google.com.au/url?sa=t&rct=j&q=&esrc=s&source=web&cd=2&ved=0CCQQFjAB&url=http%3A%2F%2Fwww.cccb.org%2Frcs_gene%2Fjoe_haldeman.pdf&ei=ef4xVfrTN4TsmAX-5YHADw&usg=AFQjCNFU2hvdysnw9J_Ty24MK3FOPTLKpw&sig2=ZLOnlhzIK7lE-M70IAMI0g&bvm=bv.91071109,d.dGY.

67. Haldeman, Joe. *Forever Peace*. 1997 (New York: Ace Science Fiction, 1998).

68. Miller, Frank. *Daredevil: Born Again* (New York: Marvel Comics, 1987), p. 126.

69. Englehart, Steve. *Captain America and the Falcon* #176 (New York: Marvel Comics, 1974), p. 7.

70. Lomax, Don. *The Punisher Invades The 'Nam: Final Invasion* (New York: Marvel, 1994).

71. Morales, Robert. *Truth: Red, White and Black* (New York: Marvel, 2003).

72. Millar, Marc. *The Ultimates*, Vol. 1: *Super-Human* (New York: Marvel Comics Group, 2002).

73. *Spider-Man*. Screenplay by David Koepp. Dir. Sam Raimi. Cast: Tobey Maguire,

Notes. Chapter 8

Willem Dafoe, Kirsten Dunst. Columbia Pictures, 2002.

74. *Hulk.* Written by James Schamus, John Turman and Michael France. Dir. Ang Lee. Cast: Eric Bana, Jennifer Connelly, Sam Elliott, Nick Nolte. Universal Pictures, 2003; *The Incredible Hulk.* Written by Zak Penn. Dir. Louis Letterier. Cast: Edward Norton, Liv Tyler, William Hurt. Universal Pictures, 2008.

75. *X-Men Origins: Wolverine.* Screenplay by David Benioff and Skip Woods. Cast: Hugh Jackman, Brian Cox. Twentieth Century–Fox, 2009; *X-Men 2.* Written by Zak Penn, David Hayter, Brian Singer, Dan Harris and Michael Dougherty. Dir. Bryan Singer. Cast: Patrick Stewart, Hugh Jackman, Ian McKellen, Brian Cox, Kelly Hu. Twentieth Century–Fox Film Corporation, 2002.

76. Claremont, Chris. *X-men: God Loves, Man Kills* (New York: Marvel, 1982).

77. *Iron Man.* Screenplay by Mark Fergus, Hawk Ostby, Art Marcum and Matt Holloway. Dir. Jon Favreau. Cast: Robert Downey Jr., Gwyneth Paltrow. Paramount Pictures, 2008; *Iron Man 2.* Screenplay by Justin Theroux. Dir. Jon Favreau. Cast: Robert Downey, Jr., Gwyneth Paltrow, Scarlett Johansson, Don Cheadle, Samuel L. Jackson. Paramount Pictures, 2008.

78. Brin, David. *The Postman* (Reading: Bantam, 1987).

79. *Universal Soldier.* Screenplay by Richard Rothstein, Christopher Leitch and Dean Devlin. Dir. Roland Emmerich. Cast: Jean-Claude van Damme, Dolph Lundgren. Carolco Pictures, 1992.

80. "Paper Clip." *The X-Files.* Script by Chris Carter. Dir. Rob Bowman. Cast: David Duchovny, Gillian Anderson, Mitch Pileggi. Fox, 1995.

81. "731." *The X-Files.* Script by Frank Spotnitz. Dir. Rob Bowman. Cast: David Duchovny, Gillian Anderson, Stephen McHattie. Fox, 1995.

82. Miller, Frank. *Daredevil: Born Again* (New York: Marvel Comics, 1987); Laurence, Charles. "'Go pills' gone if U.S. finds a way to send soldiers sleepless into battle." *Sydney Morning Herald*, 6 January 2003. http://www.smh.com.au.

83. *The Six Million Dollar Man.* TV series. Created by Harve Bennett. Cast: Lee Majors, Richard Anderson. ABC 1974–1976.

84. Morgan, Glen. Interview, 27 January 1998. *Millennium: This Is Who We Are.* http://millennium-thisiswhoweare.net/cmeacg/crew_interview.php?name= Glen%20Morgan&id=22.

85. Ibid.

86. "Pilot." *Space: Above and Beyond.* Script by Glen Morgan and James Wong. Dir. David Nutter. Cast: Morgan Weisser, Kristen Cloke, Rodney Rowland, Ronald Lee Ermey, Lanei Chapman, Joel de la Fuente. Fox, 1995.

87. "Who Monitors the Birds?" *Space: Above and Beyond.* Script by Glen Morgan and James Wong. Dir. Winrich Kobe. Cast: Rodney Rowland. Fox, 1995.

88. "Choice or Chance." *Space: Above and Beyond.* Script by Doc Johnson. Dir. Felix Alcala. Cast: Joel de la Fuente, Doug Hutchison. Fox, 1995.

89. "The Angriest Angel." *Space: Above and Beyond.* Script by Glen Morgan and James Wong. Dir. Henri Safran. Cast: James Morrison, Doug Hutchison. Fox, 1995.

90. "Pearly." *Space: Above and Beyond.* Script by Richard Widley. Dir. Charles Martin Smith. Cast: Joel de la Fuente, Doug Hutchison. Fox, 1995.

91. "Stay With the Dead" *Space: Above and Beyond.* Script by Matt Kiene and Joe Reinkemeyer. Dir. Thomas J. Wright. Perf. Morgan Weisser, Kristen Cloke, Rodney Rowland, Joel de la Fuente. Fox, 1995.

92. "R&R." *Space: Above and Beyond.* Script by Jule Selbo. Dir. Thomas J. Wright. Fox, 1995.

93. "Sugar Dirt." *Space: Above and Beyond.* Script by Glen Morgan and James Wong. Dir. Thomas J. Wright. Fox, 1995.

94. "Gropos." *Babylon 5.* Written by Lawrence G. DiTilio. Dir. Jim Johnston. Cast: Bruce Boxleitner, Claudia Christian, Jerry Doyle, Mira Furlan, Richard Biggs, Paul Winfield, Marie Marshall. Warner Bros., 1995.

95. Verhoeven, Paul. Commentary on DVD. *Starship Troopers.* Screenplay by Edward Neumeier, from the novel by Robert Heinlein. Dir. Paul Verhoeven. Cast: Casper Van Dien, Neil Patrick Harris, Michael Ironside, Dina Meyer, Denise Richards, Clancy Brown. Touchstone Pictures, 1998.

96. Ibid.

97. Ibid.

98. Neumeier, Edward. Commentary on DVD. *Starship Troopers.*

99. *Starship Troopers.* Screenplay by Edward Neumeier, from the novel by Robert Heinlein. Dir. Paul Verhoeven. Cast: Casper Van Dien, Neil Patrick Harris, Michael Ironside, Dina Meyer, Denise Richards, Clancy Brown. Touchstone Pictures, 1998.

100. *Preparing for Battle—Casting and characterization, Superior Firepower.* Special feature, *Aliens* Blu-Ray.

101. Ibid.

102. *Aliens.* Screenplay by James Cameron, story by James Cameron, David Giler and Walter Hill, characters by Dan O'Bannon and

Ronald Shusett. Dir. James Cameron. Cast: Sigourney Weaver, Michael Biehn, Lance Henriksen, Al Matthews, Jenette Goldstein. Twentieth Century–Fox, 1986.

103. *Starship Troopers*. Screenplay by Edward Neumeier, from the novel by Robert Heinlein. Dir. Paul Verhoeven. Cast: Casper Van Dien, Neil Patrick Harris, Michael Ironside, Dina Meyer, Denise Richards, Clancy Brown. Touchstone Pictures, 1998.

104. Verhoeven, Paul. Commentary. *Starship Troopers*.

105. *Ibid.*

Chapter 9

1. Bandow, Doug. "Republicans Mislead Their Base With Handwringing Over Sequester Defense Cuts." *Forbes*, 4 March 2013. http://www.forbes.com/sites/dougbandow/2013/03/04/republicans-mislead-their-base-with-handwringing-over-sequester-defense-cuts/.

2. Quoted in Logica, Mark. "JB Pearl Harbor-Hickam Sailors Preview *Battleship*." *America's Navy*, 1 May 2012. http://www.navy.mil/submit/display.asp?story_id=66884.

3. Galbreath, David. "The Technological Dimension" Lecture, "From State Control to Remote Control," University of Bath, April 2015.

4. "The 213 Things Skippy is no longer allowed to do in the U.S. Army." 12 July 2007. http://skippyslist.com/?page_id=3.

5. Ford, John M. Panel at Conspiracy, 1987 World Science Fiction Convention.

6. *Star Trek VI: The Undiscovered Country*. Screenplay by Nicholas Meyer and Denny Martin Flinn, from a story by Leonard Nimoy, Lawrence Konner and Mark Rosenthal. Dir. Nicholas Meyer. Paramount Pictures, 1991.

7. Herken, Gregg. *Brotherhood of the Bomb: The Tangled Lives and Loyalties of Robert Oppenheimer, Ernest Lawrence, and Edward Teller* (New York: Henry Holt, 2002), p. 334.

8. ABC News, 23 March 2003.

9. ABC News, 30 March 2003.

10. Gideon, Vic. "National Guardsman changed his name to a toy." 18 March 2003. http://www.wkyc.com.

11. Walker, James, Lewis Bernstein and Sharon Lang. *Seize the High Ground: The Army in Space and Missile Defense* (Washington, DC: Center of Military History, 2003), p. 12.

12. "FORCEnet." http://www.globalsecurity.org/military/systems/ship/systems/forcenet.html/.

13. George, Alexander. "The Top-Secret Aircraft That Roamed the Skies Over Area 51." *Wired* 26 March 2014. http://www.wired.com/2014/03/boeing-bird-of-prey/.

14. "Schwarzenegger to Troops: 'You Guys Are The True Terminators.'" *Fox News* 4 July 2003. http://www.foxnews.com/story/2003/07/04/schwarzenegger-to-troops-guys-are-true-terminators/.

15. Robb, David L. *Operation Hollywood: How the Pentagon Shapes and Censors the Movies* (Amherst, NY: Prometheus Books, 2004), p. 184.

16. *Ibid.*, p. 186.

17. Fleischer, Jeff. "Operation Hollywood." *Mother Jones*, 20 September 2004. http://www.motherjones.com/politics/2004/09/operation-hollywood.

18. Quoted in Debruge, Peter. "Film biz, military unite for mutual gain." *Variety*, 19 June 2009. http://variety.com/2009/digital/news/film-biz-military-unite-for-mutual-gain-1118005186/.

19. *Ibid.*

20. *Transformers*. Screenplay by Roberto Orci and Alex Kurtzman. Story by John Rogers, Roberto Orci and Alex Kurtzman. Based on Hasbro's Transformers Action Figures. Dir. Michael Bay. Paramount Pictures, 2007.

21. Quoted in Debruge, Peter. "Film biz, military unite for mutual gain." *Variety*, 19 June 2009. http://variety.com/2009/digital/news/film-biz-military-unite-for-mutual-gain-1118005186/.

22. Moynihan, Dennis. "NCMRS Miramar." https://www.facebook.com/permalink.php?story_fbid=10150821309946312&id=253972141311.

23. Quoted in Logica, Mark. "JB Pearl Harbor-Hickam Sailors Preview *Battleship*." *America's Navy*, 1 May 2012. http://www.navy.mil/submit/display.asp?story_ id=66884.

24. Quoted in Sauer, Abe. "*Act of Valor* and the Myth of an Anti-Military Hollywood." *The Awl*, 27 February 2012. http://www.theawl.com/2012/02/act-of-valor-and-the-myth-of-an-anti-military-hollywood.

25. Kang, Inkoo. "Tales of the Military-Entertainment Complex: Why the U.S. Navy Produced *Battleship*." *Movieline*, 6 February 2013. http://movieline.com/2013/02/06/military-entertainment-complex-hollywood-pentagon-relationship-battleship-zero-dark-thirty/.

26. Eagleton, Terry. *Criticism & Ideology*. 1975 (London: Verso, 1986), p. 45.

27. Suid, Lawrence. *Guts and Glory: The Making of the American Military Image in Film*, revised and expanded edition (Lexington: University Press of Kentucky, 2002), pp. 556–557.

28. Capaccio, Tony. "Navy Wanted Slimmer Sailor for Role in *Battleship* Movie." *Bloomberg*, 19 May 2012. http://www.bloomberg.com/news/2012-05-18/navy-wanted-slimmer-sailor-for-role-in-battleship-movie.html.
29. Cornet, Roth. "*Battle: Los Angeles*: Creating a Realistic War Movie With Aliens." *ScreenRant*. http://screenrant.com/battle-los-angeles-interviews-aaron-eckhart-jonathan-liebesman-rothc-104972/.
30. Scott, Mike. "Aaron Eckhart went through military training to make *Battle: Los Angeles* seem real." *Times-Picayune*, 12 March 2011. http://www.nola.com/ movies/index.ssf/2011/03/aaron_eckhart_went_through_mil.html.
31. *Godzilla*. Screenplay by Max Borenstein, story by Dave Callahan. Dir. Gareth Edwards. Cast: Aaron Taylor-Johnson, Ken Watanabe, Bryan Cranston. Warner Bros., 2014.
32. Koepp, David. Interview by Devin Faraci. *Cinematic Happenings Under Development*, 29 June 2005. http://www.chud.com/3522/interview-david-koepp-war-of-the-worlds/.
33. *War of the Worlds*. Screenplay by David Koepp and Josh Friedman, from the novel by H.G. Wells. Dir. Steven Spielberg. Cast: Tom Cruise, Tim Robbins. Paramount Pictures, 2005.
34. Hunter, Stephen. "The Great 'War.'" *Washington Post*, 29 June 2005. http://www.washingtonpost.com/wp-dyn/content/article/2005/06/28/ AR2005062801741.html.
35. Burgess, Lisa. "Gen. Jumper leaps into Stargate." *Stars and Stripes*, 12 March 2004. http://www.stripes.com/news/gen-jumper-leaps-into-stargate-1.17559.
36. Barber, Barrie. "Stargate Stars Film Movie Aboard USS *Alexandria* at the Polar Ice Cap." *America's Navy*, 18 April 2007. http://www.navy.mil/submit/display.asp?story_id=28895.
37. "Air Force to Honor Actor, Producer." *Official Website of the U.S. Air Force*, 9 September 2004. https://archive.today/6qLG.
38. Robb, David L. Interview. Fleischer, Jeff. "Operation Hollywood." *Mother Jones*, 20 September 2004. http://www.motherjones.com/politics/2004/09/operation-hollywood.
39. Card, Orson Scott. "Cross-Fertilization or Coincidence? Science fiction and videogames." In *Reading Science Fiction*. Eds. Gunn, James, Marleen S. Barr and Matthew Candelaria (Basingstoke: Palgrave Macmillan, 2009), p. 100.
40. Nemecek, Larry, and Ira Steven Behr. Commentary on *Star Trek VI: The Undiscovered Country*. Screenplay by Nicholas Meyer and Denny Martin Flinn, from a story by Leonard Nimoy, Lawrence Konner and Mark Rosenthal. Dir. Nicholas Meyer. Paramount Pictures, 1991; Liebesman, Jonathan. Commentary on DVD. *Battle: Los Angeles*. Screenplay by Christopher Bertolini. Dir. Jonathan Liebesman. Cast: Aaron Eckhart, Ramon Rodriguez, Michelle Rodriguez. Columbia Pictures, 2011.
41. Favreau. Jon. Commentary. *Iron Man 2*. Screenplay by Justin Theroux. Dir. Jon Favreau. Cast: Robert Downey, Jr., Gwyneth Paltrow, Scarlett Johansson, Don Cheadle, Samuel L. Jackson. Paramount Pictures, 2008.
42. Robb, David L. *Operation Hollywood: How the Pentagon Shapes and Censors the Movies* (Amherst, NY: Prometheus Books, 2004), p. 177.
43. Spinrad, Norman. *Science Fiction in the Real World* (Carbondale: Southern Illinois University Press, 1990), p. 25.
44. Grossman, Dave. *On Killing: The Psychological Cost of Learning to Kill in War and Society* (Boston: Little, Brown, 1996), pp. 127–128.
45. *Ibid.*, p. 128.
46. *Ibid.*, p. 162.
47. *Ibid.*
48. *Ibid.*, p. 160.
49. *Ibid.*
50. Fritz, Ben, and John Horn. "Reel China: Hollywood tries to stay on China's good side." *Los Angeles Times*, 16 March 2011. http://www.latimes.com/entertainment/la-et-china-red-dawn-20110316-story.html#page=1.
51. *Iron Man*. Screenplay by Mark Fergus, Hawk Ostby, Art Marcum and Matt Holloway. Dir. Jon Favreau. Paramount Pictures, 2008.
52. *Iron Man 2*. Screenplay by Justin Theroux. Dir. Jon Favreau. Paramount Pictures, 2010.
53. Favreau. Jon. Commentary. *Iron Man 2*. Screenplay by Justin Theroux. Dir. Jon Favreau. Cast: Robert Downey Jr., Gwyneth Paltrow, Scarlett Johansson, Don Cheadle, Samuel L. Jackson. Paramount Pictures, 2008; *Batman Begins*. Screenplay by Christopher Nolan and David S. Goyer. Story by David S. Goyer. Characters by Bob Kane. Dir. Christopher Nolan. Warner Brothers, 2005; Eick, David. Interview. "Flesh and Bone." http://en.battlestarwiki.org/wiki/Flesh_ and_Bone.
54. *Close Encounters of the Third Kind*. Screenplay by Steven Spielberg. Dir. Steven Spielberg. Columbia Pictures, 1978.
55. *The Philadelphia Experiment*. Screenplay by Michael Janover and William Gray, story by Wallace Bennett and Don Jakoby, based on the book by Charles Berlitz and William L. Moore. Dir. Stewart Raffill. New World Pictures, 1983.
56. *The Day After*. Written by Edward

Hume. Dir. Nicholas Meyer. Cast: Jason Robards, John Lithgow, Bibi Besch. ABC Circle Films, 1983.

57. *Starman.* Written by Bruce A. Evans and Raynold Gideon. Dir. John Carpenter. Cast: Jeff Bridges, Karen Allen, Charles Martin Smith, Richard Jaeckel. Columbia Pictures, 1984.

58. Contrada, Andrew. "'The Avengers' Lost Military Support Over S.H.I.E.L.D. Issue." http://screenrant.com/the-avengers-u-s-military-shield-contr-170280/.

59. *Mars Attacks!* Screenplay by Jonathan Gems, from the trading card series. Dir. Tim Burton. Cast: Jack Nicholson, Paul Winfield, Rod Steiger. Warner Bros., 1996.

60. Robb, David L. *Operation Hollywood: How the Pentagon Shapes and Censors the Movies* (Amherst, NY: Prometheus Books, 2004), p. 69.

61. *Ibid.*, p. 70.
62. *Ibid.*, p. 67.
63. *Ibid.*
64. Haldeman, Joe. *Forever Free.* 1999 (New York: Ace Books, 2000).
65. "Joe Haldeman's *War Stories.*" SFWA Pressbook.
66. Singer, P.W. *Wired for War* (New York: Penguin Press, 2009), p. 32.
67. *Ibid.*
68. *Ibid.*, p. 21.
69. Drummond, Katie. "Pentagon's Project Avatar: Same As The Movie, But With Robots Instead of Aliens." *Wired: Danger Room*, 16 February 2012. http://www.wired.com/2012/02/darpa-sci-fi/.
70. *Iron Man 2.* Screenplay by Justin Theroux. Dir. Jon Favreau. Paramount Pictures, 2010.
71. Scalzi, John. *Old Man's War* (New York: Tor Books, 2005), p. 138.
72. Scalzi, John. *The Ghost Brigades* (New York: Tor Books, 2006).
73. McCarthy, Wil. *Aggressor Six* (New York: Roc, 1994).
74. Franklin, H. Bruce. *Vietnam and Other American Fantasies* (Amherst: University of Massachusetts Press, 2000), p. 169.
75. Baen, Jim. "Enterprise Thank You to Jim Baen." 12 July 2007. http://www.baen.com/enterprise_thank_you_to_jim_baen.htm.
76. Bujold, Lois McMaster. *Young Miles* (Riverdale, NY: Baen Books, 2003).
77. Moon, Elizabeth. *Rules of Engagement* (Riverdale, NY: Baen Books, 2000).
78. Pournelle, Jerry. Quoted in Platt, Charles. *Dream Makers: Science Fiction Writers at Work* (London: Xanadu, 1987), p. 3.
79. Marvel Character Appearances. http://www.marvelappearance.com/photos.html.

80. Rosin, Hanna. "Pentagon Uses Its Spidey-Sense For The Troops." *The Washington Post*, 29 April 2009. http://www.washingtonpost.com/wp-dyn/content/article/2005/04/28/AR2005042801995.html.

81. Medved, Michael. "Captain America, Traitor." *The National Review*, 4 April 2003. http://www.nationalreview.com/comment/comment-medved040403.asp.

82. *Ibid.*
83. *Ibid.*
84. Crawford, Hubert H. *Crawford's Encyclopedia of Comic Books* (New York: Jonathan David Publishers, 1978), p. 341.
85. Brancatelli, Joe. "Captain America," in Horn, Maurice. *The World Encyclopedia of Comics* (New York: Chelsea House, 1976), p. 156.
86. Morrell, David. *Captain America: The Chosen* (New York: Marvel, 2008).
87. Kirkman, Robert, John Jackson Miller, Michael Avon Oeming, Christopher Priest and Mark Scott Ricketts. *Avengers Disassembled: Iron Man, Thor and Captain America* (New York: Marvel, 2009).
88. Brady, Matt. *Marvel Encyclopedia*, Volume 1 (New York: Marvel, 2003), p. 123.
89. Daniels, Les. *Marvel: Five Decades of the World's Greatest Comics* (London: Virgin, 1991), p. 165.
90. *Ibid.*
91. Twain, Mark. *Great Short Works of Mark Twain* (New York: Perennial Library, 1967), p. 217.
92. Fraction, Matt. *Punisher War Journal*, Vol. 2: *Goin' Out West* (New York: Marvel, 2008).
93. Franklin, H. Bruce. *Vietnam and Other American Fantasies* (Amherst: University of Massachusetts Press, 2000), pp. 105–106.
94. Shanker, Thom. "Report Cites Firefight as Lesson on Afghan War." *The New York Times*, 2 October 2009. 5 October 2009. http://www.nytimes.com/2009/10/03/world/asia/03battle.html.
95. *Ibid.*
96. *Ibid.*
97. *Forum: A Publication for the Science Fiction and Fantasy Writers of America* 191. Ed. Jim Bassett (Chestertown, MD).
98. *Ibid.*
99. Swanwick, Michael. "Against the War." 10 March 2003. http://www.michaelswanwick.com/evrel/against.html.
100. Haldeman, Joe. "War—Past, Present and Future." Speech at Cosmopolis, September 2004. http://www.google.com.au/url?sa=t&rct=j&q=&esrc=s&source=web&cd=2&ved=0CCQQFjAB&url=http%3A%2F%2Fwww.cccb.org%2Frcs_gene%2Fjoe_haldeman.

pdf&ei=ef4xVfrTN4TsmAX-5YHADw&usg= AFQjCNFU2hvdysnw9J_Ty24MK3FOPTLK pw&sig2=ZLOnlhzIK7lE-M70IAMI0g&bvm =bv.91071109,d.dGY.

101. Pournelle, Jerry. "Jacobinism and the Principle of Pursuit." 19 November 2004. 11 Jul 2007. http://jerrypournelle.com/archives2/ archives2view/view336.html#pursuit.

102. Ibid.

103. Ringo, John. "War vs. Not-War." 2005. 12 July 2007. http://johnringo.com/Unpub lished/Unpublishedopeds/warvsnotwar.asp.

104. Card, Orson Scott. "The Most Careful of All Wars." 24 March 2003. 12 July 2007. http://www.ornery.org/essays/warwatch/ 2003-03-24-1.html.

105. Card, Orson Scott. *Empire* (New York: Tor Books, 2006), p. 18.

106. *Ibid.*, p. 19.

107. *Ibid.*, p. 22.

108. *Ibid.*, p. 26.

109. *Ibid.*, p. 106.

110. *Ibid.*, p. 110.

111. *Ibid.*, p. 111.

112. Mokhiber, Jim and Rick Young. "The Uses of Military Force." *Frontline: Give War a Chance*. http://www.pbs.org/wgbh/pages/ frontline/shows/military/force/.

113. Hamrah, A.S. "Allied Forces." *Boston Globe*. 4 July 2004. 12 July 2007. http://www. boston.com/news/globe/ideas/articles/2004/ 07/04/allied_forces/.

114. Scalzi, John. "*Starship Troopers*: The Movie—A Review." 26 December 2006. 15 Jul 2007. http://www.scalzi.com/whatever/004718. html.

115. Rosenbaum, Jonathan. *Movie Wars: How Hollywood and the Media Conspire to Limit What Films We Can See* (Chicago: A Capella, 2000), pp. 69–70.

116. Swofford, Anthony. Quoted in Sauer, Abe. "*Act of Valor* and the Myth of an Anti-Military Hollywood." *The Awl*, 27 February 2012. http://www.theawl.com/2012/02/act-of-valor-and-the-myth-of-an-anti-military-hollywood.

117. Asprin, Robert. *The Cold Cash War*. 1977 (New York: Ace Books, 1992).

118. Reynolds, Mack. "Mercenary." 1962. *Study War No More*. Ed. Joe Haldeman (New York: Avon Books, 1977), pp. 145–205.

119. Effinger, George Alec. "Curtains." 1974. *Study War No More*. Ed. Joe Haldeman (New York: Avon Books, 1977), pp. 125–144.

120. Simmons, Dan. "E-ticket to 'Namland.'" 1987. *Prayers to Broken Stones* (New York: Bantam Spectra, 1992), pp. 207–231.

121. Varley, John. *Titan* (London: Futura, 1979), p. 277.

122. Grieve, Tim. "Rick Santorum and the Eye of Mordor." *Salon*, 18 October 2006. http: //www.salon.com/2006/10/17/santorum_24/.

123. "Paladin M109A6 155mm Artillery System, United States of America." Army-technology.com. http://www.army-technology. com/projects/paladin/.

124. "Crusader 155mm, United States of America." Army-technology.com. http://www. army-technology.com/projects/crusader/.

125. "Minotaur V Launch Vehicle Information." Spaceflight101.com. http://www.space flight101.com/minotaur-v-launch-vehicle-information.html.

126. "Excalibur." DARPA Microsystems Technology Office. http://www.darpa.mil/ our_work/mto/programs/excalibur.aspx.

127. Crane, David. "Fight Night: Pinnacle Armor Dragon Skin vs. Interceptor Body Armor." Military.com. http://www.military. com/soldiertech/0,14632,SoldierTech_ 060223_Pinnacle,,00.html.

128. Jameson, Frederic. *Archaeologies of the Future: The Desire Called Utopia and Other Science Fictions* (London: Versu, 2005), p. 60.

129. iRobot Press Release. 28 June 2007. 10 July 2007. http://www.irobot.com/sp.cfm? pageid=86&id=344&referrer=85.

130. Jackson, Patrick Thaddeus, and Daniel H. Nexon. "Representation is Futile?: American Anti-Collectivism and the Borg." *To Seek Out New Worlds: Exploring Links Between Science Fiction and World Politics*. Ed. Jutta Weldes (New York: Palgrave Macmillan, 2003), p. 144.

131. Singer, Peter W. "How To Be All That You Can Be: A Look at the Pentagon's Five-Step Plan for Making *Iron Man* Real." *Brookings*, 2 May 2008. http://www.brookings.edu/ research/articles/2008/05/02-iron-man-singer; Newton, Mark. "Military Hires Hollywood To Develop Real-Life Iron Man Suit." *Moviepilot*, 8 July 2014. http://moviepilot.com/posts/2014/ 07/08/military-hires-hollywood-to-develop-real-life-iron-man-suit-1687743?lt_source= external,manual.

Appendix B

1. "Eugene the Jeep" Jeepbase.com. http: //www.jeepbase.com/willys/eugene_jeep_pxl. htm.

2. "Missile. Air-to-Air. Mighty Mouse. 2.75 inch." *Smithsonian National Air and Space Museum*. http://airandspace.si.edu/collections/ artifact.cfm?object=nasm_A19660372000.

3. "Dark Star Unmanned Aerial Vehicle." *Boeing*. http://www.boeing.com/boeing/ history/boeing/darkstar.page.

4. Vanhastel, Stefaan. "F-16. net." 17 July 2007. http://www.f-16.net/articles_ article10.

html?module=pagesetter&func=viewpub&tid=2&pid=27.

5. Dryden Flight Research Center. http://www.dfrc.nasa.gov/Gallery/Photo/X-Wing/HTML/EC86-33555-2.html.

6. Walker, James, Lewis Bernstein and Sharon Lang. *Seize the High Ground: The Army in Space and Missile Defense*. Washington, DC: Center of Military History, 2003, p. 12.

7. USAICoE Command History Office. "Operation RED DAWN Meets Saddam Hussein." www.army.mil, 6 December 2013. http://www.army.mil/article/116559/Operation_RED_DAWN_nets_Saddam_Hussein/.

8. Hanlon, Mike. "PHaSR—the first man-portable, non-lethal deterrent weapon." *Gizmag*, 4 November 2005. http://www.gizmag.com/go/4815/.

9. Singer, P. W. *Wired for War*. New York: Penguin Press, 2009, p. 38.

10. "GoldenEye." *Aurora Flight Sciences*. http://www.aurora.aero/Development/GoldenEye_80.aspxLockheed Martin.

11. "HULC." http://www.lockheedmartin.com.au/us/products/hulc.html.

12. DARPA. "Ares Aims to Provide More Front-Line Units With Mission-Tailored VTOL Capabilities." DARPA.mil, 11 February 2004. http://www.darpa.mil/NewsEvents/Releases/2014/02/11.aspx.

13. Drummond, Katie. "Pentagon's Project Avatar: Same As The Movie, But With Robots Instead of Aliens." *Wired: Danger Room*, 16 February 2012. http://www.wired.com/2012/02/darpa-sci-fi/.

Appendix D

1. Suid, Lawrence H. *Guts and Glory: The making of the American Military Image in Film*. (Lexington, KY: University Press of Kentucky, 2002), p. 52.

Bibliography

Aldiss, Brian, and David Wingrove. *Trillion Year Spree: The History of Science Fiction.* London: Victor Gollancz, 1986.
Aldiss, Brian, and Harry Harrison, eds. *Hell's Cartographers.* Birkenhead: SF Horizons, 1975.
Barr, Marleen S., ed. *Envisioning the Future: Science Fiction and the Next Millennium.* Middletown, CT: Wesleyan University Press, 2003.
Bova, Ben. *Assured Survival: Putting the Star Wars Defense in Perspective.* Boston: Houghton Mifflin, 1984.
_____. *Millennium.* 1977: Glasgow: Orbit, 1978.
Boyer, Paul. *By the Bomb's Early Light: American Thoughts and Culture at the Dawn of the Atomic Age.* Chapel Hill, NC: University of North Carolina, 1994.
Brin, David. *The Postman.* Reading: Bantam, 1987.
Broad, William J. *Star Warriors—The Weaponry of Space: Reagan's Young Scientists.* New York: Simon & Schuster, 1985.
_____. *Teller's War: The Top-Secret Story Behind the Star Wars Deception.* New York: Simon & Schuster, 1992.
Burdick, Eugene, and Harvey Wheeler. *Fail-Safe.* 1962. New York: Dell, 1987.
Campbell, John W. *The Astounding Science Fiction Anthology.* New York: Simon & Schuster, 1952.
Card, Orson Scott. *Ender's Game.* 1985. London: Arrow Books, 1986.
Clarke, Arthur C. *Greetings, Carbon-Based Bipeds! A Vision of the 20th Century as it Happened.* London: Voyager, 1999.
Clute, John, and Peter Nicholls. *The Encyclopedia of Science Fiction.* 2nd Edition. London: Orbit, 1993, 1999.
Daniels, Les. *Marvel: Five Decades of the World's Greatest Comics.* London: Virgin, 1991.
Disch, Thomas M. *The Dreams Our Stuff Is Made Of.* New York: Free Press, 1998.
Eschbach, Lloyd Arthur. *Of Worlds Beyond: The Science of Science Fiction Writing.* Chicago: Advent Publishers, 1971.
Evans, Joyce A. *Celluloid Mushroom Clouds: Hollywood and the Atomic Bomb.* Boulder, CO: Westview Press, 1998.
FitzGerald, Frances. *Way Out There in the Blue: Reagan, Star Wars and the End of the Cold War.* New York: Simon & Schuster, 2000.
Franklin, H. Bruce, ed. *Countdown to Midnight.* New York: DAW Books, 1984.
_____. *Robert A. Heinlein: America as Science Fiction.* New York: Oxford University Press, 1980.
_____. *Vietnam and Other American Fantasies.* Amherst, Mass: University of Massachusetts Press, 2000.
_____. *War Stars: The Superweapon and the American Imagination.* Oxford: Oxford University Press, 1988.
Gannon, Charles E. *Rumors of War and Infernal Machines: Technomilitary Agenda-Setting in American and British Speculative Fiction.* Liverpool: Liverpool University Press, 2003.
Grossman, Dave. *On Killing: The Psychological Cost of Learning to Kill in War and Society.* Boston: Little, Brown, 1996.

Gunn, James, Marleen S. Barr, and Matthew Candelaria, eds. *Reading Science Fiction*. Basingstoke: Palgrave Macmillan, 2009.
Haldeman, Joe. *Forever Free*. 1999. New York: Ace Books, 2000.
_____. *The Forever Peace*. 1997. New York: Ace Books, 1998.
_____. *The Forever War*. 1974. London: Orbit Books, 1976.
_____. *1968*. 1994. London: Hodder and Stoughton, 1995.
_____, ed. *Study War No More*. New York: Avon Books, 1977.
Harrison, Harry. *Bill, the Galactic Hero*. 1965. New York: Avon Books, 1979.
_____, ed. *There Won't Be War*. New York: Tor Books, 1991.
Heinlein, Robert A. *Between Planets*. New York: Ace Books, 1951.
_____. *Expanded Universe*. 1980. New York: Ace Science Fiction Books, 1983.
_____. *Glory Road*. New York: Berkeley, 1963.
_____. *Starship Troopers*. 1959. New York: Ace Books, 1987.
Jameson, Frederic. *Archaeologies of the Future: The Desire Called Utopia and Other Science Fictions*. London: Versu, 2005.
Jancovich, Mark. *Rational Fears: American Horror in the 1950s*. New York: Manchester University Press, 1996.
Jenkins, Garry. *Empire Building: The Remarkable Real Life Story of Star Wars*. London: Simon & Schuster Ltd, 1997.
Jones, Gerard. *Men of Tomorrow: Geeks, Gangsters and the Birth of the Comic Book*. New York: Basic Books, 2004.
Kavenay, Roz. *From Alien to the Matrix: Reading Science Fiction Film*. London: I.B. Tauris, 2005.
King, Stephen. *Danse Macabre*. London: Macdonald Futura, 1981.
Le Guin, Ursula K. *The Word for World Is Forest*. 1972. New York: Berkley Medallion, 1976.
Lucanio, Patrick. *Them or Us: Archetypal Interpretations of Fifties Alien Invasion Films*. Bloomington: Indiana University Press, 1988.
McCarthy, Wil. *Aggressor Six*. New York: Roc, 1994.
Miller, Russell. *Bare-Faced Messiah: The True Story of L. Ron Hubbard*. London: Michael Joseph, 1987.
Morales, Robert. *Truth: Red, White and Black*. New York: Marvel, 2003.
Panshin, Alexei. *Heinlein in Dimension: A Critical Analysis*. Chicago: Advent Publishing, 1968.
Pederson, Jay P., ed. *St James Guide to Science Fiction Writers*. 1996.
Platt, Charles, ed. *Dream Makers: Science Fiction Writers at Work*. London: Xanadu, 1987.
Pohl, Fred. *The Way the Future Was: A Memoir*. New York: Del Rey Books, 1978.
Pournelle, Jerry, ed. *There Will Be War*. New York: Tor Books, 1982.
Prokosch, Eric. *The Technology of Killing: A Military and Political History of Antipersonnel Weapons*. London: Zed Books Ltd, 1995.
Rhodes, Richard. *Arsenals of Folly: The Making of the Nuclear Arms Race*. London: Simon & Schuster UK, 2007.
Robb, David L. *Operation Hollywood: How the Pentagon Shapes and Censors the Movies*. Amherst, NY: Prometheus, 2004.
Ronson, Jon. *The Men Who Stare at Goats*. London: Picador, 2004.
Rosenbaum, Jonathan. *Movie Wars: How Hollywood and the Media Conspire to Limit What Films We Can See*. Chicago: A Capella Books, 2000.
Scalzi, John. *The Ghost Brigades*. New York: Tor Books, 2006.
_____. *Old Man's War*. New York: Tor Books, 2005.
Scheer, Robert. *With Enough Shovels: Reagan, Bush, and Nuclear War*. New York: Random House, 1982.
Schelde, Per. *Androids, Humanoids, and Other Science Fiction Monsters: Science and Soul in Science Fiction Films*. New York: New York University Press, 1993.
Seed, David. *American Science Fiction and the Cold War*. Edinburgh: Edinburgh University Press, 1999.
Singer, P.W. *Wired for War*. New York: Penguin Press, 2009.
Spinrad, Norman. *The Men in the Jungle*. New York: Leisure Books, 1967.

———. *No Direction Home*. Glasgow: William Collins & Sons, 1977.
———. *Science Fiction in the Real World*. Carbondale: Southern Illinois University Press, 1990.
Suid, Lawrence. *Guts and Glory: The Making of the American Military Image in Film, Revised and Expanded Edition*. Lexington, KY: University Press of Kentucky, 2002.
Van Creveld, Martin. *Technology and War: From 2000 B.C. to the Present*. 1989. New York: Free Press, 1991.
Walker, James, Lewis Bernstein, and Sharon Lang. *Seize the High Ground: The Army in Space and Missile Defense*. Washington, D.C.: Center of Military History, 2003.
Weinberger, Sharon. *Imaginary Weapons: A Journey through the Pentagon's Scientific Underworld*. New York: Nation Books, 2006.
Weldes, Jutta, ed. *To Seek Out New Worlds: Exploring Links between Science Fiction and World Politics*. New York: Palgrave Macmillan, 2003.
Whitfield, Stephen E. *The Making of Star Trek*. New York: Ballantine Books, 1968.
Wright, Bradford W. *Comic Book Nation: The Transformation of Youth Culture in America*. Baltimore: Johns Hopkins University Press, 2001.

Index

Numbers in **_bold italics_** indicate pages with illustrations.

Aaronovitch, David 23
above-ground nuclear tests 50, 56, 67–68, 76
Action Comics 33–34, 41
Adam, Ken 134
Adams, Eddie 102
Afghanistan 2, 78, 133, 137, 164, 168, 170, 174, 178–180; Soviet occupation of 133
Aggressor Six (novel) 177
Aldiss, Brian 2, 5, 7, 22, 42, 57, 80
Aldrin, Buzz 138
Alford, Matthew 170
Alien (film) 131, 155
Aliens (film) 165
All for His Country (book) 51
All Winners Comics (comic) 54
Allen, Irwin 96, 100
Allen, Richard 141
Alley Oop (comic) 33
Allhoff, Fred 36; *Lightning in the Night* (serial) 36
The Amazing Colossal Man (film) 63, 67
Amazing Stories (magazine) 21, 32, 36, 48
American Enterprise Institute 147
The American Future (book) 58
American Legion Magazine 53
America's Army (computer game) 152
Analog Science Fiction—Science Fact (magazine) 118, 127, 184
Anderson, Martin 135
Anderson, Poul 111–112, 137
Anderson, Richard Dean 172
The Andromeda Strain (film) 155
Anthony, Piers 28, 189; *Bearing an Hourglass* (novel) 28
Anti-Ballistic Missile (ABM) Treaty 129
"The Aphrodite Project" (story) 55
Apocalypse Now (film) 132
Apollo 13 129
Appleton, Victor 136; *Tom Swift and His Cosmotron Express* (novel) 136

"Armageddon 2419 A.D." (novella) 32
Arnett, Peter 113
Arnold, Henry "Hap" 52
The Art of Star Wars (book) 135
Ashcroft, John 8
Asimov, Isaac 19, 35, 36, 37, 47, 49, 50, 57, 66, 76, 79, 111–113, 134, 139–140, 187; "By the Numbers" (essay) 111; *The Currents of Space* (novel) 66; "The Evitable Conflict" (story) 111; *Foundation* (novel) 47; "The Gentle Vultures" (story) 66; "Hell-Fire" (story) 68; "History" (story) 37; "Little Lost Robot" (story) 47; "The Proper Study" (story) 47; "Silly Asses" (story) 68; "Risk" (story) 47; "Spell My Name with an S" (story) 66; "The Weapon" (story) 19, 35; "The Weapon Too Dreadful to Use" (story) 35, 36
Aspin, Les 136
Asprin, Robert 184; *The Cold Cash War* (novel) 184
Assured Survival: Putting the Star Wars Defense in Perspective (book) 123–124, 128
Astonishing Stories (magazine) 47, 48
Astounding Science Fiction (magazine) 48, 49, 50, 52, 53, 55, 59
"The Atomic Bomb" (Eisner story) 143
The Atomic Submarine (film) 63
Autry, Gene 27
Avco Everett Research Laboratory 127
The Avengers (film) 175

Babylon 5 (TV series) 161, 163–164; "Gropos" 163–164
Back to the Future Part III (film) 31
Baen, Jim 177
Baen Books 177–178
Bailey, Charles W. 87; *Seven Days in May* (novel) 87

Bangert, Christoph 152
Barnes, Bucky 44, 54, 73, 91–92
Barnes, Steve 137
Barthes, Roland 13
"Basilisk" (Ellison story) 118
"Bat Durston, Space Marshall" (story) 28
Bates, Harry 59, 111
Batman (comic) 37, 41, 42, 44, 54
Battle Beyond the Stars (film) 31, 131
Battle: Los Angeles (film) 168, 170–171, 173
Battleship (film) 168, 170, 183
Battlestar Galactica (TV series) 30–31, 131, 147, 175; "Flesh and Bone" 175; "The Lost Warrior" 31; "The Magnificent Warriors" 31
Battlezone (video game) 152–153
Bay, Michael 169
bazooka 32
BBC (British Broadcasting Corporation) 109, 114, 151
Bear, Greg 137
The Beast from 20,000 Fathoms (film) 8, 63, 67
Ben Tre 113
Benford, Gregory 133, 137–139, 141
Bethe, Hans 135
Between Planets (novel) 76, 88, 120
"The Big Flash" (story) 118
Biggle, Lloyd 111–112, 187
Bikini Atoll 50, 67
Bill, the Galactic Hero (novel) 93–94
Binder, Otto 54
Bixby, Jerome 107–108, 110; "Day of the Dove" (*Star Trek* episode) 107–108; "Mirror, Mirror" (*Star Trek* episode) 108
blacklist see HUAC
Blazing Saddles (film) 26
Blish, James 48, 49, 77, 107, 111–112, 119, 121, 187; *The Day After Judgement* (novel) 119
Blue Beetle (comic) 73, 191
Blue Beetle (T-63 training shape) 73, 191
Bonanza (TV series) 24, 30, 31
Bond, Nelson 36; "Fugitives from Earth" (story) 36
Bone, J.F. 111–112
Boucher, Anthony 77, 111
Bourke, Joanna 24–25
Bova, Ben 123–124, 127–129, 140, 141; *Assured Survival: Putting the Star Wars Defense in Perspective* (book) 123–124, 128; *Colony* (novel) 129; *Millennium* (novel) 128–129
Bozarth, G. Richard 28; "Bat Durston, Space Marshall" (story) 28

Brackett, Leigh 111
Bradbury, Ray 6, 48, 65, 68, 74, 111; "Embroidery" (story) 68; *The Martian Chronicles* (novel) *14*; "A Piece of Wood" (story) 74; "There Will Come Soft Rains" (story) 65
Bradley, Marion Zimmer 111
Brancatelli, Joe 179–180
Brave New World (novel) 9
Bretnor, Reginald 111, 187
Brin, David 142, 159; *The Postman* (novel) 142, 159
Brooks, Mel 26; *Blazing Saddles* (film) 26
Brown, Fredric 111
Brubaker, Ed 178
Brzezinski, Zbigniew 153
Buck, Doris 111
Buck Rogers (comic) 21, 27, 30, 32, 42, 52, 122, 124, 127
Buck Rogers in the 25th Century (TV series) 131, 132
Buettner, Robert 177–178
Bujold, Lois McMaster 177–178
"bunker buster" bomb 78
Burdick, Harvey 85; *Fail Safe* (novel) 85
Burgos, Carl 43, 46
Burks, Arthur 34; "Survival" (story) 34
Burns, Ken 150
Burroughs, Edgar Rice 26, 31, 48; Barsoom series 26
Busby, F.M. 111–112, 187
Bush, George H.W. 145, 150
Bush, George W. 7, 9, 26, 150, 167
Butler, Smedley 87

Calkin, Dick 32
Campbell, John W. 5, 48–50, 59, 65, 111, 112
Cannon, Lou 63, 133–134; *President Reagan: The Role of a Lifetime* (book) 133–134
Captain America (comic) 33, 39, 41, 44, 46, 54, 57, 73, 90–92, 116–117, *137*, 145–146, 157–158, 178–180
Captain America (movie serial) 54, 145
Captain America (1990 movie) 145
Captain America (1979 TV movie) 145
Captain America and the Falcon (comic) 116–117, 146
Captain America: The Chosen (comic) 179
Captain America: The New Deal (comic) 178–179
"Captain Kirk Cold Warrior" (Wortland) 104
Captain Marvel (comic) 44, 72

Index

Carabatsos, Steven 107; "Operation: Annihilate!" (*Star Trek* episode) 107
Card, Orson Scott 147, 148–150, 151, 172, 173, 177, 181–182; *Empire* (novel) 181–182; *Ender's Game* (novel) 148–150
Carter, Jimmy 133, 153
Cartmill, Cleve 49–50, 139; "Deadline" (story) 49–50, 139
Cartwright, James "Hoss" 24
Catch-22 (novel) 86
Cat's Cradle (novel) 154
"Caught in the Organ Draft" (story) 119
censorship 43, 47, 49–50, 52
"Challenge: The Insurgent vs. the Counterinsurgent" (essay) 119
Cheney, Dick 8, 9
Childhood's End (novel) 75
Citizens Advisory Council for a National Space Policy 137–140
"The City on the Edge of Forever" (*Star Trek* episode) 104, 106, 109, 110
Civil War (Marvel Comics) 179–180
Clark, Bill 134
Clarke, Arthur C. 6, 22, 75, 129, 134, 138–140, 142, 144, 147, 154; *Childhood's End* (novel) 75; "Loophole" (story) 129; "Scenario for a Civilized Planet" (essay) 140; "Superiority" (story) 154; *2001: A Space Odyssey* (novel) 6
Clement, Hal 48, 111–112, 230
Clinton, Bill 136
Close Encounters of the Third Kind (film) 131, 147, 175
Clute, John 2, 27, 57
Cogswell, Theodore 111–112
The Cold Cash War (novel) 184
"Cold War" (Kris Neville story) 53
Collins, Larry 129; *The Fifth Horseman* (novel) 129
Colony (Bova novel) 138
Comics Code Authority 73
"Commando Raid" (story) 84, 181
Computer Space (computer game) *see Spacewar!*
A Connecticut Yankee in King Arthur's Court (novel) 6
Conrad, Pete 138
conscription 60, 77, 78–79, 108, 117–119
"The Conspiracy" (Spinrad story) 118–119
"Conspiracy" (*Star Trek: The Next Generation* episode) 110
Convergent Series (story collection) 143
Coon, Gene L. 105–106, 108, 187; "A Taste of Armageddon" (*Star Trek* episode) 108

"The Corbomite Maneuver" (*Star Trek* episode) 143
Cowboy Western (comic) 27
Cowboys and Aliens (film) 31
Crichton, Michael 155
Crowther, Bosley 87
"Curtains" (story) 184

Daigo Fukuryu Maru (Lucky Dragon 5) 67–68
Dangerous Visions (anthology) 112
Daniels, Les 35, 41, 180
Danse Macabre (book) 139
Daredevil (comic) 67, 160
Daredevil Battles Hitler (comic) 44
"Dark Outpost" (*The Invaders* episode) 102
Dark Star (film) 155, 191
DARPA (Defense Advanced Research Projects Agency) 13, 78, 147, 157, 160, 167, 176
Darth Vader 7, **8**, 9, 136, 147, 150
Davis, Chandler 52, 187; "To Still the Drums" (story) 52
Davy Crockett (nuclear weapon) 25
The Day After (film) 134, 175
The Day After Judgement (book) 119
The Day After Tomorrow (Heinlein novel) *see Sixth Column*
"Day of the Dove" (*Star Trek* episode) 107–108
The Day the Earth Stood Still (1951 film) 58, 59, 61–65, 75, 116, 134, 194
"Deadline" (Cleve Cartmill story) 49–50, 139
The Deadly Mantis (film) 63
death ray 7, 27, 52, 123–127, 145
De Camp, L. Sprague 6, 47, 48, 50, 111; *Lest Darkness Fall* (novel) 6
"Defend America Act of 1996" 136
deFord, Miriam Allen 111–112
Delany, Samuel 89, 111
del Rey, Lester 111–112
Destination Moon (film) 27, 57–58
Detective Comics (publisher) 37
"Devil in the Dark" (*Star Trek* episode) 106
Dick, Philip K. 65, 74, 81, 111, 118; "The Defenders" (story) 74, 118; *The Penultimate Truth* (novel) 118
Dickson, Gordon R. 57, 81, 136, 187; *Dorsai!* (novel) 81
Disch, Thomas M. 5, 17, 23, 111
Ditko, Steve 158
Doc Savage (comic) 32
Doctor Strangelove, or How I Learned to Stop Worrying and Love the Bomb

(film) 7, 8, 9, 12, 13, 25, 77, 85–87, 133, 134, 138, 155
Dole, Bob 136
Drake, David 84, 136, 177, 178, 189
Durston, Bat 27–28

Eagleton, Terry 2, 6, 7, 19, 170
Earth vs. the Flying Saucers (film) 63–65
Eckhart, Aaron 170–171
Edgar Allan Poe (naval vessel) 46–47
Effinger, George Alec 184; "Curtains" (story) 184
Einstein, Albert 36, 62
Eisenhower, Dwight 23, 56, 67, 74, 88
Eisner, Will 32, 35, 46, 143; "The Atomic Bomb" (story) 143
Ellis, Edward 23; *The Steam Man of the Prairies* (novel) 23
Ellison, Harlan 110, 112, 114, 118, 120, 230; *Alone Against Tomorrow* (story collection) 114; "Basilisk" (story) 118–119; "The City on the Edge of Forever" (*Star Trek* episode) 104, 106, 109, 110; *Dangerous Visions* (anthology) 112
Ellsworth, Whitney 37
Empire (novel) 181–182
The Empire Strikes Back (film) 132–133
"The Encounter" (The Twilight Zone episode) 71–72, 100
"The End of New York" (story) 21
Ender's Game (novel) 148–150
Enterprise (space shuttle) 133
Enterprise (*Star Trek*) 104, 106, 107, 109, 110, 143, 148, 154, 156
"The *Enterprise* Incident" (*Star Trek* episode) 104
"Errand of Mercy" (*Star Trek* episode) 106, 109
Evans, Joyce 59, 68, 84
Everett, Bill 36, 46
Expanded Universe (Heinlein book) 78
"Extended Performance War Fighter" 160

Fail Safe (film) 85–86, 98
Fail Safe (novel) 85–86
Fantastic Four (comic) 67, 116
Fantasy and Science Fiction (magazine) 111, 114, 119, 140
Farmer, Philip José 79, 111–112, 187
Favreau, Jon 173, 175
Ferengi 166
The Fifth Horseman (novel) 129
Fighting Aces (magazine) 47
The Final Countdown (film) 168
Finger, Bill 37
Firefly (TV series) 31

FitzGerald, Frances 134, 143–144
Five (film) 63, 66
Flash Gordon (serial) 29, 30, 57, 124, 132
Fleur, Henry 125
Flint, Eric 177
Flying Saucers from Outer Space (book) 64
Fontana, Dorothy C. 104, 107
Footfall (novel) 138
Ford, John (director) 24, 31
Ford, John M. 166–167
Forever Free (novel) 176
Forever Peace (novel) 156–157, 176
The Forever War (novel) 2, **20**, 94, 120–121, 149, 156, 160, 161, 168, 176
Foundation (novel) 47
"Four Little Ships" (Murray Leinster story) 49
Frankenheimer, John 87–88; *Seven Days in May* (film) 87–88
Franklin, H. Bruce 2, 6, 9, 25, 34, 36, 63, 78, 89, 104, 105, 111, 119, 122, 142, 143, 177, 178, 180; "*Star Trek* in the Vietnam Era" (essay) 104; *Vietnam and Other American Fantasies* (book) 119, 177; *War Stars: The Superweapon and the American Imagination* (book) 2, 21
"Friday's Child" (*Star Trek* episode) 106–107
Frontline Combat (comic) 72
Fugitives from Earth" (Nelson Bond story) 36
Full Metal Jacket (film) 87, 161
Funnies on Parade (comic book) 33
Future Force Company Commander (computer game) 152
"Future Force Warrior" 7, **16**, 185
Future Science Fiction (magazine) 49
Futureworld (film) 148, 155

Gadson, Gregory 166, 170
Galaxina (film) 30
Galaxy (magazine) 27, **28**, 111, 119, 140
Galaxy Game (computer game) *see Spacewar!*
Galbreath, David 166
Galouye, Daniel 111–112, 187
Gannon, Charles 6, 110
Gates, Robert 123
George, Peter 86; *Two Hours to Doom* (novel) 86; *see also Dr. Strangelove*
Gernsback, Hugo 32
Gerrold, David 104; *The World of Star Trek* (book) 104; *see also* "The Trouble with Tribbles" (*Star Trek* episode)
Gesell, Gerhard 135

The Ghost Brigades (novel) 177
Giesy, John 51; *All for His Country* (novel) 51
Gifford, James 79
Gingrich, Newt 136, 144–145
Glory Road (novel) 88–90, 120
Godzilla (2014 film) 168, 171
Gog (film) 63
Gold, Horace 27, 48, 50, 65, 167
GoldenEye (film) 168, 191
Goodman, Martin 34–35
Gorbachev, Mikhail 63, 123, 128, 133, 134, 136, 143–145
Gore, Al 9
Graham, Bradley 9, 144
The Great Train Robbery (film) 24
Green, Roland 178
Green Arrow (comic) 113
Green Berets 78
Greene, Lorne 31
"Gropos" (*Babylon 5* episode) 163–164
Groves, Leslie 51, 125
Guantanamo Bay 175
Gulf of Tonkin incident 91, 97, 104, 108
Guns of the South (novel) 6

Hagelstein, Peter 123, 136, 139; "Physics of Short Wavelength Design" (dissertation) 136
Haise, Fred 138
Haldeman, Joe 1, 13, 50, 84, 94, 120–121, 138, 149, 156–157, 160, 176, 181, 189; *Forever Free* (novel) 176; *Forever Peace* (novel) 156–157, 176; *The Forever War* (novel) 2, **20**, 94, 120–121, 149, 156, 160, 161, 168, 176; *1968* (novel) 13, 84
HALO (game and tie-in books) **15**, 153
Hamilton, Edmond 111
Hamner, Robert 108; "A Taste of Armageddon" (*Star Trek* episode) 108
Harak, G. Simon 143
Harrison, Harry 22, 27, 84, 93–94, 111–112, 114, 118, 181; *Bill, the Galactic Hero* (novel) 93–94; "Commando Raid" (story) 84, 181
Harryhausen, Ray 65
Hawks, Howard 24, 59–60, 164
Heinlein, Robert A. 1, 5, 19, 27, 38–39, 42, 46, 47–58, 63, 75–83, 84, 88–90, 93, 111–112, 120–122, 127, 136, 137–140, 142, 177; *Between Planets* (novel) 76, 88, 120; *Destination Moon* (film) 27, 57–58; *Expanded Universe* (book) 78; "Future History" chronology, 53; *Glory Road* (novel) 88–90, 120; "The Last Days of the United States" (essay) 51–52, 142; "The Long Watch" (story) 53–54, 58; *Rocketship Galileo* (novel) 57; *Sixth Column* (novel) 39; "Solution Unsatisfactory" (story) 38–39, 54, 58, 63; "Starship Soldier" (story) 79; *Starship Troopers* (film) 19, 164, 183; *Starship Troopers* (novel) 19, 39, 75–83, 93, 120–121, 148–149, 164, 165; *Stranger in a Strange Land* (novel) 76; *Time for the Stars* (novel) 120; *Tramp Royale* (book) 90; "Who Are the Heirs of Patrick Henry? Stand Up and Be Counted!" (advertisement) 76
"Heirloom" (Spinrad story) 117
Heller, Joseph 86, 130; *Catch-22* (novel) 86–130
Hensley, Joe 111–112, 189
Heritage Foundation 137
Herr, Michael 113
Hersch, Seymour 147
High Noon (film) 25, 31
Hill, Douglas 27
Hirohito, Emperor 44
Hiroshima 49, 50, 70
"History" (Asimov story) 37
Hitchcock, Alfred 134; *Torn Curtain* (film) 134
Hitler, Adolf 33, 35–37, 39, 42, 44, 46
Ho Chi Minh 55, 105, 120
Homer 21
HUAC (House Un-American Activities Committee) 57, 58, 63
Hubbard, L. Ron 48, 49
Hugo Award 57, 66, 81, 121, 149, 154
HULC (Human Universal Load Carrier) 11, 78, 191
Hulk (movie) 116, 158
"The Human Factor" (*Outer Limits* episode) 95
Hunter, Stephen 171
Hussein, Saddam 13, 150, 167
Huxley, Aldous 9; *Brave New World* (novel) 9
Hyde, Rod 135
Hydrogen bomb 56, 60, 138, 143

"In Praise of Pip" (*The Twilight Zone* episode) 71
The Incredible Hulk (comic) 67, 116, 158, 191
The Incredible Hulk (movie) 116, 158
The Incredible Shrinking Man (film) 67
Independence Day (film) 175
Ing, Dean 111, 137, 189
"The Inheritors" (*Outer Limits* episode) 94–95
The Invaders (TV series) 101–103; "Condition Red" 101–102; "Dark Outpost"

102; "Doomsday Minus One" 101; "The Peacemaker" 102–103
Invaders from Mars (1953 film) 63
Invasion of the Body Snatchers (film) 8, 131
Invasion USA (1952 film) 60–61, 64, 66
The Invisible Invaders (film) 63
Iran-Contra affair 110
iRobot.com 185
Iron Man (film series) 158–159, 162, 173, 174–177, 179
Iron Man (Marvel comic) 90–92, 116, 127, 179–180, 185
It Came from Beneath the Sea (film) 63, 67, 68

Jackson, Patrick T. 9, 144
Jacquet, Lloyd 33
Jameson, Frederic 2, 17, 21, 74, 112, 184; "stages of science fiction" 17
Jancovich, Mark 67
"Japanazis" 36, 41
Jarecke, Kenneth 150
Jarhead (book) 183
JEDI (Joint Expeditionary Digital Information) 11, 147, 160, 191
Jeep 12, 36, 191
Jenkins, Will *see* Leinster, Murray
John Birch Society 87
Johnny Got His Gun (book) 58, 77
Johnson, Jason 171
Jones, D.F. 154; *Colossus: The Forbin Project* 154–155
Jones, Raymond F. 50
Journey Into Mystery (Marvel comic) 92
Justman, Robert 104

Kahn, Herbert 85, 138
Kane, Bob 37
Kane, John "Killer" 42
Kang, Inkoo 170
Karig, Walter 52
Kavenay, Roz 77
Kennedy, Edward 135
Kennedy, John 78, 87–88
Kent State Four 114
Keyes, Daniel 111
Keyhoe, Donald 64; *Flying Saucers from Outer Space* (book) 64
Keyworth, George 140–141, 144
Khrushchev, Nikita 85, 88
King, Martin Luther 104, 109; "Declaration of Independence from the War in Vietnam" 104
King, Stephen 59–60, 119, 131; *Danse Macabre* (book) 131; *The Long Walk* (novel) 119

Kirby, Jack 37, 39, 46
Kissinger, Henry 85
Klein, Naomi 150
Klingon(s) 7, 9, 105–109, 148, 166, 167, 172
Knebel, Fletcher 87; *Seven Days in May* (novel) 87
Knight, Damon 2, 6, 8, 65, 111; "To Serve Man" (story) 8
Koch, Howard 33
Koepp, David 171; *The War of the Worlds* (film) 171
Kornbluth, Cyril 48, 74, 187; "The Adventurer" (story) 74; *The Space Merchants* (novel) 74
Kramer, Peter 135, 144
Kubrick, Stanley 86, 138, 183; *Dr. Strangelove, or How I Learned to Stop Worrying and Love the Bomb* (film) 86; *Full Metal Jacket* (film) 87, 138; *Paths of Glory* (film) 86
Kummer, Frederic 36; "The Foreign Legion of Mars" (story) 36; "Legion of the Dead" (story) 36
Kurtzmann, Harvey 72
Kuttner, Henry 46, 48, 187

Lady Slings the Booze (novel) 129
Lafferty, R.A. 111–112, 187
LaPierre, Dominique 129; *The Fifth Horseman* (novel) 129
laser 123, 127–129, 135–136, 138–139, 142, 156, 160, 184, 185
Laserblast (movie) 131
"The Last Days of the United States" (essay) 51–52, 142
Laumer, Keith 136, 187
Laumer, March 111–112
Lawrence Livermore laboratories 24, 123, 135, 138
Lee, Stan 34–35, 46, 54, 91–93, 127, 158
The Legacy of Hiroshima (book) 128
Le Guin, Ursula K. 111, 113–114, 181; *The Word for World Is Forest* (novel) 113–114
Leiber, Fritz 50, 111–112
Leinster, Murray 48–50, 52; *The Murder of the U.S.A.* (novel) 52
LeMay, Curtis 87
Lennon, John 104
Lerner, Frederick 32
Lest Darkness Fall (novel) 6
"Let That Be Your Last Battlefield" (*Star Trek* episode) 105
Liberty (magazine) 36
Liebowitz, Jack 37
The Lieutenant (TV series) 109
Lightning in the Night (serial) 36

Index

"limited nuclear war" 60, 128
Linebarger, Paul *see* Smith, Cordwainer
Little Big Man (film) 24
"Little Lost Robot" (Asimov story) 47
Little Orphan Annie (comic) 33
"Living in Harmony" (*The Prisoner* episode) 109–110
Loan, Nguyen Ngoc 25, 113
Lone Star Planet (novel) 27, **29**
The Long Loud Silence (novel) 65
The Long Walk (novel) 119
"The Long Watch" (story) 53–54, 58
"Loophole" (story) 129
Los Alamos 139
Lost in Space (TV series) 30, 73, 101; "West of Mars" 30
"The Lost Warrior" (*Battlestar Galactica* episode) 31
Lovecraft, H.P. 23
Lucanio, Patrick 57
Lucas, George 122, 129, 132, 135, 144, 145, 151
Lucian of Samosata 21
Lucky Dragon 5 67–68
Lundwall, Sam 181

M-16 rifle 13
MacArthur, General Douglas 25, 87
Maclean, Katherine 111
The Magnificent Seven (film) 24, 29, 31
"The Magnificent Warriors" (*Battlestar Galactica* episode) 31
Malzberg, Barry 111
"The Man Who Was Used Up" (story) 19, 160
"The Maneuver" (*Star Trek* episode) 143; "Dark Outpost" (*The Invaders* episode) 102; *Point Ultimate* (novel) 128
MARCBOT 176
Marlowe, Hugh 65
Mars Attacks! (film) 175
The Martian Chronicles (book) **14**
Marvel Comics (comic) 35–37
Marvel Comics (publisher) **18**, 67, 73, 90–93, 116, 127, 145, 157–159, 167, 174, 178–179
Marvel Mystery Comics (comic) 54
Marvel Science Stories (magazine) 34–35
Marvel Stories (magazine) 36
Marvel Tales (magazine) 35
maser 127
Matheson, Richard 57, 188
McAllister, Bruce 111–112
McCarthy, Eugene 107
McCarthy, Wil 177; *Aggressor Six* (novel) 177

McFarlane, Robert 140–141
McGarry, Byron 169
McGuire, John 27–28; *Lone Star Planet* (novel) 27–28, **29**
McKee, Robert 26
McLaughlin, Dean 77
McNamara, Robert 107
Medaris, John 58
Medved, Michael 179
The Men in the Jungle (novel) 117
Merril, Judith 111–112
Meyer, Nicholas 62
military-entertainment complex 183
military-industrial complex 56
military-scientific complex 142
military spending, U.S. 74, 133, 142–143, 182–183
Milius, John 132
Millennium (Bova novel) 128–129
Miller, Frank 157
Miller, Walter M. 66, 188; *A Canticle for Leibowitz* (novel) 66
Mills, Jane 24
"Mirror, Mirror" (*Star Trek* episode) 108–109
Missile Command (video game) 152
The Monster That Challenged the World (film) 63, 67
Moon, Elizabeth 177–178, 189
Moon Zero Two (film) 29
Moore, Alan 6, 22, 84; *Watchmen* (comic) 6, 84
Morales, Robert 158
Morgan, Glen 160–161
Morrell, David 177; *Captain America: The Chosen* (comic) 177
Morrison, Marion *see* Wayne, John
Moseley, George Van Horn 87
The Mote in God's Eye (novel) 136
Moynihan, Dennis 170
Murder in the Air (film) 126, 134
The Murder of the U.S.A. (book) 52
Murray, Doug 157
Mussolini, Benito 42, 44
My Lai 19, 113–114, 118–119
The Nam (comic) 157

NASA **13**, 107, 129, 137–138, 141
National Physical Laboratory 125
Nebula Award 121, 149
Neville, Kris 53, 111–112, 188; "Cold War" (story) 53
New Fun Comics (comic book) 33
New Scientist (magazine) 145
Nexon, Daniel H. 9, 144
"Nightmare" (*Outer Limits* episode) 96
Nineteen Eighty-Four (novel) 6, 9, 84

Index

1968 (Haldeman novel) 13, 84
Nishikado, Tomohiro 151
Niven, Larry 111–112, 136, 137–140, 177; *Convergent Series* (book) 143; *Footfall* (novel) 138; *The Mote in God's Eye* (novel) 136; *Ringworld* (novel) 136; "Rotating Cylinders and the Possibility of Global Causality Violation" (story) 143; "Transfer of Power" (story) 143
Nixon, Richard 102, 104, 117, 132, 135, 146
Nourse, Alan 111–112, 188
Nowlan, Phillip Francis 32, nuclear hand grenade 78, 164
nuclear winter 139, 140
"Null Zone" (story) 119–120

O Group (Lawrence Livermore Laboratory) 135–136
Oboler, Arch 163, 166; *Five* (film) 163, 166
Okada, Dave 129
Old Man's War (novel) 177
"The Omega Glory" (*Star Trek* episode) 105, 110
On the Beach (film) 66–67
"Operation: Annihilate!" (*Star Trek* episode) 106
Operation Desert Storm 150, 177
Operation Enduring Freedom 165
Operation Just Cause 150
Operation: Live Connections 152
Operation Paperclip 159
Operation Red Dawn 167
Operation Start Up 153
Operation Urgent Fury 150, 177
OpNav-23 48
Oppenheimer, Robert 126, 129
Organians (*Star Trek*) 106, 108
Orwell, George 6, 9, 62, 84; *Nineteen Eighty-Four* (novel) 6, 9, 84
Oswald, Lee Harvey 87
The Outer Limits (TV series) 94–96; "The Human Factor" 95; "Nightmare" 96; "The Zanti Misfits" 95–96
Outland (film) 31

Padgett, Lewis 50
The Panama Deception (film) 150
Pangborn, Edgar 48, 188
Panic in Year Zero (film) 67, 85
Panshin, Alexei 75, 77, 81, 83, 111, 189
The Paradise Crater (novella) 49
"The Paradise Syndrome" (*Star Trek* episode) 29
Paths of Glory (film) 86

Patriot missile system 145, 156
Pax Americana 38, 58
"The Peacemaker" (*The Invaders* episode) 102–103
The Penultimate Truth (book) 118
Perle, Richard 144
"permanent wartime economy" 74
The Phantom (comic) 33
The Phantom Empire (film serial) 27
PHASR (Personnel Halting and Stimulation Response) 11, 191
The Philadelphia Experiment (film) 175
"Physics of Short Wavelength Design" (dissertation) 136
Piper, H. Beam 27–28; *Lone Star Planet* (novel) 27–28, **29**
Plan 9 from Outer Space (film) 68
Platt, Charles 113
Player Piano (book) 75
Poe, Edgar Allan 19, 21, 46, 160; "The Man Who Was Used Up" (story) 19, 160
Pohl, Frederick 35, 47–49, 74, 75, 111, 113, 139, 181, 188; *The Space Merchants* (novel) 74; "The Wizard of Pung's Corners" (story) 75
Popeye (comic) 33, 36, 42, 191
Possony, Stefan 119; *The Strategy of Technology* (book) 119
The Postman (novel) 142, 159
Pournelle, Jerry 111–113, 119, 136–141, 149, 177–178, 181, 189; Falkenberg's Legion series, 178; *Footfall* (novel) 138; *Janissaries* (novel) 178; *The Mote in God's Eye* (novel) 136; *The Strategy of Technology* (book) 119
Powell, Colin 63, 134, 166; "Powell doctrine" 156–157, 176
Poyer, Joe 111–112, 119; "Challenge: The Insurgent vs. the Counterinsurgent" (essay) 119; "Null Zone" (story) 119
Pratt, Fletcher 48
President Reagan: The Role of a Lifetime (book) 133
The Prisoner (TV series) 109–110; "Living in Harmony" 109–110
"A Private Little War" (*Star Trek* episode) 104–105, 108–109
Project Horizon 58
"The Proper Study" (Asimov short story) 47
Pueblo Incident 104
The Punisher (comic) 113, 157, 167, 180
Punishment Park (film) 114–116
"The Purple Testament" (*Twilight Zone* episode) 69–70

"A Quality of Mercy" (Twilight Zone episode) 70
Quayle, Dan 145

Rayburn, Sam 61
Reagan, Ronald 12, 26, 63, 123, 126, 128, 133–146, 150, 152
Red Dawn (film) 167, 174, 191
Red River (film) 30
Red, White and Blue (comic) 38
Reiss, Edward 140
Reynolds, Mack 111–112, 184, 188; "Mercenary" (story) 184
Rice, Condoleezza 9
Richards, Thomas 29
The Right Stuff (film) 173
Riley, Arthur 50
Ringo, John 177–178
Ringworld (novel) 136
The Rise and Rise of Michael Rimmer (film) 143
"Risk" (Asimov short story) 47
Robb, David 85, 168, 172
Robinson, Kim Stanley 140
Robinson, Spider 119, 129; *Lady Slings the Booze* (novel) 129; "Unnatural Causes" (story) 119
Robocop (1987 film) 142, 156
Rocket Attack USA (film) 66
Rocketship Galileo (book) 57–58
Rocketship X-M (film) 58
Roddenberry, Gene 29, 104–105, 109–112, 188
Ronson, Jon 147
Roosevelt, Franklin D. 33, 36, 38, 87
Rosenbaum, Jonathan 82
Rosenfeld, Gavriel 37
"Rotating Cylinders and the Possibility of Global Causality Violation" (story) 143
Rotberg, Ed 152
Rucker, Rudy 135; "PAC-Man" (story) 135
Rumsfeld, Donald 136, **136**, 145, 175, 178
Russ, Joanna 111

Saberhagen, Fred 111–112, 172, 189
Sagan, Carl 128
Sagdeev, Roald 142
Salinger, Pierre 87
Samuelson, David 89
Santorum, Rick 184
Sardar, Ziauddin 26
Scalzi, John 177, 183; *Ghost Brigades* (novel) 177; *Old Man's War* (novel) 177
Schama, Simon 22, 58; *The American Future* (book) 58

Scheer, Robert 143
Schlesinger, Arthur 87
Schuster, Joe 33, 34, 37, 45
Schwarzenegger, Arnold 167
Science fiction: "Age of Silver" 57; definitions, 5–6; stages of (Jameson) 17, 21, 74, 112, 184
Science Fiction and Fantasy Research Database 81
Science Fiction and Fantasy Writers of America (SFWA) 111, 139, 181
Science Fiction Quarterly (magazine) 49
Science Fiction: The Illustrated Encyclopedia 27
SCORE (satellite) 56
SDI (Strategic Defense Initiative) 123, 134–145, 168, 182; *see also* "Star Wars" missile defense
The Searchers (film) 29
Second Amendment 90
Secrets Behind the Comics (book) 34
Seduction of the Innocents (book) 73
Seed, David 128
Segar, E.C. 36
Sellers, Peter 138
Sentinels of Liberty 44, 145
September 11 attacks 145, 165
Serenity (film) 31
Serling, Rod 69–71, 87, 188
Seven Days in May (book) 87
Seven Days in May (film) 87–88
The Shadow (Comic) 32
Shadow Complex (computer game) 181
Shane (film) 26, 31
Shelley, Mary 21
Siegel, Don 24
Siegel, Jerome 33–34, 37–38, 44–46
Silverberg, Robert 50, 111–112, 119; "Caught in the Organ Draft" (story) 119
Simmons, Dan 184; "E-Ticket to 'Namland'" (story) 184
Simon, Herbert 85
Simon, Joe 33, 37, 39, 41, 44, 46
The Six Million Dollar Man (TV series) 160
Slotkin, Richard 23–26
Smith, Cordwainer 48, 187
Smith, E.E. "Doc" 48, 49, 148, 187
Smith, George O. 48
The Smuggled Atom Bomb (book) 129
Snyder, J. William 104; "*Star Trek*: A Phenomenon and Social Statement on the 1960s" 104
Sohl, Jerry 102, 110, 112, 128, 143, 188
"Solution Unsatisfactory" (story) 38–39, 54, 58, 63

240 Index

"Son of SDI" 129
"Son of Star Wars" 136, 147
Space: Above and Beyond (TV series) 31, 160–164; "The Angriest Angel" 163; "Choice or Chance" 162; "Pearly" 163; "R&R" 163, "Stardust" 31; "Stay with the Dead" 162–163; "Sugar Dirt" 163; "Who Monitors the Birds?" 160
The Space Children (film) 68
Space Defense Initiative *see* SDI; *see also* "Star Wars" missile defense
Space Invaders (video game) 151
Space Wars (video game) *see Spacewar!*
Space Western (comic) 27, **30**
Spacewar! (computer game) 148
special forces 78, 88, 119, 150, 171, 178
"Spectre of the Gun" (*Star Trek* episode) 29
Spider-Man (film) **137**, 158
Spielberg, Steven 168, 169, 171, 183
Spinrad, Norman 5, 77, 110, 112, 114, 117–118, 134, 139, 140, 142, 149–150, 173; "The Big Flash" (story) 118; "The Conspiracy" (story) 117; Heirloom" (story) 117; *The Men in the Jungle* (book) 117
Sputnik 56, 58, 88, 143
Stalin, Josef 126
Star Trek (computer game) 148
Star Trek (TV and film series) 2, 9, 27, 29, 104–111, 131, 133, 143, 154, 161, 166, 167, 190, 191; "The City on the Edge of Forever" 104, 106, 109–110; "The Corbomite Maneuver" 143; "Day of the Dove" 107–108; "The *Enterprise* Incident" 104; "Errand of Mercy" 106, 109; "Friday's Child" 106–107; "Let That Be Your Last Battlefield" 105; "Mirror, Mirror" 108–109; "The Omega Glory" 105, 110; "Operation: Annihilate!" 106; "The Paradise Syndrome" 29; "Spectre of the Gun" 29; *Star Trek IV* (film) 168, 170; *Star Trek VI* (film) 104, 166, 172; *Star Trek: The Motion Picture* (film) 131; "A Taste of Armageddon" 108; "The Trouble with Tribbles" 106–107; "The Ultimate Computer" 110, 154
"*Star Trek*: A Phenomenon and Social Statement on the 1960s" (Wortland) 104
Star Trek IV: The Voyage Home (film) 168, 170
"*Star Trek* in the Vietnam Era" (Franklin) 104
Star Trek VI: The Undiscovered Country (film) 104, 166, 172
Star Trek: The Motion Picture (film) 131

Star Trek: The Next Generation 110, 166; "Conspiracy" 110
"Star Wars: A Critique" 128
Star Wars Dreams (documentary) 134
Star Wars Episode IV: A New Hope (film) 2, 6, 7, 13, 22, 29–30, 122, 129, 131, 132, 135, 136, 139, 144, 145, 147, 148–151, 175, 185, 191
"Star Wars" missile defense 7, 9, 13, 21, 22, 123, 134, 135, 136–145, 160; *see also* SDI
"Star Wars speech" 134–136, 138, 140, 143
Stargate (film) 171
Stargate SG-1 (TV series) 31, 171–172, 183; "Spirits" 31
Starman (film) 175
Starship Invasions (film) 131
Starship Troopers (film) 1, 19, 164–165, 183
Starship Troopers (novel) 1, 2, 19, 39, 74–83, 88–90, 93–94, 120–121, 148–149, 161, 164–165, 168
The Stepford Wives (book) 8
Stevens, Robert 56
Stimson, Henry 51
Stranger in a Strange Land (book) 76
Strategic Air Command (book) 85–86, 95
Strategic Defense Initiative *see* SDI; *see also* "Star Wars" missile defense
The Strategy of Technology (book) 119
Strick, Phillip 60
Strub, Phil 169
Stubbs, Harry *see* Clement, Hal
Sturgeon, Theodore 48–49, 52, 81; "Thunder and Roses" (story) 52–53
Super Science Stories (magazine) 47, 48
Superman (comic) 2, 33–34, 37–38, **40**, 41–42, **43**, 44–46, **45**, **46**, 49, 54, 93, 191
Superman: The Movie (film) 131
Superman II (film) 131
"Survival" (Burks story) 34
Swofford, Anthony 183; *Jarhead* (book) 183
Szilard, Leo 36

T-63 training shape 73
Tales of Suspense (Marvel comic) 59, 91–92
Taser 11, 185
"A Taste of Armageddon" (*Star Trek* episode) 108
Technology and War (Van Creveld) 11–12
"technoporn" 144
"technowonders" 6, 9, 14, 33, 180
Teller, Edward 36, 128, 138–140, 167; *The Legacy of Hiroshima* (book) 128

Index

The Terminator (film) 7, 153, 155
Terminator2: Judgment Day (film) 167
Tet offensive 102, 104, 111
Thatcher, Margaret 123
Them! (film) 63, 67–68
Theurer, Dave 152
Thieu, Nguyen Van 104
The Thing from Another World (1950 film) 56, 58–62, 64, 100, 131
Things to Come (film) 51
Thomson, Elihu 125
"Thunder and Roses" (story) 52–53
THX-1138 (film) 151
Time for the Stars (novel) 120
Timecop (film) 31
Timely Publications 34–37, 54, 72
Timerider (film) 31
"To Still the Drums" (story) 52
Tobey, Kenneth 59–60
Tojo, Hideki 42
Tom Swift and His Cosmotron Express (book) 136
Torn Curtain (film) 134
"Transfer of Power" (story) 143
Transformers (TV cartoon, film series) 167, 169, 172, 183, 191, 195
Trinity A-bomb test 68
"The Trouble with Tribbles" (*Star Trek* episode) 106–107
Truffaut, François 183
Truman, Harry 55, 87, 88
Trumbo, Dalton 58, 77; *Johnny Got His Gun* (novel) 58, 77
Truth: Red, White and Black (comic) 158–159
Tucker, Wilson 65; *The Long Loud Silence* (novel) 65
Turtledove, Harry 6, 129; *Guns of the South* (novel) 6; *Worldwar: Upsetting the Balance* (novel) 129
Tuskegee syphilis experiment 153
Twain, Mark 6, 180; *A Connecticut Yankee in King Arthur's Court* (novel) 6
The Twilight Zone (TV series) 8, 69–72, 100; "The Encounter" 71–72, 100; "I Shot an Arrow Into the Air" 71; "In Praise of Pip" 71; "*King Nine* Will Not Return" 69; "The Last Flight" 71–72; "The Purple Testament" 69–70; "A Quality of Mercy" 70; "The Thirty-Fathom Grave" 69; "To Serve Man" 8; "Two" 70–71; "Where Is Everybody?" 69; "The 7th Is Made Up of Phantoms" 71
Two-Fisted Tales (comic) 72
Two Hours to Doom (novel) 86
2001: A Space Odyssey (book) 6

"The Ultimate Computer" (*Star Trek* episode) 110, 154
Ultimate X-Men (comic) 113
Ultimates (comic) 147
Union of Concerned Scientists 128; "Star Wars: A Critique" 128
Universal Soldier (film) *21*, 113, 159
"Unnatural Causes" (story) 119
U.S. Naval Air Experimental Station 47
USA Comics (comic) 54

Vance, Jack 111
Van Creveld, Martin 11–12; *Technology and War* (book) 11
Varley, John 184; *Titan* (novel) 184
Verhoeven, Paul 1, 19, 164–165; *Starship Troopers* (film) 1, 19, 164–165
Verne, Jules 17
Vietnam and Other American Fantasies (book) 148, 177
"Vietnamization" 104
"The Village" (Kate Wilhelm short story) 19, 118
Vincent, Harl 111–112
von Braun, Werner 56, 58, 138, 154
Vonnegut, Kurt 75, 80, 81, 154, 188; *Cat's Cradle* (novel) 154; *Player Piano* (novel) 75, 80; *The Sirens of Titan* (novel) 81

Waldrop, Howard 58–59, 189
Walker, Alexander 86
Walker, Edwin 87
The War Game (documentary) 114
War Machine (comic) *18*, 159, 173, 176
War of the Worlds (1953 film) 64
War of the Worlds (2005 film) 168–169, 171–172
The War of the Worlds (novel) 1, 123–124, 151
"The War of the Worlds" (radio play) 1, 33–34
War Stars: The Superweapon and the American Imagination (book) 2, 21
WarGames (film) 97, 133–134, 153, 155
Watchmen (book) 6, 84, 113
Watkins, Peter 114–116; *Punishment Park* (film) 114–116; *The War Game* (documentary) 114
Watson-Watt, Robert 125
Wayne, John "Duke" 23–27, 30, 31, 59, 60, 131, 140, 185
"The Weapon" (Asimov story) 19, 35
"The Weapon Too Dreadful to Use" (story) 35, 36
Weber, David 177–178

Welles, Orson 1, 33–34; "The War of the Worlds" (radio play) 1, 33–34
Wells, H.G. 36, 37, 51, 151; "Berlin Should Be Bombed" (essay) 37; "A Prophetic Trilogy" (serial) 51; *Things to Come* (film) 51; *The War of the Worlds* (novel) 1, 123–124, 151; *The World Set Free* (book) 36
Wertham, Frederic 73; *Seduction of the Innocents* (book) 73
"West of Mars" (*Lost in Space* episode) 30
Westworld (film) 31, 148
Wheeler, Eugene 85; *Fail Safe* (novel) 85
Wheeler-Nicholson, Malcolm 33
Wigner, Eugene 36
Wilhelm, Kate 19, 111–112, 118; "The Village" (story) 19, 118
Williamson, Jack 36, 48, 111–112, 188
Williamson, Michael Z. 177
Willis, Connie 1
Wills, Garry 23–25, 31
Wilson, Richard 111–112, 188
Wingrove, David 2, 5, 42, 57
Wise, Robert 59, 61–63, 155; *The Andromeda Strain* (film) 155; *The Day the Earth Stood Still* (1951 film) 58, 59, 61–65, 75, 116, 134, 194
Wonder Woman (comic) 44, 54
Wong, James 160–161
Wood, Lowell 135–136
The Word for World Is Forest (book) 113–114
The World of Star Trek (book) 104
The World Set Free (book) 36
Worldwar: Upsetting the Balance (book) 129
Wortland, Rick 104; "Captain Kirk Cold Warrior" (essay) 104
Wright, Bradford 72, 116
Wu, David 9
Wylie, Philip 49, 50; *The Paradise Crater* (novella) 49; *The Smuggled Atom Bomb* (novel) 129

X Files (TV series) 159–160; "Paper Clip" 159; "731" 159–160
X-ray laser 123, 135–136, 138–139
X-wing (prototype aircraft) *13*, 147, 191

"The Zanti Misfits" (*Outer Limits* episode) 95–96

www.ingramcontent.com/pod-product-compliance
Lightning Source LLC
Chambersburg PA
CBHW020808230426
43666CB00007B/912